MANAGEMENT OF FINANCIAL INSTITUTIONS IN INDIA

By the Same Author

- Financial Services in India
- Portfolio Management
- Financial Markets and Institutions
- Research Methodology

About the Author

Dr. G. Ramesh Babu, Lecturer in Commerce, S.S.R. Jyothi College, Khammam, has vast teaching experience of 18 years at U.G. and P.G. levels. Academically, he is Ph.D. in Industrial Finance. He has published many papers in various management and commerce journals of repute and has also presented papers in various conferences. He is an active member of the All India Management Association, New Delhi; Associate Member of Society for Capital Market and Research, New Delhi; and Associate Member of Indian Institute of Public Administration, New Delhi. His areas of interest include Financial Systems and Capital Market.

Dedicated to Lord Ganesh

My Family Members

Lakshminarayana-Kasturi
Ramesh-Vani
Srinivas-Janaki
Suresh-Rani
Mahesh-Narmada
Buchibabu-Joythi

Our Little Masters

Gowthami-Harish
Srinadh-Sriharsha
Supriya-Sumanth
Nitheesh-Dinesh
Sowmya-Ramya

PREFACE

"Put not your trust in money, but put your money in trust"

— **O.W. Holmes**

Banking has been witnessing radical changes all over the globe in this digital era. As Banks thrive on public trust, depositor's interest, accountability, strategic objectives, managerial oversight, audit-role, risk management and the like concerns are predominant. Policy compliance and regulation bound conduct are essential preconditions. Economic reforms brought in their wake, a plethora of norms for income recognition, asset classification, appropriate provision which are to be meticulously complied with other overbearing concerns are freed interest rate structure, consolidation and overseeing financial conglomerates finding synergies and so on.

Banks are playing a vital role in the economy. After globalisation, privatisation and liberalisation drive, the entire Indian economic scenario has been changed. A rapid development in Information Technology enables the banking sector, to perform their duties with more sophisticated machines. Now everything will be done through a click of mouse. Internet has changed the lifestyle of a layman. Commercial banks are reducing their operational cost by establishing ATMs. Banks explored innovative things to perform customer's functions more easily and conveniently. ATMs can be utilised for further functions to reduce the workload of the banking sector. All payment utilities may be done through this kind of machines. Before IT revolution everything is inline, after IT revolution everything is "online". India is emerging as qualified, competent and challenging nation to the competitors in the IT environment. However the banks should focus on fee based services more sophisticatedly. Even they should enter into "chit fund" sector to provide safety to the chit holders.

In this book an attempt is made to give a comprehensive coverage of banking aspects. It has been written as per the syllabus prescribed for the MBA (Finance), M.Com., MFA, CFA, MFC and MS (Finance). I am confident that this book will help the students, faculty members executives in banking sector and as well as those individuals who desire to upgrade their knowledge and skills.

Since the book is synthesis, I am indebted to all the authors who have contributed to the world of banking sector. I hope that I have interpreted their views correctly. I am also indebted to my seniors and professionals and impossible to list them all. Anyhow for evincing personal interest in undertaking a project of this magnitude and making invaluable suggestions from time to time. I would like to thank all those who had directly and indirectly encouraged in completion of this book. I received valuable suggestions from many luminaries. Though it is difficult to thank all of them individually, it is my pleasure to express grateful thanks to Late Sri K. Ram Mohan, President, Jyothi Education Society. He was the person who inspired the crew members of the Jyothi Education Society. He spent his entire life to create miracles in the education sector. He folds the lives of thousands human beings in un-compromising environment. Dr. D. Ramachandra Bose, Principal, SSRJ College, Khammam is always an inspiring force behind the talent. Sri P. Raghurama Rao, Treasurer, Jyothi Education Society, Khammam is a motivational factor in every assignment. Sri K. V. Kameswar Rao, former principal, SSRJ College , Khammam who provided excellent information regarding banking sector aspects. I am also thankful to all my professors, Prof. P. Madhusudan Rao, Prof. V. Gangadhar, Prof. Narasimhamurthy, Prof. S. Ravi Prakash, Prof. A. Shankaraiah, Prof. Sudarshan, Prof. Rajeswar Rao, Prof. Krishna Reddy, whose elderly advice has been of immense use to me. I am also placed on record my sincere thanks to my teachers Sri P. V. Anjaneyulu, Sri G. Satyanarayana and Dr. K. Srinivasa Rao.

I owe my gratitude to Sri Ashok Kumar Mittal and Sri S. P. Sinha of Concept Publishing Company giving their personal attention in expediting the publishing of this book.

Dr. G. Ramesh Babu
E-Mail: rameshbabu_6317@rediffmail.Com
Mobile: 9849623310, 9848449377

CONTENTS

bill – Bill market in India – Certificate of deposit – Introduction – CDs in India – Original scheme – Modified scheme – Commercial paper – Salient features – CDs in abroad – CDs in India – Guidelines issued by the RBI – Collateral loan market – Unorganised money market – Indigenous bankers – Money lenders – Chit funds – Functions of indigenous bankers – Accepting of deposits providing loans to customers – Hundi business – Other functions – Characteristics of indigenous bankers – Defects of indigenous bankers – Banking commission reforms – Money lenders – Operations – Defects of money lenders – Licences of the Indian money market – RBI and money market – Measures for improvement in the money market – Vaghul Committee – Present structure – Recent measures taken by the RBI – Primary dealers – Satellite dealers – Money market – Mutual funds – Capital market – Introduction – Functions – Coordinator – Motivation to savings transformation to savings – Transformation to investment – Enhances economic growth – Stability – Advantageous to the investors – Barometer – Importance of capital market – Players in the capital market – Companies – Financial intermediation – Investors – Capital market before independence – After independence – Raising level of income and investment – New financial institutions – Expansion of commercial banks – Dynamic growth of specialised financial institutions – Distinction between money and capital market – Structure of capital market in India – Components of the capital market – Primary market – Capital market – New issue market – Introduction – Effectiveness of capital issues – Sources of raising of funds – Features of new issue market – Functions of NIM – Investigation – Underwriting – Distribution – **Indian financial system – Development financial institution** – Industrial Development Bank of India – Introduction – Management – Role – I phase – II phase – III phase – Industrial Credit and Investment Corporation of India – Introduction – Financial resources – Share capital – Reserves – Borrowings – Public deposits – Business operations – Lending operations – Industrial Finance Corporation of India – Introduction – Financial resources – Business activities – **Financial institutions** – Introduction – Banking – Non-banking – Reserve Bank of India – Functions – Authorities – Monetary authority – Bankers to the government – FERA – Promoting authority – Monetary policy of the RBI – Techniques of the monetary control – Open market operations – Refinance and bank rate – CRR – SLR credit planning – Regulation of interest rates – Credit norms – Credit authorisation scheme – Selective credit control – Banking institutions – Financial institutions – Interest rates.

Unit I

- Management of Financial Institutions
  (a) Introduction
  (b) Financial Institutions
  (c) Interest Rates

Unit I

MANAGEMENT OF FINANCIAL INSTITUTIONS

Introduction

A well-regulated modern financial sector is essential in a globalised economy. Financial innovation has been contributed to the economic development. Market based economies have in general done better, because of the constant identification and improved satisfaction of consumer needs.

Finance has a tendency towards boom bust cycles. Markets can discover prices and reveal information in about the future trends but the information is suspected because of the bandwagon effects, market participants follow each other and are uncertain about fundamentals. So both micro and macro policy should be geared to encourage competition and innovation. The justification of finance lies in improving real sector productivity.

Reforms offered a real opportunity for India to catch up to leap from being extremely backward to being more state of the art than many countries which are locked into older, less efficient technology. Good progress has been made in market microstructure but the small investor has disappeared from the market and finance is contributing less to the real economy. In most of the countries financial reforms led to the over expansion of credit regulators were not able to keep up since regulatory skills often lack and major crises followed.

Financial system is the base for the capital formation. Capital formation creates asset formation. The asset creation is the most important factor for the development of a nation. Adequate capital formation is required to a speedy economic development. The flow of funds from the capital market lead to the growth of the industrial sector. The capital market is the collection of savings from the investors and diverting it towards the productive ways. The asset creation accelerates the process of economic growth. The process of capital formation in any country depends upon the following factors:

(a) Savings
(b) Finance
(c) Investment

There is a close relationship between economic growth and accumulation. Capital formation is accompanied by a rapid growth in productivity and income. It is an essential determinant of the economic growth. It is quite necessary to determine the desirable rate of capital formation. Capital has been defined by **Prof. Nurkse:** "Capital is a necessary but not a sufficient condition of progress".[1]

Capital formation is the most important factor for the development. The real physical assets growth will be treated as capital formation. It does not include financial assets such as shares, bonds, currently notes and bank deposits. It is only the increase of real capital which stimulates the productive potential of the society. It is an addition to the stock of the goods such as machines and equipment, transport facilities. The capital formation can be classified into two kinds: (a) **Physical capital formation**, (b) **Human capital formation**. The physical capital formation has the close relationship with the economic growth. Most of the theories believe in stepping up the peace in a short period of time. A minimum level of quantum of investment is a necessary condition for getting success. The process of physical capital accumulation is a function of three factors such as:

(a) An increase in the volume of real domestic savings.
(b) The creation of adequate banking and financial institutions facilities.
(c) The creation of strong entrepreneurial base for utilising the savings into channels of productive investment.

Savings are the accumulated surplus which is available presently by postponing the consumption. Planned economies aim at achieving a high rate of domestic savings by imposing curb on consumption. Domestic savings are derived from **the household sector, private corporate sector and public sector**. The savings of the household sector are classified into two categories: (a) financial savings, (b) savings in the form of physical assets. Financial savings are associated with currency, deposits, shares, debentures, net claims of government life insurance funds, UTI, PF and pension funds. Savings in the form of physical assets such as real estate, ornaments, jewellery etc. In order to accelerate the process of growth in an economy, a nation has to boost its level of investment. This investment can be procured from the savings. The savings may be available in the form of domestic and external. The savings which are financed through internal are called as domestic savings. The savings which are mobilised from abroad is known as external savings. They have to be repaid with interest.

The household sector comprises productive economic units. These units either run on industrial basis or partnership or unincorporated business. It comprises urban and rural household savings. The savings of the private corporate sector are available from non-government corporate sector, banks and societies. In comparison with the most advanced nations, the share of the corporate sector in total savings is very negligible. The corporate sector contributes a less amount to national income in the kind of savings. All the savings of the corporate sector in the form of **depreciation, retained earnings or development funds** are usually used for their own expansion. In a mixed economy the savings of the corporate sector may largely be used for their expansion. Generally the corporate sector shows interest towards the direct investment in high profit industries. The savings of the public sector are largely derived from taxes surplus of the public enterprises and mobilisation of the internal debt and deposits. The government has embarked on a policy of lower direct tax rate with stricter enforcement. Taxation of agricultural income is one of the sources, which remained untapped. The public sector can increase its contribution by the extension of provident fund, compulsory life insurance and mobilisation of small savings from rural areas. Therefore, these measures will help for more inflow of savings from the public sector.

The share of the corporate sector in total savings of the nation is negligible. The corporate sector contributes very less amount of national income in the form of savings. Its contribution depends upon the peace of industrialisation. Its savings in the form of depreciation, retained profits are usually used for its expansion. Hence the contribution of the corporate sector should be improved to stimulate the growth of the economy. In a mixed economy both the private and public sectors are to co-exist. The savings of this sector may largely be used for its expansion. The profit will guide the corporate sectors investment.

India's Total Debt. During 1989-2000: Components of Centres Outstanding Debt

(Rs. in crores)

S. No	Items	1989-90	1990-91	1991-92	1992-93	1993-94	1994-95	1995-96	1996-97	1997-98	1998-99	1999-2000
I	**Multilateral**	32886	40386	68262	77758	82199	89819	98173	105066	116904	129674	136584
A.	Government borrowing	31575	38429	63787	72286	75617	82223	89428	94824	104218	114531	119722
(1)	Concessional	21760	25849	40990	48206	50250	55963	60425	63418	70560	78979	82864
(a)	IDA	21055	25221	40017	47167	49238	54897	59349	62343	69392	77725	81590
(b)	Other's	705	628	973	1039	1012	1066	1076	1075	1168	1254	1274
(ii)	Non-concessional	9815	12580	22797	24080	25367	26260	29003	31406	33658	35552	36858
(a)	IBRD	9752	12161	21134	21602	22518	22442	23721	24354	25438	25747	25924
(b)	Others	63	419	1663	2478	2849	3818	5282	7052	8220	9805	10934
B.	Non-Government borrowing	1311	1957	4475	5472	6582	7596	8745	10242	12686	15143	16862
(i)	Concessional	0	0	0	0	0	0	0	0	0	0	0
(ii)	Non-concessional	1311	1957	4475	5472	6582	7596	8745	10242	12686	15143	16862
(a)	Public Sector	158	303	1424	1777	2786	3248	4628	4738	8765	10711	12184
	IBRD	158	303	962	1300	2158	2013	2942	3341	5217	6349	6933
	Others	0	0	462	477	628	1235	1686	1397	3548	4362	5251
(b)	Financial institutions	799	1270	2345	2883	2718	2559	2464	2391	2171	2720	3101
	IBRD	503	872	1720	1791	1667	1605	1643	1618	1011	1057	999
	Others	296	398	625	1092	1051	954	821	773	1160	1663	2102
(c)	Private Sector	354	384	706	812	1078	1789	1653	3113	1750	1711	1578
	IBRD	313	330	628	709	953	1610	1244	1639	1321	1312	1172
	Others	41	54	78	103	125	179	409	1474	429	399	406
II	**Bilateral**	22993	27378	47603	50258	54580	63761	65740	62891	67104	74297	78749
A.	Government Borrowing	19444	23065	40371	42220	45387	52965	53119	49092	51420	57106	60819
(i)	Concessional	19444	23065	40371	42220	45387	52965	52078	48165	50583	56425	59280
(ii)	Non-concessional	0	0	0	0	0	0	1041	927	837	681	1539
B.	Non-Government Borrowing	3549	4313	7232	8038	9193	10976	12621	13799	15684	17191	17930
(i)	Concessional	441	514	928	1243	1453	1896	3088	3409	1770	2738	4025
(a)	Public Sector	7	0	0	0	190	654	376	1054	192	526	1489
(b)	Financial Institutions	431	514	928	1243	1263	1242	2712	2355	1578	2212	2536
(c)	Private Sectors	3	0	0	0	0	0	0	0	0	0	0
(ii)	Non-concessional	3108	3799	6304	6795	7740	8900	9533	10390	13914	14453	13905
(a)	Public Sector	2581	2957	4472	4726	5475	6120	5602	5216	5360	5190	4590
(b)	Financial Institutions	271	527	1236	1571	1718	1883	2197	2436	4216	4362	4108

(Contd.)

S. No	Items	1989-90	1990-91	1991-92	1992-93	1993-94	1994-95	1995-96	1996-97	1997-98	1998-99	1999-2000
(c)	Private Sector	256	315	596	498	547	897	1734	2738	4338	4901	5206
III.	**International Monetary Fund**	2572	5132	8934	14985	15812	13545	8152	4714	2662	1218	113
IV.	**Trade Credit**	8002	8374	12418	13484	16307	20876	18432	21044	25783	28809	29006
(a)	Buyer's Credit	1877	2230	3566	3989	5474	6227	7216	11184	15453	18099	18188
(b)	Suppliers Credit	950	933	1380	2050	4129	6432	5382	4791	5453	5534	5581
(c)	Export Credit Component	1340	1390	2428	3671	3947	4604	4529	4189	4399	4901	5154
(d)	Export Credit for defence	3835	3821	5044	3774	2757	3613	1305	880	498	276	83
V.	**Commercial Borrowing**	15988	19727	35711	36367	38782	40915	47642	51454	67086	89521	84476
(a)	Commercial Bank Loans	11453	13200	20933	20156	18694	18384	23120	29968	39419	43891	43391
(b)	Scrutinised Borrowings	4227	5840	13219	13990	16557	16935	19790	17320	23786	41964	37736
(c)	Loans with Multilateral Guarantee	308	687	1512	2105	2430	2998	3050	3521	3451	3433	3235
(d)	Self Liquidity loans	0	0	47	116	1101	2598	1682	645	430	233	113
VI.	**NRI & FC (B & O) Deposits**	15719	20030	27384	34941	39729	39006	37802	39527	47050	52382	63585
(a)	NRI Deposits	15719	19843	26737	34113	39729	39006	37802	39527	47050	52382	63585
(b)	FC (B & O) Deposits	0	187	647	828	0	0	0	0	0	0	0
VII.	**Rupee debt**	19075	25199	31956	33149	31634	30316	28150	26978	23204	20078	19128
(a)	Defence	17276	22875	28796	30177	28735	27603	25602	24590	20976	18005	17211
(b)	Guilian	1799	2324	3160	2972	2899	2712	2548	2388	2228	2073	1917
VIII.	**Total Long Term Debt**	117235	146226	232268	260942	279043	298237	304091	311674	349573	395979	411641
IX.	**Short Term Debt**	12964	16775	20642	19804	11375	13448	16637	24153	19929	18616	17630
(a)	NRI Deposits (upto 1 year)	5589	7018	6517	8131	4078	7176	9896	13547	8657	9331	6449
(b)	FC (B & O) deposits (upto 1 year)	0	328	924	2433	1672	0	0	0	0	0	0
(c)	Other Trade Related	7375	9429	13201	9240	5625	6272	6741	10606	11272	9285	11180
(d)	Inc Dept. of 6 Months	3472	4976	4736	5601	5625	6272	6741	10606	11272	9285	11180
X.	**Total External Debt**	130199	163001	252910	280746	290418	311685	320728	335827	369682	414595	429271
	Concessional Debt	60720	74627	114245	124818	128724	141139	143741	141970	146117	158220	165297
	As % of Total	46.6	45.8	45.2	44.5	44.3	45.3	44.8	42.3	39.5	38.2	38.5
	Short Term Debt	12964	16775	20642	19804	11375	13448	16637	24153	19929	18616	17630
	As % of Total	10	10.3	8.2	7.1	3.9	4.3	5.2	7.2	5.4	4.5	4.1
	External Debt as % of GDP	26.7	28.7	38.7	37.6	33.8	30.9	27.1	24.7	24.4	23.5	22
	Debt Service Ratio (%)	30.9	35.3	30.2	27.5	25.8	26.2	24.3	21.2	19	18	16
XI.	**Total Internal Debt**	133193	154004	172750	199100	245712	266467	307869	344476	388998	459696	728627
	Internal Debt as % of GDP	27.3	27.1	26.4	26.6	28.6	26.4	26	25.3	25.7	26.1	37.3
XII.	**Total Debt (Internal + External)**	263392	317005	425660	479846	536130	578152	628597	680303	758680	874291	1157898
	Total Debt as % of GDP	54	62.4	65.1	64.2	62.4	57.3	53.1	50	50.1	49.6	59.3

Source: *The Economic Times*, 5-4-2001, p. 3.

Statement Showing the GDP Growth-International

Sl. No.		(Average percent per year) 1965-80	1980-90	Comparison 1990-2000
1.	China	6.4	9.5	10.3
2.	Korea	9.5	9.7	5.7
3.	Malaysia	7.4	5.2	7.0
4.	Thailand	7.4	7.6	4.2
5.	Indonesia	7.9	5.5	4.2
6.	India	3.7	5.3	6.0

Source: World Bank Reports, *EPW*, 12-10-02. p. 4189.

Statement Showing the Structure of Domestic Savings

S.No.	*Country*	*Period*	*Public*	*Private*
1.	Indonesia	1981-88	7.7	14
2.	Malaysia	1981-90	10.3	19.1
3.	Thailand	1980-85	14.3	4.7
		1986-87	8.6	14.6
4.	Japan	1981-88	5.1	15.8
5.	India	1961-70	2.7	9.89
		1971-80	3.7	13.7
		1981-90	3.02	16.16
		1991-2000	1.01	22.04

Source: World Bank Reports, *EPW*, 12-10-02, p. 4189.

Statement Showing the Investment and GDP Growth Rates Cross Country Comparison Average per cent per year

Sl. No.	*Name of the Country*	*Changes in Investment Rate*		*Change in GDP Growth*	
		1980-90	*1990-95*	*1980-90*	*1990-95*
1.	China	11	15.5	10.2	12.8
2.	Malaysia	2.6	16	5.2	8.7
3.	Indonesia	7	16.3	6.1	7.6
4.	Thailand	9.4	10.2	7.6	8.4
5.	Turkey	5.3	2	5.3	3.2
6.	Argentina	–0.3	5.7	–4.7	16
7.	India	6.5	5.3	5.8	4.6
8.	Venezuela	–5.3	3.8	1.1	2.4
9.	Brazil	0.2	3.5	2.7	2.7

Source: World Bank Reports, *EPW*, 12-10-02, p. 4189.

Statement Showing the Country/Statewise Break-up of Foreign Direct Investments Approved During August 1991 to March 2002

Sl. No.	Countrywise Position	Investment (Rs. in crores)	% to Total
1.	USA	56616	20.4
2.	Mauritius	32918	11.9
3.	UK	21405	7.7
4.	Japan	10858	3.9
5.	South Korea	9798	3.5
6.	Germany	8950	3.2
7.	Netherlands	8636	3.1
8.	Australia	6734	2.4
9.	Malaysia	5682	2.0
10.	France	6234	2.2
11.	Singapore	4945	1.8
12.	Italy	4779	1.7
13.	Israel	4244	1.5
14.	Belgium	4162	1.5
15.	Cayman Island	3861	1.4
16.	Switzerland	3011	1.1
17.	Canada	2726	1.0
18.	Thailand	2726	1.0
19.	Hong Kong	2261	0.8
20.	South Africa	1906	0.7
21.	Sweden	2039	0.7
22.	NRIs	10408	3.7
23.	Euro Issues	48447	17.4
24.	All Others	14346	5.2
		277692	100

Sources: *EPW*, 31-8-2002, p. 3567.

Statement Showing Industry Break-up of Foreign Collaboration Approvals from August 1991 to March 2002

Sl. No.	Statewise Position	No. of Approval	Amount (Rs. in crores)	% of Total
1.	Maharashtra	3854	48409	17.4
2.	Delhi	1857	33470	12.1
3.	Tamil Nadu	2113	23202	8.4
4.	Karnataka	1891	21413	7.7
5.	Gujarat	1032	18265	6.6
6.	Andhra Pradesh	975	12753	4.6
7.	Madhya Pradesh	225	9227	3.3
8.	Orissa	136	8229	3.0
9.	West Bengal	584	8730	3.1
10.	Uttar Pradesh	730	4790	1.7

(*Contd.*)

(Contd.)

Sl. No.	Statewise Position	No. of Approval	Amount (Rs. in crores)	% of Total
11.	Haryana	769	3518	1.3
12.	Rajasthan	319	3005	1.1
13.	Punjab	181	1968	0.7
14.	Kerala	259	1525	0.5
15.	Pondicherry	110	1241	0.4
16.	Bihar	47	740	0.3
17.	Himachal Pradesh	96	364	0.1
18.	North Eastern Region	30	63	0.0
19.	Rest of the Country	6294	76577	27.6
	Total	21502	277597	100

Sources: *EPW*, 31-8-2002, p. 3567.

Statement Showing Industry Break-up of Foreign Collaboration Approvals from August 1991 to March 2002

Sl. No.	Name of the Industry	Amount Approval (Rs. in crore)	% of Total
1.	Basic goods industries	107576	38.8
2.	Capital goods industries	25117	9.0
3.	Intermediate goods	4993	1.8
4.	Consumer non-durable	27623	10.1
5.	Consumer durable	9357	3.4
6.	Service	102928	37.1
		277597	100

Sources: *EPW*, 31-8-2002, p. 3567.

According to **S.L. Shetty** and **K.L. Menon**[2] "The increase in saving ratio is possible by following three factors:

(a) There has been a record increase in inflationary financing which has helped to accelerate saving in the form of financial assets.

(b) There has been a movement of terms of trade against agriculture and this has helped to increase the savings of the non-farm sectors.

(c) There has been a sharp increase in the distribution of money incomes and this has given a sharp boost to savings in the form of financial assets."

All these factors have resulted in a sharp increase but it may not lead to make a perceptible impact on economic growth. The saving and investment relation indicates the following situations:

1. The escalation in projects costs without any enhancement in investment in real terms.
2. There has been increase in the price of investment goods at a faster rate than the rise in general price level.
3. Increase in savings of the community has been to a large extent absorbed by the projects.
4. Increase in inefficiency of management of public sector undertakings.
5. The pattern of investment should be changed.
6. There is a strong need to remove infrastructural bottlenecks, investment in power, transport and irrigation.
7. There must be sufficient attention paid to maintenance and fuller utilisation of investment projects.
8. There must be more emphasis on productivity of industrial sector.

Finance is the most important factor for the economic development of a nation. It is an activity by which claims to resources are either pooled by domestic savings or procured from abroad. In the **digital economy** the funds can be raised throughout the world on competitive interest rates basis. The capital formation can be found with the help of **financial innovations**. The growth of financial technology led to various innovations. The part played by the financial innovation depends upon the following elements:

(a) Traditional Economy
(b) Direct Finance
(c) Indirect Finance

(a) Traditional Economy

India had a strong historical economic record. Its financial system has transformed in many ways. The finance which is in the traditional economy is known as the **Rudimentary finance**. It refers to the financial system that is an economy in which the per capita income is very low and declining over a spell of time. It is the period where the absence of different financial assets or instruments in the economy. But these financial assets would stimulate savings and allocate resources competitively to the investment centres. These assets are treated as a claim against other economic units. They are held as a store of value and for the expected return on shares, debenture and bonds are the best examples for financial instruments. The economic unit mobilises the small savings, and invest in business activities. The savings are raised from individuals, corporates, financial institutions and the government. In this traditional economy once upon a time, there are no financial assets other than **cash**. This situation led to an economy to invest in new tangible assets. The absence of financial instruments led to inefficient allocation of resources. Therefore, inferior investment projects are undertaken and others are rejected.

In this traditional economy, the financial markets were non-existed. The business concerns could compete for informal savings or private savings. The private savings have been always financing for higher interest rate. There were no organised market existed to capture the accumulated savings from the individuals. Therefore, there must be different kinds of financial markets for the transaction in securities. These are necessary to accelerate the process of capital formation. A new financial structure is essential to break the old system. The new structure must bring together the investors and savers. The saving and investment process can be speeded up by establishing new forms of dynamic financial organisations.

(b) Direct Finance

The financial organisations collect the savings directly from the savers. There are no mediators in this procurement. It represents an improvement to the traditional economy. It provides a better way for efficient capital formation. In this method of procurement of finance, the firms can mobilise a heavy amount of financial resources. The capabilities are derived from the introduction of three innovations such as **Financial Instrument Brokers, Investment Bankers** and **Stock Exchanges**. In rudimentary finance, there is no existence of financial instruments. The growth of financial technology led to the introduction of various financial assets. All the problems associated with rudimentary finance are eliminated as a result of introduction of financial innovation. The growth of industrial sector depends upon the peace of industrialisation. The firm can issue financial assets in the form of **primary security**. Primary security is described as a financial asset issued by non-financial economic undertaking. The economic units function is to produce and purchase current output by issuing shares, preference shares and debentures. The introduction of financial assets is a historical trend in the financial sector. It has shown a great impact on the business concerns. The financial assets do two functions: (a) It facilitates the savers that their savings do not remain idle with them, (b) The savings will be diverted towards profitable investment opportunities. Therefore, the financial assets stimulate the capital formation and contribute to fasten economic development. The capital formation alone cannot stimulate the growth.

Brokers constitute the element of direct finance. They mobilise small savings from the savers and divert the fund towards the economic units which need fund. They are the financial intermediary with a vast network of clients and influence the investment decisions of the investors. The information technology has changed the communication channel between brokers and investors which resulted in increased attractiveness of primary securities or direct loans. They have more effect of improving the flow of savings to users of funds. They work for brokerage. They procure the funds from various channels and charge the brokerage from parties. They underwrite primary issues. They also contribute to the efficient flow of funds for the smooth functioning of the corporate sector. Underwriting involves the risk of selling the issue to the public. The financial intermediary will undertake the unsubscribed portion of the issue. This situation may lead to the unit for the guaranteed flow of funds and it can go ahead according to its project implement action. They are an important contributory factors in the process of transfer of financial resources.

Another important element in the direct finance is **stock exchanges**. Stock exchanges serve the needs of the saving surplus units and fund needed units. It enhances the efficiency of the flow of savings. It increases the liquidity of existing securities by trading arrangements continuously for buying and selling. It provides liquidity and market ability to the industrial investment. It provides flexibility and encourages more risk bearing on the part of the investors by removing psychological hurdles. Therefore, surplus units are encouraged to deploy the savings for wonderful economic development through the financial system. The stock exchange plays an important role in the construction of a good industrial empire in the country. It can create wonderful things in the financial sector. It has the capacity to build modern India to compete the developmental nations. **Bombay Stock Exchange** is the world premier institution and has the world-class standard services. The

National Stock Exchange is also becoming very popular in India and it has world level capacity skills. These two exchanges are more competent with global premier exchanges such as **New York Stock Exchange, Tokyo Stock Exchange, Singapore Stock Exchange**. The bulk of trade happens online through the BSE and NSE. The direct finance has some development over rudimentary finance. All these innovations are responsible for considerable value to both the savers and investors the direct finance is expensive, inconvenient, risky and ineffective as a means of promoting mass flow of savings into the investment. This is because the direct finance is largely confined to the relatively richer sections of the community. Before investing in a financial asset, the investor requires a careful selection of securities, a diversification of risk, continuous monitoring of portfolio, changing economic and financial conditions of government etc. The investor should have knowledge, experience, thorough understanding of the economy. These are needed to construct and successfully administer an investment portfolio. All these skills may not have the small investors and it is impossible to cope with these requirements of the investment management. But the large investors are able to well-equipped with efficient skilled persons as their advisers. The NSE introduced screen based trading across the country in November 1994. It did trading more transparent and was done much the same way on par with world standards. In 1991 there were 2471 companies listed on 23 Indian stock exchanges,[3] 500 of these were traded actively. But in 2001, there were **5937** companies listed on the bourses, less than 150 of them were traded actively. By the turns of this decade **24 hour** stock exchanges will come into being. Investors in India can trade in bluechip securities around the world. The NSE has revolutionised trading in India through its network of **3075 VSAT** exchanges across **379 cities**. In 2000-2001, its total turnover of **Rs.17,70,457** crores was higher than the BSEs **Rs.10,00,054 crores**[4]. The New York Stock Exchange has its Dow Jones Industrial, BSE has the **Sensitive Index**. The index first made its appearance in 1986. The Sensex movement information has been presented below[5] (in points).

Year	Sensex (Average)	Sensex High for the Year
1986-87	570	659
1987-88	455	536
1988-89	613	719
1989-90	730	798
1990-91	1050	1559
1991-92	1845	4285
1992-93	2899	4286
1993-94	2895	4467
1994-95	3975	4631
1995-96	3289	3598
1996-97	3469	4069
1997-98	3812	4548
1998-99	3295	4281
1999-2000	4659	5934
2000-2001	4270	5542
2001-2002	NA	3742

The BSE has put online trading system in 1995 in place allowing brokers to trade from their offices. In 2000-01 the average daily volume was **Rs.4775 crores**. The information regarding the BSE is presented below:[6]

BSE: A Numerical Journey

Year	Average Daily Turnover (Rs. in crores)
1989-90	134.80
1990-91	188.54
1991-92	332.30
1992-93	238.00
1993-94	387.78
1994-95	292.02
1995-96	215.79
1996-97	517.85
1997-98	851.00
1998-99	1283.95
1999-2000	2729.20
2000-2001	4775.77

(c) Indirect Finance

Indirect finance means the flow of small savings from the savers to the Corporate Sector through the indirect method. The financial intermediary will help the corporate sector by mobilising the small savings from the savers and channelise them into productive way. In this method of finance the intermediary play an important role in arranging the resources. The intermediary financial institutions such as **Mutual Funds** and **Insurance Companies** collect savings from others and issue in return claims against themselves. Therefore, the raised fund will be utilised to purchase ownership or debt claims. Mutual funds occupy a dominant role in the mobilisation of small savings. The small investors who do not have stock market operations expertise automatically tend towards mutual funds by purchasing of small units. Mutual funds generally raise the financial resources by selling units to the unit holders through different schemes. They offer various schemes to the unit holders to suit their needs and conveniences. Therefore, the procured amount of money will be deployed in the stock market by the mutual funds with the help of stock market specialists. They play an important role in economic development through the capital formation. They contribute to the **Initial public offer** made by the new companies and encourage new business units. They take an active role in the asset creation of the nation. The asset creation is the most important factor for the economic development of a nation. The history of mutual fund in India has begun in 1964. **The Unit Trust of India** launched **US 64**. There are several mutual funds in private and public sectors offering various schemes to the unit holders. Commercial banks promote the mutual fund through their subsidiaries. **For example: Canbank Mutual Fund, SBI MF, BOMF, PNBMF, IDBI, ICICI Prudential**. Recently the private sector mutual funds emerged as a strong financial intermediaries in the market. **For example: Prudential ICICI, ILEFS MF, HDFC MF, Sun F&C, JMMF, DSP Merry Lynch MF, Alliance MF etc**. The mutual funds have a strong team of experts, those who are specialist in this field can utilise their services for getting huge amount of profits from the stock market operations. The individual cannot become an expert in all walks of life of the stock market operations. In India, there are 34 mutual fund houses managing 614 schemes and **Rs. 94,571 crores** in assets. The information regarding mutual fund industry is presented below:[7]

Year	Assets (Rs. in crores)
1964-69	65
1969-74	172
1974-79	402
1979-84	1261
1986-87	4563
1987-88	6738
1988-89	13455
1989-90	19110
1990-91	23060
1991-92	37480
1992-93	46988
1993-94	61301
1994-95	75050
1995-96	81026
1996-97	80539
1997-98	68984
1998-99	68472
1999-2000	107946
2000-2001	90587
2001	94571

Indirect financing system occupies an important role in the capital formation of a country. The financial intermediaries play an important role in the indirect finance system. They are attractive because they prepare the various schemes to suit the requirements of the investors. They are able to provide better satisfactory services to the unit holders. The pooling of funds leads to a number of benefits such as **Lower risk, expert's advices, suitability, large scale economies**. They provide lower risk to the unit holders because of the benefits of diversification. By diversification, a portfolio can avoid risk and increase return. This facility is available in this system. They provide better expert advices to both large and small investors. The benefits of highly specialised, skilled, trained, experienced talent is available to the mutual fund organisation. The specialised experts are in continuous supervision and monitoring of the portfolio. Therefore, the small investors cannot avail these facilities due to the financial limitations. The financial intermediaries mobilise the fund by dividing a small piece of units. It is a more convenient vehicle for the mobilisation of savings. It provides divisibility and flexibility. Because the share capital of the mutual fund is divided into small units such as unit one is Rs. Ten, leads to attract lakhs of small investors. The unit holders have the chance to exist from the scheme whenever they think by surrendering the units to mutual funds. Mutual funds provide economies of scale because they pool the small amounts which will become a huge amount. They exploit economies of scale in lending and borrowing. Therefore, the financial intermediaries play a crucial role in the mobilisation of resources to capital formation.

Investment refers to use money to earn interest or bring profit for a specific period of time. The volume of capital formation depends upon the availability of investment surplus among the public. The investment habits in India are very low while compared with developing nations. During the second half of the 1990s, there was a significant shift of investor's interest from shares towards high quality bonds like bonds of development financial institutions. While retail investors are showing a great appetite for high quality bonds, not many of them want to touch the bonds of private sector companies except a few of the most reputed ones. **The society for Capital Market Research** conducted a survey about the retail investor's attitude regarding the investment patterns.[8] The findings of the study are presented below:

(a)	IDBI bonds	81%
(b)	Government company bonds	65%
(c)	Private sector bonds	15%

The investors perceived each category as safe, showed wide difference. The study provides reasons why most of the household investors abhor private sector bonds despite there being a general shift towards the fixed income investments. The study has found that the investors cannot afford to have adequate diversification of the bond portfolio and hence the riskier type of bonds are not suitable for such investors.[9] In India the investors make their decisions after taking the consideration of the company management. The study found that the company management, auditor's name, credit rating agencies certification, stock exchange members recommendation will hold key elements. The survey further found that the new issues no more favoured over the secondary market purchases. The investors showed strong preference for sub-striving to new issues rather than buying from the secondary market[10] has disappeared.

Share Trading Volume in India[11] 1994-95 to 1999-2000

Year	*Rs. in crores*
1994-95	1,62,905
1995-96	2,27,368
1996-97	6,46,116
1997-98	9,08,691
1998-99	10,23,381
1999-2000	20,76,031

Public and Rights Issue of Share and Bonds[12] 1994-95 to 1999-2000

Year	*Rs. in crores*
1994-95	27,632
1995-96	20,804
1996-97	14,276
1997-98	4,570
1998-99	5,586
1999-2000	7,817

Therefore, the investment activities in India depends upon many factors.

INDIAN FINANCIAL SYSTEM

Introduction

A well-developed financial system is necessary for the rapid economic growth of any country. The economic growth is invariably followed by a strong parallel growth of financial organisations. The financial system is largely influenced by political economic environment. The economic planning had greatly influenced the rapid growth of the development of a nation. The financial system refers to the process of borrowing and lending of funds. Finance refers to funds of monetary resources required by individuals, business concerns and the government. The individuals need funds for meting their present requirements. A business concerns need funds for making their disbursements towards salaries, wages, buying raw materials, purchasing of new machinery etc. The businessmen require finance for buying and producing goods in their routine function. The agriculturist requires finance for different purposes in different times. The government needs funds to meet its expenditure for various development programmes to the welfare of citizens. Therefore, the funds are needed by all the individuals, business concerns and governments to meet their current commitments. Usually the financial system is classified as:

(A) Industrial finance
(B) Agricultural finance
(C) Development finance
(D) Government finance

Industrial finance refers to the funds required for the smooth functioning of the trade and industry. **Agricultural finance** provides funds to the conduct of agriculture and allied activities. The farmers and cultivators need funds in different times for different purposes for the production of agricultural commodities without interruption. **Development finance** makes provision for the development of industry and agriculture sector. **Government finance** relates to the demand and supply of funds to meet the growing needs of government for the developmental activities as per its policies. The government is also required to mobilise its resources through various sources like a common man. Thus the financial system may affect the generation of savings by the citizens for the investment purposes. The Indian financial system is composed of banking system, insurance companies, mutual funds, investment funds and other institutions. Hence, the Indian financial system can be categorised as:

(A) Indian Financial System I – Commercial Banking
(B) Indian Financial System II – Money and Capital Market
(C) Indian Financial System III – Development of Financial Institutions

A. COMMERCIAL BANKING

Introduction

The origin of commercial banking can be found in the early times. In India the commercial banking began in 1770 with the establishment of the first joint stock bank, namely as **Bank of Hindustan** in Kolkata. But the real commercial banking started with the establishment of **Bank of Bengal** in 1806. Later on the Bank of Bombay and the Bank of Madras were also set up in 1840 and 1843 respectively. These banks are called as **Presidency Banks**. The first Indian bank came in 1881 named as **Oudh Commercial Bank**. It was followed by the establishment of Punjab National Bank in 1894. The people's bank was established in 1901. The commercial banks mobilise savings in urban areas and make them available to industrial houses for their working capital requirements. The Swadeshi movement of 1905 encouraged the growth of banking system in India. During 1913-48 about **1100** banks failed. The commercial banks in India can be classified into two kinds:

(a) Public Sector Banks
(b) Private Sector Banks

(a) Public Sector Banks: The public sector banks are also known as scheduled banks. The scheduled banks have been developed in India in four stages. In the first stage the Imperial Bank was nationalised and renamed as the State Bank of India in 1955. The SBI was reconstituted into seven subsidiary banks of the SBI. These banks are now called as the associates of the SBI. They are State Bank of Hyderabad, State Bank of Patiala, State Bank of Travancore, State Bank of Mysore, State Bank of Bikaner, State Bank of Indore, and State Bank of Saurashtra. Later on July 19, 1969, 14 major commercial banks were nationalised. Again the Government of India nationalised 6 more commercial banks on April 15, 1980. These banks were Allahabad Bank, Andhra Bank, Bank of Baroda, Bank of India, Bank of Maharashtra, Canara Bank, Central Bank of India, Corporation Bank, Dena Bank, Indian Bank, Indian Overseas Bank, Oriental Bank of Commerce, Punjab and Sind Bank, Punjab National Bank, Syndicate Bank, UCO Bank, Union Bank of India, United Bank of India, Vijaya Bank and SBI. The Regional Rural Banks have been established in 1974.[13] At present their numbers are **196**. At present there are 298 commercial banks functioning as scheduled banks. Of the scheduled banks, **223** are in public sector. In post-nationalisation period no new private sector bank was allowed to be set up. But in 1993, 10 new private sector banks were set up to introduce greater competition. The competition has led to higher productivity and efficiency of the banking system. The commercial banks in India are joint stock banks. They are registered with under the Indian Companies Act. They are controlled and regulated by the RBI. They are eligible for their re-discounting facilities. The development of banking industry leads to the better credit facilities to the public after nationalisation. The RBI introduced lead bank scheme in 1969 to provide bank credit to all the districts of the country. The objective of the lead bank scheme is to coordinate the operations of commercial banks, cooperative banks and other financial institutions for the purpose of development. In India in two episodes of nationalisation between 1969 and 1980, the banking system virtually came to be under state ownership and the objectives and presented below:

(a) to mobilise small savings of people to the largest possible extent and to utilise them for productive purposes,
(b) to ensure that the operations of the banking system are guided by a larger social purpose and are subjected to close public regulation,

(c) to ensure that the legitimate credit needs of private sector, industry and trade big or small are met,

(d) to ensure that the needs of productive sectors of the economy and in particular those of farmers small scale industrialists and self-employed professional groups are met,

(e) to actively foster the growth of new and progressive entrepreneurs and create fresh opportunities for hitherto neglected and backward areas in different parts of the country, and

(f) to curb the use of bank credit for speculative and other unproductive purposes.

(b) Private Sector Banks: These banks are promoted by the private individuals or corporations. These banks can be divided into two kinds (i) old private sector banks; and (ii) new private sector banks. In India, there are 23 old private sector banks such as Bharat Overseas Bank, The Bank of Rajasthan, The Sangli Bank, Vyshya Bank, United Western Bank, The Karur Vyshya Bank, the Catholic Syrian Bank, The Karnataka Bank, The Nedungudi Bank, etc. **The New Private Sector Banks** are such as Bank of Punjab, Centurian Bank, Global Trust Bank, UTI Bank, HDFC Bank, ICICI Bank, IndusInd Bank, etc.

The Composition of the Indian Banking System. The organised banking system can be divided into three categories: (a) Central Bank, (b) Commercial Banks, and (c) Cooperative Banks. The Central bank in India is Reserve Bank of India. The RBI is supreme authority in the banking system. It has the responsibility to control the entire banking system in the country. Commercial banks mobilise savings and facilitate the resources to the industrial sector. The **Regional Rural Banks** came into existence with a view to provide credit and deposit facilities to the small farmers, agricultural labourers, artisans and entrepreneurs in villages. They have the responsibility to develop agriculture, trade, commerce and industry in rural areas. They are commercial banks but their area of operation is limited to a district horizon.

A detailed explanation of the banking system in India is presented below:

(A) Indigenous banking

(B) Progress of banking since 1969

(C) Lead bank scheme

(D) Performance of banks

(E) Reforms of the banking sector
(F) The securities scam – banking system

(A) Indigenous banking refers to ancient banking system. It existed in age-old banking operations in different parts of the country. Under different names, these bankers were known as **Chettys** in Chennai, **Sahukars** in North India, **Shroffs and Marwaris** in Mumbai, **Seth and Banias** in Bengal. The indigenous banker is defined as "an individual or private firm which receives deposits, deals in hundies or engages itself in lending money".[14] They can be divided into three kinds: (1) Those persons who deal only in banking business activities. They are known as **Multani bankers.** (2) The persons those who combine banking activities with their regular routine business. They are known as **Marwaris.** (3) Those persons deal mainly in trade and also participate in limited banking activities. These indigenous bankers are different from money lenders. The money lender is not a banker, he lends money from his own resources. But the indigenous banker mobilises deposits from the public and lends the public. They occupy a key role in Indian money market. They are popular in same areas only, where the banking facilities do not exist. The activities of the indigenous bankers have declined considerably after the development of the banking system. They provide better services and flexible credit. They give loans to small business units who are fully ignored by the commercial banks. They maintain close relations with the customers and fully acquainted with their needs and financial problems. They provide not only money but also friends and advisers. Their functions are presented below:

(a) Accepting deposits
(b) Lending money
(c) Miscellaneous activities

(a) Accepting deposits: The indigenous bankers work like commercial bankers. They accept deposits from the public. They are available to the public around the clock and do not require any business hour. They procure funds from the public and pay higher rate of interest than the commercial bankers. They accept two kinds of deposits (i) Demand deposits, (ii) Time deposits. **Demand deposits** are repayable on demand by the customers. The accepted deposits shall be repayable whenever the customer desires. **Time deposits** are repayable after a fixed period. The fixed period will be indicated by the customer. They are also called as **Fixed deposits.** Accepting deposit is the basic function of indigenous bankers. According to the Indian Central Banking Enquiry Committee, indigenous banker is defined as "any individual or private firm receiving deposits and dealing in hundis or lending money."[15] There were about 2500 indigenous bankers in the country in 1971. They had concentrated in the western and southern parts of India. Most of these bankers were confined to urban areas.

(b) Lending money: They advance loans to their customers against securities. They will undertake all types of securities such as land, crops, gold and silver. They will also grant loans as the basis of personal security. They also grant loans to the small scale industrialist and small traders who are unable to fulfil the loan conditions of commercial banks. They provide loans to all the persons those who are completely neglected by the commercial banks.

(c) Miscellaneous activities: They also deal in hundies and non-banking functions. They involve in hundis transactions such as buying and selling. They also discount hundis and meet the financial needs of the internal traders. They actively participate in transfer of funds from one place to another place. They do this business in addition to their routine business. They also act as agents to large business concerns and charge commission for their services. They participate in speculative transactions.

(B) Progress of banking since 1969: The Indian banking system has recorded excellent growth after the independence. It was achieved through a planned economic growth, increase in money supply, growth of banking habit, control and guidance by the RBI. The banks were nationalised in July 1969. The nationalisation was a historic event in the history of banking in India. The nationalisation of banks would enable the government to obtain all the large profits of the banks as its revenue, it provided a new resource for providing the financial resources to the government.

Before nationalisation, the banks were controlled by a group of industrialists and businessmen. They used public funds to build their private industrial empires. Small scale industries and common men were continuously ignored and starved of funds.

The aim of the nationalisation of banks was to provide credit facilities to small tiny cottage and village industries, and agricultural sectors. The public funds were used to support anti-social and illegal activities against the interest of the public. The following factors showed impact due to nationalisation of banks in the economy:

(a) Branch expansion
(b) Mobilisation of resources
(c) Expansion of bank credit
(d) Development banking
(e) Priority sector lending
(f) Social banking

(a) Branch expansion: After the nationalisation of banks, branch expansion gained momentum for rapid economic development. Initially, the banks were concentrated mainly in **Mumbai, Chennai, Kolkata and Delhi** and other major cities. The branches of commercial banks had been established in the rural areas. The massive branch bankings show the magnitude of the problem before the banking villages are covered by banks directly.

(b) Mobilisation of bank resources: Planned economic development led to the increase in the banking deposits. Mobilisation of resources by banks has been an important feature in recent years. Banks have contributed greatly to the development of banking habit among the people by making prompt service to the customers. The nationalisation made the way to mobilise resources from the depositors adequately. The trend of increase in deposits and credit of scheduled banks presented below:[16]

(Rs. in crores)

Particulars	*1999-2000*	*2000-01*	*2001-02*	*2002-03*
(a) Money supply M_3	143154	189046	186783	172191
(b) Currently with public	20138	20468	31849	23238
(c) Deposits with banks	123779	167983	155712	148236
(d) Bank credit to commercial sector	90574	92654	77047	91887
(e) Scheduled commercial bank deposits	99319	149274	140742	142609
(f) Scheduled commercial bank advances	67121	75476	78288	91526

So many factors influenced the mobilisation of resources such as rapid branch expansion, circulation of money increased in volume, the CRR, favourable business environment, high rate of interest. Recently the banks have been facing stiff competition from the mutual funds, housing banks, leasing and investment companies. The development financial institutions offer higher interest rates and have tried to mobilise the savings of the household.

(c) Expansion of bank credit: After the liberalisation, the bank credit has been expanded exponentially. It is freely available to well-established houses of business concerns. But the tiny and small-scale business concerns are still neglected by the banks with the increase in bank deposits. There has been continuous expansion of bank credit to the corporate sector. The flow of funds towards the corporate sector made the industrial development. The industrial development is the most important factor in the financial architecture of the nation. A careful financial planning may lead to the well-structured industrial empire.

(d) Development banking: Traditionally, there has been good relations between banks and industries. Some traditional industries are well-linked with commercial banks for their financial requirements. These industries are cotton textiles in Western India, jute industries in Eastern India, sugar industries in Northern India. Previously, banks were unwilling to venture into the new fields of industries. The concentration of banks in large and commercial areas was responsible to the virtual neglect of the non-commercial sector. Presently, the banking sector moved away from the traditional sector to another diversion. This concept of banking has widened towards development. Bankers are now financial to small industries, artisans and other neglected groups in the country. After liberalisation, lending also became hospitality management. In every stage the customer case will be taken. Now-a-days banking is becoming like **shopping**. The new breed banks changed the entire banking environment, they are able to provide more facilities to their valuable customers. They treat the customer like a well-dignified guest. Now the customer is the **king** in the market, if he has the right intention to borrow money. Financial discipline is the most important factor for every nation, every individual, every business concern. Financial discipline can be maintained by every honest person, every good-reputed firm and every sincere nation. It can be described as the weapon for building a strong economy for the country. If there is no financial discipline for any one, it will be like the beautiful women without moral values. Therefore, the financial discipline will definitely enhance the status of a person/concern country.

(e) Priority sector lending: Before the nationalisation of banks, the commercial banks completely neglected the agriculture sector which is the mother status to our nation. We cannot ignore the foundation because our country depends upon agriculture. Agriculture is the basic foundation to the industrial sector. Therefore, we must recognise the status of agriculture in our economy. Our economy is entirely dominated by $\mathbf{H_2O}$. Because, there is no rain, there will be no economy, our entire industrial sector will be collapsed. The farmers in India need money for their agricultural operations and for land development. At present, even the farmers are borrowing money from the unorganised market at higher rate of interest. They are even charged with 120% rate of interest per annum. Soon after the nationalisation, the commercial banks are asked to provide finance to the priority sectors such as agriculture, small industry business and small transport operators, professional and self-employed persons. They are also directed to grant loans for education, housing loans for weaker sections and consumption loans. In 1980 RBI issued certain directives to the banks for granting the loans to priority sectors.

(f) Social banking: The commercial banks also have social responsibility. They are working for profit motive. They should mix the services with profit. The government has introduced schemes for the commercial banks to eradicate poverty. The following elements have been used to encounter the poverty problems:

(i) Differential Interest Rates
(ii) Integrated Rural Development Programme
(iii) Lead bank scheme

The Government of India introduced the differential interest rates scheme in 1972. This scheme covers 162 districts and later it was extended to the entire nation. According to the scheme guidelines, the public sector banks give loans at a concessional interest rate of 4% to the weaker sections of the community. The scheme is aimed to promote gainful employment among the weaker sections. Under this scheme, the banks are directed by the RBI to finance:

(a) Scheduled Castes and Scheduled Tribes and others engaged in agriculture and allied activities.
(b) The physically handicapped people by offering loans for cottage and rural industries such as sewing garments, running way side stalls, basket making etc.
(c) People engaged in elementary processing of forest products.
(d) Village artisans.

In April 1983, the Government of India set up a task force as this scheme to examine the various provisions of the scheme and to suggest any modifications. The Task Force Committees report was considered by the Finance Ministry and the following decisions were made:

(i) The scheme will continue to operate by charging interest at the rate of **4% p.a.** to the beneficiaries.

(ii) The beneficiaries of this scheme should be selected on the basis of government directions.

(iii) The beneficiaries should not be recipients of benefits under any other subsidised schemes of the government.

(iv) The ceiling of annual family income of beneficiary for eligibility for assistance is raised from **Rs. 2,000 to Rs. 6,400** in rural areas and from **Rs.3,000 to Rs.7,200** in urban areas.

Integrated Rural Development Programme is a pioneering programme introduced by the Central Government. This programme is to rectify imbalance in rural economy. It is also aimed for all-round progress and prosperity of the downtrodden rural masses. This programme is a social obligation on the part of the commercial banks. This is a poverty alleviation programme and single largest anti-poverty programme introduced by the Government of India since 1978.

(C) Lead bank scheme is a new strategy introduced by Central Government. It is aimed to develop banking sector in the post-nationalisation era. This scheme is the brainchild of **The Gadgil Study Group** in October 1969. It was enabled the commercial banks for assuming the role of leadership for better credit facilities throughout the country as the basis of area approach. According to regulations of this scheme, all the districts in the nation have been allotted to the State Bank group, nationalised banks and private Indian banks. A lead bank is a dynamic agent for economic development through the expansion of branches, and diversification of credit facilities in the district allotted to it. The lead bank is responsible for surveying the financial resources and potential for banking development in the concerned district. The basic objectives of a lead bank are:

(a) to widen the bank branches in all important localities of the lead district.

(b) to provide maximum credit facilities for the development of entire lead district.

(c) to mobilise the small savings from the public through entire district.

(d) to coordinate all the activities of cooperative banks, commercial banks and financial institutions in the district.

(e) to survey about the industrial units activities and which do not have banking facilities.

(f) to conduct a survey about the marketing facilities for agriculture produce, storage and warehousing, etc.

(g) to provide facilities for stocking of fertilisers and other agricultural inputs.

(h) to maintain cordial relations with government and semi-government agencies.

(D) Performance of banks: The commercial banks face a triple jeopardy. They are losing market share, their profitability is being seriously squeezed. Their balance sheets are not strong and their sovereign support which has buttressed them so far, is becoming a questionable situation. A key element of the process of economic reforms and liberalisation in the decade of the 1990s in India recognising the financial sector to be something more than merely an adjunct of the so-called real sector. The financial performance of the banks were presented below:[17]

Statement Showing the Financial Contours of Banking (1990-91)

(Rs. in crores)

Particulars	*All Scheduled Commercial Banks*	*Public Sector Banks*	*SBI Group*	*Nationalised Banks*	*Private Banks*	*Foreign Banks*
(a) Interest Income	27,521	24,756	9,061	15,695	885	1,880
(b) Interest Expenses	18,968	17,109	5,673	11,436	552	1,307
(c) Net Interest	**8,553**	**7,647**	**3,388**	**4,259**	333	**573**
(d) Operating Expenses	7,596	6,883	2,556	4,327	318	395
(e) Net income after operating expenses	957	764	832	- 68	15	178
(f) Provisions and Contingencies (Incl. Tax)	3097	2,685	1,640	1,045	68	344
(g) Non-Interest Income	2883	2,397	958	1,439	88	398
(h) Profit after tax	743	476	150	326	35	232
(i) Total assets	2,84,162	2,59,308	93,012	1,66,296	8,869	15,985
(j) Share of total assets (%)	-	91.3	32.7	58.5	3.1	5.6
(k) Share of profits	-	64.1	20.2	43.9	4.7	31.2
(l) Interest Income (%)	9.7	9.6	9.7	9.4	10	11.8
(m) Interest Expense (%)	6.7	6.6	6.1	6.9	6.2	8.2
(n) Net profit after tax (%)	0.26	0.18	0.16	0.20	0.39	1.45

Statement Showing Financial Contours of Banking 2000-01[18]

Particulars	All Scheduled Commercial Banks	PSB	SBI Group	Nationalised Banks	Old Private Indian banks	New Pvt.. Banks	Foreign Banks
(a) Interest income	1,14,951	90,984	34,017	56957	8,052	6,444	9,471
(b) Interest expense	78,152	61,693	22,903	38,790	5,932	4,759	5,768
(c) Net interest	36,799	29,291	11,114	18,178	2,120	1,685	3,703
(d) Operating expense	34,179	28,013	10,730	17,284	1,679	1,376	3,111
(e) Net income after operating exp.	2,620	1,278	384	894	441	309	592
(f) Provisional and contingencies (Incl. tax)	13,323	9,476	3,518	5,958	957	730	2,160
(g) Non-Interest income	17,127	12,515	5,356	7,159	1,039	1,060	2,513
(h) Profit after tax	6,424	4,317	2,222	2,095	523	639	945
(i) Total assets	1,294,974	10,29,770	4,02,878	6,26,892	84,607	78,776	1,01,824
(j) Share of total assets (%)	-	79.5	31.1	48.4	6.5	6.1	7.9
(k) Share of profits (%)	-	67.2	34.6	32.6	8.1	10	14.7
(l) Share of net NPA (%)	-	86.1	29	57	8.5	2.9	2.5
(m) Interest income (%)	8.9	8.8	8.4	9.1	9.5	8.2	9.3
(n) Interest expense (%)	6.0	6.0	5.7	6.2	7.0	6.0	5.7
(o) Net interest (%)	2.8	2.8	2.8	2.9	2.5	2.1	3.6
(p) Operating expenses (%)	2.6	2.7	2.7	2.7	1.9	1.7	3.0
(q) Net income after operating expenses (%)	0.20	0.12	0.10	0.14	0.52	0.39	0.58
(r) Provisions and contingencies (Incl. tax) (%)	1.03	0.92	0.87	0.95	1.13	0.93	2.12
(s) Non-interest income (%)	1.32	1.22	1.33	1.14	1.23	1.35	2.47
(t) Profit after tax (%)	0.50	0.42	0.55	0.33	0.62	0.81	0.93
(u) Gross NPA (%)	11.4	12.4	12.7	12.2	11.1	5.1	6.8
(v) Net NPA/Total assets (%)	2.5	2.7	2.3	3.0	3.3	1.2	0.8
(w) Net NPA/net worth (%)	47.9	56	54.2	56.9	60.9	21.5	8.9

Statement Showing Phases of Recapitalisation of Nationalisation of Banks[19]

Particulars	*No. of banks recapitalised*	*Rs. in crores*
Phase I		
1985-86	19	400
1986-87	19	400
1987-88	18	200
1988-89	18	200
1989-90	08	700
1990-91	11	700
1991-92	15	700
1992-93	13	700
		4,000
Phase II		
1993-94	19	5,700
1994-95	13	5,287
		10,987
Phase III		
1995-96	06	850
1996-97	06	1,509
1997-98	03	2,700
1998-99	03	400
1999-2000	0	0
2000-2001	0	0
		5,459
Phase I		4,000
Phase II		10,987
Phase III		5,459
		20,446

Statement Showing Groupwise Financial Performance[20] during 1994-95 to 2000-2001(%)

Group	1994-95	2000-2001
1. Nationalised banks	56	48
2. State Bank group	31	31
3. Old private sector banks	05	07
4. New private sector banks	0	06
5. Foreign banks	08	08
Deposits		
1. Nationalised banks	58	52
2. State Bank group	28	30
3. Old private sector banks	07	07
4. New private sector banks	0	06
5. Foreign banks	07	06
Net Profit		
1. Nationalised banks	13	33
2. State Bank group	40	35
3. Old private sector banks	15	08
4. New private sector banks	0	10
5. Foreign banks	33	15
Advances		
1. Nationalised banks	55	50
2. State Bank group	30	29
3. Old private sector banks	07	07
4. New private sector banks	0	06
5. Foreign banks	08	08

Statement Showing the Bank Groupwise Return on Total Assets[21]

Bank Group	1997-98	1998-99	1999-2000	2000-01
1. Public sector banks	0.77	0.42	0.57	0.42
2. Nationalised banks	0.62	0.37	0.44	0.33
3. State Bank group	1.06	0.51	0.80	0.55
4. All private banks	1.04	0.68	0.88	0.71
5. Old private sector banks	0.81	0.48	0.81	0.62
6. New private sector banks	1.55	1.03	0.97	0.81
7. Foreign banks	0.97	0.69	1.17	0.93
8. All banks	0.82	0.49	0.66	0.50

Statement Showing Non-performing Assets of Public Sector Banks During the Period 1993-2001[22]

Year	Gross NPAs						Net NPAs					
	Nation-alised Banks	% to Advances	SBI Group	% to Advances	Total	% to Advances	Natio-nalised Banks	% to Advances	SBI Group	% to Advances	Total	% to Advances
1993-94	27064	25.84	13977	22.94	41041	25%	13254	16	6436	12	19690	14
1994-95	25114	19.98	13277	18.50	38385	19%	11789	12	5778	9	17567	11
1995-96	28366	19.52	13295	15.46	41661	18%	12935	10	5362	7	18297	9
1996-97	29209	19.05	14368	15.81	43577	18%	13903	10	6382	8	20285	9
1997-98	30130	16.88	15522	14.57	45652	16%	14497	9	6735	7	21232	8
1998-99	33069	16.02	18641	15.67	51710	16%	15794	8	8417	7	24211	8
1999-2000	33521	13.91	19773	14.08	53294	14%	17435	8	8753	7	26108	7
2000-01	34180	12.19	20593	12.73	54773	12%	18491	7	9445	6	27936	7

NPA: Non-performing Assets

Statement Showing Select Parameters of Nationalised Banks 1996-97 and 2000-01 (percent)[23]

Name of bank	Capital Adequacy Ratio		Return on Assets		Net NPA/Net Advances		Spread/Total Assets	
	1996-97	2000-01	1996-97	2000-01	1996-97	2000-01	1996-97	2000-01
1. Allahabad Bank	10.57	10.50	0.51	0.18	14.84	11.23	3.05	3.09
2. Andhra Bank	12.05	13.40	0.01	0.59	4.10	2.95	2.98	2.45
3. Bank of Baroda	11.80	12.80	0.73	0.45	7.53	6.77	3.21	3.06
4. Bank of India	10.25	12.23	1.01	0.44	6.93	6.72	3.00	2.78
5. Bank of Maharashtra	9.07	10.64	0.57	0.24	9.66	7.41	3.67	2.93
6. Canara Bank	10.17	9.84	0.44	0.43	9.32	4.84	3.19	2.83
7. Central Bank of India	9.41	10.02	0.65	0.10	14.40	9.72	3.17	3.07
8. Corporation Bank	11.27	13.30	1.66	1.55	3.63	1.98	3.87	2.95
9. Dena Bank	10.81	7.33	0.81	0	9.38	18.37	3.85	2.51
10. Indian Bank	**–18.81**	–	–	–	25.24	10.06	0.71	1.84
11. Indian Overseas Bank	10.07	10.24	0.58	0.38	7.64	7.01	2.38	2.91
12. Oriental Bank of Commerce	17.50	11.81	1.60	0.80	5.64	3.60	3.89	2.92
13. Punjab & Sind Bank	9.22	11.42	0.29	0.10	12.04	12.27	2.60	2.51
14. Punjab National Bank	9.15	10.24	0.71	0.73	10.38	6.69	3.47	3.21
15. Syndicate Bank	8.80	11.72	0.43	0.91	7.53	4.05	3.17	3.87
16. UCO Bank	3.16	9.05	–1.46	0.14	13.73	6.35	1.93	2.42
17. Union Bank of India	10.53	10.86	1.01	0.40	6.98	6.87	3.41	3.13
18. United Bank of India	8.20	10.40	–	0.10	19.20	10.50	1.54	2.39
19. Vijaya Bank	11.50	11.50	0.30	0.53	9.56	6.23	2.91	3.23

Statement Showing Net Interest Spread as a Proportion of Total Assets – Public Sector Banks (percentage)[24]

Year ending March 31	*SBI Group Banks*	*19 Nationalised Banks Group*	*All Public Sector Banks*	*Old Indian Private Sector*	*New Indian Private Sector*	*Foreign Banks*
1995	3.26	2.73	2.92	3.04	1.17	4.24
1996	3.34	2.92	3.08	3.14	2.84	3.74
1997	3.48	2.97	3.16	2.93	2.88	4.13
1998	3.14	2.78	2.91	2.57	2.23	3.93
1999	2.85	2.77	2.80	2.15	1.98	3.47
2000	2.76	2.66	2.70	2.33	1.95	3.92
2001	2.76	2.90	2.84	2.51	2.14	3.64

(E) Reforms of the banking sector: India has witnessed a phenomenal expansion during the last decades. The commercial banks spread throughout the country with their branch expansion. They occupy a dominant role in the financial system. The development of the financial sector is a major achievement and it has contributed significantly to stimulate the level of savings and household sector. The banking sector is still in problems and as a result, productivity and efficiency of the sector have suffered. Therefore, the profitability of the banking sector has been eroded. The public sector banks have become weak financially and incurring losses year after year. They rendered poor service to customers and adopted outdated technology and they are unable to meet the growing challenges of a competitive environment. Hence the Central Government set up a High Level Committee with **Mr. Narasimhan, a former Governor of the RBI** as Chairman. The Committee had been appointed to examine all the aspects such as structure, organisation, functions and procedures of the financial system. The Committee submitted its report to the Government in November 1991. The Committee found that there were poor directions to the banks from the policy framers. The system has been influenced by political interference. The Committee has acknowledged the spectacular success of the banks since nationalisation of banks. It has also suffered serious decline in productivity and efficiency. The Committee has pointed out that directed investment and directed credit programme are the two major causes for the state of affairs.

Recommendations of the Committee on the banking sector: The Committee's recommendations are based on the assumption that the financial resources of the banking sector come from the public and they have to be deployed for the maximum benefits to their owners. The Committee recommendations aim at:

(a) Providing better operational environment.
(b) Providing full autonomy for the banks in their decision-making process.
(c) Providing a ground for greater degree of professionalism in banking sector.
(d) Providing setting up of Asset Reconstruction Fund.
(e) Removing dual control of the sector.
(f) Adjustments regarding SLR and CRR.
(g) Providing prudential norms by the RBI.

(F) Banking system—the securities scam: The Central Government introduced many innovative methods after the stock exchange crash in 1988-89, such as liberalisation of licensing, liberal fiscal measures, and positive export-import policy and greater scope for the private sector. Therefore, there was an upward swing in the Stock Market, spearheaded by excellent performance by market leaders and best industrial policies. This upward trend led by the market was given a big boost by Dr. Manmohan Singh's 1991-92 budget with a series of dynamic market activities, the ordinary share prices rose from 189 at the end of March 1988 to 528 at the end of March 1991 and exceeded 1000 in February 1992. The budget 1992-93 sent the stock market, and led to booming into a frenzy. The two budget sessions alone, Sensex flare up by 360 points. The Sensex crossed 3350 on March 9 and crossed 4,300 in April 20, 1992. The RBI conducted preliminary investigations about the aspects of securities trading by banks that led to the exposure of serious irregularities and frauds in the securities transactions of several banks. The members of the stock exchange by colluding with some bank officials violated the rules and regulations and diverted funds for speculative business in the stock market. These malpractices and violations are popularly known as **"securities scam"**. This situation led to the most worst manipulated booms in the market and later led to huge losses. The banks were responsible for the huge amount of losses and revealed serious weaknesses of internal control and supervision of banks. Hence, the RBI set up a high level authority known as **"Janaki Raman"** Committee to find out several types of irregularities in this aspect. The Committee found the following irregularities of the banks:

(a) The banks purchased the securities through the brokers and the amount was credited to their accounts directly or indirectly.
(b) The banks showed the ready forward transactions either on their own or clients accounts with brokers. These funds were used for speculation business.
(c) The brokers in the stock exchange were patronised by the bank officials through discounting bills, which were not genuine transactions.
(d) The banks also misused the funds through call money system. They showed large payments to other banks which in turn were transferred to the brokers accounts. On the due date the banks showed repayment of money by themselves only not by brokers.
(e) The Merchant Banking Wings of the public sector banks misused the Inter-Corporate deposits and passed on to the brokers through **Ready Forward** transactions.

There were so many types of irregularities and the Committee estimated that there would be unreconciled amount of **Rs. 4,000 crores**. All these irregularities were made by the banking community. According to the Committee reports the irregularities took place in three factors.

(A) The public sector banks made these irregularities to earn more profitable avenue of investment.
(B) The banking community burdened with **CRR** and **SLR** commitments and priority lending sector were faced with the problem of low interest income and possible losses and they took the opportunity to show higher profits by this way.
(C) Brokers of the stock exchange needed funds during this period to finance their overbought positions availed this situation.

Definition

The RBI describes the money market as "The centre for dealings, mainly of a short-term character, in monetary assets; it meets the short-term requirements of borrowers and provides liquidity or cash to the lenders".[25]

According to Crowther, "The money market is the collective name given to the various firms and institutions that deal in the various grades of near money".[26]

Money market is like the commodity market. In money market the funds are available at a certain price. The funds are supplied by the lender and the funds are borrowed by the borrower. It refers to lending and borrowing activities of banking, financial institutions and individuals. It includes legal tender and near money. Commercial banks and Discount Houses deal in short term loans. It provides facilities for the adjustment of liquidity positions of commercial bankers. NBFIs corporate sectors and other investors. It also facilitates the flow of funds to the most important uses in the economy. It provides funds to the finance production and distribution. It promotes the economic growth of the nation. It constitutes a highly efficient mechanism for credit control. The features of money market are presented below:

1. Constituents.
2. Dealers of money market.
3. Near money asset.
4. No need of personal contact.
5. Short-term funds.
6. Heterogenous market.
7. Fluctuations.
8. Different from capital market.

1. Constituents: Money market has three constituents such as (a) It has borrowers and lenders, (b) It deals with short-term credit instruments, and (c) It has a price in the form of rate of interest.

2. Dealers of Money Market: Generally the markets are participated by lenders and borrowers. The borrowers in the money market are manufacturers, traders, speculators and government institutions. Generally, the lenders in the money market are commercial banks, Central banks and non-banking financial intermediaries.

3. Near Money Asset**:** Money market deals in short-term financial instruments which are called as "near money asset". These assets are liquid and readily marketable. These assets are useful and against which the funds can be borrowed from the money market. These near money assets include bills of exchange, BRs, short-term government securities.

4. No Need of Personal Contact: Money market is not restricted to a particular place. It is a place where the borrowers and lenders meet each other. But in normal practice it is not necessary that the borrowers and lenders should have personal contacts with each other at a specified place. The parties may carry on their deals through telephone or mail. Therefore, the money market relates to arrangement for transfer of funds between lenders and borrowers.

5. Short-term Funds: Money market provides fund to the needy party for short-term period. The borrowers can obtain funds for periods ranging from a day to six months.

6. Heterogenous Market: The money market consists of several sub-markets. Each market deals with a specified short-term credit instrument for example, bills market, call money market.

7. Fluctuations: Money markets change with time. The functions of money markets in different countries are broadly the same. But the financial institutions and the instruments vary considerably from country to country.

8. Different from Capital Market: Money market is a market for short-term credit and capital market is a long-term market. It is different on the basis of maturity period. Money market deals with short-term lending and borrowing of funds. The capital market deals with long-term borrowing and lending of funds.

Functions and Importance of Money Market

Money market plays an important role in the process of industrial and commercial progress of the nation. A well-developed money market is essential for a modern digital economy. Money market has important role to play in the economic development of a nation. The importance of a developed money market and its various functions are presented below:

(a) Financing Trade and Industry
(b) Profitable venture
(c) Help to Central bank
(d) Help to Government
(e) Capital formation

(a) Financial Trade and Industry: Money market provides fund to the commercial enterprises on short-term basis. It plays a crucial role in financing both domestic and international trade. Short-term funds are available to the traders through bills of exchange. The bills are discounted by the bill market. In International trade the activities are carried out by the **acceptance house**. The money market also finances the industry by various methods. It contributes to the growth of the corporate sector. It helps the industries through the system of bills and commercial paper. It arranges loans to meet the working capital requirements of the industry. The working capital is more useful to the smooth functioning of the production schedule of the industry. The long-term requirement of the fund will be supplied by the **Capital market** to the industry. But the capital market depends upon the nature of the money market. The interest rates of the money market influence the capital market. Therefore, the money market indirectly helps the industries. Hence, the short-term requirements of the industrial sector may be fulfilled by the money market.

(b) Profitable Venture: The commercial banks play an important role in the money market. Generally, the commercial banks function is accepting deposits from the public and advancing the loans to the borrowers. Sometimes the banks will have some idle funds at their disposal. Therefore, the banks will earn profit by deploying the surplus fund into the money market. Hence, the main objective of the commercial banks can be achieved. The money market provides liquidity to the investment made by the banks. Usually the excess reserves of banks are invested in near money assets. The near money assets are highly liquid and can be easily converted into cash. The commercial banks can reduce the loss by participating in money market. The money market provides a short-term assignment to the commercial banks. The money market is a best place when the banks need funds in emergency. If the commercial banks have scarcity of funds, they need not to approach the Central bank at higher interest rate. The banks can meet their requirements by recalling their investments from the money market. Therefore, the money market creates an opportunity for income generation to the commercial banks. The banks also become self sufficient with the help of the money market. The commercial banks can take the advantages of the money market according to their routine requirements.

(c) Help to Central Bank: The Central bank is the supreme authority in the banking system. The Central bank plays an important role in the economy of a nation. The existence of a developed money market smoothens the functioning of the Central bank. The money market increases the efficiency of the Central bank. The money market helps the Central bank in two methods.

(i) The indication of short-term rates of interest of the money market will reflect the monetary and banking conditions in the country. This situation will guide the Central bank to adopt an appropriate banking policy.

(ii) The money markets are highly sensitive and integrated, they help the Central bank to secure quick and wide spread influence on the sub-markets.

(d) Help to Government: The money market helps the government. It provides the short-term funds at low cost to the government through treasury bills. The government has the borrowing capacity from other modes, which are inflationary in nature. The money market helps the government in floating long-term loans. The changes in the short-term interest rates of the money market influence the interest rates on long-term capital.

(e) Capital Formation: The money market plays a vital role in accelerating the process of capital formation. The money market tends to establish equilibrium between saving and investment. The development of the money market leads to the development of the capital market. The capital market provides a strong base for the long-term nature of investments. The development of the capital market reflects the overall economic position of a nation. The capital market will be flooded with the new issues of equity. The primary market has the only one to accelerate the growth of capital formation. The New issue market depends upon the number of factors.

Characteristics of Money Market

The characteristics of the money market are presented below:

(a) In this market the short-term funds are borrowed and lent.
(b) In this market the parties mutually agree on the terms and conditions of the exchange of funds.
(c) The interest rate is determined on the basis of demand and supply of money.
(d) The fund suppliers in the market are commercial banks and financial institutions.
(e) The borrowers in this markets are government, commercial banks, manufacturing concerns and firms.

Characteristics of Developed Fund Underdeveloped Money Market

A strong money market is an indication to the growth of the economy. The money market influences the capital market. Ultimately the capital market accelerates the growth of the economy. Therefore, the money market is the basic element for all other markets. The money market is more sensitive and integrated. The development of money market refers to a better organised and systematic market. The developed money market has greater responsibilities to change the demand and supply of short-term funds in all of its segments. The extent of development of a money market is associated with the level of degree of economic development of a nation. The examples for developed money markets are **UK and USA**. The underdeveloped or developing countries are the examples of underdeveloped money market. **India** is the best example for under-developed money market. The following characteristics persist in the developed money market. If any of the following characteristics is not present the money market will be treated as underdeveloped.

1. Participation of Central bank.
2. Strong banking system.
3. Availability of financial instruments.
4. Active sub-markets.
5. Structure of the market.
6. Adequate Resources.
7. Faith in the money market.

1. Participation of Central Banl : A market is said to be a developed market when the Central bank involves fully which functions as monetary and banking authority in the country. The Central bank's presence is necessary to guide, control and regulate the money market. It is an essential prerequisite for a developed money market. A powerful Central bank guides all the affairs of the money market. The **monetary policy** of the government will be prepared and implemented by the Central bank of the concerned nation. The Central bank formulates a suitable monetary policy to meet the needs of the money market. The Central bank assists the banking system to flourish and maintain the economic stability in the country. It enables the money market to secure adequate funds through open market operations. An efficient and experienced Central bank can properly guide, control and lead the money market towards better achievement. The Central bank is the lender of the last resort. It keeps the cash reserves of the banks and provides funds in times of emergency by granting them funds through re-discounting the eligible securities. In underdeveloped money market the Central bank is unable to take effective steps to influence the money market.

2. Strong Banking System: A developed market only exists when there is a strong infrastructural banking system in the country. However, the citizens should also have the banking habits. The commercial banks are the **oxygen** to the developed money market. They are the basic suppliers of short-term funds. Therefore, the functioning of the commercial banks will have its effect on the money market. The commercial banks serve as a connecting link between the Central bank and various sectors of the money market. The origin of the money market is closely associated with the banking system. If the more development occurs in the banking sector, the more will be the development in the money market. If the Central bank closely associates with the money market it will be easy to become a developed money market. If the commercial banks are efficiently organised, the various compartments related with them will be strongly organised. A highly organised system will enhance the level of the money market capabilities. Therefore, the development of the money market is closely associated and reflected by the structure of the banking system. Any policy regarding the financing pattern of the commercial banks has direct impact on the money market. In the underdeveloped money markets the number of developed Commercial banks is very less and their business are restricted to the urban areas the citizens of the underdeveloped countries have not fully developed the banking habits.

3. Availability of Financial Instruments: A strong money market demands a regular and adequate supply of a variety of financial instruments. The financial instruments in the money market are bills of exchange, treasury bills, short-term government bonds etc. The developed money market consists of adequate number of dealers and brokers. They actively involve in the money market. They buy and sell these assets. An underdeveloped market consists of inadequate dealers and brokers. The various types of financial instruments are not available in the under-developed market. The various forms of securities should be available to every segment of money market in developed markets. This is possible only when the experienced dealers with such securities.

4. Active Sub-markets: Developed money market consists of well-organised sub-markets. Each and every sub-market has specialised in a particular type of financial asset. **For example**: The New York money market has commercial paper market, certificate of deposit market, treasury bills market, banker's acceptance market. Federal fund market specialised in repurchase agreement market. The money market can flourish and develop only when the sub-markets are fully developed and are associated with each other. If the sub-markets are not developed and are not co-ordinating to each other, the money market may not develop with full swing.

5. Structure of the Market: The developed money market has an integrated structure. The sub-market are very closely associated with each other. The information and funds move easily and quickly from one market to another market. There will be free movement of borrowers and lenders from one segment to another. In developed money market, all the sub-markets are highly sensitive. They influence each other in all the segments of the money market. There is no interrelation between segments of the sub-markets of the underdeveloped money market. There is no co-ordination between sub-markets in the underdeveloped money markets.

6. Adequate Resources: In developed markets the sub-markets have adequate resources. The underdeveloped money market is unable to mobilise the required funds. If the money market is able to attract foreign funds it will be developed money market. **New York and London money markets** are the examples of developed markets.

7. Faith on the Capital Market: The money market can develop only with the faith in it. The dishonesty and malpractices may spoil the foundation of the money market. The political condition, viable economic growth absence of discrimination cause the up serving of the money market.

Importance of Developed Money Market

The money market plays an important role in the economic development of a nation. The importance of the developed money markets are presented below:

(a) Large amount of lending.
(b) Trade and industry.
(c) Cyclical fluctuations.
(d) Service to government.

(a) Large amount of lending: The money market consists of borrowers and lenders. They play an important role in a developed money market. A large amount of borrowing is possible. Crores of rupees are transferred from lenders to the borrowers. The commercial banks are main suppliers of the fund. The whole economy could get a large amount of funds for development. The scarcity of funds is removed quickly. Because the commercial banks can fill the gap in shortage of funds in the money market. The banks can provide huge funds without reducing their liquidity. The money market is a suitable place for banks to park their idle fund in the market. The investment in financial instruments of the money market can earn certain income on the near liquid assets. The banks are able to get back the money income immediately at a short notice. The money market is useful to all the players such as commercial banks, financial institutions, manufacturing concerns and society.

(b) Trade and industry: The money market can provide financial assistance to trade and industry. The business concerns get their short-term requirements from money market. The money market provides working capital to the corporate sector. The individual businessmen are mostly benefited by the acceptance house and discount house. The traders can easily get money from the bill market. The bill market is a part of money market. The discount houses or acceptance houses can discount the bills which are issued by the traders. Businessmen and producers get adequate funds for their purposes through the money market. The commercial banks also can benefit from the money market. Because they lend the money whenever they have surplus funds and they can procure the funds in case of scarcity of their funds. The global markets developed due to the money market.

(c) Cyclical fluctuations: The developed money market can reduce the cyclical fluctuations. The money market is highly sensitive and mechanised. The Central bank has the authority to control the economy through money market operations. The government can inject new credit to the economy in depression and siphon it off in boom. The Central bank is the supreme authority in the monetary aspects. It can control the credit through quantitative and qualitative measures. It can reduce considerably the dangerous effects of depression and crisis. The controller of the money market is **Central bank**. It can diffuse the effects of the cyclical fluctuations which are raised in the normal economy. These effects are possible only in a developed money market. The performance of the money market is the barometer of monetary and banking conditions in the country.

(d) Service to the Government: The developed money market can service the government in every monetary aspect. The development of the economy can considerably be materialised by the government. The government can easily mobilise the funds by issuing treasury bills. The treasury bills are one of the most important financial instruments in the money market operations. The treasury bills can reduce additional pressure on the inflation. Because in the absence of treasury bills the government shall print the currency notes which causes the inflationary pressure on the economy.

Indian Money Market

The financial markets are the combination of money market and capital market. Money market refers to short-term finance. It deals with relatively liquid and quickly marketable assets. The money deals with the financial instruments such as **Treasury Bills, Government Securities, Bills of Exchange** etc. The money market in India consists of two sectors.

(A) Organised sector.
(B) Unorganised sector.

(A) Organised Sector

The Indian money market originated after the establishment of the RBI in 1935. The organised sector comprises the RBI, SBI with its 7 associates, 20 nationalised banks, scheduled banks, non-scheduled commercial banks, foreign banks and RRBs. The RBI is the apex body of the money market. The biggest lender of the money market is the RBI, which controls the entire banking sector in India. All these organisations involve in the money market, which are controlled and guided by the RBI. Therefore, the sector is known as **organised sector** of the money market. It is called organised because its parts are coordinated by the RBI. The other institutions also involve in this sector. They are LIC, GIC, UTI operating in this market indirectly. The large companies and quasi-government organisations also make their surplus funds available to the organised sector through banks. The cooperative institutions also participate in the organised sector of the money market. The organised sector of Indian money market can be further classified in the following way:

1. Call Money market.
2. Treasury bill market.
3. Commercial bill market.
4. Certificate of deposits.
5. Commercial paper markets.
6. Collateral Loan market.

1. Call Money Market

Call money deals in call loans or call money granted for one day. The important component of organised money market is the call money market. The participants in the call money market are mostly banks. It is also known as inter-bank call money market. The suppliers of the fund in the call money market is the banks and demand comes from the banks also. Call money market is the part of national money market. The day to day surplus funds of banks are traded in the call money market. The call money market is a short-term nature. The maturity of the call market varies between one day and a **fortnight.** The loans of the call market are repayable on demand and at the option of either the lender or the borrower. They are highly liquid. The nature of this market in different countries varies from each other. The nature of the call market in the US and UK as per their acts and regulations. Call loans and short notice in the balance sheets of banks is a highly liquid asset. They are unsecured in India. The money and credit situation in India every year is subject to seasonal fluctuations. The trading on the call market is influenced by seasonal fluctuations. The seasonal ups and downs are reflected in the volume of money at call and short notice and the rates are at different times of the year. The call money borrowings are highest around March every year. Because the withdrawals of deposits in March to meet year end tax payment. The financial institutions also withdraw the money to meet their statutory obligations. If the banks CRR increases, automatically there will be increase in call money borrowings.

Participants: The important players in the call money market are scheduled commercial banks, non-scheduled banks, foreign banks, Urban banks, Cooperative banks, Discount and Finance House of India, and Securities Trading Corporation of India. The DFHI and STC borrow as well as lend like banks and primary dealers in the call market. The foreign banks borrow money from this market due to difficulties in tappings deposits and increase in the cost of servicing FCNR deposits. The large commercial banks have been regularly participating in this market excluding SBI. The SBI kept itself away from the call market till 1970. During 1970s a new development arises in the market that the direct participation in it by the term lending institutions like GIC, UTI and LIC. The indirect participation by other institutions such as IDBI, IFCI and ICICI. The continuous participation in the call market by the players would help to integrate the long-term and short-term money markets in the economy.

Geographical Location: Call markets are located in commercial centres like **Mumbai, Kolkata, Chennai, Delhi and Ahmedabad**. The stock exchanges are also located in these cities. Mumbai and Kolkata dominate call markets in India. **Mumbai** is the financial capital of India and the head offices of RBI, LIC and UTI are located there. It also has the biggest stock exchange in Asia. The development of IT has facilitated for the flow of funds. The call rates are prevailing in different centres in different rates. There are a large number of local call markets developed and marketed by in indigenous local bankers. **For example**: in Gujarat the large payments or remittances are made, the local banks charge the price of overnight money is **02 paise** per hundred rupees per night.

Turnover of the Call Market: The turnover of the call market in India has been smaller than that of the US and UK. Because the bill market in India is underdeveloped. The call loans to bill market cannot be available. The volume of call loans depends upon the extent of trading in bills of exchange, treasury bills etc. The banks in India are not willing to offer loans to brokers and dealers in bills and securities. The another important factor is that the commercial banks can re-discount their bills from the RBI as a result of which they have much less interested towards the loans from the money market. The commercial banks hold fairly large cash reserves. Therefore, there is no need to get the funds from the call market. The other factor is that the government securities are directly sold by the RBI without much intervention by brokers and dealers. The turnover in securities traded on the stock exchanges is also relatively small. There is no scope in our financial system to extend support to the stock exchanges by the banks. So many regulations have been imposed by the RBI on banks in respect of loans against shares. Hence the trading activities on stock exchanges are carried out by the members using their own funds. Therefore, the turnover in stock exchange has been derived by the members from private sources. There are fluctuations in the volume of demand and for supply of call loan due to various factors. The following are the causes for volatility of call market:

1. The financial resources in the banking system depends on the extent of deposits accruals.
2. Any increase in deposits with banks, needs to explore possibilities of investment overseas.
3. The bank resources flow to call market in which some of overseas for investment would increase.
4. All the banks accrue deposits, then there will be an increase in volume of inter-bank call loan transactions.
5. In a case such as the supply of funds to the outside of the banking system borrowers would increase.
6. The differential growth in the deposits of different banks would lead to increase in volume of Inter-bank call loans market.
7. The demand for call loans would depend upon the stock market situation, industrial sector needs and commercial requirements.
8. The turnover of call market is determined by the possibility of quick investment or liquid assets.
9. The opening of subscriptions to government loans would lead to increase for the demand to call loans.

10. Usually the demand for call money tends to broaden in December, March, June.
11. The velocity of the remittance and clearance system in the country leads to show an impact on the day-to-day volume of call loans.
12. The policies of the RBI leads to show an impact as the volume of call market.
13. The pressure on call money market reaches a peak towards the end of banking week, i.e., Friday.
14. The foreign exchange market activity becomes a significant factor in the turnover of call market.

The annual statement of monetary and credit policy released on April 19, 2001 projected a GDP growth of **6% to 6.5%** for 2000-01. These projections are based on the assumptions of a reasonable monsoon, good performance of exports and a revival of the industrial sector. The annual policy statement also indicated that under normal circumstances and baring emergence of any adverse and unexpected developments in domestic or external sectors. The overall stance of monetary policy for 2001-02 will be as follows regarding call market.

(a) The average call money rate came down sharply from **8.6%** in early April to **7%** in mid October 2001. During this period, The repo rate also came down from 7% to 6.5%.
(b) The call market with average daily gross lending improved to Rs.19,000 crores during May-September 2001 from **Rs.10,900 crores** during the corresponding period of the previous year. Therefore, the Central bank feels that planned phasing out of non-banking participants from the call market has not caused any strain on the market.

Call Rates: The call rate means, the rate of interest which will be paid on call loans. The call rates in the market are highly volatile from day-to-day and sometimes even from hour to hour. The rates vary from one market to another also. The call rates are very sensitive to changes in any demand and supply of call loans. The call rates in India are generally determined by the market forces till 1973. But in May 1973, the policy of credit squeeze introduced by the RBI leads to control the call market rates. According to the policy, the RBI tightened the refinance and re-discount facilities, then the call rates have been reacting as high a level as 30% immediately. Therefore, the banks defaulted in a

Statement Showing the Average Daily Turnover in Call Money Market

Fortnight ended	*Turnover per day (Rs. in crores)*	*Fortnight ended*	*Turnover per day (Rs. in crores)*
May 5, 2000	48,056	Dec. 1, 2000	47,310
May 19, 2000	39,214	Dec. 15, 2000	46,747
June 2, 2000	40,056	Dec. 29, 2000	43,568
June 16, 2000	38,300	Jan. 12, 2001	50,396
June 30, 2000	38,357	Jan. 26, 2001	49,039
July 14, 2000	42,465	Feb. 9, 2001	50,675
July 28, 2000	39 797	Feb. 23, 2001	45,987
Aug. 11, 2000	39,275	March 9, 2001	51,550
Aug. 25, 2000	35,973	March 23, 2001	50,314
Sept. 8, 2000	41,797	April 6, 2001	44,630
Sept. 22, 2000	42,933	April 20, 2001	50,957
Oct. 6, 2000	44,635	May 4, 2001	48,008
Oct. 20, 2000	45,776	May 18, 2001	41, 935
Nov. 3, 2000	47, 321	June 1, 2001	46, 156
Nov. 17, 2000	46,805	June 15, 2001	44,790

Sources: *RBI Bulletin*, October 2001, p. S-997.

major way in respect of cash and liquidity requirements at that time due to high cost of call money. Then it become necessary to monitor and regulate call rates within reasonable limits. Hence, the Indian Banks Association fixed a ceiling of 15% in 1973. This confirmation has no legal sanction. The IBA further reduced this ceiling to 12.5% in March 1976. Again the IBA modified the ceiling rate 10% in June 1977, and 8.6% in March 1978 and 10% in April 1980. The actual call rate level in India since 1973 had remained within the ceiling fixed by the IBA. The ceiling rates became a hurdle to many large banks. Afterwards the call rate was freed in two stages. In October 1988, the operations of the Discount and Finance House of India were exempted from the ceiling. From May 1989, the ceilings on the call rate were withdrawn. The inter-bank term money rates were also withdrawn. From 1989 onward the call rate has been freed. The call rates were determined by the market forces. In India there are now two call rates, one the inter-bank call rate and the other DFHI lending rate. In India the call rates are usually highest in Kolkata and lowest in Mumbai. In Kolkata market, there will be relatively higher demand for funds than supply in the call market. The supply of funds in call market is greater in Mumbai market due to the location of various head offices of the different financial and non-financial institutions. The demand in Kolkata is because there is greater business than Mumbai. The large number of organisations concentrated in Kolkata like jute, tea, coal absorb a large amount of finance. Therefore, usually the funds will flow from Mumbai to Kolkata. The extreme fluctuation in the call market is based on the following factors:

1. The mechanism of CRR makes fluctuation in the call market.
2. The credit operations of some banks tend to fluctuate the market.
3. Any disruption in the banking industry may lead to change the call market.
4. On 31st March, most of the large business concerns withdraw the money from the banks to pay the advance tax. This volatiles the call market.
5. The liquidity and illiquidity crisis in money markets may show an impact on call market.
6. The mismatch between assets and liabilities of the commercial banks leads to volatility in the market.
7. The change in Forex market also leads to volatility in the call market.
8. The window dressing of the banks may also lead to volatility.

The present call rates are presented below:

Daily Call Money Rates from 1.8.2001 to 12.8.2003

As on	*Range of Borrowings*	*Rates of Lending*	*Weighted Borrowings*	*Average Rate Lending*
August 1	5.47-7.10	4.92-7.50	6.90	6.92
August 2	5.89-7.10	4.89-7.40	6.86	6.88
August 3	5.85-7.10	4.85-7.00	6.92	6.87
August 4	6.15-7.05	5.39-7.05	6.82	6.96
August 6	5.80-7.05	4.80-7.10	6.78	6.80
August 7	5.45-7.20	4.90-7.10	6.88	6.89
August 8	5.70-7.65	5.10-7.90	7.11	7.12
August 9	5.75-7.60	5.20-7.60	7.18	7.26
August 10	5.94-7.50	6.25-7.50	6.93	6.97
August 11	5.90-7.25	5.54-7.25	6.97	6.97
August 13	5.21-7.25	4.97-7.90	6.92	6.99
August 14	6.00-8.30	5.11-8.30	7.05	7.06
August 16	5.59-7.30	5.09-7.30	7.04	7.08
August 17	5.55-7.30	5.03-7.30	7.02	7.01
August 18	5.96-7.15	6.50-7.25	6.97	7.00
August 20	5.59-7.34	5.06-7.90	7.04	7.04
August 23	5.61-7.25	5.06-7.25	7.04	7.08
August 24	6.00-7.50	5.75-7.25	7.04	7.05

(Contd.)

(Contd.)

As on	Range of Borrowings	Rates of Lending	Weighted Borrowings	Average Rate Lending
August 25	6.86-7.20	5.42-7.80	6.86	6.88
August 27	5.85-7.05	4.85-7.05	6.84	6.85
August 28	5.30-7.30	4.75-7.10	6.74	6.75
August 29	5.26-7.30	4.75-7.80	6.73	6.78
August 30	5.44-7.40	4.89-7.10	6.90	6.93
August 31	5.53-7.55	4.96-7.55	6.95	6.98
September 01	5.92-7.10	6.10-7.15	6.91	6.92
September 03	5.45-7.45	4.90-7.50	6.89	6.91
September 04	5.85-7.00	6.00-7.15	6.85	6.86
September 05	5.43-7.25	4.89-7.25	6.98	6.90
September 07	6.00-7.95	5.89-7.95	7.14	7.17
September 08	6.08-7.40	6.60-7.40	7.08	7.08
September 10	6.05-7.75	5.05-7.75	7.02	7.15
September 11	6.10-7.80	5.10-7.50	7.06	7.06

Source: *RBI Bulletin*, October 2001, p. S-996.

2. Treasury Bills Market

Introduction: Treasury bills are the main financial instruments of money market. These bills are issued by the government. The borrowings of the government are monitored and controlled by the Central bank. The bills are issued by the RBI on behalf of the Central Government. The RBI is the agent of Union Government. They are issued by tender or tap. The bills were sold to the public by tender method upto 1965. These bills were put at weekly auctions. A treasury bill is a particular kind of finance bill. It is a promissory note issued by the government. Until 1950, these bills were also issued by the State Governments.

After 1950 onwards the Central Government has the authority to issue such bills. These bills are greater liquidity than any other kind of bills. The treasury bills are highly liquid because these bills are guaranteed by the Central Government. The RBI is always willing to purchase or discount them. These bills are claims against the government. They do not require any endorsement or acceptance. These bills are issued to meet the short-term financial requirements of the Central Government. These bills have become a permanent source of funds to the government. Every year the Central bank, a portion of bills are converted into long-term bonds. These bills are of two kinds: (a) *adhoc*, (b) regular. *Adhoc* treasury bills are issued to the State Governments, semi-government departments and foreign Central banks.

They are not marketable. The *adhoc* bills are not sold to the banks and public.

The Regular Treasury bills are sold to the general public and banks. They are freely marketable. These bills are sold by the RBI on behalf of the Central Government. The treasury bill market in India is underdeveloped. The treasury bills markets are well-developed in USA and UK. In the developed market these bills occupy a key role in their economy.

The *adhoc* treasury bills were introduced in India in 1937. The government and RBI made an agreement in 1937 and 1955 between them for functioning of the treasury bills market in India. According to their agreement, the Central Government shall maintain with the RBI a cash balance of not less than Rs.50 crores on Friday and Rs.4 crores on other days. It involves free of obligation to pay interest thereon and if the balance falls below these minimum levels the government account may be replenished by the creation of *adhocs* in favour of the RBI. These bills are financed by the created money. But these bills are quickly replaced by borrowing against dated securities from the market. The *adhoc* treasury bills became permanent sources of many for the government. These bills reduce the currency circulation in the market. These bills provide an opportunity to the State Governments and semi-government to invest their surplus funds. These organisations helped to eliminate undesirable fluctuations in the discount rate at the treasury bills market. The *adhoc* bills became the vehicle for automatic monetisation of the budget deficit. The government and RBI entered into an agreement on September 9, 1994, to phase out the system of *adhoc* bills.

The treasury bills are issued by the RBI on behalf of the Central Government at a discount. The RBI is the agent of Central Government. It will look after all the needs of the banking activities for the Central Government. The treasury bills are not a source of financing budget deficit. It is a mechanism to cover day-to-day mismatches in receipts and payments of the Central Government. It implies periodic vocation of advances made and not their accumulation year after year. The RBI introduced a system of ways and means. Advances with effect from 1.4.97 to adjust temporary mismatches in receipts and payments of the Central Government. The interest rate on WMA and the limit will be mutually agreed upon by the government and RBI. There is not much difference between the *adhoc* treasury bills and WMA. The *adhoc* treasury bills became a source of fund. The WMA became a source of funds to the State Governments also. The treasury bills are sold to the public by tender or at weekly auctions. The issue of treasury bills will be announced in a press communique and tenders which quoted the lowest discount rate would be accepted. If any remaining portion was available, it was allotted to other tenders. There were no restrictions on the class of tender. Every tender will be called for a minimum amount of Rs.25,000 or a multiple of that amount. Until 1965, these were known as intermediate treasury bills. These bills had a maturity period of 91 days and were sold at rates fixed by the RBI. With effect from 12.7.65, the treasury bills were available on tap throughout the week at rates announced from time to time accordingly. This system of selling treasury bills facilitated investment in them by the commercial banks as and when their resources increased. The *adhoc* bills are issued in favour of the RBI only. The *adhoc* bills are not sold through the tender system. These bills purchased by the RBI on tap and are kept in its issue department the RBI may issue currency notes against these bills. These bills are nationally discharged and renewed on maturity. The government raised the funds through *adhoc* bills are a short-term nature but these bills will be renewed from time to time. But in practice these bills are to be treated as long-term finance. These bills can be compared with the cash credit and overdraft system followed by the commercial banks at the private sector.

The treasury bills are issued in the form of promissory note. The bills can be purchased by any business concern. From August 1994, the State Governments, State pension fund, eligible provident funds have been allowed to participate in caution on a non-competitive basis. Therefore, they are not allowed to bid, they should apply to the RBI and pay at the cut off rate decided by the RBI. The amount of participation may also be decided by the RBI. These parties cannot avail rediscounting facility with the RBI for this treasury bills. There are no limits on individual bids subject to notified amount. These bills are useful as eligible security for the purpose of SLR in case of banks. Any shortfall in bids in relation to notified amount is taken up by the RBI. These bills have no automatic rediscounting facility. But the RBI may provide limited rediscounting facility to the holders of these bills.

The turnover of the treasury bills market caused changes that have occurred in it over the period. The volume of treasury bills sold every year and the amount of outstanding at the end of each year. The treasury bills market in India is limited and narrow. But this market is active in UK. In UK, the banks deal in this market because they can buy or sell them to discount houses for settling their adjustments. The volume of transactions between banks and discount houses has been the large banks prefer to approach the discount houses rather than their Central bank. The discount houses themselves also involve in this market. They have ample opportunities for business in treasury bills. The discount houses also hold treasury bills because they can offer them as security for getting call loans from banks. In India, the discount and finance house of India have been established for the purpose to enter in this segment as par with discount houses in UK. But the DFHI does not deal in some specific bill transactions. Now in India there is no discount house. The treasury bills market provides extremely low rate of return on this investments. The treasury bill rate in India has been the lowest rate of interest in the entire interest rate structure. Therefore, the corporate sector in India is away from this market due to low rate of return on investments. Hence, the **Chakravarty Committee** has stated that the discount rate is too low, the general investors are not willing to hold these bills and only the banks and financial institutions purchase them. They hold these bills for short-term before re-discounting them with the RBI. If the return on treasury bills increase, the banks, general investors and financial institutions will tend to be purchased. They will deploy their surplus fund temporarily in this market and this situation may lead to reduction of re-discounting pressure as the RBI. Another important factor is that the relationship between the treasury bills market and the government securities market. The RBI put a policy that every bank should maintain SLR position. The RBI considers the government securities to fulfil the SLR situation. Hence, the government securities hold a good demand among banks. It dominates the treasury bill market. The government securities market has reduced the importance of treasury bills as an investment medium. The RBI also encourages the government securities market by maintaining a stable prices without any risk. The LIC and other financial institutions are also required to invest a large amount of funds in this market. They have freedom to invest the remaining amount in assets which offer a better return. The treasury bills can be categorised as follows:

1. 14 days Treasury bills.
2. 28 days Treasury bills.
3. 91 days Treasury bills.
4. 182 days Treasury bills.
5. 364 days Treasury bills.

1. 14 days Treasury bills: The 14 days T-bills has been introduced from 1996-97. These bills are non-transferable. They are issued only in **book entry system they would be redeemed at par. Generally, the**

participants in this market are State Government, specific bodies and foreign Central banks. The discount rate on these bills will be decided at the beginning of the year quarter. The yield on **this market is on par with the interest as ways and means.** These bills are not popular in India due to some limitations. These bills are issued every week.

2. 28 days T-bills: These bills were introduced in 1998. The treasury bills in India issued on auction basis. The date of issue of these bills will be announced in advance to the market. The information regarding the notified amount is announced before each auction. The notified amount in respect of T-bills auction is announced in advance for the whole year separately. A uniform calendar of T-bills issuance is also announced. The State Governments have been allowed to enter into this segment for investment of their surplus funds as non-competitive bidders. They are also allowed to avail the special ways and means advances against the collateral of their investment in this bills market.

3. 91 days T-bills: The 91 days treasury bills were issued from July 1965. These were issued tap basis at a discount rate. The discount rates vary between **2.5 and 4.6% p.a.** from July 1974 the discount rate of 4.6% remained uncharged the return on these bills were very low. However, the RBI provides re-discounting facility freely for these bills. The commercial banks also invest their surplus fund into these instruments for a short-term period. Generally they will park their idle funds in these instruments for **1 or 2 days** respectively. There will be high fluctuations in the volume of outstanding treasury bills. Therefore, the RBI introduced measures. They are (a) recycling of the T-bills, (b) additional early rediscounting fee. The recycling of the T-bills was introduced from October 1986. Under this scheme the bills which were re-discounted by the RBI could be resold to the banks. Therefore, once re-discounted by the RBI can be sold to the banks. Another factor is that an additional early re-discounting fee was imposed from November 1986, in case the banks re-discounted the T-bills within 14 days of purchase. The fluctuations declined in the bills market could not become an integral part of the money market.

4. 182 days T-bills: The 182 days treasury bills were introduced in November 1986. The Chakravarty Committee made recommendations regarding 182 days treasury bills instruments. There was a significant development in this market. These bills were sold through monthly auctions. These bills were issued without any specified amount. These bills are tailored to meet the requirements of the holders of short-term liquid funds. These bills were issued at a discount. These instruments were eligible as securities for SLR purposes. These bills have re-discounting facilities. These instruments could be purchased by individuals firms, companies and corporate bodies. The bill market was not emerged as part of the money market.

5. 364 days T-bills: The 364 days treasury bills were introduced by the government in April 1992. These instruments are issued to stabilise the money market. These bills were sold on the basis of auction. The auctions for these instruments will be conducted for every fortnight. There will be no indication when they are putting auction. Therefore, the RBI does not provide re-discounting facility to these bills. These instruments have been instrumental in reducing the net RBI credit to the government. These bills have become very popular in India. These bills provide higher yield with liquidity position. The reputed financial institutions such as IDBI, ICICI and other financial assets. These instruments have widened the money market. They provide an innovative parking place for idle funds. These bills have been to auction on monthly basis since October 1988. The RBI does not purchase these bills. The response for these bills depends upon many factors such as the uncertainty in government securities market. Variations in SLR and the yield.

The treasury bills market will show an impact on the functioning of banks and monetary policy of the government. The buying of treasury bills by the banks will affect on reduction of credit creating capacity of the banks. In this situation large holding of treasury bills by banks lead to a dangerous situation. The banks always plan for the make up of loss by re-discounting bills with the Central bank. The banks participation in the treasury bills market have been increased due to the tight money policy of the RBI. There will be another dimension to study the treasury bills market is that, the banks which purchased the treasury bills will increase the power of deposit creation of banks. These bills are treated as securities for calculation of the SLR position.

3. Commercial Bill Market

Introduction: The Corporate sector requires two kinds of capital, they are (a) fixed capital, (b) working capital. The fixed capital can be procured by the companies by issuing shares, term loans from all India financial institutions and other long-term nature of the sources. The working capital of the corporate sector are mainly provided by banks through cash credit, overdrafts, and purchase or discounting of the commercial bills. In abroad the bill finance is the major source of income for the banks. But in India, the bill system is yet to became popular. The financing of bill method is flexibility to the money market. The financial instrument which is traded in the bill market is known as the bill of exchange. The bills are used for financing a deal in goods that takes sometime to complete. The bill of exchange reveals that the liability to make the payment as a fixed date when the goods are bought on mercantile basis. The bill of exchange will be treated as negotiable instrument. **The Indian Negotiable Instruments Act, 1881** has defined the bill. It is a written instrument containing an unconditional order, signed by the maker, directing a certain person to pay a certain sum of money only to or to the order of a certain person or to the bearer of the instrument.

The bills of exchange are drawn by the seller **(drawer)** on the buyer **(drawee)** for the value of the goods delivered by him. These bills are called as trade bills. If the trade bills are accepted by the commercial banks they are known as commercial bills. If the seller provides sometime for the payment the bill payable at a future date is known as **usance bill.** If the seller party is in need of finance he may approach the bank for discount of the bill. The commercial banks generally finance the business community through bill discounting method. The commercial banks can finance the seller at a negotiated discount rate therefore, the bank collects the maturity proceeds of the discounted bills from the drawee. In this situation, if the bank needs emergency fund it can re-discount the bills already discounted in the commercial bill discount market. The bill is a negotiable instrument and can change ownership conveniently during its currency. It provides a clear legal safeguard. This instrument will be treated as self-liquidating paper on the money market. The liquidity position of this instrument is being next only to cash, call loan, treasury bill and commercial bills. It carries a low degree of risk of loss. It is different from other commercial loans by banks. In the US the bills are known as **Banker's Acceptance.**

In the bill market, there are a number of bills available and can be categorised on the basis of their maturity. Some bills are due for payment whether the documents to title of goods accompany them or not, the type of activity they finance some bills are known as demand bills. A demand bill is payable immediately at sight or on presentment to the drawee. The bills are payable on demand and those payable on fixed date such as payable 30 days after date or on the date of the happening of a certain event, need not be presented by the holder for acceptance. A bill which has no time for payment specified is also known as **demand bill.** The time bill is payable in a specified later date. The bills also can be classified as clear bill and documentary bills. The documentary bills are accompanied by the document of title to goods. The document of title is RR or bill of lading. Further the bills are also classified as DA and DP bills. The DA bill refers to document against acceptance. The DP refers to document against payment. The DA bill becomes as a clean bill after delivery of the documents. The bills further can be classified as **Inland bills and foreign bills**. Inland bill means a bill must drawn in India and it must be payable in India. The bill must be drawn upon any person when he is resident in India. The inland bill may even be endorsed in a foreign country. Foreign bills are drawn outside India and payable outside India by a party. The foreign bill may be payable in India or drawn on a party resident in India. The foreign bill may be drawn in India and payable outside the country. Another classification of bills can be made as export bills and import bills. The export bills are drawn by the exporters on any foreign country. Import bills are drawn on importers in India by the exporters from abroad. The commercial bills can be utilised for financing the movement of goods and storage of goods. The bill of exchange was originated in UK and USA. The growth of bill financing took place mainly for international trade. The bill of exchange was used for a limited extent. The turnover of the bills market depends upon many factors such as foreign trade sector, international transactions economy of the respected country. But in India, the bill of exchange is not popular in case of the financing of agricultural operations, cottage and small scale industries etc. Agricultural bills are drawn for financing agricultural operations. The agriculture is mainly a seasonal activity and the financing to these sectors for marketing of crops. The small sector industries bills are drawn for the purpose of financing the production and marketing activities. The Indian agriculture system is based on monsoon position. This sector is a highly risk area. The agricultural sector, a variety of bill of exchange or promissory note known as **Hundi**. The Hundi system has a long tradition of use in India. Hundi is used to raise money or to remit funds. They are used for financing inland trade by indigenous bankers. The following are the various kinds of bills of exchange:

(a) Darshini Hundi.
(b) Muddati Hundi.

(a) **Darshini Hundi** is also known as Bill at sight or demand. This Hundi again is classified as **Shahjog, Naurjog, Dekharnar jog, Fermani jog, Jokhami, and Dhanjog**. This bill is used for the payment of goods originating from one country to another places. The bill payment place may be different from its place of origin.

(b) **Muddati Hundi** is useful for local geographical specification areas and its use is diminishing. The maturity period of this bill varies between **30 days** and **120 days.**

The bill of exchange is also associated with indigenous bankers. The Multani Shroffs and the Chettiars have been mainly dealing in hundi. Generally the banks discount their hundis. But the SBI has stopped since 1965. The other commercial banks have been continuing to extend such facilities to the Multanis. The banks involved in discounting these hundis with reference to the personal credibility of the indigenous bankers. The authorities should make arrangements for taking advantage for the development of the bill market in the country. After the nationalisation of commercial banks, they have to meet the credit requirements of the various sectors. The banks will have to provide credit to the small scale and cottage industries, small borrowers and artisans. The bank shall reduce the bad debts, delays in recoveries, increasing administrative expenses. They shall have to concentrate on increasing the level of profitability. All these problems can be rectified by the banks with proper allocation of funds to all the categories of borrowers. The banks should make to efforts to improve the assessment procedure of the credit-worthiness of the indigenous bankers. The commercial banks have a wide geographical locations to extend discounting facilities on the credit standing of indigenous bankers.

The bills of exchange further can be categorised as **accommodation bill** and **supply bills**. The accommodation bill is also known as wind bill or a kite. The accommodation bill is defined as one in which a person known as an accommodation party. The bill contains a name to accommodate another person without obtaining any consideration. The **supply bill** is a bill drawn by the suppliers or contractor on the government. These bills are issued by the parties concerned with the supply of goods or materials provided under contract to the concerned department. The suppliers of the goods or the materials can get advance from the banks on the basis of these bills. These bills are more useful to the suppliers and contractors. Because these parties could not get funds from the government or concerned company. Therefore, the parties will make adjustments through their supply bills. These bills do not have the status of a negotiable instrument. They are not accepted by the government departments. These bills are not accompanied by documents of title to goods. The bank advances on the basis of supply bills are known as clear advance.

The Process of Bill: The bill of exchange contains an order from the creditor to the debtor in a transaction to pay a certain sum to a specified person after a certain period. The bill of exchange can be defined as "An instrument in writing containing an unconditional order signed by the maker, directing a certain person to pay a certain sum of money only to, or to the order of a certain person or to the bearer of the instrument".[27] Therefore, a bill is always drawn by the creditor on the debtor. The person who draws the bill is known as the **drawer**. The person on whom the bill is drawn is known as the **drawee**. The drawee is also called as acceptor. The person drawer is called as **Payee**. The payee is entitled to get the bill amount on maturity date. A bill must be in writing only. A bill is always drawn on a certain person. A bill cannot be made payable to bearer on demand. A bill may be payable at sight or after the expiry of a certain specified time. There will be 3 days of grace period for a bill. The following example can reveal the process of a bill, usually in business community:

For example: Mr. A sells goods to buyer B. The buyer will have to pay the money to the seller. But Mr. B does not have money at present and Mr. A is in need of the money. Therefore, to solve this problem the bill of exchange comes into picture between these two parties. Mr. A draws a bill on B for a certain period of maturity. In this situation Mr. A is known as creditor and Mr. B is called as Debtor. The creditor is known as **drawer** of the bill and the debtor is called as the **drawee** of the bill. Hence Mr. A sends the bill to B and in turn Mr. B acknowledges his responsibility by accepting the bill. After the acceptance of the bill by Mr. B the transaction is closed for time being. In the meanwhile Mr. A can take the accepted bill to a bank for getting money by discounting it. The difference between ready money paid by the banker and the face value of the bill is called as **discount**. The discount is calculated by the bank at a rate per cent per annum on the basis of maturity value. The discounting of a bill with the bank is not a borrowing on the security of the bill and it is an act of selling the bill. Theoretically the process of bill finance is described as simple. But in practice it is quite complex. A bill has to pass through many hands before its maturity period. Acceptance is the most important element in bill financing system. The commercial banks accept these bills for earning income through commission. The discount amount on the trade bill becomes income to the commercial banks. It is an income generating activity for the banks. The acceptance business of commercial banks is very small. For development of this bill market, the banks and indigenous bankers must involve in accepting business. The RBI introduced a Bill market scheme in 1952. According to this scheme, the banks are required to select the borrowers after careful examination of their credit worthiness and reputation. The dealings with these selected parties may convert their advances into bills. In India the maturity periods for bills in general are 30, 60, 90 or 120 days. The export bills may have a maturity period of **180 days.** Agriculture finance bills may have a maturity period of **15 months.** The bill for financing cottage industries may have a maturity period of **120 months.** The RBI has fixed a longer eligible maturity period for different bills. A bill with maturity period of **90 days** is the most popular in India. Bills are self liquidating and they promote efficient use of credit. They provide liquidity to the assets of banks.

The Bill Market in India: The bill market in India is yet to be developed. The bill market depends upon the volume of credit transactions occurred in the market. The banks also should give preference to these instruments for providing credit to the business customers. The market may be developed by popularising these instruments among the business community. The market provides re-discounting facility for these instruments. The involvement of the Central bank may develop the market. The secondary market for the bills is also quite developed. The velocity of the bill reveals the development of the market. The acceptance facility is available in India at a low cost. The participation of brokers and bankers in this market is expected for smooth functioning of the process. Therefore, the bill market in India is treated as under developed. There is no real bill market in India. The following factors indicate for non-development of bill market in India:

1. The discounted bills were not actual bills.
2. They are created by banks by converting OD/CC accounts of the customers.
3. Bill finance is made by the banks by way of **loans** only.
4. They are provided credit as the bills were security.
5. The re-discounting facilities for bills market do not exist in India.
6. The acceptance service is much restricted in India.
7. There is no bills habit to the business community towards the bills of exchange.

Therefore, the RBI has taken the innovative steps to develop this market in June 1974. It permitted the commercial banks, LIC, UTI, GIC and ICICI to re-discount the genuine trade bills. Hence this has increased the number and types of institutions taking part which play the role in this market.

The bill market in India is based on the suggestions of the **Narasimhan Committee** in 1970. The RBI freed the bill re-discounting rates from **May 1, 1989**. The specified ceiling in the re-discount rate was freed, the banks and financial institutions can re-discount the bills with the Discount and Finance House of India **(DFHI).** The DFHI was permitted to fix its own discount rates for the bills according to the market position. The government has taken a decision for the abolition of stamp duty to activate the market. The RBI promoted a drawee bill scheme to help the small scale units. The RBI made same efforts to develop the bill market by introducing the following schemes:

(a) The scheme of 1952.
(b) The scheme of 1970.

The salient features of the 1952 scheme was presented below:

1. All licensed schedule banks were permitted to re-discount the bill with RBI from July 1954.
2. RBI permitted the banks for the lodgement of bill as security for loans.
3. RBI made the funds available at concessional rate for their market.
4. The scheme was extended to cover export bills.

The salient features of the scheme of 1970 are presented below:

1. The re-discounting facility provided to all licensed scheduled banks.
2. The scheme covers only genuine trade bills.
3. The produced bills must bear the endorsement of a licensed scheduled bank.
4. The bill should bear atleast two good signatures.
5. The refinance facility available throughout the year.
6. There is no minimum value of a single bill.
7. The RBI excluded some of the transactions covered by selective credit controls.

The bill discounting and re-discounting system in India is yet to take root in the financial system. These schemes do not contain any concrete and direct measures to develop all the aspects of the developed bill market. The RBI has made efforts to activate the bill market and provided re-discounting facility to all the eligible banks. Generally, the business customers of the banks prefer to get finance through cash credit. But the Central bank permitted all the banks to convert their CCS into bill financing system. But this situation did not help to the market. These schemes aimed primarily for providing liquidity facility for the market.

The government has also made efforts to develop this market. It appointed various Committees to study the problems and for suggestion. They play a major role in development of this market.

(A) Tandon Committee
(B) Chore Committee
(C) Chakravarty Committee
(D) Vaghul Working Committee.

As a result of the recommendations of these Committees the RBI has taken some measures to develop this market. They are presented below:

(a) The abolition of stamp duty on bills of exchange.
(b) The setting up of DFHI as a major financial institution.
(c) The acceptance service comes under credit monitoring scheme.
(d) The procedures and documentation process shall be simplified.
(e) The RBI made access to a large number of financial institutions to develop this market.
(f) The RBI permitted the following institutions to enter into this market from May 1990:
   1. All scheduled commercial banks.
   2. ICICI.
   3. UTI.
   4. IRBI.
   5. LIC and its subsidiaries.
   6. IDBI.
   7. SIDBI.
   8. GIC.
   9. NHB.
   10. DFHI.
   11. LIC Mutual Fund.
   12. NABARD.
   13. EXIM Bank.
   14. Select Urban Cooperative Banks.
   15. IFCI.
   16. SCICI.
   17. Canbank Mutual Fund.

18. ECGC.
19. SBI Mutual Fund.

Reasons for Non-development of Bills Market: The government had made all efforts to develop this market through RBI. The RBI also appointed various expert Committees to develop this segment in spite of the encouraging official policy. The bill market has not developed in India. The bill market was developed in UK and the US. But in developed markets, the volume of business regarding the bill has tend to decline in the developed markets also. The following are the factors for non-development of the bills market:

(a) The government does not prefer to finance its activities through bills of exchange.
(b) The quick discounting and collection of bills by the branches of banks, quick transfer and remittances of fund have tend to narrow down the basis for using the creation of bill.
(c) The bill markets were mostly established for the financing of foreign trade which were not developed.
(d) Bill discounting was a costly mode of financing system.
(e) The banks were not showing interest to finance through bill of exchange.
(f) The trade and industry have shown reluctance to the discipline of the bill finance.
(g) Bill of exchange requires the endorsement of reputed institution.
(h) The bill market has been dominated by indigenous bankers, those who rely on their own sources of funds.
(i) The complicated processing loss of interest on the part of banks, absence of specialised credit information acquires, the growth of other instruments in money markets.

In order to develop a sound bill market, the RBI introduced a number of measures to strengthen the market.

4. Certificate of Deposits

Introduction: The scheme of certificate of deposits has been introduced by the RBI in June 1989. This financial instrument has been introduced in order to widen the money market and its instruments. This scheme provides greater flexibility in the parking of their idle funds. The certificate of deposits can be issued only by the scheduled commercial banks. These will be issued in multiples of Rs.25 lakhs. The minimum size of the issue is Rs.1 crore. The maturity period will vary between three months and one year. It will be issued at discount to face value. The discount rate will be freely determined according to the situation. It will be freely transferable by endorsement. They are subject to stamp duty. The RBI is the supreme authority in this segment. The RBI prescribes a limit to each bank for funds to raise under this scheme. It is a negotiable instrument. It provides maximum liquidity. The DFHI dominates the trading in CDs market. These instruments have large size of the market in primary but there is no room for the secondary market. Liquidity and marketability is the hallmarks of these instruments. They are in bearer form. They are known as **Negotiable Instrument**. They are also called as Negotiable Certificates of Deposits.

Certificate of Deposit means, an amount of money deposited in a bank for a specified period at a specified rate of interest. The concerned bank will issue a receipt which is transferable and marketable in the market. The receipts may be either in bearer form or in registered form. They are documents of title to time deposits with banks. Technically they are a part of banks time deposit. These are riskless in terms of payment of interest and principal amount.

The CDs have been introduced by many developed and developing countries. They were introduced in 1961 in the US and UK. The CDs in the form of dollars were issued in 1966 and pounds in 1968. The CDs have been emerged in many countries based on different forces and factors. They have been emerged for widening the money market in many countries. They have been introduced to restore intermediation function of banks, to strengthen the market, to innovative financial system, to mop up excess liquidity in the monetary system and as a part of financial reforms. They will be treated in global markets as **Euro Certificates of Deposits**. They are issued in different countries to meet the competition. They have some advantages over the time deposit. The banks issued them as a competitive tools against other financial intermediaries.

The CDs were introduced in Japan 1979, France 1985, West Germany 1986, Australia 1969, New Zealand 1971, South Korea 1974, Malaysia 1979, Indonesia 1971. Many factors have contributed to the evaluation of CDs in different countries. They are introduced as a part of marketing strategy in the financial markets by the commercial banks. In the US, the CDs are issued in any denomination from $1,00,000 to $10 millions. In UK they are not eligible collateral security for loans from the bank of England.

CDs in India: The introduction of CDs in India was being seriously assessed from the beginning of 1980s. The RBI appointed a Committee to study the feasibility of CDs in India. The **Tambe working group** studied the market and recommended against it for the reasons. There were no secondary money markets in the country. There was the administered system of interest rates. The CDs may rise to fictitious transactions. The **Vaghul Committee,** appointed in 1987 made recommendations for the introduction of CDs in India. They are provided short-term deposit rates. The RBI formulated and launched in June 1989, a scheme permitting the banks to issue CDs with a view to widen the money market.

Original Scheme: The RBI formulated a scheme for the introduction of CDs in the form of new promissory notes. These notes are payable on a fixed date without any grace period. They were issued with a maturity period of 3 months to one year. These instruments would be issued at a discount, to face value. They are transferable by endorsement and can be delivered only after the **lock in period of 45 days** after the date of issue. The total outstanding of all CDs issued by bank to any point of time should not exceed **1%** of its fortnightly average deposits. All CDs are subject to the usual CRR and SLR requirements. The banks have to report about the issue of CDs to the RBI. The banks are not allowed to buy back their own CDs. The banks were not allowed to grant loans against CDs. The CDs has to bear the stamp duty at the rate **0.25 per cent** *advalorem* for a maturity of over **3 to 6 months of 0.375 per cent** for a maturity of over 6 months to 9 months and 0.5 per cent of a maturity of over 9 months to 12 months. They are issued to individuals corporations. Trusts companies funds and associations they are issued to NRIs also on a non-reputation basis. The discount rates may be determined by the market forces. The regional rural banks and scheduled banks were not eligible to issue CDs they are issued in multiples of Rs.25 lakhs subject to a maximum of issue of Rs.1 crore.

Modified Scheme: The above original scheme has been modified by the RBI and the rules and regulations have been framed by the RBI from time-to-time. These regulations are in force in 1997-98, they are badly presented as follows.

(a) The minimum denomination is **Rs. 5.00 lakhs**.
(b) The minimum size of issue at a single time is **Rs. 10.00 lakhs**.
(c) The maturity period varies from **3 months to 1 year**.
(d) They are issued at a discount to face value.
(e) The discount rate of CDs are determined by the market forces.

(f) They are freely transferable after lock in period of 30 days after issue.
(g) All scheduled banks can issue them.
(h) Anyone can purchase CDs.
(i) They can be issued by banks without any ceiling.
(j) They are subject to CRR and SCR requirements.
(k) Term lending institutions can also issue them with a maturity of 1 to 3 years.

The development of CDs is based on its secondary market. The secondary market for these instruments has not developed well. Because the CDs is priced high. The holders in primary market prefer to hold them to maturity. The DFHI is key partner in the market. It quotes daily bid discount rate on CDs. Most of the CDs are said to be in replacement of the existing current account or short-term deposits. In India there will be a potential for the growth of CDs in primary and secondary markets. The CDs can get support from various sources. The **demand and supply** sides of the CDs market as presented below:

Large public sector undertakings and private sector corporate bodies are believed on demand side of the CDs market. UTI also has gathered huge investible funds and they do not have ready investment outlets. There are inter-corporate funds of substantial amount to be invested in this segment. On the supply side, the banks are facing stiff competition from foreign banks and in need of exploring the use of innovative means such as CDs to occupy their share in the market. The supply and demand and favourable factors and with the support of RBI and DFHI made a good potential for growth in the coming years. The interest rates offered on CDs are high. The maturity period of 3 months at the short-term end is generally popular with the investors. The organisation replace their current account with CDs. The CDs is not fresh accrual of deposits. Hence, it appears to be that the banks are retaining their deposits at higher cost. This situation adversely affects the banks earnings. Because the operating expenses of the banking sector increases by the way of interest charges. Hence, the banks should be allowed to buy and sell CDs in the secondary market. The rates of Interest on CDs ranges from 5.40% to 9.20%.[28]

CDs are the obligations of banks. They are issued on discount basis and similar to treasury bills or commercial bills. They are just like bonds. They may be issued directly to the investors or through the dealers. They can be issued at discount that can be freely determined. The formula for the discounted value as follows:

$$D = \frac{F}{1+\dfrac{(I\times N)}{(100\times 365)}}$$

D = Discounted value of the CDs,
F = Face value of the CDs,
I = Interest rate per annum, and
N = Usual period.

5. Commercial Paper Market

Introduction: Money market consists of many financial short-term instruments. Commercial paper is one of the financial instruments of the money market. It provides an opportunity to well-rated companies/ good track record companies for raising funds on short-term basis honesty is the best element to all track the funds. The Market always provides funds to sincere companies. The companies which maintain **financial discipline** can procure funds from the market confidently. The investor or the fund suppliers always put. Their funds at the doors taps of the good-reputed companies and sincere organisation. In the financial market credibility is the most important factor at present. The financial discipline leads to credibility. The credibility has the borrowing capacity from the market. In the recent period many good-reputed companies have accursed the commercial paper market for meeting their working capital requirements.

Commercial paper is an unsecured promissory note. They are issued by well-rated companies for a minimum of 3 months and maximum of **six months**. They are regulated by non-banking companies directions. Those directions were issued by RBI in 1989. The directions came into force on 1.1.90.

Salient features: The salient features of CPs are presented below:

(a) They are unsecured promissory notes.
(b) The issuing company shall have current ratio **1.33: 1**.
(c) They have maturity period from 90 days to 180 days.
(d) The minimum issue shall be **Rs.25 lakhs**.
(e) They are transferable by endorsement and delivery.
(f) The issuing company shall have tangible net wealth of Rs.5 crores.
(g) They can be issued at discount to face value.
(h) The discount value may be decided by the issuing company.

(i) They require floating expenses.
(j) They may be issued to individuals, banks, companies registered, corporate bodies and union corporate bodies.
(k) They are also issued to NRIs on Non-repatriable basis.
(l) The issuing company shall get rating from CRISIL before issue as P_2 or A_2 from CRISIL or ICRA respectively.

CPs in Abroad: Commercial paper is totally new in India. They are not yet fully developed. It is quite a new instrument in the money market. The market has not developed even in the advanced nations except in the US, the CPs are known as **Industrial paper**, finance paper, or corporate paper. The CPs have been introduced in **UK in 1986, France 1985, Spain 1982, Hong Kong 1982, Singapore 1984, Netherlands 1986, Sweden 1980, Canada 1950** respectively. They have a very flexible maturity period. In the US, the maturity period shall not be more than **270 days**. Generally in the US the maturity period is 90 days or three months. In UK the maturity period will be **7 to 364 days**, in France 10 days to 7 years, 30 days to 365 days in Canada. In Australia they have 185 days maturity period. They are issued in domestic as well as international financial market. They are known as **Euro commercial papers**. They are normally issued in a bearer form on discount to face value basis. They are issued in larger denominations. They may be issued through banks or merchant banker or dealers or brokers in the open market. Some times they may be sold through placement directly to the lenders or investors. In US they are sold through dealers who are specialised in this market. They are cheaper sources of finance than bank loans. It is at the same time a more impersonal and therefore, more unreliable sources of finance. The primary market for them is active but the secondary market is yet to be developed even in advanced nations. Because the investors who purchased in the primary market will hold this instrument till maturity period. Hence there is no need of secondary market operations in the market. Another factor is that these instruments have shorter maturity period. They are issued only for short-term needs of the corporate sector. The rise and popularity of CPs in abroad has been a matter of spontaneous response by the large corporations. The rising cost of the bank loans leads the large companies towards the CPs market. They found to be cheaper, simpler and flexible sources of funds The raising short-term CPs represents the weakening process of intermediation. It strengthen the process of securitisation. It brings the large borrowers and large investors together and reduces the existence of the brokers or dealers.

They are primarily issued by public utilities, bank holding companies, insurance companies, transportation companies and finance companies. The buyers of the CPs are **banks, liquid business concerns, and NBFCs.**

The Industrial paper refers to the paper which is issued by a manufacturing concern or commercial or industrial concern. The finance paper means it is the liability of the finance company issued by it. Corporate paper is a wider term and reveals that it is issued by companies which may be either financial or non-financial. The CPs are regarded as highly safe and liquid instruments. They are like treasury bills but unlike CPs they are close competitors of the treasury bills. They have a buy-back facility, they are issued in a bearer form. They are useful to meet the current needs of the funds for the corporate sector. They will fulfil the needs of the seasonal business.

The banks are one of the major buyers of CPs.

In India the CPs were introduced on the suggestions of the working group on Money market in 1987. The RBI has the supreme authority in this segment. It announced a scheme in March 1989 for the introduction of the instrument in the Indian Money Market. It issued a notification which came into effect from 1.1.90. It framed the guidelines which apply to all the NBFCs and Non-financial companies. The FEMA related companies shall take the permission from the RBI to issue CPs. The CPs have the maturity period of 30 days. They may be issued on a single date or in parts. The RBI has not permitted the banks either to undertake or to co-accept the issue of CPs. The issuer of this instrument shall have to bear the stamp duty, dealer fee, rating agency fee, fee to banker, standby facility and other concerned expenses.

Guidelines Issued by the RBI: The RBI issued guidelines in respect of the sale of CPs. They are presented below:

1. The rules come into force in 1997-98.
2. The issuing company shall have the tangible net worth of **Rs. 4 crores.**
3. The issuing company working capital limit should not be less than Rs.4 crores.
4. The company can issue CPs up to 75% of its working capital.
5. The CPs shall have a minimum denomination of **Rs.5 lakhs.**
6. The minimum size of an issue to a single investor is **Rs.25 lakhs.**
7. The issuing company shall have $\mathbf{P_2}$ & $\mathbf{A_2}$ rating from CRISIL and ICRA.
8. The issuing company directly issue CPs.

9. There is no need to take RBI permission.
10. The holder shall present the CP for payment to the issuer.
11. There is no need of underwriting the issue of CPs.
12. The issue of CP must be meant for working capital requirement only.
13. There is no need for co-accepting issue of CPs.

The subscription to CPs is open to all investors. The investors in this market is consisting of large corporate bodies operating in the inter-corporate funds market trusts with substantial funds and public sector corporations. Sometimes the banks also invest in this market.

Though CPs have some advantages but they have some limitations also. The intercorporate lenders and borrowers would prefer to tax free bonds rather than CPs. They have some administrative hassles. The big institutional investors like UTI, GIC and LIC are not interested towards these instruments because their investment patterns are determined by the government. They do not get any tax incentives on investment in CPs. Generally the real major holders of CPs are banks. The market for CPs will grow when there exists a secondary market. The DFHI is created for the purpose of developing the secondary market for CPs. The DFHI can acquire the CPs in primary and provide them in secondary market. CPs finance is not an additional finance.

CPs are likely to prove restrictive time consuming and costly. The borrower will lose the bank credit for their working capital requirement. They are unsecured instruments. It leads to a disincentive.

6. Collateral Loan Market

Introduction: Collateral loan market is a market where the loans are secured against collateral securities like stocks and bonds. The collateral securities are returned to the borrower when he repays the loan if the borrowers fail to pay his loan. The collateral asset becomes the property of the lender. These are mostly granted by the banks to the private parties. These are provided for a short period of a few months.

Unorganised Money Market. The unorganised sector of money market contains different agencies. These agencies have diverse policies and lack of uniformity. They are not following uniformity in lending activities. The unorganised sector of the Indian money market includes the following:

(a) Indigenous bankers

(b) Money lenders
(c) Chit funds.

(a) Indigenous Bankers. The Indigenous bankers are the part of unorganised Indian money market. It is mostly confined to certain castes like **Khatries, Jains, Marwaris and Chettis**. They are known as the banking cast in India. There were about 2,500 indigenous bankers in the country in 1971. They are active in commercial centres. The Indian Central Banking Enquiry Committee defined the Indigenous banker as **any individual or private firm receiving deposits and dealing in Hundis or lending money**. The Indigenous bankers have concentrated mostly in the southern and western parts of India. They have been active in the rural money market. The **Multani** bankers play an important role in the market. They grant loans against unsecured to the traders. A Multani banker involves in business transactions with atleast 300 parties every-day.

They represent ancient banking system of India. They have been carrying their traditional and historical operations in different parts of the country. They spread throughout the country. They are called **Chettys** in Chennai, **Sahukars, Mahajans and Khatries** in North India. In Mumbai they are known as **Shroffs and Marwaris** and in Kolkata they are called as **Seths and Banias**. Any individual or private firm which receives deposits, deals in hundis or engages itself in lending money business. They can be divided into three categories: (1) **Multani bankers,** (2) **Marwaris and Bengalis,** (3) **limited business**.

The Multani bankers deal only in banking business operations. Marwaris and Bengalis involved in banking business with trade also. Some indigenous bankers deal mainly in trade and participating in limited business transactions. The indigenous banker lends and also accepts funds from the public.

Importance of Indigenous Bankers: They occupy an important place in the Indian money market. They play a vital role in financing the trade sector. They are more popular where the banks neglected certain geographical locations of the country. Some areas have not been served properly by the banks. After nationalisation of the banks, their transactions had been declined significantly. They have control still in the market where the finance is required more demand. They become more popular due to the following reasons:

(a) They provide finance to their friends and relatives.
(b) They provide excellent service to the customers.

(c) They give loans to the persons those are neglected by banks.
(d) They have good relations with customers.
(e) They are not merely bankers to the customers.
(f) They know the customers' needs and their requirements and pulse.

Functions of Indigenous Bankers: The indigenous bankers are mixed with the society. They provide service to their customers 24 hours. The main functions of the indigenous bankers are presented below:

1. Accepting Deposits from the public.
2. Providing loans to the customers.
3. Hundi business.
4. Other functions.

Accepting Deposits from Public: The indigenous bankers perform the same functions as performed by the commercial banks. They accept deposits from the public at a specified rate of interest. These deposits are of two kinds:

1. The demand deposits
2. Fixed deposits

The demand deposit: They accept the deposits from the public and the amount will be repayable whenever the customer demands. They pay higher rate of interest than commercial banks. **Fixed deposits are** repayable only after a fixed date. They will not be paid in advance. The depositor will have to wait till the maturity period. The collected deposit will be circulated in the market at higher interest rate.

Providing Loans to the Customers: They provide loans to customers against a security. The desired security may be in the form of **land, silver, gold and crops**. They lend the money against personal security. They sanction loans to small industrialists who were ignored by the commercial banks.

Hundi Business: They deal hundis also. They buy hundis and sell them in the market. Sometimes they may also write hundis. They discount hundis. They meet the needs of small traders. They transfer the funds from one location to another location through discounting of hundis.

Other Functions: They also carry other business functions along with banking. They generally do their retail trading business. Sometimes they act as agents to large firms. They earn income in the form of commission. They are involved in speculative transactions. The following are the characteristics of the indigenous bankers.

Characteristics of Indigenous Bankers:

1. Indigenous bankers accept deposit from the public.
2. They lend their own funds in the market.
3. They do not require any complicated formalities.
4. They are available to the public whenever they need money.
5. Their establishments are small and economical.
6. They provide finance to all types of borrowers.
7. They conduct the banking activities on the basis of their experience.
8. They maintain simple accounts.
9. They know about their customers thoroughly.
10. They observe the activities of their borrowers.
11. They have good relations among the trade community.
12. Their presence in the rural cannot be eliminated.

Effects of Indigenous Bankers: The indigenous banking system suffers from the following defects:

1. Basically they are traders but a sound banking principle requires a higher specialised skill.
2. The indigenous banking system is entirely unorganised. They are working independently without any coordination among them.
3. The transfer of fund is not possible in this system.
4. Their financial capability is very low due to low resources.
5. They do not mobilise savings on large scale from the public.
6. They charge higher interest rate than banks.
7. They do not follow the sound banking principles.
8. They grant loans even without sufficient security.
9. They do not observe the purpose of the loan issued.
10. They also provide loans to unproductive activities.
11. They provide loans to speculation activities also.
12. They do not maintain books of accounts in proper way.
13. They will exploit the customers.
14. Their activities cannot be regulated by the RBI.

Indigenous Bankers and Reserve Bank: The RBI is the supreme authority in the banking sector. It has been making efforts to change the unorganised system into organised system. It has been trying to bring them into its control. It has been making environment to integrate them with the modern banking system. The RBI prepared a scheme in 1937 for direct linking with indigenous bankers under certain conditions. These conditions are presented below:

1. Every indigenous banker should have a minimum working capital of Rs.1.00 lakh.
2. The working capital should be increased to Rs. 600 lakhs.
3. They should concentrate on banking business only.
4. They should leave their non-banking business activities.
5. They should maintain accounts properly.
6. Their accounts should be audited by authorised auditors.
7. They should submit their records to the RBI.
8. They should submit periodical report like scheduled banks.
9. The Reserve Bank should have the right to regulate them.
10. The scheme was not in practice because they did not agree to accept its various conditions.

Banking Commission: The banking commission has appraised the services which are rendered by the indigenous bankers. They play a very useful role in the lives of millions of people. They cover all categories of the public in the society. The segments which they cover are ignored by the banks. The commission feels that the indigenous banking system should work properly and it can be utilised for society. They should be regulated and institutionalised. The commission strongly feels that they should bring under the purview of the RBI for functioning of the banking sector more effectively. The commission thought that the indigenous bankers should bring indirect control though commercial banks. The RBI should frame the rules and regulations for the commercial banks to deal with them. The banks should provide rediscounting facility to the indigenous bankers on satisfying the following norms:

(a) They should involve fully to the banking business only.
(b) They should have own capital of not less than Rs.1.00 lakh.
(c) They should not borrow from more than a single bank.
(d) They should maintain regular books of account.
(e) They should submit annual report to the RBI.
(f) They should monitor the loans.

Reforms: In Indian economy the indigenous bankers occupy a great role in the lives of public. They should be reformed and integrated with the original system of banking. The following are the suggestions to reform them:

(a) They should be linked with the RBI.
(b) They should run the banking business separately.
(c) They should convert their business to modern banking system.
(d) They should eliminate the competition from banks.
(e) They should maintain proper accounts and get them audited regularly.
(f) There should be convergence between banks and indigenous banks.
(g) They should stop various malpractices.
(h) The licensing system should be introduced for them.
(i) The commercial banks might discount their hundis easily.
(j) They should form association.
(k) The benefits of the banker shall pass on them.
(l) They should develop bill broking business.
(m) They should adopt modern accounting records.
(n) They should change their attitude in the modern world.
(o) They should have a positive approach.
(p) They should become more professional and formal in their operations.

(b) Money Lenders: In the unorganised money market sector, the money lenders play an important role in the economy. Their basic activity involves money lending. The indigenous bankers also do this money lending. But their primary business is not banking. The money lenders can be classified as follows:

(a) Professional money lenders.
(b) Non-professional money lenders.

Professional money lenders basic business is money lending. They are known as ***"banias"***, ***"mahajans"***, ***"sahukars"***. They hold licences for money lending activities. Their main source of income is lending money.

Non-professional money lenders means occasionally they do lending business. They do not depend entirely on money lending business. They do this business in addition to their routine work. They consist of landlords, agriculturists, traders, pensioners, rich vendors etc. They have no licence to carry this business.

The money lenders can also be classified into two kinds. They are: (a) Rural money lenders, (b) Urban money lenders. The money lenders those who operate in villages are called as **Rural money lenders**. The lenders who operate in urban areas are known as **Urban money lenders**. They provide loans to poor labourers, factory workers, low paid employees.

Operations: The money lenders are the part of society. They know the needs of various kinds of people. They will help the people by providing loans to meet their requirements. They possess good knowledge of the borrowers and have a minimum risk. They provide loans against security. The loans may be for the borrower's family expenditure. They have good personal contacts with their customers. They have good social contacts with their clients. In this system there is less chance for default in repayment of the loan. Because the rural system will pressure the borrowers to repay that amount. There is no uniform interest rate in this system. There are different rate of interest charged in different parts of the country. They also resort to undesirable practices.

Features of Money Lenders: The following are the salient features of money lenders:

(a) They deploy their own funds.
(b) They provide money to mainly illiterate and economically weaker sections of the society.
(c) They provide highly exploitative nature of the loans.
(d) They are unregulated.
(e) The loans may be secured or unsecured.
(f) Their operations are prompt, informal and flexible.

Defects of Money Lenders: The money lending system has the following defects:

1. The money lenders have limited resources to meet the needs of the rural people.
2. They charge very high interest rates.
3. They adopt all possible types of malpractices in business.
4. They provide unproductive purpose loans.
5. They provide crop loans to the farmers. They compel the farmers to sell their produce at low prices to them.

Chit Funds

Chit Fund is one of the elements of the unorganised sector of the money market. Chit funds are recognised by law. They are required to be registered under the Companies Act. The Central Government has proposed to introduce a special legislation called Chit Fund Act.

Characteristics of the Unorganised Sector of Indian Money Market

The Unorganised Indian money market has the following characteristics:

1. It consists of indigenous bankers, money lenders and chit funds.
2. They conduct the mixed business of money lending and trading.
3. They have good personal relations with the borrowers.
4. They know the historical background of each and every borrower.
5. They keep their accounts in a simple manner.
6. They keep their business affairs very confidential.
7. They provide loans according to the needs of the borrowers.
8. Their operations are flexible in nature.
9. They locate in rural and urban centres.
10. They lend the money to all types of borrowers.
11. They cater to the credit needs of the rural economy.

Efficiencies of the Indian Money Market: The money market in India has not developed. It suffers from a number of drawbacks. They have been presented below:

(a) The Indian money market is categorised into organised and unorganised sector. The organised sector works under the control and guidance of the RBI. The unorganised sector looks for scientific organisation. It is an unorthodox approach.
(b) There is coordination between organised and unorganised system of the Indian money market.
(c) There is wide divergence between two parts of the money market system in many factors such as structure of interest rates, lending policies.
(d) The RBI has no control over the unorganised sector of the Indian money market.
(e) In Indian money market, the organised sector consists of bill market. The bill market is undeveloped in India. The bill market is well-developed in advance countries.
(f) The Indian banking has neglected the agriculture finance.
(g) In the unorganised sector, the financial agencies do not lend money only. They usually carry on retail trade and other activities along with lending operations.

(h) There is no co-ordination in unorganised money market system.
(i) The Indian money market suffers from the seasonal stringency of credit and higher interest rates during a part of the year.
(j) Indian money market suffers from the shortage of capital funds.

RBI and Money Market

The Indian money market operates within the legal environment of the RBI. It has all the authorities regarding all the aspects of borrowing and lending of the money.

1. The RBI introduced two schemes for the development of the bill market. They were introduced in 1952 and in 1970. It has made efforts to encourage the usage of bills in the banking system.
2. It has taken a number of measures to improve the functioning of the indigenous banks.
3. The RBI has been able to reduce the differences in the interest rates between different sections as well as different centres of the money market.
4. The RBI has taken measures to amalgamate and merge banks into few strong banks.
5. There are certain problems faced by the RBI in controlling the money market, i.e., absence of bill market, hurdle in the way of strengthening the unorganised money market.
6. Inadequate development of call money market in India.
7. There is no co-ordination among the different components of money market.

Measures for Improvement in the Money Market: The RBI and the Union Government are keen on removing the deficiencies of the Indian money market. The following are the measures for improving the organisation of the money market:

1. Money lenders required to obtain licences for carrying lending business through an usurious Loans Act, 1918.
2. In order to alternate credit of the indigenous bankers, the RBI encouraged the credit cooperative societies to provide credit facilities to the rural areas. The cooperative societies have a wide network and they spread throughout the country and cover all the needs of agriculturists, artisans and others. Cooperative

banking is regarded as the only practice answer to the problem. The Banking Laws Act was passed in 1964 for scientific banking business to regulate property.

3. The government made efforts to meet the needs of the agriculturists more comprehensively. The government established Agricultural Refinance Corporation in 1963 to provide credit facilities to the agriculturists. The ARC refinances the term loans furnished by **Land Mortgage Banks** and other institutions. The ARC was replaced by the **National Bank for Agriculture and Rural Development** in 1982. It is established for the purpose of providing adequate credit to the agriculture sector in India.
4. The government established rural banks in 1970 with a view to finance primary agricultural credit societies through commercial banks. The government created a link between cooperative and joint sector banks. Therefore, the banking commission proposed to establish rural banks in India. The affairs and control of the RRBs are made responsible to the banks. The RBI extended the credit guarantee scheme to coop banks.
5. The RBI made efforts to create a link between indigenous banks and commercial banks. As a result the indigenous bankers are entitled to get cash credit from the approved list of joint stock banks and the SBI against demand promissory notes.
6. The RBI has taken some steps to encourage the bill market. It introduced two schemes: (a) The bill market scheme 1952, (b) The new bill market scheme 1970. But they have no impact on the bill market.
7. The Government of India made efforts to strengthen the Indian money market and capital market through commercial banks. Therefore, it nationalised a number of banks to provide the credit facilities in the rural areas for the priority sector.
8. The RBI introduced a lead bank scheme in December 1969 to provide more credit facilities by eliminating banking deficiencies in rural areas. The scheme is based on area approach. The scheme entrusted the individual banks to develop a particular area in their jurisdiction.
9. The Central Government has proposed to introduce a special legislation called the Nidhis and Chit Funds Act with a view to control and regulating their activities. The banking commission has suggested uniform fund legislation for the entire country.

Vaghul Committee of Money Market

The RBI made a comprehensive review of the money market. It appointed a working group in September 1986 under the chairmanship of **Shri M. Vaghul**. The group was appointed to study the money market system and recommend specific measures for their development. The group submitted its report in January 13, 1987. The group was appointed for the following purposes:

(a) The group was appointed to examine money market instruments and recommended specific solutions for their development.
(b) To recommend the market interest rates.
(c) To assess the impact of changes in the cash credit system.
(d) To study the possibility of increasing the players in the money market.

The group made a number of recommendations and observations for strengthening the market.

(a) Present structure of the money market.
(b) Recommendations.

Present Structure

1. The financial markets consists of money market and capital market. The money market is a market for short-term market.
2. The short-term financial assets are near to money.
3. The instruments are liquid and can bc transferable quickly.
4. They help in equilibrating the short-term surplus funds of lenders.
5. The Indian money market is narrow with a limited number of players.
6. There is also a need of new money market instruments.
7. The money market interest rates regulated by RBI and Indian Bankers Association.
8. The interest rates of the unorganised sector is more than the organised sector's market.
9. In the organised sector, the volume of the business in the call money market has been increased.
10. The RBI has taken several measures for the development of the bill scheme, there has not been satisfactory progress in this sector.

11. The treasury bills are the part of organised money sector.
12. The inter-corporate market providing short-term liquidity.

Recommendations: The Vaghul group made the following recommendations for the development of the money market:

(a) The call money interest rates should be freely determined by market forces.
(b) The call market should be like an inter-bank market.
(c) The government should take some steps for developing a genuine bill market.
(d) The bill discounting market should not exceed 16% rate of interest.
(e) The re-discounting of bills should be freely allowed to all the institutions.
(f) In commercial paper market, no restrictions should be imposed on the participants.
(g) The rate of interest on commercial papers should be left to the market forces.
(h) The 182 TBs market should be developed and more players should be allowed to participate in the auctions.
(i) The stamp duty involved in the bill transactions must be abolished.
(j) The government should pay all credit purchases through bills of exchange.
(k) The treasury bill refinance facility should be introduced. The refinance rate should be 1.5% higher than the prevailing TBs rate.
(l) An autonomous body should be incorporated to deal in short-term money market instruments. It should be jointly started by the RBI. The public sector banks and the financial institutions.
(m) A short-term commercial paper should be introduced.
(n) The factor service should be encouraged by the banks and non-bank financial institutions.
(o) Every new instrument must be approved by the RBI in money market.

Recent measures taken by RBI: The RBI is the supreme authority in the money market. It has the powers to regulate, coordinate and guide the money market. The Vaghul Committee had submitted its recommendations on 1.1.1987. based on the recommendations submitted by the group, the

RBI has taken several steps to develop the money market. The following measures are recently taken by the RBI to strengthen the market:

(a) The RBI has taken steps to promote the discount and finance house of India with a view to increase the liquidity of the money market.
(b) The RBI permitted in 1991 to set up money market mutual fund by the scheduled commercial banks and their subsidiaries. This mutual funds would provide additional short-term funds to the money market.
(c) In April 1987, the RBI introduced an effective interest rate on bill discounting. The ceiling rate has been raised from **11.5% to 12.5%.**
(d) The RBI has been taking several steps to increase the players in the bill rediscounting market.
(e) The RBI has been introducing several treasury bills in the money market. In 1987, 182 day TBs.; in 1992-93, 364 day TBs were introduced. These bills were taken into consideration for SCR.
(f) The RBI had been taking total deregulation of money market interest rates with effect from 1.5.1989.
(g) The RBI permitted the CDs into the money market in June 1989.
(h) The RBI liberalised the credit authorisation in July 1987.
(i) The RBI promoted the DFHI with a view to increase the liquidity of the money market instrument.
(j) As a result of various measures taken by the RBI, the money market became more organised and diversified.

Discount and Finance House of India

The Vaghul group submitted its report in 1987. As per the recommendations of the group, the RBI made efforts to establish the DFHI. The DFHI was set up in April 1988. It is the apex body in the Indian money market. It has been set up in collaboration with the public sector banks and financial institutions. Its establishment is a major step towards developing the secondary market for Indian money market. It commenced its operations in April 25, 1988. It deals in short-term money market instruments. The ultimate aim of the DFHI is to increase the turnover of the money market. The initial paid up capital is Rs.150 crores. It has the refinance and credit facility from the RBI. It is also entitled to get support from the consortium of public sector banks. It encourages the participation of several institutions in the money market. The players in the market are scheduled commercial banks, and their subsidiaries, state and urban cooperative banks and all India financial institutions. It provides an equilibrium place for these institutions surplus and deficit position. It opened its branches at Delhi, Kolkata, Chennai, Ahmedabad and Bangalore. It decentralised its operations in order to provide better facilities to the Indian money market. In accordance with the announcement of the monetary policy by the RBI in April 1994, a system of primary dealers was introduced on May 14, 1994, in the money market. The RBI had also introduced the system of **Satellite Dealers** on 31.12.96. The PDs and SDs made institutional development in the money market more liquid and broaden.

Primary Dealers: The monetary policy of 1994 introduced the system of primary dealers. RBI framed the guidelines for efficient and smooth functioning of the money market.

Objectives: The primary dealers objectives are presented below:

(a) To strengthen the money market and government securities market to make more liquid and broad.
(b) To conduct open market operations more effectively.
(c) To improve the secondary market trading system in the money market.
(d) To provide the underwriting facilities to the government securities market outside the RBI.

Any subsidiary of scheduled commercial bank and all India financial institutions are eligible to apply for primary dealership. These institutions shall be related to government securities market. Any company which is incorporated under the Companies Act, 1956 are also eligible to primary dealership. But they should be engaged in government securities market. The company institutions shall have a minimum net worth of **Rs. 50 crores**. The net worth shall consist of paid up equity, free reserves, premium account balance and capital reserves. If they play an important role in the government securities market both in primary and secondary market segments. The RBI is the supreme authority and the PD is required to have a standing agreement. The PD shall bid for government dated securities and auction T-bills at a specified amount. The PDs will underwrite a portion of the issue upto a minimum fixed percentage of shortfall in subscriptions against the notified amount. A PD offers a firm two way quotation either through phone a recognised stock exchange. Every PD has to maintain the minimum capital standards at all points of time. The annual turnover of PD in a financial year should not be less than 5 times in government dated securities and 10 times in treasury bills. A PD is subject to all prudential and regulation guidelines by the RBI. They should submit periodic returns as prescribed by the RBI. They should provide all rewards to the RBI. They should have a sufficient internal control system for the smooth functioning of the business. They should have physical infrastructure facilities and skilled manpower for efficient participation in primary issues.

Satellite Dealers: The RBI has introduced the satellite dealer system for the development of the supporting infrastructure for dealing and distribution arrangements in government securities and money market instruments. The subsidiaries of commercial bank/all India financial institutions and companies are eligible to become satellite dealers. They must be predominantly in government securities market. They should have a minimum net worth of **Rs. 50 crores**. They should be registered with the RBI as SD. The net worth means paid up equity, free reserves, balance in share premium account and capital reserves, if any. They are designed to work with the PDs in primary and secondary segment of the government securities market or money market. They would generate a turnover of Rs. 30 crores annually. The annual turnover should not be less than 5 times in the government securities market and should not be less than 3 times in respect of outright transactions. The RBI will sanction permission to the SDs in money market operations. The SD should achieve a portfolio of not less than 20% in government securities in relation to the total assets. They should maintain minimum capital requirements at all times as prescribed by the RBI from time-to-time. They should have good infrastructure facilities.

Money Market Mutual Funds (MMMFs): The RBI is the supreme authority in the money market. The MMMF dealt with wholesale transactions involving large amount of transactions. They were issued to large corporates and institutional inventors. The RBI prepared a broad framework for selling up these institutions. The RBI announced in April 1992 about the introduction of MMMFs. But the scheme was finally introduced in December 1995. The scheme was introduced with a view to provide greater liquidity and depth to the market. The scheme was made more flexible and attractive to the commercial banks, financial institutions and institutional investors. The MMMF can be established by any scheduled commercial banks, public financial institutions and companies. The Mutual fund can also be eligible for setting up of MMMF. The MMMF can be operated through a trust or in the form of department. Its assets and liabilities form a part of the eligible institutions and balance sheets. It is a parking place for cash reserve. The private sector mutual funds also have been allowed to set up MMMFs with the approval of the RBI and SEBI. They can invest in any money market instruments without any ceiling. The lock in period in case of these schemes was 30 days. The RBI also allowed to set up these funds by UTI, IDBI MF, Amro Bank and Bank of Madurai. The first MMMF was set up by Kothari Pioneer in 1997. But the fund did not succeed. The UTI MMMF had mobilised Rs.30 crores from the market in 1997. The scheme is offered to resident individuals, HUFs, trusts, societies and corporates, the minimum amount of investment is Rs.10,000. The NAV will be calculated on daily basis.

CAPITAL MARKET

Introduction

The Financial Markets are the centres that made provisions for buying and selling of financial claims and services. Financial markets are classified as Money Markets and Capital Markets. Money Market deals in short-term finance with a period of maturity of one year or less. **Capital Market** is a market for long-term securities. It contains financial instruments of maturity period exceeding one year. It involves in long-term nature of transactions. It is a growing element of the financial system in the Indian economy. It differs from the money market in terms of maturity period and liquidity. It is the financial pillar of industrialised economy. The development of a nation depends upon the functions and capabilities of the capital market.

Capital market is the market for long-term sources of finance. It refers to meet the long-term requirements of the industry. Generally, the business concerns need two kinds of finance.

(a) Short-term funds for working capital requirements.
(b) Long-term funds for purchasing fixed assets.

Therefore, the requirements of working capital of the industry are met by the money market. The long-term requirements of the funds to the corporate sector are supplied by the Capital Market. It refers to the institutional arrangements which facilitate the lending and borrowing of long-term funds. In this market long period maturity securities are exchanged. Generally every market is based on supply and demand forces. In capital market, the corporations require the funds on long-term basis. They are leading borrowers of funds in the capital market for their business. They mobilise the funds by issuing various financial instruments. These financial instruments will have a long-term maturity period. On the demand side the Central Government, State Governments and local bodies are also included. All of these institutions need the fund to meet their development activities. The business concerns, farmers, unincorporated business firms are other demanders of the Capital Market Fund. On the supply side of the capital market, the individuals are the bulk suppliers of fund. Their investment is done through financial intermediaries, financial institutions, banking institutions or directly. The individuals have the largest potential savings in the country. They tend to keep their surplus funds in savings according to the prevailing interest rates. In addition to individual investors, the other suppliers in the capital market are companies, MFs, NBFCs, financial institutions. Many organisations are both demanders and suppliers of capital market funds in a large size. Capital markets are very dynamic. They play an important role in mobilising resources.

These mobilised resources are diverted towards productive way. Therefore, it not only mobilises the savings but also helps in industrial development of the country. The success of a country depends upon the **financial architecture** of the strong capital market. A strong capital market is required for the process of economic growth in the country. A developed and competitive capital market tends to establish equilibrium between saving and investment. The borrowers of the capital market raise funds through various instruments like **equity, preference, bond and mortgages.**

Functions of Capital Market

Capital market plays a vital role in the development by mobilising the savings to the needy corporate sector. In recent years there has been a substantial growth in the Capital Market. The Capital Market involves in various functions and significance. They are presented below:

(a) Coordinator.
(b) Motivation to savings.
(c) Transformation to investment.
(d) Enhances economic growth.
(e) Stability.
(f) Advantages to investors.
(g) Barometer.

(a) Coordinator: The Capital Market functions as coordinator between savers and investors. It mobilises the savings from those who have surplus fund and divert them to the needy persons or organisations. Therefore, it acts as a facilitator of the financial resource. In this way it plays a vital role in transferring the surplus resources to deficit sectors. It increases the productivity of the industry which ultimately reflects in GDP and national income of the country. It increases the prosperity of the nation.

(b) Motivation of Savings: The Capital market provides a wide range of financial instruments at all times. India has a vast number of individual savers and the crores of rupees are available with them. These resources can be attracted by the capital market with nature. The banks and non-banking financial institutions motivate the people to save more and more. In less developed countries, there are no efficient capital market to tap the savings. In underdeveloped countries there are very little savings due to various factors. In that countries they invest mostly in unproductive sector.

(c) Transformation of Investment: The capital market is a place where the savings are mobilised from various sources, is at the disposal of businessmen and the government. It facilitates lending to the corporate sector and the government. It diverts the savings amount towards capital formation of the corporate sector. It creates assets by helping the industry. Thus it enhances the productivity and leads to industrialisation. The industrial development of the country depends upon the dynamic nature of the capital market. It also provides facilities through banks and non-banking financial institutions. The development of financial institutions made the way easy to capital market. The capital has become more mobile. The interest rate falls lead to an increase in the investment.

The Industrial Investment Proposals (August 1991 to March 2002)

Sl. No.	*States/UTs*	*Total Investment (Rs. in crores)*	*Percentage*
1.	Maharashtra	2,21,750	20.60
2.	Gujarat	1,79,702	16.70
3.	Tamil Nadu	69,012	6.41
4.	Uttar Pradesh	76,081	7.07
5.	Andhra Pradesh	1,17,310	10.90
6.	Haryana	32,874	3.05
7.	Rajasthan	40,278	3.74
8.	Punjab	53,255	4.95
9.	West Bengal	36,135	3.36
10.	Madhya Pradesh	43,777	4.07

(Contd.)

(Contd.)

Sl. No.	States/UTs	Total Investment (Rs. in crores)	Percentage
11.	Karnataka	54,490	5.06
12.	Dadra & Nagar Haveli	19,960	1.85
13.	Daman and Diu	4,054	0.38
14.	Chattisgarh	26,882	2.50
15.	Kerala	10,513	0.98
16.	Pondicherry	7,464	0.69
17.	Delhi	6,480	0.60
18.	Goa	6,357	0.59
19.	Himachal Pradesh	9,428	0.88
20.	Orissa	26,946	2.50
21.	Jharkhand	10,786	1.00
22.	Uttaranchal	5,881	0.55
23.	Assam	7,586	0.70
24.	Bihar	4,468	0.42
25.	Meghalaya	741	0.07
26.	Jammu and Kashmir	804	0.07
27.	Chandigarh	458	0.04
28.	Tripura	1,834	0.17
29.	Sikkim	33	0.00
30.	Andaman and Nicobar	332	0.03
31.	Arunachal Pradesh	68	0.01
32.	Nagaland	207	0.02
33.	Lakshadweep	04	0.00
34.	Manipur	0	0.00
35.	Mizoram	0	0.00
36.	More than one state	377	0.04
	Total	10,76,327	100%

Source: *EPW*, 17.08.02, p. 3387.

The Statement Showing Year on Year Growth Rates of GDP at Factor Cost at Current Prices

(per cent)

Sl. No.	Sector	1998-99	1999-2000	2000-01	2001-02
1.	Agriculture Forestry and Fishing	18.8	0.1	2.5	9.6
2.	Mining and Quarrying	5.0	15.4	10.2	7.1
3.	Manufacturing	8.5	6.0	12.3	4.7
4.	Electricity, gas and water supply	20.4	3.3	12.9	17.6
5.	Construction	18.1	14.7	10.4	7.4
6.	Trade, hotels transport and communications	15.1	8.8	9.3	9.4

(Contd.)

(Contd.)

Sl. No.	*Sector*	*1998-99*	*1999-2000*	*2000-01*	*2001-02*
7.	Financing, insurance, real estate and business services	15.8	21.5	7.3	11.6
8.	Community social and personal services	23.6	16.0	10.0	10.0
	GDP at Factor Cost	16.3%	8.6%	8.0%	9.1%

Source: *EPW*, 6.7.2002, p. 2671.

The Statement Showing Year on Year Growth Rates of GDP at Factor Cost at 1993-94 Prices

(per cent)

Sl. No.	*Sector*	*1998-99*	*1999-2000*	*2000-01*	*2001-02*
1.	Agriculture Forestry and Fishing	7.1	0.5	-0.2	5.7
2.	Mining and Quarrying	1.3	3.5	3.3	1.8
3.	Manufacturing	2.5	4.4	6.7	2.8
4.	Electricity, gas and water supply	6.4	6.7	6.2	4.6
5.	Construction	6.1	8.2	6.8	3.6
6.	Trade, hotels transport and communications	7.1	8.3	5.3	6.2
7.	Financing, insurance, real estate and business services	8.4	9.6	2.9	7.8
8.	Community social and personal services	9.9	12.1	6.0	5.9
	GDP at Factor Cost	6.6%	6.0%	4.0	5.4%

Source: *EPW*, 6.7.2002, p. 2671

Statement Showing the Annual GDP from 1998-2002 at 1993-94 Prices

(Rs. in crores)

Sl. No.	*Sector*	*1998-99*	*1999-2000*	*2000-01*	*2001-02*
1.	Agriculture Forestry and Fishing	2,88,401	2,89,842	2,89,194	3,05,818
2.	Mining and Quarrying	25,996	26,908	27,796	28,306
3.	Manufacturing	1,84,263	1,92,404	2,05,220	2,11,021

(Contd.)

(*Contd.*)

Sl. No.	Sector	1998-99	1999-2000	2000-01	2001-02
4.	Electricity, gas and water supply	26,831	28,637	30,406	31,804
5.	Construction	54,342	58,815	62,801	65,081
6.	Trade, hotels transport and communications	2,34,022	2,53,506	2,66,817	2,83,369
7.	Financing, insurance, real estate and business services	1,33,130	1,45,865	1,50,051	1,61,696
8.	Community social and personal services	1,36,069	1,52,523	1,61,637	1,71,137
	GDP at Factor Cost	10,83,054	11,48,500	11,93,922	12,58,232

Source: *EPW*, 6.7.2002, p. 2671.

The Statement Showing the Annual GDP from 1998-2002 at Current Prices

(*Rs. in Crores*)

Sl. No.	Sector	1998-99	1999-2000	2000-01	2001-02
1.	Agriculture Forestry and Fishing	4,59,899	4,60,547	4,71,981	5,17,354
2.	Mining and Quarrying	35,105	40,520	44,648	47,807
3.	Manufacturing	2,51,793	2,66,890	2,99,753	3,13,877
4.	Electricity, gas and water supply	42,480	43,886	49,526	58,218
5.	Construction	91,922	1,05,440	1,16,431	1,25,014
6.	Trade, hotels transport and communications	3,36,038	3,65,735	3,99,623	4,37,366
7.	Financing, insurance, real estate and business services	1,81,575	2,20,561	2,36,645	2,64,124
8.	Community social and personal services	2,17,219	2,52,059	2,77,236	3,05,050
	GDP at Factor Cost	16,16,031	17,55,638	18,95,843	20,68,810

Source: *EPW*, 6.7.2002, p. 2671.

The Statement Showing Statewise Breaking-up of Foreign Direct Investment Approvals During August 1991 to March 2002

States	*No. of Approvals*	*Amount (Rs. in crores)*	*Percentage*
I. Northern Region:			
(a) Delhi	1,857	33,470	12.1
(b) Haryana	769	3,518	1.3
(c) Himachal Pradesh	96	364	0.1
(d) Punjab	181	1,968	0.7
II. Western Region:			
(a) Gujarat	1,032	18,265	6.6
(b) Maharashtra	3,854	48,409	17.4
(c) Rajasthan	319	3,005	1.1
III. Eeastern Region:			
(a) Bihar	47	740	0.3
(b) Orissa	136	8,229	3.0
(c) West Bengal	584	8,730	3.1
IV. North Eastern Region	30	63	0.0
V. Central Region:			
(a) Madhya Pradesh	225	9,227	3.3
(b) U.P.	730	4,790	1.7
VI. Southern Region:			
(a) A.P.	975	12,753	4.6
(b) Karnataka	1,891	21,413	7.7
(c) Kerala	259	1,525	0.5
(d) Tamil Nadu	2,113	23,202	8.4
(e) Pondicherry	110	1,241	0.4
(f) Others	6,294	76,577	27.6
	21,502	**2,77,597**	**100%**

Source: *EPW*, 31.8.02, p. 3567.

The Statement Showing Foreign Investment Approvals and Actual since 1991 August Countrywise Break-up

Sl. No.	*Country*	*Investment (Rs. in crores)*	*Per cent to Total*
1.	USA	56,616	20.40
2.	Mauritius	32,918	11.90
3.	UK	21,405	7.7
4.	Japan	10,858	3.9
5.	South Korea	9,798	3.5
6.	Germany	8,950	3.2
7.	Netherlands	8,636	3.1
8.	Australia	6,734	2.4
9.	Malaysia	5,682	2.0
10.	France	6,234	2.2

(Contd.)

(*Contd.*)

11.	Singapore	4,945	1.8
12.	Italy	4,779	1.7
13.	Israel	4,244	1.5
14.	Belgium	4,162	1.5
15.	Clayman Island	3,861	1.4
16.	Switzerland	3,011	1.1
17.	Canada	2,726	1.0
18.	Thailand	2,726	0.98
19.	Hong Kong	2,261	0.8
20.	South Africa	1,906	0.7
21.	Sweden	2,039	0.7
22.	NRIs	10,408	3.7
23.	Euro Issues	48,447	17.4
24.	All others	14,346	5.2
		2,77,692	100

Source: *EPW*, 31.8.2002, p. 3567.

The Statement Showing Savings and Investment
(As a Per cent of GDP at Current Market Prices)

Year	*Gross domestic capital formation*	*Gross domestic savings*	*Public savings*	*Private savings*	*Household savings*	*Corporate savings*
Average 1985-90	22.7	20.4	2.4	18.0	16.0	2.0
1990-91	26.3	23.1	1.1	22.0	19.3	2.7
1991-92	22.6	22.0	2.0	20.1	17.0	3.1
1992-93	23.6	21.8	1.6	20.2	17.5	2.7
1993-94	23.1	22.5	0.6	21.9	18.4	3.5
1994-95	26.0	24.8	1.7	23.2	19.7	3.5
1995-96	26.9	25.1	2.0	23.1	18.2	4.9
1996-97	24.5	23.2	1.7	21.5	17.0	4.5
1997-98	24.6	23.1	1.3	21.8	17.6	4.2
1998-99	22.7	21.7	-1.0	22.6	18.9	3.7
1999-2000	24.3	23.2	-0.9	24.0	20.3	3.7
2000-01QE	24.0	23.4	-1.7	25.1	20.9	4.2

Source: *EPW*, 13.7.2002, p. 2903.

The Statement Showing the Index of Gross Fixed Capital Formation (at 1993-94 Prices) by Industry of Use (Base 1993-94 = 100)

Sl. No.	Sector	1993-94	1994-95	1995-96	1996-97	1997-98	1998-99	1999-2000
1.	Agriculture	100	108.3	114.1	115.3	115.6	120.2	133.6
2.	Industry	100	116.3	158.2	159.5	152.9	143.8	139.8
3.	Manufacturing	100	114.7	186.0	194.4	179.4	165.1	153.4
4.	Mining & Quarry	100	193.8	123.4	76.8	77.4	70.4	79.8
5.	Electricity, water, gas	100	91.4	86.2	94.1	94.4	101.7	112.5
6.	Construction	100	164.4	244.2	130.3	277.9	238.4	252.2
7.	Services	100	123.5	131.2	124.2	116.0	119.2	131.0
8.	Trade, Hotels and Restaurants	100	146.2	189.6	133.3	119.2	118.8	116.9
9.	Transport & storage	100	123.8	131.0	131.3	106.0	101.2	118.2
10.	Financing Insurance	100	118.7	124.6	119.4	121.1	119.8	121.6
11.	Community Services	100	123.1	121.8	199.8	199.6	142.4	168.8
12.	Total 1+2+3.	100	118.5	143.9	141.9	135.2	132.1	135.8

Source: *EPW*, 13.7.2002, p. 2903.

The Statement Showing Industry-wise Break-up of FDI Approvals Since August 1991 to March 2002

Sl. No.	Name of Industry	No. of approvals	Amount of approval	% to No. of total
1.	Basic goods industries	3,459	1,07,576	38.8
2.	Capital goods industries	6,538	25,117	9.0
3.	Intermediate goods industries	811	4,993	1.8
4.	Consumer Non-durable industries	4,363	27,623	10.1
5.	Consumer durable industries	159	9,357	3.4
6.	Services	6,172	1,02,928	37.1
	Grand Total	21,502	2,77,597	100

Source: *EPW*, 31.8.2002, p. 3567.

The Statement Showing Industry-wise for Investment Proposals (August 1991 to March 2002)

Sl. No.	Industry	Total Investment (Rs. in crores)	Percentage
1.	Textiles	1,19,464	11.10
2.	Chemicals	1,89,036	17.56
3.	Metallurgical	1 6,46541	13.61
4.	Miscellaneous	84,494	7.85
5.	Electrical Equipment	50,818	4.72

(Contd.)

(Contd.)

Sl. No.	Industry	Total Investment (Rs. in crores)	Percentage
6.	Food Processing Industry	33,889	3.15
7.	Veg. Oil and Vanaspati	18,409	1.71
8.	Drugs and Pharma	15,926	1.48
9.	Sugar	43,964	4.08
10.	Paper and Pulp	40,442	3.76
11.	Telecommunication	30,201	2.81
12.	Mechanical and Engg.	15,853	1.47
13.	Industrial Machinery	16,275	1.51
14.	Cement and Gypsum	67,972	6.32
15.	Transportation	26,098	2.42
16.	Fermentation Industries	8,819	0.82
17.	Prime Movers	6,030	0.56
18.	Rubber Goods	11,247	1.04
19.	Fertilisers	21,688	2.02
20.	Fuels	92,834	8.63
21.	Leather	4,038	0.38
22.	Ceramics	3,742	0.35
23.	Soaps Cosmetics	3,477	0.32
24.	Scientific Instruments	4,124	0.38
25.	Office Equipment	4,149	0.39
26.	Glass	6,448	0.60
27.	Machine Tools	1,950	0.18
28.	Timber Products	2,629	0.24
29.	Photographic Film	1,137	0.11
30.	Agriculture Machinery	1,843	0.17
31.	Earth Moving Machinery	1,074	0.10
32.	Glue and Gelatin	353	0.03
33.	Dyestuffs	357	0.03
34.	Medical and Surgical	575	0.05
35.	Industrial Instruments	134	0.01
36.	Defence Industries	265	0.02
37.	Map Survey and Drawings	4	0.00
38.	Boiler and Steam Generators	28	0.00
	Total	10,76,327	100.00

Source: *EPW*, 17.08.02, p. 3387.

(d) Enhances economic growth: The development of the capital market is influenced by many factors like the level of savings with the public, per capita income, purchasing capacity, and the general condition of the economy. The capital market smoothens and accelerates the process of economic growth. The capital market consists of various institutions like banking and non-banking financial institutions. It allocates the resources very cautiously in accordance with the development needs of the country.

The balanced and proper allocation of the financial resources lead to the expansion of the industrial sector. Therefore, it promotes the balances regional development. All regions should be developed in the country.

(e) Stability: The capital market provides a stable security prices in the stock market. It tends to stabilise the value of stocks and securities. It reduces the fluctuations in the prices to the minimum level. The process of stabilisation is facilitated by providing funds to the borrowers at a lower interest rate. The speculative prices in the stock market can be reduced by supply of funds. The flow of funds towards secondary market reduces the prices at certain level. Therefore, the capital market provides funds to the stock market at a low rate of interest.

(f) Advantages to the Investors: The investors who have surplus funds can invest in long-term financial instruments. In capital market, a number of long-term financial instruments are available to the investor at any time. Hence the investors can lend their money in the capital market at reasonable rate of interest. The capital market helps the investors in many ways. It is the coordinator to bring the buyer and seller at one place and ensure the marketability of investments. The stock market prices are published in newspapers everyday which enables the investor to keep track of their investments and channelise them into most profitable way. The capital market safeguards the interest of the investors by compensating from the stock exchange compensating fund in case of fraud and default.

(g) Barometer: The development of the capital market is the indicator of the development of a nation. The prosperity and wealth of a nation depend upon the dynamic capital market. It not only reflects the general condition of the economy but also smoothens and accelerates the process of economic growth. It consists a number of institutions, allocates the resources rationally in accordance with the development needs of the country. A good allocation of resources lead to expansion of trade and industry. It helps both public and private sector.

The term Capital Market has been defined by different authors. According to Gitman and Joehnk, "Capital Market is the market where transactions are made in long-term securities such as stocks and debentures".[29]

Capital Market has been defined "The market for relatively long-term (greater than one year original maturity) financial instruments".[30]

Generally, the corporate sector requires funds not only for meeting their long-term requirements of funds for their new projects modernisation, expansion and diversificatin programmes but also for covering their operational needs. Therefore, their requirement of capital is classified as given below:

(A) Long-term capital
(B) Short-term capital
(C) Venture capital
(D) Export capital

Long-term capital represents the amount of capital invested in the form of fixed assets. Fixed assets are such as land, building, plant and machinery necessary for every company at the initial stage of the commencement of the production. Heavy amount of capital is required by the companies when they are going for modernisation or expansion or diversification. Therefore, the requirement of long-term capital is supplied by the capital market. The long-term capital is also known as **Fixed Capital**. Usually the corporate sector mobilises the fixed capital from the capital market through various long-term maturity financial instruments. Therefore, it provides adequate funds to the corporate sector by offering various financial instruments. They mobilise the funds through issue of **Equity shares, Preference shares, Debentures, Bonds etc.** These financial instruments have a longer maturity period and they are treated by the companies as permanent capital. Some instruments have no maturity until the close down of a business unit.

Short-term capital represents the amount of capital invested in current assets. The Current Assets consist of cash, bank balance, inventory, debtors etc. The short-term capital is required to meet the need of working capital of the corporate sector. Working capital is required for meeting the operating cost of the business concern. They are required to pay different amount to different parties as per their schedule. Hence they procure the working capital from the commercial banks. In India a majority of the corporate sector is funded by commercial banks for working capital needs. The working capital may be sanctioned by the banks through different modes of finance. The working capital is known as circulating capital. An adequate supply of working capital leads to smooth functioning production of the goods. There are some other avenues available to the corporate sector to meet the needs of the working capital.

Venture capital is the capital which invested in highly risky ventures. It is also known as seed capital. It is a quite recent entrant in the capital market. It has great significance in helping technocrat entrepreneurs at the commencement stage of the concern. It has technical expertise. But it lacks finance.

Export capital refers for making payment in international trade. The payment of international trade involves in bills of exchange and other instruments.

Importance of Capital Market

Capital market deals with long-term funds. These funds are subject to uncertainty and risk. It supplies long and medium term funds to the corporate sector. It provides the mechanism for facilitating capital fund transactions. It deals in ordinary shares, bond debentures and stocks and securities of the government. In this market the funds flow will come from savers. It converts financial assets into productive physical assets. It provides incentives to savers in the form of interest or dividend to the investors. It leads to capital formation. The following factors play an important role in the growth of the capital market:

1. A strong and powerful Central Government.
2. Financial dynamics.
3. Speedy industrialisation.
4. Attracting Foreign Investment.
5. Investments from NRIs.
6. Speedy implementation of policies.
7. Regulatory changes.
8. Globalisation.
9. The level of savings and investment pattern of the household sectors.
10. Development of financial theories.
11. Sophisticated technological advances.

Players in the Capital Market

Capital market is a market for long-term funds. It requires a well-structured market to enhance the financial capability of the country. The market consists of a number of players. They are categorised as:

1. Companies
2. Financial Intermediaries
3. Investors

1. Companies: Generally every public company can access the capital market. The companies which are in need of finance for their projects can approach the market. The capital market provides funds from the savers of the community. The companies can mobilise the resources for their long-term needs such as project cost, expansion and diversification of projects and other expenditure items. In India, the companies should get the prior permission from the Securities and Exchange Board of India to raise the capital from the market. The SEBI is the most powerful organisation to monitor, control and guide the capital market. It classifies the companies for the issue of share capital as **new companies, existing, unlisted existing listed companies.** According to its guidelines a company is a new company, if it satisfies all the following conditions:

(a) The company shall not have completed **12 months** of commercial operations.
(b). Its audited operative results are not available.
(c) The company may set up by entrepreneurs with or without track record.

A company can be treated as existing listed company, if its shares are listed in any recognised stock exchange in India. A company is said to be an existing unlisted company if it is a closely held or private company.

2. Financial Intermediaries: Financial intermediaries are those who assist in the process of converting savings into capital formation in the country. A strong capital formation process is the **oxygen** to the corporate sector. Therefore, the intermediaries occupy a dominant role in the capital formation which ultimately lead to the growth of prospering to the community. Their role in this situation cannot be neglected. The government should encourage these intermediaries to build a strong financial empire for the country. They can also be called as **financial architectures** of the Indian **digital economy**. Their network cannot be ignored. Their financial capability cannot be measured. They take active role in the capital market. The major intermediaries in the capital market are:

(a) Brokers.
(b) Stock-brokers and sub-brokers.
(c) Merchant bankers.
(d) Underwriters.
(e) Registrars.
(f) Mutual funds.
(g) Collecting agents.
(h) Depositories.
(i) Agents.
(j) Advertising agencies.

3. Investors: The capital market consists of many numbers of investors. All types of investors basic objective is to get good returns on their investment. Investment means, just parking one's idle fund in a right parking place for a stipulated period of time. Every parked vehicle shall be taken away by its owners from parking place after a specific period. The same process may be applicable to the investment. Every fund owner may desire to take away the fund after a specific period. Therefore, safety is the most important factor while considering the investment proposal. The investors comprise the financial and investment companies and the general public companies. Usually, the individual savers are also treated as investors. **Return** is the reward to the investors. **Risk** is the punishment to the investors for being wrong selection of their investment decision. Return is always chased by the risk. An intelligent investor must always try to escape the risk and capture the return. All rational investors prefer return, but most investors are risk averse. They attempt to get maximum capital gain. The return can be available to the investors in two types they are in the form of revenue or capital appreciation. Some investors will prefer for revenue receipt and others prefer capital appreciation. It depends upon their economic status and the effect of tax implications. The institutions and companies raise the resources from the market by designing various schemes to meet the needs and convenience of the investors. The schemes can be framed to attract all types of investors, who are sailing in the capital market. The main objectives of any type of investors are **safety, profitability, liquidity** and **capital appreciation**.

Before Independence

The capital market in India was not scientifically developed before independence. The following are basic reasons for non-development of the capital market in India:

(a) Agriculture was the basic occupation of the people but there was no proper long-term lending to this sector.
(b) The British rulers were concentrated more on London market rather than Indian capital market.
(c) The number of companies were small and the number of scrips traded on stock exchanges also were smaller.
(d) Individual investors were very few and limited.
(e) The government had imposed many restrictions on the institutional savers.
(f) The absence of specialised financial intermediaries in pre-independence period.

The capital market had not been developed properly because of the British rulers.

Indian Capital Market Post-Independence

The Indian capital market has been growing significantly after 1951. After independence many regulations have been changed for the smooth functioning of our economy. Some acts have been abolished and others have been amended according to the needs and convenience of the public. Therefore, many factors have contributed to the capital market growth.

(a) Raising level of Income and Investment.
(b) New Financial Institutions.
(c) Expansion of Commercial Banks.
(d) Dynamic growth of specialised financial Institutions.

Raising level of Income and Investment: After 1951, there has been increase in the volume of saving and investment in the country. The capital market entirely depends upon the savings of the community. The government has taken some measures to strengthen the capital market. It provided all kinds of encouragement and tax relief to promote savings in the country. It concentrated on the investors problems and many steps have been taken to promote the welfare of the investors. After 1951, there was a spectacular growth in the joint stock companies which is an important indicator of the market. There was an increase in the growth of public borrowing for investment purpose. The insurance sector also led to the promotion of savings and supply of funds in the market. The provident fund collections have been increased significantly which leads to the promotion of capital market. The increased number of financial institutions and intermediaries encouraged mobilisation and channelisation of country's savings.

New Financial Institutions: The financial institutions occupy an important role in the capital market. They have not only accelerated the growth but also improved its efficiency and competitiveness effectively. The following institutions provide special types of financial services:

(a) Merchant banking.
(b) Leasing and hire purchasing companies.
(c) Mutual funds.
(d) Venture capital.
(e) Other institutions.

Expansion of Commercial Banks: Commercial banks are the financial nerves of the Indian economy. The Indian economic growth has been linked with the commercial bank system. They are the important constituents of the capital market. Their operations in this market are limited to purchase and sale of the government securities. Their holdings of industrial securities are very small. Recently the banks have been increasingly participating in term lending directly or indirectly through subscription of shares and debentures. This situation encourages investment in industrial securities.

Dynamic growth of specialised financial Institutions: After independence, the Government of India had taken a number of steps to assist the private sector industries in the matter of finance. The initiative of the government lead to promote the **Industrial Finance Corporation of India** in 1948. It was the first financial institution, which was established by India after the independence. It was the premier financial institutions to provide the financial assistance to the corporate sector. After the formation of the IFCI, it was followed by state finance corporations set up by State Governments. These SFCs provide financial assistance to small and medium industrial units. The following institutions had been established after the independence at the initiative of the Central Government:

(a) Industrial Credit and Investment Corporation of India (ICICI) 1956.
(b) Industrial Development Bank of India (IDBI) 1964.
(c) Unit Trust of India (UTI) 1964.
(d) Life Insurance Corporation of India (LIC) 1956.

These financial institutions have been rendering excellent services to the existing new and old companies. They provide finance in the form of loan assistance, underwriting new issues, and subscription to shares and debentures. These institutions are engaged in the channelising of resources to private sector.

Distinction between Capital and Money Market

There are some differences between money market and capital market. Money market is different from the capital market on the basis of the following characteristics:

(a) Period of time.
(b) Financial instruments.
(c) Purpose of loan.
(d) Risk.

(e) Market regulation.
(f) Liquidity.
(g) Monitoring.
(h) Players.

(a) Period of Time: The money market is a market for lending and borrowing of the short-term finance. The term short-term period refers to finance available for one year or less to the borrowers. Generally the borrowers will procure the fund for meeting their working capital requirements. Usually the working capital of the corporate sector is supplied by mostly commercial banks and players of the money market. While the capital market is a market where the long-term funds are available at reasonable rates of interest to the borrowers. Usually the fixed capital of the corporate sector will be met by the long-term nature of financial instruments. These financial instruments are available in the capital market only. The corporate sector will also be supplied the fund by the capital market for the purpose of their **project expansion, diversification and other needs.**

(b) Financial Instruments: The companies generally raise the fund from market by issuing a number of financial instruments. The money market consists of short-term financial instruments such as **call money, CDs, Bills and collateral loans etc.** On the other hand the main instruments are used in the capital market for long-term basis. These financial instruments such as **shares, debentures and bonds** are issued by the companies for their requirements.

(c) Purpose of Loans: The companies enter the money market to meet the needs of their short-term finance. The money market issues different types of financial instruments for one year period to meet the needs of working capital. The working capital arrangements will be adjusted by the money market while the fixed capital by the capital market. The long-term needs of finance will be adjusted by the capital market to the corporate sector.

(d) Risk: Generally the financial markets involve some degree of risk. The level of degree of risk depends upon the nature of market. The money market involves less risk level while the capital markets consist of higher level of risk. The money market maturity period is one year giving little time for default to occur. On the other hand the capital market caters to the long-term credit needs of the corporate sector and arrangements will be made for fixed capital to buy land or machinery.

(e) Market Regulation: In India, the market is closely observed by the prudential authorities. It is necessary to regulate the market operations for better functioning of the financial system. In the capital market the institutions are not much regulated. The money market is regulated by RBI, SEBI and Ministry of Finance.

(f) Liquidity: Liquidity is the most important factor in the money market. The role of money is creation of liquidity. The money market is a ready market for its financial assets. The basic role of capital market is providing funds to work on long-term basis. The financial instruments which are available in the capital market are productive employment and generation of assets in the economy. Asset formation is made by the capital market.

(g) Monitoring: The money market is closely associated with the Central Bank of the country. The Central Bank in India is RBI. The RBI is the supreme authority in the money market. It is directly linked with the Central Bank of India. But the capital market is regulated, observed and monitored by the SEBI. The RBI has less control on capital market.

(h) Players: The important players in the money market are Central Bank, Acceptance house, Commercial banks, non-banking financial institutions, Bill brokers etc. But in capital market stock exchanges, insurance companies, mortgage banks, non-banking institutions are important players.

The secondary market for money market is not active in India. But the secondary market for capital market is very active. The investment in money market is highest safety whereas the investment in capital market is not so safe. The accessibility to money market by individual is not possible but capital market provides easy accessibility to the individuals.

Structure of Capital Market in India

The structure of the capital market has undergone vast changes in recent years. The Indian capital market has transformed into a new appearance over the last four and half decades. Now it comprises an impressive network of financial institutions and financial instruments. The market for already issued securities has become more sophisticated in response to the different needs of the investors. The specialised financial institutions were involved in providing long-term credit to the corporate sector. Therefore, the premier financial institutions such as ICICI, IDBI, UTI, LIC and GIC constitute the largest segment. A number of new financial instruments and financial intermediaries have emerged in the capital market. Usually the capital markets are classified in two ways.

(a) On the basis of Issuer.
(b) On the basis of Instruments.

On the basis of issuer the capital markets can be classified again into two types.

(a) Corporate securities market.
(b) Government securities market.

On the basis of financial instruments the capital markets are classified into two kinds.

(a) Equity market.
(b) Debt market.

Recently there has been a substantial development of the Indian capital market. It comprises various sub-markets.

Equity market is more popular in India. It refers to the market for equity shares of existing and new companies. Every company shall approach the market for raising of funds. The equity market can be divided into two categories: (a) primary market, and (b) secondary market. Debt market represents the market for long-term financial instruments such as debentures, bonds etc. The structure of Indian capital market is shown below:

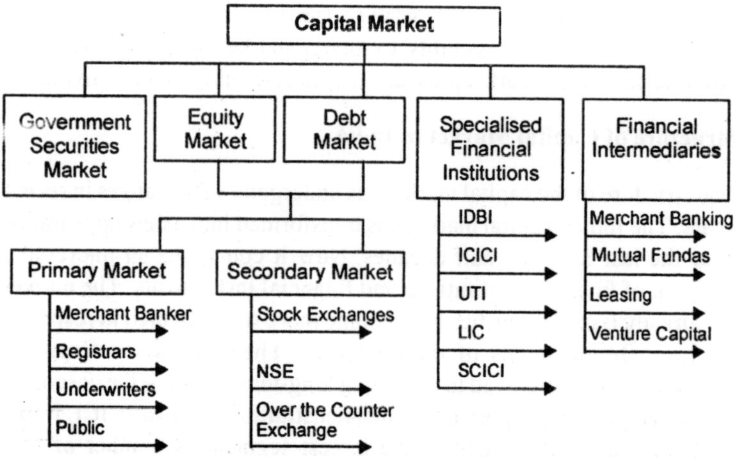

Structure of Capital Market

Components of the Capital Market

Indian capital market has a vast growth potential. It has most powerful avenue for household savings. India has a vast middle class families potential, they occupy a dominant role in mobilisation of resources. They play an important role in capital market. The corporate sector had been attracted 10% household savings of the community. In the developed countries more than 20 to 25 per cent of householdings are tapped by their capital markets. In the developed countries 25% of population go for shareholdings but in India such percentage is just less than 5%. The Society for Capital Market Research and Development conducted a shareholders survey in 1990. It placed the total number of share owners at around **90-100 lakhs**.[31] The survey also traced the past growth of share owning population since 1955. The total number of individual share owners at the end of 1977 in India is at around 2 crores. Most of the growth after 1990 took place during the boom years 1991-94. The analysis showed that the growth of share owners tapering of since 1995 had come to a near halt in 1997 due to persistent depression in the share market and investors bad experiences with many scrupulous company promoters and managements.

The capital market in India consists of two components.

1. New issue market or primary market
2. The secondary market

1. PRIMARY MARKET OR NEW ISSUE MARKET

Introduction

The capital market in India consists of two kinds: (a) primary market (b) secondary market. Primary market is known as new issue market. The new issue market is also called as "public issue". In the primary market, new securities are sold or exchanged for cash credit or other securities. The new securities that can be issued by the existing companies are newly floated companies. The primary market can be defined as "A market where new securities are bought and sold for the first time".[32]

Primary market is a new issue market. The funds are raised through the sale of new securities flow from the buyers of securities to the issuer of securities. The financial institutions play a key role in moving funds from the savings sector to the investment sector. A large manufacturing company requires bulk amount of capital for its needs. It raises funds both publicly and privately with more confident. Raising funds from the public is known as public issue. Public issue can be defined as **"Sale of bonds or stock to the general public".**[33] **The securities are sold to the lakhs of investors under a formal contract overseen by the government authorities. The required funds can also be raised privately to a limited number of investors. This process is known as private placement".** The primary market creates financial claims. In this market the public can only buy the shares. Two parties are involved in this market, they are lenders and the borrowers. The funds are flown from the lenders to the borrowers.

Objectives of Capital Issues: Generally the companies require two kinds of capital. They are (a) fixed capital, and (b) working capital. Fixed capital is in need of financing the capital assets. It is raised for buying of fixed assets like machinery, plant, equipment, land, building at the initial stage of a project. Sometimes existing companies can also raise funds from the primary market. The issue of capital can be raised for any of the following purposes:

(a) Promotion of new project.
(b) Expansion of the existing capacity.
(c) Diversification.
(d) Capitalisation of reserves.
(e) Regular working capital requirement.

Sources for raising Funds

The corporate sector usually raises funds from the market for their needs and convenience. They can procure the funds through the following sources:

(a) Issue of equity at par or premium.
(b) Issue of bonus shares.
(c) Issue of debentures.
(d) Issue of bonds by public sector undertakings.
(e) Issue of cumulative preference shares.

In the primary market, funds are available from lenders to park their funds on long-term basis. The companies, government, semi-government bodies, PSUs and a number of other institutions borrow issue of securities by the way of shares and debentures.

Features of the NIM: The major features of the primary market are as follows:

(a) The capital market is freely accessible by any company for raising funds from the public.
(b) The corporates have freedom in fixing of issue price of a share subject to some SEBI guidelines.
(c) The companies approach capital market rather than banks and financial institutions for raising of funds.
(d) The mushroom growth of companies and a spate of new issue by both new companies as well as existing companies.

Classification of New Issues

The new issue market is to facilitate transfer of funds of those who have surplus income and are willing to invest to entrepreneurs. The new issues in this market may be classified as follows:

(a) First issue of new companies (entrepreneurs without a track record).
(b) First issue of new companies (set up by existing companies with a track record).
(c) First issue by existing private/closely held company (without 3 years track record).
(d) First issue by existing private/closely held company (with 3 years track record).
(e) First public issue by existing private/closely held/existing unlisted/without 3 years track record but promoted by existing companies (with 5 years track record).
(f) Existing private/closely held and other unlisted companies without three years track record of consistent profitability seeking disinvestment by offer to public without issuing fresh capital).
(g) Existing private closely held or other existing unlisted company with 3 years track record of consistent profitability seeking disinvestment by offer to public without issuing fresh capital.
(h) Public issue by existing listed companies.

Transactions of Primary Market

The primary market is a market, where the companies found money as per their requirements. It is to facilitate the transfer of resources from savers to entrepreneurs. The general function of NIM can be split from the operational view into three services, they are:

(a) Investigation.
(b) Underwriting.
(c) Distribution.

(a) Investigation: The new proposals of the company may be investigated by the specialised agencies. The preliminary investigations entail a careful study of investigations regarding technical economic, financial and legal aspects of the issuing companies. The specialised agency renders the following services for improving the quality of capital issues. These services include advice on such aspects of capital issues as:

(a) Determination of the class of security and the price of the issues in the light of market conditions.
(b) The timing and magnitude of issues.
(c) Methods of flotation.
(d) Technique of selling.

(b) Underwriting: Underwriting is a guarantee about the success of an issue. The issuing company can eliminate the uncertainties of the public issue by making an agreement with the underwriter. The provision of underwriting is of crucial significance to the issuing company as well as investing public.

(c) Distribution: The success of a public issue depends upon many factors. The sale of securities to the ultimate investors is called as distribution. These specialised job can be handled by a highly specialised persons. These specialised persons are called as brokers and dealers in securities. They are highly specialised persons in dealing securities and debentures. They are powerful intermediaries in selling the shares to the public. They maintain regular contacts with the ultimate investors. The investors are the regular customers to the broker. They know about the buying habits and investment attitudes of the investors. They play an important role in investment decisions of the investors. They guide, direct and motivate the ultimate investors in taking a decision with regard to investment decisions.

Issue Process: The public issue is the most important event in the life of a company. The success of an issue depends upon the issue process. The issue of shares can be made by anyone of the following methods:

(a) Public issue through prospectus.
(b) Book building method.
(c) Private placement.
(d) Offer for sale.

(e) Rights issue.

Anyone of the above methods can be adopted by the issuing company. The companies have freedom to select anyone of the options to enter into the market. Let us discuss each method, advantage and their role in market.

(a) Public Issue through Prospectus: Public issue is more popular in India. It is one of the best methods available to the corporate sector. Generally the corporate enterprises raise capital through the issue of securities by means of a prospectus inviting subscription from the public. In this method, the issuing company invite the public by issue of prospectus. The prospectus is a document which contains all the particulars about the issuing company. The prospectus is an evidence document to the investors. The investors can be informed about the future activities of the company and past information. The issuing company offers directly to the general public, a fixed number of shares at a stated price. The public issues are generally underwritten to ensure success without any uncertainty at the market.

The prospectus is the base for investing money into a company by the ultimate investor. Therefore, the contents of the memorandum shall contain the information, according to the Companies Act. The disclosure of information in the prospectus shall be legal aspects of the Companies Act. Every care should be taken while preparing the prospectus. It also provides both civil and criminal liability for any mis-statement in the prospectus. The additional information also be furnished according to the SEBI guidelines. The prospectus shall contain the following information:

1. Company name and registered office address.
2. Present activities and proposed activities.
3. Location of the industry.
4. Particulars regarding capital such as authorised capital, subscribed and proposed issue of capital to public.
5. Date of opening and closing of subscription list.
6. Minimum amount of subscription.
7. Name of brokers, underwriters and others.
8. Name of underwriters along with directors opinion regarding underwriters capabilities.
9. A statement regarding the listing arrangements to the concerned stock exchanges.
10. Other legal information about the company.

The public issue method has some advantages and disadvantages. This system has the advantage that the transactions are carried on in the full light of publicity. In public issues, the shares are allotted to a wide range of the investors. The share ownership is widely diffused thereby contributing to the prevention of concentration of wealth and economic power. The issues are widely distributed and the threat of an artificial restriction on the quantity of shares available is avoided. The issue of shares publicly is a highly expensive method. The cost of flotation involves underwriting expenses, brokerage, printing charges of prospectus, advertisement changes, accountancy charges, legal charges, bank charges, stamp duty, listing fee, registration charges, travelling expenses, filling of document charges, mortgage deed, charges and postal charges. Therefore, the public issue is suitable only to large companies for **Mega issue**. It cannot be useful to small issues for even large companies. It involves in preparation of prospectus printing of share application distribution of forms throughout the nation. It is a time consuming process.

(b) Book Building Method: The book building is one of the sale procedures of fresh equity. In this method, the price of the issue is left to the investors. It is also on par with the system of public issue. Public issue refers to issue of shares to the public. But in this method the issuing company incorporates all the information of the issue proposal in the offer document. The offer document will be prepared on the lines of the public issue method which includes the reserve or minimum price. The investors are required to quote the number of shares and the price at which they are willing to acquire. It is very popular method for raising finance in abroad. In India this method has not been widely accepted.

(c) Private Placement: Private placement is another method of new issue of capital. In this method the shares are offered privately to the investors or to the issue houses. Placing of securities which are unquoted is known as private placing. Generally the securities of a particular company are acquired by the issue houses and the issue houses in turn will sell to the individual and institutional investors. The issue houses have a list of private and institutional investors who are potential to subscribe to any security which is issued in this manner. The shares will be transfered to the individual/institutional investors with a margin by the issue houses. This method of selling new issues made by the companies are cheap. Because there is no involvement of any flotation expenses like brokerage, underwriting expenses, advertising charges and printing and distribution of stationery.

(d) Offer for Sale: Offer for Sale means, the shares are offered through the intermediaries, i.e., Merchant banks, Investment banks, firms stock-brokers, issue houses. In this method, they will follow the process of public issue by drafting the prospectus. The prospectus contains the prescribed minimum contents which is the basis for the sale of securities. The shares are distributed to the applicants in a non-discriminatory manner. However, these issues are underwritten to avoid the possibility of the issue being left largely in the hands of financial intermediary. The offer for sale involves two stages. They are:

(i) In the first stage the issuing company sells the securities enbloc to the financial intermediary at an agreed fixed price. Therefore, the shares are acquired by the financial intermediary.
(ii) In the second stage the acquired financial intermediary will sell the shares to the ultimate investors. The securities which are offered to the public is generally higher than which they acquired from the issuing company. The difference between buying and selling price of equity is known as **"turn"**. The term is known as remuneration of the issuing houses. Generally the turn, the remuneration of financial intermediary involves underwriting commission, prospectus cost, advertisement cost etc. The main advantage of this method is that the issuing company will not feel trouble in selling of the shares.

(e) Rights Issue: All of the above methods can be used by both new companies and existed companies. The existed companies shares are already listed and widely held shares can be offered to the existing shareholders. This method is known as **Rights Issue**. According to this method, the existing shareholders are offered the right to subscribe to new shares in proportion to the number of shares as previously they hold. This offer will be made to existing shareholders only by a circular. Section 81 of the Companies Act reveals that a company shall issue right shares in the following situations:

(i) The company can issue rights offer after two years of its formation, or
(ii) After one year of first issue of shares.

From the above situation whichever is earlier these have to be first offered to the existing shareholders with a right to renounce them in favour of a nominee. A company can dispense with this requirement by passing a special resolution to the same effect. They are not normally underwritten.

The merit of rights issue is that it is an inexpensive companies method. This method can be used only by existing companies. In this method the general investing public has no opportunity to participate in the new companies. Generally the rights issue was not underwritten. But some organisations will take care to underwrite the issue. It is only a precautionary measure. The experience of underwritten companies reveals that there is no need of the services of the underwriters in Rights issue. Therefore, the company can reduce its expenses by avoiding underwriting. The other usual expenses like brokerage administrative expenses and advertising changes are of very small extent. However, it is more economical exercise for the issuing companies.

All of the above methods of flotation of new issues are suitable in different situations to different organisations.

2. SECONDARY MARKET

Difference between NIM and Secondary Market

1. The NIM deals with the fresh issue of securities to the investing public for the first time. The secondary market is a market for already issued securities. In this market the shares are moving with some velocity.
2. The NIM provides funds directly to the Industrial projects. They are involved in capital formation but secondary market does not create any additional fund directly to the corporate sector. They provide liquidity to the market.
3. The NIM is a market which does not have a physical existence and administrative set up. But the stock exchanges have excellent physical infrastructure and are located at various geographical areas throughout the nation.
4. The NIM is a market where the securities are made available the first time to the public. The secondary market serve all the sectors in India. It also makes a continuous valuation of securities traded in the market.
5. The NIM exists in the market and it is recognised by the services that it renders services at a particular time only. But the secondary market provides all facilities in the form of a market place. It consists of dealers of security where they regularly meet at an appointed time.

Relationship between the NIM and Secondary Market

(a) The NIM is the facilitator for corporates, borrowers and lenders. These securities are listed on a recognised stock exchange. The listing of securities creates a facility of convenience holdings of new securities which expand the initial market for them.
(b) The stock exchanges regulate the organisation of new issues for fair dealings.
(c) The NIM and secondary markets are complimentary in nature in providing capital to the industrial sector through securities.
(d) The infrastructural facilities are provided with the combination of various financial intermediaries. They provide excellent first hand information about the functioning of the corporate sector. They supply all the financial literature, information and supply of daily stock exchange lists to the investors.
(e) The response to the public issues is mainly dependent on the conditions pertaining in the stock market. If the secondary market is in active and shows a better movement then it will be reflected in the NIM. Therefore, the NIM is dependent on the secondary market. If the secondary market is dull and not quite encouraging, then there is no market for new issues.

Factors to be Considered for Investment to Primary Market

Primary market is a market where the funds are available to the borrowers from savers. It is the place where the funds are at disposal of corporate sector. The market is now regulated by the SEBI. According to the SEBI guidelines the issue has the right to fix its DWN issue prices. The SEBI also issued guidelines to the corporate sector for raising of funds from the market. The SEBI guidelines reveal that the issuer companies shall disclose full information about them to the investors. The guidelines provide protection to the investors which shall be followed by the corporate sector. The investors in stock market shall behave more cautiously. They are responsible for their own decisions which are taken by them with the lack of awareness. The set of guidelines is intended to educate the investors about certain aspects which they normally should look for in the memorandum of association. They should check the contents which are disclosed by the issuing company in the memorandum of association. The memorandum shall contain all the information of prospectus accompanying all application forms before making investment in any issue. The investor may contact the company or merchant banker if he requires any additional information relating to the issue. The investors shall assess the situation and should look into the following matters:

(a) Promoter's history
(b) Objectives of the present issue
(c) Project information
(d) Product or market observation
(e) Financial information
(f) Forecasting
(g) Pricing of issue
(h) Litigations
(i) Risk factors
(j) Auditor's Report
(k) Statutory dues
(l) Statutory clearances
(m) Careful observation
(n) Problems of New Issue Market
(o) Regulatory Framework.

(a) Promoter's History: The investors should look into the proper disclosures on all the aspects of promoters involvement in the proposed project. They should check the background of the promoters, their qualification, technical experience, past experience in the market, business capabilities, tactics, their reputation in the market etc. Therefore, the investors shall make a proper assessment about the abilities of the promoters before making an investment decision. The promoters are the most important persons in running the business activities. They occupy a dominant role in the discharge of functions of the business concern. They shall procure the information with reference to the companies earlier promoted by the promoters and their track record. In business sector, the past performance is the indicator to the future performance. Therefore, the investors shall observe the past performance of the promoters. The investors are also required to gain some knowledge in all areas of functional management. The investors shall make independent enquiries about the promoters work culture, attitudes, philosophy and morality. They shall get the information through other sources of information such as financial magazines, business journals and media reports. The investors awareness in India is to be increased. They generally do not have any idea about the corporate sector and its structure. They burnt their fingers in the market by investing innocently. They have no minimum knowledge before taking an investment decisions. Having money with them and investing blindly in wrong companies at the wrong times at wrong prices is quiet natural in

India. Some investors do not know even some simple fundamentals about the corporate sectors. Promoter's track record is the most important factor in selecting a proper portfolio by the investors. The investors in the market shall move more cautiously before taking investment decisions. The good track record of the promoters may consists of the MD's background and experience in the field and composition of board of director. The board of directors are the most important members in smooth functioning of the companies. The profitability of the corporate sector depends upon the abilities of the Board of Directors. The company shall have a professional management team. The management of the company shall be left to the professional managers.

(b) Objectives of the Present Issue: The investors shall check the contents of the prospectus. They shall verify that the present issue of capital may increase in profitability or not? These issues of shares may reflect in enhancement of the profitability in future or not? A close observation of the prospects content can reveal all the things about the present issue of capital. The objects of the issue of capital is more important before making investment in that company. Therefore, the investors are required to check the objectives of the present issue and take the decision in this regard.

(c) Project Information: Generally the prospectus contains all the information about the proposed project/existing project. The project information is useful to the investors in evaluating their investment proposed. The projects information which is provided in the prospectus may be helpful to know about the tax incentives available or not? The location of the project also influences the profitability of the corporate sector. The investor shall observe the following aspects:

(i) Location of the project, availability of tax concessions, availability of infrastructure facilities, raw materials etc.
(ii) Whether the issuing company obtained appraisal of the project by financial institutions and banks or not?
(iii) Whether the appraisal agency has any financial stake in the project or not?
(iv) The provisions which made to monitor the project by financial institutions and banks or any other agency.
(v) Any special advantage to that project.

(d) Product or Market Observations: Generally every investor shall aware about the companies and their activities. They should know about the demand and supply position of the product which they are producing.

Whether the prospectus discloses the information about the demand and supply gap for the product or not? The investor shall observe about any marketing arrangement for the sale of the product. The investor shall also make an enquiry about the technology which the company adopted. The present technology obsolete the company product. The availability of substitutes in the market having a bearing on the demand for the product. The investors shall observe about the export potential for the product in case of an export oriented project. The arrangement which is made by the company with the foreign collaborator or agency for purchase of products.

(e) Financial Information: The investors before making investment decisions, shall observe the financial data of the issuing company. The data relating specifically to capital, reserves and surplus, turnover, profits dividend declared and distributed, profitability ratios, book value, EPS and other information. The financial data reflects the future trend of the company.

(f) Forecasting: The guess work about the companies activities are more important while predicting a company's future. The investor shall observe about the profitability projections made by the company or the appraisal agency. The investor may also be made enquiries about a particular product or a company. The past performance is the indicator of the future prospect.

(g) Pricing of Issues: The share capital can be issued to the public by offering discount or premium, or at par. A good-reputed company with strong background of the experience and professionals consisting of board of directors with managerial capabilities leads to fix high premium. The price fixed by the company must be in reasonable level. The justification for pricing with reference to the past performance and future projections. It should be most important to note that these projections are based on company's own estimates or by an independent appraisal by financial institutions and banks etc. In case of existing companies movement of prices immediately before the issue to ascertain, whether prices are fair market prices or there has been rigging of the market prices.

(h) Litigations: Usually the business activities are involved without any dispute. The business operations are routine activities of the corporate sector. Any dispute with another company shall be indicated in the prospectus. The disputes in the business may not settle immediately. The conflicts between two organisations will be kept in pending under court supervision. The pending litigations having a bearings on the profitability of the company or likely to result in winding up of the company for inability to pay debts or any other costs.

(i) Risk Factors: The risk is an important factor in the evaluation of a company. Generally every business concern faces risk. There is no business without risk component. Therefore, the investors shall observe the prospective of the issuing company. The prospectus indicates the risk level involved in that project. The investors shall make an enquiry about the risk component in the market from market intelligence system.

(j) Auditor's Report: Auditor's report is one of the sources of information to know about the affairs of the issuing company. The report is the part of offer document especially with reference to significant notes relating to accounting system of the issuing company. The auditor of the company could analyse all the financial data and put his remarks for better functioning of the business concern. The audited figures are the legal evidence of the financial affairs of a company. These figures are reflected in balance sheet, where the balance sheet stands for the financial status of the company as on a particular date.

(k) Statutory Dues: The offer document shall indicate, statutory dues, if any, defaulted by the issuing company. The statutory dues include bank dues and institution defaults. The document shall also indicate about payment of interest to debenture holders. Any default made by the company shall inform to the prospecting investors through prospectus. Any failure to show such dues, the SEBI has the authority to take action in this regard. Therefore, the investors must be aware about the financial discipline of the issuing company. **Financial discipline** is the most important element in the growth of a business concern. The raising of finance depends upon the financial morality of the company. **For example,** some companies are raising crores of rupees from the market which is based on their financial discipline. Reliance Industries Ltd. is one of the examples for Mega issues.

(l) Statutory clearances: The investor confirms himself whether the company fulfilled all the formalities for the implementation of the project or not? Sometimes the company may not be in a position to get such clearances at the time of public issue. So such information should be disclosed by the company to the public. The current status of such clearances may be indicated to the public. In our country there may be a number of clearances which shall be obtained to commerce a project.

(m) Careful observation: The investors shall make careful observation before making their investments commitment in a particular business concern. Investment means, not simply handover a cheque to the brokers but they should know about the parking place of their funds. The surplus savings of the savers, park their idle fund in a safe parking place when it may be taken back by the investors. They shall take all precautions before investing the funds in the market. The management of new issues is the responsibility of merchant bankers, lead managers and co-managers.

(n) Problems of New Issue Markets: The new issue market is the important factor in capital formation of the country. The market creates financial assets in the society. This market can be defined as **financial architecture** of the digital economy. India is a country, where the large number of individuals, avail the savings at their disposal, but the NIM is unable to attract the investments from the public less than 10% of the savings. A large portion of the capital requirements of corporate sector is placed on market privately or provided by the financial institutions. The NIM suffers from functional and institutional gaps particularly in terms of the new instruments to appeal the investing community. Therefore, the wholesale market for new issues is yet to develop in India and the merchant banking is in fluid stage. The merchant bankers play a leading role in the NIM. They are the pillars of the NIM. They involve in the public issue from drafting the prospectus stage to closing of the public subscription time but they are presently not playing a developmental role. They should pay proper attention towards project preparation and other allied activities. The development of the NIM in India is based on the performance of the merchant bankers, if they fail to perform effectively the small investors may be duped by the companies. Therefore, they have social responsibility to the small investors. Another important factor is that, the absence of merchant bankers leads to diversions of savings towards the companies as fixed deposits. A fixed deposit with the company means a high risk component involved in that segment. The floating cost is very high in case of public issue. In India, the public issue means just like a social function. It requires an elaborate arrangements throughout the country participation of many players are necessary. It involves a physical strain to the small companies because the small companies generally raises a low amount of capital. Therefore, the public issue is not useful to small companies. It is useful to large companies where they offer Mega issues. The new and small companies are not in a position to bear this much of flotation costs.

The public issue involves a high expensive exercise to the small investors. Because the semi-urban and rural investors have to send the application forms to the centres where the banks are authorised to accept them. Then the investor has to spend in obtaining a demand draft, postal charges for sending and suffer loss of interest and collection charges for refund orders. In public issues there are inordinate delays in allotment of shares, refunding of application money, posting of share certificates. All these activities will not be carried out by the companies as per schedule time. They do not pay interest for the delayed period as per the law.

All these problems may not be possible to face by the small investors. If the investors bear all these problems. They are again to face some problems such as **dividend warrants, refund orders, interest payment** not being encashable at par in all centres. Therefore, they feel inconvenience in the activities which are carried out by consultants. The time taken for allotment of shares is often 2 to 3 months or even more. There is considerable loss of interest to the investors. The government issued orders in this regard that the shares allotment process shall be completed within 30 days.

In public issues, the existing companies with a good track record only receive good response from the market. The underwriters support the issue which is offered by the well-known companies only. The new companies face moral support problem from the financial intermediaries. Generally the investors do prefer to debentures to equities. Therefore, SEBI recently imposed new regulations on merchant banks which may improve the investment climate in the NIM.

The free pricing of issue created some problems in the market. The companies at the initial period of this implication fixed over price for their issues. Soon after few months the investors became more discrete in making investments in NIM with hefty premiums. If the premiums are unreasonable, many new issues would have become flops in raising public subscription. Thus, the SEBI has imposed one condition in fixing of premiums by the companies for their issues.

(o) Regulatory Framework: The legal framework in India consists of many regulations. A business concern shall fulfil all the legal formalities which are framed by the government. The SEBI is the powerful organ in the primary. It has the controlling authority to regulate and guide the market from time-to-time. The corporate sector in India is regulated by **3 organs** of the Central Government. They are:

A. Companies Act.
B. Securities Contract Act.
C. Securities and Exchange Board of India (SEBI).

A. COMPANIES ACT

The company law deals with the issue formalities of securities. The shares in India are issued by public limited companies. The public is generally interested in buying shares. The shares which are offered by the companies will be purchased by the investors in public issue. The issuing company shall have to fulfil some formalities before coming to the public. The following factors will reveal about the issue of shares process before approaching the public for raising finance:

(a) Issue of shares.
(b) Buy-back the shares **(Repurchase of shares)**
(c) Issue of shares certificates.

(a) Issue of Shares: In India every company shall be incorporated under the Companies Act as public limited company or company without share capital. All public limited companies have the chance to issue shares for financing their business operations. The companies while registering with the government shall submit three important documents such as **Memorandum of Association, Articles of Association and Prospectus**. The memorandum of association must state the amount of share capital with which it is to be registered. It is known as **"Authorised capital"**. The authorised capital is an amount of shares which can be raised at any time by issuing shares. The share capital which is issued for public offer is called as **Issue Capital**. The company can collect the amount by issue of shares from the subscribers. It is known as **paid up capital**. The share capital may be refunded by only winding up the company. A share is the right to a specified amount of the share capital of a company. It carries certain rights and liabilities which are issued to the shareholders. A share is treated as a movable property and transferable. The transfer may be effective between the transferee from the date of transfer. The transfer of share transaction must be made with the company. On transfer of the share, the transferee becomes a shareholder with the company. The shareholder has all the rights only when the transfer is registered in the register of the members of the company. The shareholders will get a share certificate in evidence of his ownership under the company seal. The share certificate contains the name of the person in whose favour the certificate is issued. A company which is incorporated as public company can issue two types of shares. They are **equity and preference shares**. Equity shares are the permanent capital of the company. In India equity shares are more popular, preference shares carry a preferential right to fixed dividend and the refund of the share capital when it is wounded up. The preference shares are redeemable after 10 years. They can be converted into equity shares.

The authorised share capital, can be altered by the company with the acceptance of shareholders at the general meeting through an ordinary resolution. The company can exercise the following changes in the capital structure, with the acceptance of shareholders:

(a) A company can increase its share capital by issuing new shares.
(b) A company can convert shares into stock and stock into shares.
(c) A company can reduce its face value of share capital.
(d) A company has the authority to cancel the shares, if the person has not been taken delivery.
(e) A company can consolidate the shares with the larger denomination.

All of these changes can be made by the company with the acceptance of shareholders at the AGM with an ordinary resolution. Any reduction in share capital is possible with special resolution and confirmation by the court.

The policy matters and business strategies are framed by the board of directors. The board of directors is the powerful organ in the corporate sector. The board has the authority to make any changes in the company subject to rules and regulations. The board of directors has the power to issue new shares to the public. The board of directors has the power to increase the share capital for the advantage of the companies with them. These chances should not be utilised by the board for their own purpose. Usually, the companies can issue shares of 3 types. They are:

(A) Issue of shares at par.
(B) Issue of shares at premium.
(C) Issue of shares at discount.

The companies can issue shares at par. But sometimes they offer premium. A company has the right to issue shares at premium. The share premium collected by the company shall be kept in share premium account separately. The amount of share premium can be utilised for the following purposes:

(a) Issue of fully paid bonus shares.
(b) Writing off the preliminary expenses.

(c) Writing off the flotation charges.
(d) Provision for premium which is payable on the reduction of any redeemable preference shares or debentures.

The companies can be issued shares at discount subject to the fulfilment of the following conditions:

(a) The issue of shares at discount must be authorised by the Company Law Board.
(b) The company shall make a resolution to this effect the rate of discount shall be below **10%**. If the CLB permits, the discount rate can be beyond 10%.
(c) After completion of one year of the business commencement the company can issue discount.
(d) The company shall issue discount within two months of the sanctioning by the CLB. Sometimes the CLB may specify the period of time for offering shares to the public.
(e) The prospectus shall indicate the rate of discount.

Buy-back the Shares: Generally the public limited companies are not permitted for purchasing their own shares. However, there are two exceptions to this permission. They are:

(a) The purchase of its own shares shall be made for the benefit of its employees by the trustees of the company.
(b) The company can make advances to its employees by way of beneficial ownership. Such loans could not exceed 6 months salary of the employee.

The company shall not violate any restriction posed on it. If it violates any restriction it will be punishable with a fine of **Rs. 1,000**. After October 1988 the companies have been allowed to buy-back their own shares or other specified securities. The companies are allowed to buy-back their shares from out of

(a) its free reserves.
(b) the premium account.
(c) the proceeds of an earlier issue other than fresh issue of shares made particularly for buy-back purposes.

After the liberalisation of policy, the government made efforts to liberalise all the earlier restrictions. The corporate sector has been provided to some extent of freedom. A company can purchase its own share only if it satisfies the following conditions:

(a) Articles of Association shall permit for buy-back of its own shares.
(b) A special resolution should be passed in general meeting to this effect.
(c) The buy-back of shares should be completed within a period of **12 months** from the date of passing the special resolution.
(d) The buy-back of shares do not exceed **25%** of the total paid up capital **plus** free reserves of the company.
(e) The process shall be done in accordance with the SEBI regulations.
(f) The debt equity ratio does not exceed **2:1**.

The buy-back of shares can be made from the following parties:

(a) The company can procure shares from the existing shareholders on proportionate basis.
(b) It can mobilise the shares from the open market.
(c) From odd lots.
(d) It can repurchase from its employees.

The companies are required to file a declaration of solvency in a prescribed proforma before they making buy-back of its shares. The solvency certificate should be submitted to the Registrar of Companies and SEBI. The solvency certificate in the prescribed proforma and an affidavit to that effect that the board of directors have made a full inquiry into the affairs of the company. The inquiry shall be made to this effect and found it is capable of meeting its liabilities and will not become insolvent within a period of one year from the date of declaration made by the board of directors. The statement shall be signed by atleast two directors of the company, one of the persons should be Managing Director. The unlisted companies need not file the declaration of solvency with the SEBI or Registrar of Companies.

After completion of buy-back of shares the company shall destroy physically the share certificates within 7 days of the last date of completion of buy-back shares. The companies which are completed by buy-back of its shares, not allowed for further issue of shares within a period of two years. However, they can make bank issues or other conversion processes.

The companies shall record all the transactions regarding the buy-back affairs. The company shall report to the ROCs and SEBI after completion of the process within 30 days. If any company violates this condition it is liable to punish with imprisonment upto two years or with fine upto **Rs. 50,000** or with both. Therefore, the companies shall follow all these rules and regulations strictly. The companies are not allowed to buy-back securities through its subsidiaries or through its group companies etc.

Generally the companies will collect the share capital amount on instalment basis. After the collection of application fee, the allotment fee and the remaining balance will be collected by the company on instalment basis. The balance payable on application each year cannot be less than 5% of the nominal value. The remaining will be collected by the company in kind of calls of shares. Call on shares will be made on the basis of all shares of the same class. The call must be made by the Board of Directors by a resolution passed at its meeting. The company shall make calls as per the provisions laid down in Articles of Association. If any shareholder fails to pay the call amount on his shares may lead to **forfeit the shares**. The Board of Directors has to serve a notice to the defaulter requiring the payment of unpaid amount together with accrued interest and a resolution of the directors to that effect. The forfeiture of shares can be done only after careful implementation of legal provisions.

Any individual can become a member of a company by the following methods:

(a) The person can subscribe its memorandum of association before its registration.

(b) Buying shares from the company and placed on the register of members.

(c) Purchasing in secondary market and placed on the register of members.

(d) Permitting his name to be on the register of members.

The member of a company can attend the meetings and cast his vote. The members of a company can have some privileges. Equity shareholders are entitled to vote on every resolution placed at any general meeting of the company.

Issue of Share Certificates: After the completion of issue process every issuing company shall issue share certificates to the shareholders. It is the *prima facie* evidence of the title of the members to such shares.

The shareholder can use this certificate as a proof of evidence for his ownership claim. The share certificate shall contain the stamp, issued under the common seal of the company. It should be signed by the director or an authorised person. It is to be delivered within 3 months after the allotment of shares and within two months after the application for registration of transfer.

Prospectus: Prospectus is the most important document in the life of the company. There are three important documents for the formation of a company. They are: **(a) Memorandum of Association, (b) Articles of Association, (c) Prospectus**. The Memorandum of Association is like the constitution of the company. It reveals the relationship between company and outside world. All the company affairs shall be carried out according to MA. There should not be any deviation from it. **Articles of Association** is related to internal management of the company. It contains all the rules and regulations of Directors, Managing Director, Managers and others. **Prospectus** is an important document while entering into the capital market. The prospectus is the basic document for the shareholders. It refers to any document by which a capital is offered to the public and on the basis of which the applicants actually subscribe. It is issued to invite the public for the subscription of any security of a company. Every company shall draft a prospectus before approaching the public and it should be prepared according to the Companies Act. The Companies Act framed the prescribed proforma for drafting of prospectus is a document which contains past information and credit future of the company. It provides some promises to the prospecting investor. The contents of a draft prospectus prescribed by the Act are as follows:

(A) Part I
(B) Part II
(C) Part III

The prescribed form of schedule must be as per IInd Schedule of the Companies Act.

(A) Part I

The contents of Part I shall contain the information regarding the following aspects:

1. General Information.
2. Capital structure of the company.
3. Terms of the present issue.

4. Particulars of the issue.
5. Company management and project.
6. Disclosure of the particulars of public issues.
7. Disclosure of particulars of outstanding litigations.
8. Risk factors.

(1) General Information: It should contain the information regarding the general business affairs. The company shall inform the public about the following aspects:

(a) Name and address of the Registered office of the company.
(b) Consent of the SEBI for the present issue and declaration of SEBI about non-responsibility for financial soundness or correctness of statements.
(c) Letter of Intent/industrial licence and declaration of the SEBI about non-responsibility for financial soundness or correctness of statements.
(d) Names of Regional stock exchanges and other stock exchanges where application made for listing of present issue.
(e) Provisions of Section 68(A) of the Companies Act relating to punishment for the fictitious applications.
(f) Statement of declaration about refund of the issue of minimum subscription of 90% is not received within 90 days of closure of the issue.
(g) Declaration about the issue of allotment letters/refunds within a period of 10 weeks and interest in case of any delay in refund at the prescribed rate under Section 72(2)/(2A).
(h) Date of opening of public issue, date of closing of the issue, date of earliest closing of the issue.
(i) Name and address of auditors, and lead managers.
(j) Name and address of trustee under debenture trust deed (in case of debenture issue).
(k) Whether rating from CRISIL or any rating agency has been obtained for the proposed debentures/preference shares issue.
(l) Underwriting of the issue. Name and address of the underwriters and the amount underwritten by them. Declaration by Board of Directors that the underwriters have sufficient resources to discharge their respective obligations.

(2) Capital Structure: The company shall indicate the following aspects:

(a) Authorised, issued, subscribed and paid up capital.
(b) Size of the present issue giving separately reservation of preferential allotment to promoters and others.
(c) Paid up capital:
  (i) after the present issue.
  (ii) after conversion of debentures.

(3) Term of the present Issue: The term of the present issue shall be indicated as follows:

(a) Terms of payment.
(b) Rights of the instrument holders.
(c) How to apply availability of forms, prospectus and mode of payment?
(d) Any special tax benefit for the company and its shareholders.

(4) Particulars of the Issue: The following aspects shall be disclosed to the public in the prospectus:

(a) Objects of the issue
(b) Project cost
(c) Means of financing (promoters' contribution)

(5) Particulars about Company Management and Project: The following information shall be provided by the company for understanding the company activities and other aspects:

(a) History and main objects and present business of the company.
(b) Particulars regarding subscriptions.
(c) Subsidiaries of the company.
(d) Promoters and their background.
(e) Names, addresses and occupations of manager, managing director and other directors including nominees.
(f) Location of project.
(g) Details about plant and machinery technology and process.
(h) Details about collaborations agreement.
(i) Particulars about the infrastructural facilities.
(j) Schedule for implementation of the project and progress so far, details for land acquisitions, civil works, installation of plant and machinery, trial production and commercial productions.

(k) Particulars of products and nature of the products consumer or industrial and end users.

(l) Approach to marketing and proposed marketing set up.

(m) Particulars about export possibilities and export obligations, if any.

(n) Details about future prospects, expected capacity utilisation during the first three years from the date of commencement of shares/debentres production and the expected year when the company would be able to earn cash profits and net profits.

(o) Details about the stock market data for shares/debentures of the company (high low price in each of the last three years and monthly high low during the last six months).

(6) Disclosure of Particulars of Public Issue: The company shall disclose all the information to the public. The Companies Act, Section 370(1B), reveals about the information which is required to be given includes the year and type of issue, amount of issue, date of closure, date of completion of delivery of share/debenture certificates, date of completion of project where the issue was made for financing a project and rate of dividend paid.

(7) Disclosure of Particulars of Outstanding Litigations: A company which makes public issue is required to state in the prospectus outstanding litigation pertaining to matters likely to affect operation and finances of the company including disputed tax liabilities of any nature. Particulars of any criminal prosecution launched against the company and its directors for alleged offences under the enactments, specified in Para 1 of Part I of Schedule XIII of the Act are also required to specify particulars of default, if any, in meeting statutory dues, institutional dues and towards instrument holders like debentures, fixed deposits and arrears of cumulative preference shares in relation to the company and other companies promoted by the same promoters which are listed on stock exchanges.

(8) Risk Factors: According to the SEBI guidelines every issuing company shall indicate in prospectus about the risk involved in this investment. The management should submit its views, regarding its risk factors. The risk may belong to foreign exchange rate fluctuations, difficulty in availability of raw materials or in marketing or products.

(B) Part II

The prospectus shall disclose in this part about the general information and other allied information. The company shall indicate the following aspects in the prospectus:

(a) General information.
(b) Financial information.
(c) Statutory and other information.

(a) General Information: The company should disclose the information about routine activities of the administration and other functions. The following aspects should cover in this part of the prospectus:

(a) Consent of directors, auditors, solicitors, advocates, managers, to issue, Registrar of issue, bankers to the company, bankers to the issue and experts.
(b) Expert opinion obtained, if any.
(c) Changes, if any, in directors and auditors during the last three years and reasons thereof.
(d) Authority for the issue and details of resolution passed for the issue.
(e) Procedure and time schedule for allotment and issue of certificates.
(f) Names and addresses of the company secretary, legal advisers, lead managers, co-managers, auditors, bankers to the company, bankers to the issue and brokers to the issue.

(b) Financial Information: The company should disclose the following information in the prospectus:

(i) A report by the auditors of the company with respect to the profits and losses for the five financial years preceding the issue of prospectus. The report should also show the rates of dividend paid on each class of shares for each of the said years. If the company has been carrying on business for less than 5 years, the figures are to be given for the actual period if the five financial years immediately preceding the issue of the prospectus cover a period of less than five years, the reports should cover as financial years as may be necessary, so that the aggregate period covered is not less than 5 years. The report should also give statement of assets and liabilities as at the last date of the latest financial year. The report should indicate the nature of any provision or adjustments made or yet to be made as respects the figure of any profit or loss and liabilities assets and liabilities of the subsidiaries as the last date to which the accounts of the company are made up must also be shown in the like manner.

(ii) If the company proposes to acquire any business, a report by a chartered accountant upon the profits and losses of the business for each of the five financial years preceding the issue of prospectus and the assets and liabilities of business.

(c) Statutory and other Information: The following information shall disclose by the company:

(a) Minimum subscription.
(b) Expenses of the issue, payable to advisers, registrar managers, trustees for the debenture holders.
(c) Underwriting commission and brokerage.
(d) Previous issue for the cash.
(e) Previous Rights issue (during last 5 years).
   (i) Date of allotment, closing date, date of refunds, date of listing of the stock exchange;
   (ii) If the issues at premium or discount and the amount thereof; and
   (iii) The amount paid or payable by way of premium.
(f) Commission paid or brokerage on previous issue.
(g) Issue of shares other than for cash.
(h) Debentures and redeemable preference shares and other instruments issued by the company outstanding as on the date of prospectus and terms of issue.
(i) Option to subscribe.
(j) Purchase of property and its details.
(k) Details of directors proposed directors, whole time directors, their borrowing powers and qualification shares.
(l) Full particulars about the contracts made by the company.
(m) Full particulars of the nature and interest of the promoters or every director in the contract.
(n) The powers and rights of members regarding voting, dividend, lien of shares and the process of modification of such rights and forfeiture of shares.
(o) The method and process of transfer of shares and transmission of shares.
(p) Revaluation of assets if any during last 5 years.
(q) Particulars about material contracts.

(C) Part III

The financial information which was submitted by the company in the prospectus, made by the qualified Chartered Accountant. The Chartered Accountant should not be an officer or servant or a partner in the company or in employment of an officer or servant of the company or in any of its subsidiary or holding companies.

The time and place at which the copies of the balance sheets, profit and loss accounts materials, contracts and documents can be inspected.

The prospectus must end with a declaration by the directors that all the relevant provisions of the Companies Act, 1956 and guidelines issued by the SEBI have been complied with and that no statement made in prospectus is contrary to the provisions of the Companies Act, 1956 and rules thereunder.

The contents of the prospectus must be true and accurate if any false statement or information contains it, the directors and promoters of the company are liable to all persons who subscribe for shares on the faith of the prospectus they are also punishable with imprisonment for a term which may extend to two years or fine which may extend to Rs.5,000 or both.

Prospectus and Application Form: The issuing company shall distribute application forms to the investors. Usually every company provides application forms to the investors in the new issue market. The Companies Act, Section 56(3), states that every application form shall be accompanied by the prospectus. The prospectus is the basic document to the investor for making investment in this company. Therefore, every issuing company shall follow this rule. However, there are four exceptions to this rule, they are:

(a) If the shares or debentures are not offered to the public.
(b) If the issue is Rights issue.
(c) If the shares or debentures offered are in all respects uniform with shares or debentures already issued and quoted on a recognised stock exchange.
(d) If the offer is made in connection with the bona fide invitation to a person to enter into an underwriting agreement with respect to the shares or debentures.

Legal Framework on Rights Issue

Rights issue means, the shares are offered to the existing shareholders.

The Companies Act framed some rules and regulations for issuing of rights shares. According to the Companies Act, the rights issue may be offered in the following two situations, whichever is earlier, must be offered at the date of the offer:

(a) The company shall offer only after the expiry of two years from the incorporation of a company.
(b) A company shall issue the offer to existing shareholders after expiry of one year from the first allotment of shares.

The rights offer must be made in the form of a notice, specifying the number of shares offered. The shareholders are provided a time less than 15 days from the date of the offer to accept. If they did not respond to the notice, it is deemed to have been declined. The shareholders have also inclusive of the option/right of renunciation. The board has the right to dispose of the shares if they think that it is advantageous to the company.

Issue of Debentures: The issue of debentures by a company vests powers with the Board of Directors. The board has the authority to take decision to this effect. The board should take the consent of the shareholders. The shareholders must pass an ordinary resolution. If the amount borrowed exceeds the aggregate of the paid up capital and free reserves. The debentures are of different types such as Redeemable, Mortgage, Convertible and Non-convertible. Large companies issue Redeemable and Mortgage debentures. The debenture holders are not entitled of any voting rights. They are not entitled to receive a copy of accounts and reports of the company. They have the right to get a copy of trust deed.

The debenture holders have the following rights which are to be disclosed in the prospectus:

(a) Debentures are transferable.
(b) They are transmittable on par with the same manner of equity shares.
(c) They are entitled to inspect the register of debenture holders.
(d) The rights and privileges of the debenture holders can be modified with the consent of atleast **3/4th** of the amount outstanding or by a special resolution passed at the meeting of the debenture holders.
(e) The debentures are subject to other usual terms and conditions.
(f) The debentures are incorporated in the trust deed between the company and the debenture trustee.

The debentures may or may not be secured. There is no provision in the Act requiring the secured charge of the debentures. However, it is usual to secure the debentures by a mortgage or charge on the company's assets. The general tradition is to secure debentures by a trust deed which contains a charge. The debenture trust is created by an instrument of trust the trustees hold properties in trust for the benefit of the beneficiary. These properties will be useful in the event of default of payment of interest of the principal amount of debt advanced under terms agreed upon and by selling such properties in the hands of the trustees. The mortgage to secure debentures must be registered with the Registrar of Companies within 30 days of the creation of charge. Every company shall be registered with the Registrar of Companies for every issue of mortgage debentures. All the other provisions of the Act concerning with the issues of securities, allotment and listing etc., are applicable to shares are also equally applicable to the debentures.

Legal Framework in Allotment of Shares: The allotment process is the most important factor in raising of funds from the market. The company shall not be made allotment. If the company is unable to raise the minimum subscription from the public the minimum subscription amount should be stated in prospectus. The application money cannot be less than 5% of the nominal amount of each share. If the company fails to procure the minimum subscription amount within 120 days from the date of the first issue of prospectus, that collected amount must be refunded. If the company fails to refund the amount within 130 days after the issue of the prospectus, the company is liable to pay interest at the rate of 6% the allotment should be made by the directors within a reasonable time. The company shall commence the allotment process after the completion of 5th day from the day of the opening of such subscription list. If company violates this rule, it is liable to a fine upto Rs.5,000.

Every issuing company shall apply to the concerned recognised stock exchange before making public issue, for permission to list these securities. The company shall also get permission for allotment of shares from the stock exchange. If it is not granted by the stock exchange, on expiry of 10 weeks from the date of the closing of the subscription list the company is required to refund that amount to the applicants. If such amount is not paid by the company within 8 days, it will have to pay interest at 4% and not more than 15%. After the completion of the allotment process the company shall file a return of allotment with the Registrar of Companies within 30 days from the date of allotment. The Registrar of Companies can grant the permission to submit the return for the extension of time.

B. SECURITIES CONTRACT ACT

The Securities Contract Act regulation provides the broad framework of the functioning of stock exchanges in India. The first legislative measures were enacted in 1925. This Act is known as **The Bombay Securities Contracts Control Act, 1925**. The Act was to regulate and control certain contracts for the sale and purchase of securities in the Bombay city. The government had appointed an Expert Committee in 1951. Under the Chairmanship of A.D. Gorawala, the Committee had prepared a draft bill on the Stock Exchange Regulation in India. Another Committee was appointed in 1954 under the Chairmanship of **Gorawala**. The recommendations of the Committee were culminated in the enactment of Securities Contract Regulation Act, 1956. It provides the broad framework of the present scheme of the stock exchange regulation in India. Stock exchange means, it is a place where the securities are purchased and sold by the investors in a specified time. It regulates the business of buying, selling or dealing in securities.

The objectives of the SCRA is to present malpractice in securities transactions by regulating the business. The Act specifies the following instruments as "securities":

(a) Shares, scrips, stocks bonds, debentures stock or other marketable securities like a nature in or of any incorporated company or other body corporate.
(b) Government securities.
(c) Rights or interests in securities.
(d) Derivatives, units or any other instrument issued by any collective investment scheme.
(e) Any other instrument such as specified by the SEBI.

A **Derivative** means a security derived from a debt instrument, share, loan (secured/unsecured), risk instrument or contract for differences or any other form of a security. It is a contract which derives its value from the index of prices of underlying securities. Derivatives may also be regulated outside transactions of the stock exchange through the licensing system of security dealers. The SCRA framed the general framework of control regarding the market. It provides the government with a flexible apparatus for the regulation of stock market in India. The Securities Contract Regulation Act can be divided into the following aspects:

(i) Recognised stock exchanges **(Sections 3-12)**

(ii) Contracts and options in securities **(Sections 13-20)**
(iii) Listing of Securities **(Sections 21-22A)**
(iv) Penalties **(Sections 23 to 26)**
(v) Miscellaneous or other matters **(Sections 27 to 30)**

Recognised Stock Exchanges

The stock exchanges are the most important organs in the capital market. They play a vital role in the efficient functioning of capital market. It is the place where the securities are brought and sold. It is the market place for second hand securities. It does not help in the capital formation of the corporate sector. There is no creation of additional financial assets. It provides liquidity to the securities which are already issued. The main provisions relating to the stock exchanges for grant of recognition is based on the following factors:

(a) Applications to the SEBI
(b) Conditions
(c) Terms and period
(d) Cancellation
(e) Periodical returns
(f) Enquiries
(g) Submission of annual reports
(h) Amendments
(i) Bye-laws of recognised exchanges
(j) Powers of the SEBI

(a) Application to the SEBI: The stock exchange authorities shall apply to the SEBI for the grant of recognition in a prescribed proforma. The application form shall be accompanied by a copy of the bye-laws of the stock exchange. The SEBI has the full authority to grant the recognition to the stock exchanges. The following information shall be furnished by the exchange authorities for granting of recognition to the SEBI:

1. The full information about the governing body of stock exchange.
2. The powers and constitution of governing body.
3. The powers and duties of the office bearers of the stock exchange.
4. The admission process of various class members into stock exchange.
5. The qualification required for becoming member in the stock exchange, member's suspension, expulsion and re-admission.

6. The procedure of registration of partnership firm as members of the stock exchange.

(b) Conditions: After receipt of the applications from the stock exchange the SEBI will scrutinise the information and may impose the following conditions for the better functioning of the stock exchange:

1. The required qualification for the membership of stock exchange.
2. The procedure for contracts made between members of the stock exchange.
3. The representation of the SEBI by its nominees on the stock exchanges.
4. The accounting procedure to be followed by the members of the stock exchanges and their periodical audit by Chartered Accountants.
5. All of the rules of any stock exchange shall be amended by it with the approval of the SEBI.

(c) Terms and period: After the receipt of application form in prescribed manner from the stock exchange, the SEBI will commence its process. The application will be closely scrutinised by the SEBI and impose some regulations on the part of the stock exchanges. If the concerned stock exchange satisfies all the conditions, the SEBI will grant the recognition to the stock exchange. The recognition of stock exchange will be made either on permanent or temporary position. The temporary recognition is not for less than a year. The temporary recognition can be renewed further. If the stock exchange is granted the recognition, its rules can be amended with the approval of the SEBI.

(d) Cancellation: If any malpractice is made by the concerned stock exchange, the SEBI has the full authority to take any action against such institution. The SEBI is the most powerful organisation in monitoring and controlling the activities of the stock exchanges in India. It can take action in the interest of the trade or in the public interest, after due notice, giving sufficient opportunity to show cause against withdrawal of the recognition. The SEBI may be giving notification to this affect withdraw the recognition given to a stock exchange. Therefore, the stock exchanges should be more cautious because their recognition may be cancelled at any time, if they are not working properly.

(e) Periodical returns: After getting the recognition to the stock exchanges, they have to work within the control limits of the SEBI. The

SEBI is the watchdog of the stock market. It controls, regulates, monitors and guides the activities of the secondary market. Every recognised stock exchange in India shall have to furnish the periodical returns to the SEBI. The affairs of the stock exchanges shall be informed to the SEBI. In stock exchange, every member has to maintain such books of accounts and other documents as prescribed by the SEBI in the interest of trade or the public. The SEBI has the authority to inspect the books of accounts at any time without any notice. It has also powers to call for information or explanations from recognised stock exchanges or from any member of exchange. For discharging all the monitoring activities, the SEBI shall inform in writing to all the stock exchanges and members.

(f) Enquiries: The SEBI has all the powers to make an enquiry into the affairs of the governing body is of any stock exchange or any member's affair. The SEBI will appoint an Enquiry Committee consisting of one or more persons as it thinks fit. The appointment of Enquiry Committee depends upon the nature of the situation. However, in case of an inquiry is concerned with the affairs of a member, the SEBI can give directions to the governing body of the stock exchange to conduct the inquiry in the manner as it is directed. The person/persons, who are appointed for the purpose have to submit a report of the result of the inquiry to the SEBI. In such an inquiry the following persons are responsible to produce all such books of accounts, documents and any other information to the Enquiry Committee:

1. Every director/manager/secretary/officer of the stock exchange.
2. Every member of the stock exchange.
3. If the member of the stock exchange is a partnership firm every partner, manager, secretary or officer.
4. Any other person who is directly or indirectly related to the above persons.

It is their duty to submit all the information whenever required by the Enquiry Personal Committee. They shall cooperate the Committee for smooth functioning of the inquiry.

(g) Submission of the Annual Reports: The recognised stock exchanges in India shall have to follow the statutory regulations. Every recognised stock exchange in India has to furnish to the government of its annual report. Generally every stock exchange will prepare annual report. The copy of the annual report may be submitted to the SEBI for favour of kind information. These reports shall contain the information as prescribed by the SEBI.

(h) Amendments: The SEBI has the full authority on the functioning of the stock exchanges and concerned members. It can make or amend any rule or direct the recognised stock exchanges for the better functioning of the stock market. The SEBI has the authority to impose rules while granting the recognition for the stock exchanges. It has the power to direct the stock exchanges to make or amend any rule thereof. Hence, it is the duty of concerned stock exchange to make or amend the rule within two months from the date of direction. If any stock fails to comply with the guidance, the SEBI itself makes or amends the rule through an order. Therefore, the SEBI and the concerned stock exchanges have to approve the modification.

(i) Bye-laws of Recognised Stock Exchange: Every stock exchange in India shall get recognition from the SEBI. The SEBI is the regulatory authority in the stock exchange's affairs. The recognised stock exchange may get the prior approval from the SEBI for its bye-laws. The bye-law is the constitution of the stock exchange. It has the sets on conditions. Every stock exchange shall function according to its bye-law. The bye-law contains all the information about the better functioning of the stock market. It contains the regulation and control of contracts to provide for the activities, such as:

1. The opening and closing time of stock exchange.
2. The trading hours of the exchange.
3. Periodical settlement of contracts through clearing house.
4. The particulars about the process of delivery and payment of securities, passing of delivery orders and the regulation.
5. Maintenance of clearing house.
6. Periodical reports to be submitted by clearing house to the SEBI. The periodical reports shall contain the following information:
   (i) The total number of each category of security carried over from one settlement period to another.
   (ii) The total number of each category of security contracts in respect of which have been squared up during the course of each settlement period.
   (iii) The total number of each category of security actually delivered at each clearing.
7. The particulars about the publication by the clearing house.
8. The details regarding prohibition of blank transfers or its regulation process.

9. The full information about the baldly or carryover settlements.
10. The process for fixing or altering or postponing settlements.
11. The procedure for determination and declaration of market rates.
12. The full information about the terms, conditions and incidents of contracts.
13 The process for regulation of the entering into making, performance, recession and termination of contracts.
14. The particulars about the listing of securities on the stock exchange.
15. The method and process for the settlement of disputes.
16. The methods of levy and recovery of fees, fines and penalties.
17. The process for fixing a scale of brokerage and other charges.
18. Regulation of dealings by members of their own account.
19. Separation of the function of jobbers and brokers.
20. Any other matter in relation to emergency of trade.

(j) Powers of the SEBI: The bye-laws made under this section is void and render the member concerned liable to fine, expulsion from membership for a specified period or any other penalty not involving the payment of money. The SEBI is the most powerful organ in the capital market. It is the representative of the Central Government. It can make bye-laws or amend all or any of the above aspects of the stock exchanges. It has the supreme authority. It can supersede the governing body of the stock exchange. It can also appoint any person to exercise and perform all the powers and duties of the governing body. It can also suspend the business of a concerned stock exchange for a period not exceeding seven days. It can also extend the period from time-to-time for the benefit of the general investors.

Contracts and Options in Securities

Generally the stock exchanges are the vehicles of community savings. They mobilise the funds and diverts the funds towards the productive ways. They channelise the small savings and facilitate the funds at the disposal of the corporate sector. Usually the transactions in stock exchanges can be made between two members through contracts. The legal provisions relating to contracts and options can be presented as follows:

(A) Nature of contracts.
(B) Options in securities.

The contracts in the stock market plays an important role. The major transactions are being settled in the form of contracts. Contract in securities can be done only between the members of a recognised stock exchange or through the members of a recognised stock exchange. The spot delivery contracts cannot be made between members. All other contracts are illegal.

Spot delivery contracts: They have the following characteristics:

(a) Spot delivery contracts provide actual delivery of securities.
(b) The payment for these delivered securities will be made on the day of the contract or the next day.
(c) The securities will be transferred through depository system to the buyer.

The SEBI has the authority to prevent undesirable speculation in specified securities in any area. It can prohibit any contract in any specific security by any person. Any contract made after the prohibition would be illegal. The SEBI has the full authority to prohibit any contract or can permit any contract to enter into an agreement. The members of the recognised stock exchange shall get licence from the SEBI. Every person doing such business has to acquire a licence from the SEBI.

Options in securities were illegal and void. The enactment of Securities Contract Regulation Act has been permitted since February 1995. Section 20 of the SCRA was amended for this purpose. The contract in derivatives is valid and legal since 1999 if they satisfy the following conditions:

(a) They shall be traded on a recognised stock exchange.
(b) They shall be settled on the clearing house of the recognised stock exchange in accordance with its rules and regulations.

Listing of Securities

The legal provisions relating to the listing of a security with the stock exchange was stipulated in SCRA. The **Sections 21 and 22A** of this Act deals with the process of listing a share with the recognised stock exchange. **Listing** means, an admission of a scrip to trade on a stock exchange officially. It denotes like a registration of security for dealing or trading on a stock exchange. The listing is not compulsory under the Companies Act but it is necessary under **Section 73** of the Act. The main objective of listing a scrip with the stock exchange is to provide ready marketability and liquidity to the scrips. It ensures proper supervision and control of dealings and protects the interest of investors and general investing community. The Securities Contract Regulation Act, Section 21, empowers the SEBI to compel a company to list securities with the stock exchange in the interest of the trade or public. The SEBI has the authority to impose conditions for listing of securities with the concerned stock exchanges. **Sections 22** of the SCRA reveals that a company has the right to appeal the SEBI, if its application for listing is refused by any recognised stock exchange in India. The ultimate decision will be taken by the SEBI and the recognised stock exchange shall obey the listing of a scrip. Further the corporate sector can appeal to the securities appellate tribunal against refusal. Therefore, listing of a security with the stock exchange is the most important factor in the management of an issue. The listed securities are bought and sold through the members of recognised stock exchanges. The members of recognised stock exchanges are known as **"Brokers"**. The prices at which the securities are bought and sold are called as **"quotations"**. The quotations are the official prices of the scrips on a particular stock exchange. **Section 73** of the Companies Act reveals that listing of security is compulsory if a company makes public issue of securities. The legal provisions stipulates various conditions for the listing of a security with a recognised stock exchange. The following kinds of listing is made with the recognised stock exchange:

1. Listing of securities (first time).
2. Offer of sale of existing issued capital.
3. Listing of Rights Issue.

Listing of Securities First Time

Generally the public limited companies will raise resources from the market through public issue. Public issue is becoming more popular and widely accepted process. It provides sufficient financial resources for the reputed, honest sincerity companies. Honesty is the best policy for the achievement of business goal. The public always trust the good business enterprises. The reputed business concerns mobilise funds through **Mega issues**. Therefore, the companies seeking the enlistment of their securities for the **first time** have to apply in the prescribed form along the listing agreement and listing fee. The following documents shall be submited while applying for listing:

(a) Memorandum of Association (for shares issue).

(b) The debenture trust copy (for debenture issue).
(c) Copies of all prospectus.
(d) Copies of offer for sale.
(e) Circular for advertising offering securities for subscription or sales during last 5 years.
(f) Copies of balance sheets and audit reports for the last 5 years.
(g) In case of new companies accounts for shorter periods.
(h) Full particulars about dividends and cash bonuses paid during last 10 days.
(i) Information about dividends or interest in arrears, if any.
(j) Agreement copies with vendors/promoters, underwriters and sub-underwriters, brokers and sub-brokers.
(k) Particulars about agreements made with selling agents, managing directors and technical directors.
(l) The following documents shall be submitted for the last 5 years:
    1. Audit Report.
    2. Balance sheet.
    3. Valuation contract.
    4. Court orders.
    5. Offer for sale.
    6. Any circular for offering securities for issue of securities.
    7. Material contracts.
(m) Full information about the history of the company since its incorporation.
(n) All particulars regarding issue of shares and debentures for cash and other than cash. Other particulars about premium on par issue.
(o) The full information shall be submitted for any payment of commission, brokerage, discount for the present issue of shares.
(p) The following certified copies shall be submitted:
    1. Acknowledgement from SEBI.
    2. Agreements made with IDBI, IFCI, ICICI, if any.
(q) The full information about the company's ten highest holders of securities of each class of shares or debentures along with their addresses.
(r) Particulars about the arrangements for listing of securities with a recognised stock exchange.

In addition to the above information a company before listing its securities has to satisfy the following conditions through its articles of association:

1. The company shall use a common form of transfer.
2. The AGM shall permit any person that the option or the right to call off shares.
3. The fully paid shares will be free from all lien. In case of partly paid shares, lien will be restricted to mono called.
4. Any amount paid up in advance of calls may carry interest but shall not be eligible for dividend.
5. There will be no forfeiture of unclaimed dividends before the claim becomes barred by law.

The following conditions shall be fulfilled by a company to become eligible for its securities for listing:

I. Minimum public offer.
II. Other conditions.

Minimum Public Offer: Every company which approaches the public for raising of finance shall satisfy the rules and regulations as per the legal provisions. Every company while making public issue shall offer now **25%** of each class of security offered for subscription through advertisement in newspapers for atleast **two days**. These conditions are not applicable to a government company and to public financial institutions. The minimum offer of **25%** does not form part of the minimum public offer from the following agencies:

(a) Subscriptions made by the Central Government.
(b) Subscriptions made by the State Governments.
(c) Subscriptions made by investment agencies of the State Governments.
(d) Subscriptions made by the developmental financial institutions such as **IDBI, ICICI, IFCI, UTI, and GIC**.

The minimum capital limit for listing was raised to **Rs.10 crore** in April 1995. Usually the legal provisions will make sure about a wide distribution of shares among the general investing public. A related requirement is the minimum number of shareholders to the allotted shares in a fresh issue of capital and offer for sale of existing capital. The present legal stipulation is that there should be atleast **10 and 20 public shareholders for every Rs.1.00 lakh** fresh issue of capital and offer for sale of existing capital respectively. Therefore, public offer means only the offer made to the public. If the issue is offer for sale, and it is entire underwritten by PFI, banks, the conditions of minimum number of shareholders do not apply. A company may be listed after giving a six months notice. If the number of public shareholders for every **Rs.1.00 lakh** of capital offered to the public is less or if the public shareholding falls below **50%** of the public offer.

Other Conditions: The legal provisions have to be fulfilled by the companies according to the rules and regulations imposed by the government from time-to-time. The companies having a paid up value of **Rs.10 crores** and above are required to get their listed on more than one stock exchange. It is in addition to the regional stock exchange listing. Therefore, all existed listing companies are required to be listed on the stock exchange, where its Registered office is located.

There is another important legal provision which is imposed by the Central Government, that the company shall pay interest on excess application money for the delayed period 10 weeks from the date of closure of subscription at a specified rate. It is a prerequisite condition for listing of securities on stock exchanges. The companies are not permitted to transfer the shares which are sold under the promoters quota. These shares will be kept in lock in period and cannot be transferred.

The company cannot advertise in the media during the period when the subscription is open. But after closing of the issue, the company can say thanks to the investors. If any violation is made by the company listing can be refused by the concerned stock exchange.

Therefore, the companies are required to fulfil the needs of statutory provisions which are imposed by the Central Government through its various organs in many aspects. The companies which are proposing to enlist their securities should follow some legal provisions to the stock exchange requirements relating to prospectus and public issue of share capital. The legal aspects are presented below for the clear understanding about the legal framework regarding the public issue.

1. The company should draft the prospectus according to the Companies Act, 1956 and it should be thoroughly scrutinised and approved by its legal advisers.
2. The company shall appoint brokers/managers to the issue. The appointed person should not be a member of recognised stock exchange.
3. The company should appoint an efficient, experience and capable person as underwriter. The persons must be from public financial institutions, banks and approved investment bankers only. They

should have a strong financial background exchange.

4. The prospectus shall contain only the facts as highlights of the issue.
5. The prospectus should be advertised in the media atleast **10 days** in advance to the opening of the subscription list.
6. The prospectus shall indicate that the subscription list may be kept for atleast 3 working days.
7. The prospectus shall also indicate that the subscription list would not be kept open for a period exceeding **10 working days**. If the issue is underwritten by all India public financial institutions the subscription list shall be opened for a period exceeding 21 days if the issue is underwritten.
8. Copies of all the publicity material relating to the public issue should be filed with the stock exchange.
9. The advertisement process for the public issue shall closely be monitored by the company, managers and advisors to the issue. Any violation of these directions will result as to be disqualified for an official quotation on the stock exchange. The company should abide the advertisement code which is issued by the SEBI.
10. The company shall take care of about providing the prospectus copies available to all the recognised stock exchanges atleast **three weeks** before the opening of the subscription list. The company should ensure strict compliance with the relevant directions.
11. The company shall indicate in the prospectus about the application forms which have been made to the stock exchanges available at concerned places.
12. The company should make arrangements to provide the applications at specified 30 centres if the company's issue is more than **Rs.10 crores**.
13. The prospectus shall indicate about the mode of payment by the shareholders for subscription of share capital. It should also state that refund orders process in the prospectus for non-allottees of shares.
14. The company shall take all precautions in printing of application forms. The application forms should bear a printed identification number of six or seven digits. It should also have all the columns, for the smooth functioning of the public issue process.
15. The application form should contain a column from showing details about the applicants tax payers **PAN** with the instructions that it should be filled up if the application is for shares/

debentures of a total value of **Rs.20,000** or more.

16. If the applicant does not have any PAN, the other information about his income tax circle district/ward should be filled up for further reference.
17. The prospectus should contain some provisions, namely—an applicant should submit only one application and not more than one for the total number of shares/debentures required. Applications may be made in single or joint names or more applications in single and/or joint names will be deemed to be multiple applications. If sole and/or the first applicant is one and the same the board of directors reserves the right to reject in its absolute discretion, all or any multiple applications with a view to discourage multiple applications.
18. The company shall make arrangements for the acceptance of allotment and call moneys through the bankers at all centres.
19. The company shall also match arrangements for sending allotment letters or refunding orders. These activities must be completed within the stipulated time.
20. The company shall send the share certificates/debenture certificates within **two months or 10 weeks from the date of closure of the subscription list**.
21. The company should pay the brokerage and underwriting commission to the financial intermediaries within **70 days** from the date of closing of the subscription list.
22. The company shall get the share certificates, which are designed by the concerned stock exchange authorities. The company should be issued a lot of **100** equity shares of Rs.10 each or Rs.100 each in case of debentures. The draft format shall be sent to the stock exchange in advance to get approval.
23. The company shall satisfy the **Section 73** of the Companies Act in the following aspects:
    (i) It should submit the letter of application before filing the prospectus with the Registrar of Companies.
    (ii) It shall also submit 5 copies of the prospectus and a cutting of newspaper advertisement to the stock exchange.
    (iii) The other listing particulars should be submitted to the exchange.
24. Generally all reputed companies will get tremendous response from the market. In the event of over subscription, the company shall made allotment of shares in consultation with the concerned

stock exchange. The company should follow the directions which were issued by the SEBI. It should made allotment with the help of the SEBI nominated public representative if the company gets over subscription 5 times or more for at par issues and two times for premium issues.

25. If the company gets over subscription, the company should furnish a certificate from its auditors that the allotment processes are completed as per the legal provisions of the stock exchange.
26. The company shall inform the stock exchange about the date of completion, posting of refund orders, posting of allotment letters, certificate of shares or debentures etc.
27. The company shall confirm that all the activities were completed.
28. The company should furnish a certificate from its auditors regarding the expenditure involved in the public issue. Therefore, the company shall take all precautions not to involving the ceiling amount.
29. The company should obtain a certificate from its banker regarding the number of applications received, amount collected etc.
30. The company should file a statement with the director of the stock exchange within 5 working days of the expiry of stipulated period containing the information that all the legal formalities have been followed as per scheduled period of time.
31. After completion of the process, the company should appoint a member of stock exchange as a market matter to look after the listed securities.
32. Finally, the company shall submit a certificate from its auditors or a practising company secretary that all legal formalities have been complied according to the law.

Public issue involves so many legal implications. The company has to comply rules and regulations at every stage. There are some fines and penalties, if the company violates any regulation. Therefore, the companies shall follow all the precautions during the public issue. The issuing company shall follow the legal provisions before applying for listing of its security with the recognised stock exchange.

(a) The letters of allotment/refund letters will be issued accordingly.
(b) The letters of rights will be issued accordingly.

(c) The company will issue receipts for all securities deposited with it whether for registration or any other purpose.
(d) The share certificates will be made subdivision or consolidate through the clearing house of the stock exchange.
(e) The company will make transfer of shares on production of necessary documents by the shareholders.
(f) The transfer process will be completed within the period of **one month** from the date of lodgement of transfer.
(g) The information will be submitted to the stock exchange about the date board meeting, declaration or recommendation of a dividend or the issue of rights or bonus shares.
(h) The company will send the information to the stock exchange regarding dividend or cash bonuses atleast 5 days before the commencement of the closure of its transfer books or the record date fixed for this purpose.
(i) The company will inform the stock exchange if there is any change in general character of the nature of business.
(j) The company will inform the stock exchange if any change arises in the board composition. The change regarding the company auditor may also be informed.
(k) The company will forward the copies of statutory and annual reports to the stock exchange.
(l) The company will inform the stock exchange authorities regarding the affairs of all kinds of meeting which are to be conducted in the normal duration of the business.
(m) The company will bring the following affairs to the notice of the stock exchange authorities:
   1. Re-issue of any forfeited securities.
   2. Any alteration of share capital.
   3. Book closure dates.
   4. Annual returns after general meeting.
   5. Any privilege to be granted to the shareholders.
   6. Any change regarding securities listed on the stock exchange.

Offer of Sale of Existing Issue Capital

Generally the companies will approach the capital market for raising the finance for their long-term needs of requirements. The companies can make arrangements to list their shares on a recognised stock exchange through an offer for sale of their existed issued capital. This offer for sale can also be combined with a new issue. The public offer shall comply with the provisions of governing the listing of securities on recognised stock exchanges. The following conditions shall be fulfilled by the company for an offer for sale:

1. The net worth of the company should not be less than its existing paid up capital.
2. While making an application for listing its securities it should not have incurred a loss in each of 3 years in preceding time.
3. The offer must be in a position to a wide distribution of shares among the general public.
4. While making an offer for sale the number of public shareholders should be atleast 20 for every **Rs.1.00 lakh** worth of shares.
5. If the share is offered at premium, it must be accepted by the SEBI.
6. The offer should be made containing all material particulars relating to the company.

Listing of Rights Shares

A listed company can also raise the finance through the issue of right shares. **Right share** means offering of additional shares to the already existed shareholders in the company. Generally it is customary that every issuing company will ask at first instance the existing shareholders to subscribe for further share capital the shareholders have also the right to get the additional shares at a specified rate fixed by the company. Rights shares are the privilege for the existed shareholders for a reputed company. The following **formalities** have to be complied with by a listed company for listing of Rights shares debentures:

1. Section 81 (1) of the Companies Act reveals that a company can issue right shares in the following two situations whichever is earlier:
   (a) At any time after the expiry of two years from the formation of a company, **or**
   (b) At any time after the expiry of two years from the allotment of shares in that company made for the first time after its formation.
2. Whether the concerned stock exchanges have notified the date of rights issue of shares is to be considered.
3. The concerned stock exchange authorities shall give a notice of atleast one day in advance for transacting securities of the company by its members, before board meeting.

4. After the approval of board meeting for issue of rights shares, the company has to intimate the stock exchange immediately by a letter or telegram.
5. For issue of rights shares, the company has to obtain a formal consent from the equity shareholders in the form of a **Special Resolution** in its general meetings.
6. The company shall announce the closure of register of members and intimate the stock exchange.
7. The company shall issue a letter of offer to the existing shareholders. The following aspects are to be incorporated in the letter of offer:
   (a) The letter of offer should indicate the shareholders right in favour of the nominees.
   (b) The company has the right to reject any nominee of whom it does not approve.
   (c) The shareholders should be entitled to apply for additional shares.
   (d) The shareholders who have renounced their rights would not be entitled to apply for additional shares.
   (e) The shares will be allotted on a fair and equitable basis.
   (f) The letter of offer should provide the freedom to the directors.
8. The company will have to make arrangements for the acceptance of application forms from the centres through its bankers.
9. If any company fails to make its arrangements, the company should borne the outstation cheque **collection** expenses.
10. The company shall issue letter of offer within 6 weeks of the record date.
11. The company shall give sufficient time not being less than four weeks to exercise their rights.
12. The company should provide forms of renunciation to all the shareholders freely on request.
13. The company shall provide freedom for splitting of the letter of rights.
14. The shareholders may be provided atleast **2 to 3 weeks** to apply for sub-division.
15. There should not be any restriction on the number of split letters of rights.
16. The company shall intimate the last date for submission of rights application to the concerned stock exchange.

17. A specimen copy of the letter of offer and application form for the rights issue should be forwarded to the stock exchange.
18. After the allotment of new shares, the company shall despatch the share certificates within **six weeks** of the last date.
19. After the despatch of share certificates to the shareholders, the company should make a letter of application in the prescribed form accompanied by other related documents. At the same time a listing application in prescribed form should be submitted to the stock exchange for official quotation of the new shares issued by it.
20. In addition to the above forms, the company has to file in duplicate with the stock exchange a distribution schedule an analysis form etc. A new issue statement form to be obtained from the stock exchange.
21. After completion of all the legal formalities with the stock exchange, it will enlist the new shares for official dealings by its members within 3 days.

Legal Formalities after Listing of Securities: After the listing of securities with the concerned stock exchange, the company has to follow many legal provisions in smooth functioning of the stock exchanges. Every listed company is required to furnish the unaudited financial results to the stock exchange authorities on a half yearly basis in a prescribed proforma. The unaudited financial statements should be submitted within **two months** of the expiry of the period. After the listing of its security with the stock exchange, the company shall make announcement in atleast one national language and one English daily newspaper within **48 hours** of the conclusion of the board meetings. The board of directors must sign on unaudited half yearly results and inform the stock exchange atleast 15 days in advance and issue immediately a press release in atleast one national newspaper and one regional newspaper. The company shall take all precautions in preparing the unaudited financial results. It should also not substantially differ from the audited results of the company. Any deviation found in first and second half year's unaudited results of any item varies by **20%** compared with the audited results for the full years. Therefore, the company shall give its explanation to the concerned stock exchanges.

If any violation is made by the company the concerned stock exchange can suspend or withdraw admission to dealings in securities of a company. If any company fails to comply with the above legal provisions in listing of securities. It leads to suspend the trading or withdraw the admission of the security. Any action will be taken by the concerned stock exchange after giving to the company a reasonable opportunity through a notice in writing stating the reasons to show cause against the proposed action. Therefore, if a stock exchange takes an action against a company for a continuous period not exceeding **three months**. Then the company may appeal to the SEBI. The SEBI has the full authority in this regard. The SEBI will give sufficient time to the concerned stock exchange, it may vary or set aside the decision of the stock exchange.

Delisting of a security means withdrawal of admission to a security by the stock exchange authorities. The scrip will not be permitted to trade on the stock exchange floor. A listed company may be delisted by a recognised stock exchange in the following situations:

(a) If the number of public shareholders falls below 5 for every Rs.1.00 lakh share capital offered to the public.
(b) If the public shareholding falls **below 50%** of the public offer.

The above requirements are not applicable if the infractions are due to the holdings of development financial institutions. The stock exchanges have the authority to admit the delisted securities if they fulfil the following conditions:

(a) The company has incurred losses during the proceeding three consecutive years and its net worth has been reduced to less than its paid up capital.
(b) The security of the company has remained infrequently traded during the proceeding three years.
(c) The security of the company may remain listed atleast one of the concerned exchanges.

C. SECURITIES AND EXCHANGE BOARD OF INDIA (SEBI)

Introduction

The Securities and Exchange Board of India was established in April 1988. It has been functioning under the overall administrative control of the Government of India. It works under the guidance of Ministry of Finance. It is the agent of the Central Government in capital market. It is established for the regulation and orderly functioning of the stock exchanges. It also works for protecting the investors rights, prevents malpractices in security trading and promote healthy growth of the capital markets. It was granted statutory status in 1992 under SEBI Act. It has the full authority to control, regulate, monitor and direct the capital markets. It is the watchdog of the securities market. It is the most powerful organ of the Central Government in the capital market.

After the repeal of the Capital Issue Control Act and abolition of the CCI the SEBI was given full powers on the new issue market and stock market. It has been issuing guidelines since April 1992 for all financial intermediaries in the capital market. The guidelines have been issued with the objective of investor protection. The guidelines also include the obligations of merchant bankers in respect of free pricing, disclosure of all correct and true information and to incorporate the highlights and risk factors in investment in each issue through the prospectus. It has been established for the healthy development and regulation of the capital market.

Objectives of the SEBI: The main objectives of the SEBI is to protect the interest of the investors in the securities market. It has three objectives by its Act:

(a) to protect the interests of the investors in securities market
(b) to promote the development of securities market.
(c) to regulate the securities market.

The powers of the SEBI can be exercised by the way of regulations. It is an implementing agency of policy matters by the Central Government from time-to-time. It has to report every year to the Central Government about its activities, policies and programmes. It shall submit a report to the government which in turn will be placed before Parliament.

The Powers of SEBI: The following powers have been given to the SEBI with the enactment of SEBI Act, 1992:

1. Regulating the business activities in the capital market.
2. Power to grant registration to financial intermediaries.
3. Registering and regulating the working of the depositories, custodians, FIIs, credit rating agencies.
4. Registering and regulating the working of venture capital funds and mutual funds.
5. Power to grant approval to bye-laws of recognised exchanges.
6. Power to prohibit insider trading.

7. Power to compel listing of securities by public companies.
8. Power to control and regulate stock exchanges.
9. Power to call for any information or explanation from recognised stock exchanges or its members.
10. Power to levy fee.
11. Power to regulate substantial acquisition of shares and take over of companies.
12. Power to promote and regulate self regulatory bodies.
13. Prohibiting fraudulent and unfair trade practices relating to the securities markets.
14. Promoting investors, education and training of intermediaries of the securities market.
15. Performing any other functions as may be assigned by the government from time-to-time.

Delegation of Powers: The Government of India has delegated some powers to the SEBI subject to such limitations. The government retains the power in relation to any matter under the Act. The **Securities Contract Regulation Act, Section 28,** reveals that the SEBI has been authorised to exercise powers on the following aspects:

(a) It has power to call periodical returns from the exchange.
(b) It has the power to regulate and control activities in spot delivery contracts.
(c) It has the power to grant of recognition to the exchanges.
(d) It has the powers to withdraw the recognition of the exchange.
(e) It has the powers to suspend the business of a recognised exchange.
(f) It has the powers to amend the rule with regard to **Section 3(2)** of the Act.
(g) It has the powers to give directions to the recognised exchanges.
(h) It has the powers to compel a public limited company to show lists.
(i) It has the powers to grant licensing to the dealers in securities market.
(j) It has the power to hear the appeals made by companies.
(k) It has the power to exercise the legal provisions of SCRA.
(l) It has the power to make or amend rules or articles of association of a stock exchange regarding the voting rights of members of a stock exchange.

Powers to make Rules: The Central Government delegated the power to the SEBI with effect from 1995. Now the SEBI is the supreme authority in the capital market. Prior to 1995 the Central Government had the authority to make rules for carrying out the purposes of the SEBI Act. It includes the SEBI constitution, maintenance of its accounts, manner of inquiry to impose penalty for defaults and constitutions of the securities appellate tribunal. Now the SEBI has the authority to make rules relating to the following intermediaries:

(a) Brokers and sub-brokers.
(b) Merchant bankers.
(c) Portfolio managers.
(d) Registrars to issue.
(e) Share transfer agents.
(f) Underwriters.
(g) Debentures trustees.
(h) Bankers to an issue.

Powers to make Regulations: For the smooth functioning of the capital market the SEBI is empowered to make regulations with the approval of the government. All regulations which are made by the SEBI must be published as notification in the official gazette.

The SEBI will make the regulations which include:

(a) The registration process of financial intermediaries, cancellation or suspension of registration.
(b) The matters belonging to the issue of share capital and transfer of securities.
(c) The powers for the regulations in respect of the registration of the following financial intermediaries:
    (a) Merchant bankers
    (b) Lead managers
    (c) Brokers and sub-brokers
    (d) Portfolio managers
    (e) Registrars to issue
    (f) Share transfer agents
    (g) Bankers to the issue
    (h) Underwriters
    (i) Debenture trustees

Organisation of the SEBI

The SEBI is the most powerful organ in the capital market. It is the representative of the Central Government. It is a statutory body in the capital market. It leads, monitors, regulates and controls the activities of the capital market. The organisation has divided its activities into the five operational departments. The each department will be headed by an executive director. The legal department and investigation department also are headed by the executive directors. The following are the main departments which are functioning in the organisation:

1. Primary Market Department
2. Issue Management and Intermediaries Department
3. Secondary Market Department
4. Institutional Investment Department
5. Legal Department

1. Primary Market Department: The Primary market department is the most important division in the organisation of the SEBI. It deals with the new issue market activities. It is headed by a division chief with specific responsibilities. It relates to the policy matters of the public issues. It looks after all the regulatory issues for the primary market in India. It also involve in regulatory matters with regard to the financial intermediaries. It also looks after the investor grievances. It deals with the investor complaints for refund of application money for non-allottees refund of excess money, non-receipt of dividends, non-receipt of share certificates etc. Therefore, it has the full authority with reference to the public issues.

2. Issue Management and Intermediaries Department: This department will take care about the scrutiny of offer document. The offer document is the most important paper in public issue. It is the tool for attracting the investors. It is the basic document which are promised by the company to the newly becoming shareholders. The offer document should contain only facts and a right projection about the future. Some companies can misguide the investors by creating a gloomy picture about their product and company. Therefore, this department shall closely monitor the contents of the offer documents. This department also involve in the registration of the financial intermediary. It also monitors the activities of various financial intermediaries.

3. Secondary Market Department: The secondary market department occupies an important role in the regulation of the capital market operations. It involves in framing the policy matters regarding stock exchange activities. It regulates the secondary market activities. It guides and monitors the stock exchange administration. It continuously monitors the price movements in the stock market. It involves in the development of new investment products. It closely observes the market movements and gathers information through market surveillance. It also looks about the insider trading practices. It frames the policy and regulatory matters for the secondary market in India. It also issues directions to the stock exchange administration authorities on various matters. It also looks into the affairs of stock exchanges administration inspection by making inquiry towards financial intermediaries. It also regulates the sub-brokers activities.

4. The Institutional Investment Department: This department frames the policy matters regarding the institutional investors. The institutions investors are more important in the capital market. They will put the higher amount of investment in the stock markets. They involve in buying and selling of shares on daily basis with crores of rupees investment. The following members will be treated as institutional investors:

(a) Mutual funds.
(b) Foreign institutional investors.
(c) Corporate investors.
(d) Institutional investors.

It looks after mergers and acquisitions of the corporate sector. It also concentrates on research and publications. It maintains international relations in the process of globalisation. It frames the policy matters for institutional investors.

The Legal Department: It will take care of all the legal matters under the supervision of **General Counsel**. The investigation wing is also the part of institutional investment department, the investigation using carry out inspections and investigations under the supervision of the chief.

In addition to the above departments the SEBI has two Advisory Committees. Each committee works for primary and secondary market. These Advisory Committees helps in framing policies and regulations. These Committees are constituted with market players, recognised investor associations and experts in the capital market. But these Committees will have no statutory power and the SEBI may or may not bound the suggestions made by them. Further the SEBI has also expanded its activities by opening their regional offices at **New Delhi, Chennai,**

Kolkata and Mumbai. The regional offices shall cover all operations in northern, southern, eastern and western effectively.

Composition of the SEBI: The government proposes to make more in strengthening the SEBI. It granted additional powers for the smooth functioning of the capital market operations. The SEBI Act provides for the establishment of a statutory board constituted by **6 members**. The board will constitute with a chairman and two members who are appointed by the Central Government. The another member is to be appointed by the **RBI**. The remaining two members will be drawn from securities market with those persons having rich experience in that field. Therefore, the board will maintain the best talented expertise for the better functioning of the operations of the capital market. The Central Government has sanctioned the SEBI as an autonomous body status with perpetual succession and common seal. The preamble of the Act states that it has been established to protect the interest of the investors in securities and to promote the development and regulate the securities market. Section 11 of the Act deals with the powers of the board. It clearly states that the board has to work to protect the interest of the investors. The statutory board was established on **21.2.1992**. The Act further lays down that the various rules and regulations will be issued to enable the SEBI to register, regulate and monitor various financial intermediaries in the capital market.

Licensing Authority

The SEBI is the most powerful organisation in the capital market. It has the right to grant the licences to the financial intermediaries. All financial intermediaries dealing in security markets must compulsorily registered with the SEBI in accordance with the regulations made under the SEBI Act. The financial intermediaries, without licence do not have an opportunity to take up the business activities in the capital market. Therefore, every financial intermediary shall get licence from the SEBI. The following intermediaries are required to get licence from the SEBI for commencing business activities in the capital market:

(a) Stock-brokers
(b) Share transfer agents
(c) Bankers to an issue
(d) Registrar to an issue
(e) Underwriters
(f) Merchant bankers
(g) Trustees of trust deed

(h) Portfolio managers
(i) Investment advisers
(j) Depositories
(k) Custodians
(l) FIIs
(m) Credit rating agencies
(n) Venture capital funds
(o) Mutual funds
(p) Other intermediaries

An application made by the above intermediaries in a prescribed proforma to the SEBI. SEBI will scrutinise the application form and if found satisfaction, then it will grant the certificate of registration. **The Certificate of Registration** contains the rules and regulations for the conduct of business by the intermediaries. Every financial intermediary shall apply in a prescribed form with a fee to the SEBI. The SEBI has the right to **cancel/suspend** a certificate of registration issued to the financial intermediaries in accordance with rules and regulations. If an intermediary dissatisfies with the behaviour of the SEBI, can appeal to the Central Government. The Central Government issues various orders from time-to-time to implement the rules strictly in accordance with the provisions of the Act. The Central Government may also issue various directions to the SEBI matters relating to the policies in writing from time-to-time. The SEBI has to implement the orders, which are received from the Central Government for the smooth functioning of the capital market. The Central Government has the fall authority to review the policy matters relating to the capital market.

Penalties: The Central Government has the authority to instruct the SEBI to follow the rules and regulations from time-to-time. It has provided freedom to the SEBI to implement all the directions which are issued by the government. The SEBI has been empowered to impose penalties on various intermediaries in non-compliance with the rules and regulations which are in force from time-to-time. The SEBI is the supreme authority in regulating and monitoring the capital market. It has the powers to impose fines and penalties. If any intermediary does not follow the rules strictly it has the right to call any information from any intermediary. If the intermediary fails to furnish certain information to the SEBI it can impose the following penalties:

(a) for failure to furnish any document, return report is liable to pay **Rs.1,50,000**.

(b) for failure to submit the return/information or document within the specific time not exceeding **Rs.50,000** for each day.

(c) If any intermediary fails to maintain proper books of accounts or records not exceeding **Rs.10,000** each per day.

In addition to the above failures, the intermediaries would have to pay penalty for failure to enter into agreement with the clients. A registered intermediary will have to pay a penalty not to exceed **Rs. 5 lakhs** for every failure. If any intermediary fails to redress the investors grievances called upon by the SEBI to pay a fine not to exceed **Rs. 10,000** for each such failure the SEBI has the authority to impose the fines and penalties in case of institutional investors for failure of statutory guidance. It has the right to impose the penalties for mutual funds also. The following are the different penalties if a mutual fund fails to comply with the legal provisions:

1. If any mutual fund fails in obtaining a certificate of registration from the authorities is liable to pay the following penalty whichever is higher:
   (a) not to exceed **Rs.10,000** for each day or
   (b) **Rs.10,00,000.**
2. If any mutual fund default is not complying with the terms and conditions of the Certificate of Registration is liable to pay the following penalty whichever is higher:
   (a) not to exceed **Rs.10,000** for each day, or
   (b) **Rs.10,00,000**.
3. If any mutual fund fails to make an application for listing of schemes with authorities is liable to pay penalty whichever is higher.
   (a) not to exceed **Rs. 5,000** per day.
   (b) **Rs. 5,00,000 lakhs.**
4. If any mutual fund has became default in not despatching the Unit certificates to the unit holder is liable to pay penalty not to exceed **Rs. 5,000** for each day default.
5. If any mutual fund fails to refund the application money not to exceed **Rs.1,000** each day of default.
6. If any mutual fund fails to invest the collected money in portfolio, is liable to pay penalty not to exceed **Rs. 5,00,000** for each such default.

In addition to the above penalties, the Assets Management Company of the mutual fund is also liable to pay penalty for failure of rules and regulations not to exceed **Rs. 5,00,000** for each failure.

Stock-Brokers: The stock-brokers are also important persons in the capital market. The investors are the regular customers to the brokers. They play an active role in the capital formation of the country. They are able to guide, inspire and motivate the investors. Because they are regular customer, they know the pulse of the investors and guide them towards the active participation in the capital market. The stock-broker is an intermediary in the capital market. He has to abide by the rules and regulations which were issued by the SEBI from time-to-time. The SEBI closely observes the brokers activities. If any broker involves in malpractices, he has to face severe penalties which are levied by the SEBI. The following penalties have to be paid by the brokers if they do not comply with the legal provisions:

(a) If any broker fails to issue contract notes to the client in the prescribed proforma is liable to pay not to exceed **5 times** the amount for which the contract note was required to be issued.
(b) If any broker fails to deliver any security or payment, the amount due to the investor in the manner and within the stipulated period of time, not to exceed **Rs. 5,000** for each day of default.
(c) If any broker charges excess amount of brokerage from the client prescribed by the regulation not to exceed **Rs. 5,000** or **five times** the excess charge whichever is higher is payable as fine.

Insider Trading: Insider trading is one of the methods of undesirable activity. It is not permitted by the Act. Insider trading is possible to carried out by the company's top level management. It is a highly specialised speculative activity. It may be defined as "sale or purchase of securities by persons who possess price sensitive information about the company." It is made possible of their status in the company. It is an unfair and unhealthy practice. It damages the integrity of the market. It is an opportunity when the companies face the favourable and unfavourable trends, the violation of the provisions of the SEBI. Insider Regulations 1992 is treated as committing the offence of insider trading. If an insider deals in securities on his behalf or on behalf of others on the basis of an unpublished price sensitive information or any insider communicates any unpublished price sensitive information except as required in the course of business or under any law, is liable to pay penalty up to **Rs. 5,00,000.**

Takeovers: Takeover means acquiring shares in a company at a specified price by a person or another company. It implies acquisition of controlling interest in a company by another company. It simply means a change of controlling interest in a company through the acquisition of its shares by another group. The company which fails to disclose the aggregate of shareholding in a company before acquiring any shares of that company and also to make a public announcement is liable to a penalty not exceeding **Rs. 5,00,000**.

All the above penalties will be levied by the SEBI if anyone violates the legal provisions. It is empowered to conduct any inquiry into the affairs of the market.

Steps taken by SEBI: SEBI is the legal entity to look after the welfare of the common investors. The main objective of the SEBI is to provide better facilities and protection to the common investor. Therefore, several steps have been initiated to promote, develop and regulate the capital market. These steps have been included in both the primary and secondary markets. The following steps have been taken by the SEBI to strengthen the capital market:

Primary Market

1. Introduced an innovative product **"Stock Invest"**.
2. Flexibility in issue pricing.
3. Vetting of prospectus and letter of offer by SEBI.
4. Abridged prospectus.
5. Fixation of promoters contribution.
6. All financial intermediaries brought under the purview of SEBI.
7. Public sector bonds brought under the purview of SEBI.
8. Deployment of Issue proceeds.
9. Guidelines for preferential allotment of shares.
10. Risk factors shall be disclosed prominently in prospectus.
11. Companies permitted to open private collection centres.
12. Guidelines to develop financial institutions for disclosure and investor protection.
13. Obligations on Merchant bankers and underwriters.
14. Fixation of lock in period for promoters quota shares.
15. The allotment process must be finalised in the presence of the SEBI representative.
16. Registration of FIIs for the development and growth of the market.
17. In public issue, the number of minimum shares increased to **500 shares.**

18. Code of conduct to advertisers are announced.
19. Proportional allotment permitted in case of over subscription.
20. Substantial firm allotment to institutions in public issues.
21. Shareholders to decide price and time of conversion.
22. Underwriting for issues are made mandatory.
23. Credit rating is made compulsory.
24. Reduced the validity period of stock invest.

Secondary Market

1. Registration of share shops for spot trading shares.
2. Insider trading is declared as illegal.
3. Forward and carryover system banned.
4. Odd lot trading facilities provided at stock exchanges.
5. Financial requirement and norms for corporate members.
6. Uniform settlement system.
7. Introduction of Jumbo transfer deeds.
8. Regulations and transactions between brokers and clients.
9. Introduced circuit broker system at stock exchanges to check wide fluctuations.
10. Private mutual funds have been permitted for the welfare of the small investors.
11. Private placement of shares banned.
12. Capital adequacy norms are prescribed for stock-brokers and other intermediaries.
13. NSE was introduced in July 1994.
14. Steps to ensure transparency in secondary market operations.
15. Brokers shall keep client's money in separate account.
16. Constitution of governing council of stock exchange.
17. Appointment of an Executive Director.
18. Audit inspection for members of the stock exchange.
19. Precautions in transactions between clients and brokers.
20. Norms for multiple membership of stock exchange.
21. Issue of contract notes is made compulsory.

Factors to be Considered for Investment in Primary Market: At present the investors must be aware that the free pricing environment makes the issuers free to fix the issue price subject to some conditions. These conditions are levied by the SEBI to regulate the primary market activities. The set of guidelines issued to educate the investors to be cautious while investing in the primary market. They are advised to check the contents of prospectus before making investment in any issue. For every details relating to the issue. They should study the detailed prospectus which is available with the company or merchant banker. The merchant bankers play an important role in making success of public issue by a company. They have to make more efforts about the public issue. Public issue involves so many organisation and activities. The merchant bankers are responsible for drafting a prospectus. Therefore, they must take care about the disclosure of all the relevant information in the prospectus. The following factors are to be examined by the investor before making investment in any public issue:

(a) Promoter's record.
(b) Professional management of the company.
(c) Objects of the present issue.
(d) Analysis of project details.
(e) Product analysis.
(f) Government stability.

Therefore, the investors are advised to go through the contents of the prospectus and avail the advises of the experts from media in this regard.

PRIMARY MARKET IN INDIA

Introduction

The primary market is also known as **New issue market**. It is the market where the capital formation process will take place. The huge amounts of financial resources are mobilised by the corporate sectors through public issues. A well-reputed, goodwill organisation can procure the funds from the market very cheaply. The crores of funds are available at the disposal of this market. However, newly established companies cannot raise sufficient resources from this market. At the same time some companies are also cheating the investors by issuing share capital with fictitious names. The new issue market faced some emerging trends in the Indian financial system. The nation's development depends upon the activeness of this market. It is an asset creation market. The capital formation in the country leads to the enhancement of productivity and per capita income. It is the growth engine for other allied markets. But at present the primary market is not very active.

The organisation of the primary market earlier suffered from many problems. In earlier decade there were no separate primary market exists. It was in unorganised system. No one can lead this market. Therefore, the study of primary market can be done through the following manners:

A. Primary Market (Structure) basis.
B. Primary Market Activities basis.

A. Primary Market (Structure) Basis

Primary market involves a number of financial intermediaries. The structure of the primary market a decade earlier suffered from structural lacunae. The primary market is backed by the developmental of financial institutions. There were no organisational structure arrangements for the organisation of the issue of share capital. At the earlier stage the gap was filled by ICICI and a few commercial banks such as **SBI, ANZ Grindlays Bank**. They did set up their merchant banking divisions and rendered the services to the investors. But their services had not made any significant impact due to some problems. The primary market suffered a serious drawback of the system. It was the **absence** of an in-built provision for distributing the securities to the investing public. In developed countries like USA, the investment bankers provide a unified and comprehensive package of service. They render all the services whichever required by the issuing company during public issue time. The primary market in India has to set up merchant banking institutions with high skill and better expertise being its main sources. The primary market in India faced the organisation weakness in the following ways:

(a) Barriers to the small companies.
(b) Poor response from public.
(c) Unorganised system of market.
(d) Lack of institutional demand for industrial securities.
(e) Crowding of new issues at sometimes.

The liberalisation of the regulations made the new issue market more active. The abolition of the CCI in 1992, the protection of the investors in securities market and the promotion of the development and regulation of the market by the SEBI has changed the new issue market structure. The SEBI has the full authority in the new issue market to regulate, monitor and guide the market forces. To tone up the operations of the new issues in the country, The SEBI has put in place rigorous measures. The intermediaries have to conform to regulations designed by the SEBI. The financial intermediaries play an important role in the process of selling new issues. The legal framework for their operations has been prescribed by the SEBI. The new issue market involves many intermediaries participation. Without the cooperation of many intermediaries, it is not possible to raise finance from the market. The following intermediaries occupy an important role in the primary market. Their legal framework, operational work and other matters will be explained in detail.

1. Merchant Bankers
2. Lead Managers
3. Underwriters
4. Bankers to an Issue
5. Brokers to the Issue
6. Registrars to an Issue/STA
7. Debenture Trustees
8. Portfolio Managers

Therefore, the above intermediaries will play an important role in the primary market. The success of the issue will depend upon the participation of the various intermediaries. The public issue depends upon the coordination activities of the issuing company. The primary market is a combination of many intermediaries.

1. Merchant Bankers

Merchant bankers play a vital role in the public issue. They work as sponsors of the capital issues. They render major services to the issuing company. They involve in determining the composition of the capital structure of the issuing company. They are able to guide the client company to give suggestions about different types of securities to be issued at a lowest cost. They involve in public issues right from drafting of prospectus and application forms, compliance with legal formalities, appointment of registrars, underwriters, bankers to issue, listing of securities, selection of brokers, publicity and advertising agents, printers etc. The issuing company can rely on merchant banker upto the closing of issue. Therefore, the importance of the merchant bankers in the process of capital issues have been increasing day by day. It is now mandatory that all the public issues should he managed by the merchant bankers functioning as the **Lead Managers**. The SEBI is the most powerful organ in the primary market. It is the controlling authority to the merchant bankers who handles the public issues on behalf of his client company. Hence, the merchant banker shall follow the guidelines which are issued by the SEBI. The following conditions should be fulfilled by the merchant bankers:

1. Registration
2. Capital adequacy requirements
3. Obligations

1. Registration: The registration is compulsory for every merchant banker to carry out his activities. They should register with the SEBI. SEBI is the licensing authority to the merchant bankers. According to the SEBI guidelines the merchant bankers can be classified into four categories. They are:

(A) Category I	Merchant Banker
(B) Category II	Merchant Banker
(C) Category III	Merchant Banker
(D) Category IV	Merchant Banker

Category I Merchant bankers may carry any activity relating to public issue. They involve in preparation of prospectus, determining capital structure, arrangements of intermediaries, final allotment of securities and refund of subscriptions. They will participate in all activities relating to the public issue. They also act as advisor, consultant, managers, underwriters or portfolio managers. They could act as lead managers to an issue. From 9.12.97 onwards only Category I Merchant bankers are required to get registration with the SEBI. They should get a separate registration of certificates to carry on the activities of underwriters and portfolio managers.

The Category II Merchant bankers could act as advisors, consultants, managers, underwriters and portfolio managers. The Category III Merchant bankers can act as an underwriter, adviser and consultant only. The Category IV Merchant banker could act as stipulated by the law. Therefore, the merchant banker has to work in public issues in different ways. He must coordinate all the issue related activities. The SEBI has the authority to grant a certificate of registration on consideration of all matters which are furnished by the merchant bankers. The Merchant banker shall fulfil the following conditions to get the registration of certificate from the SEBI:

(a) The merchant banker should be a body corporate.

(b) The primary dealer or satellite dealer who were registered with the RBI can also carry out the activities of a merchant banker.
(c) The satellite dealer or primary dealer shall not accept deposits from the public.
(d) The merchant banker should have necessary infrastructure like adequate office staff, manpower and equipment.
(e) They should appoint atleast two persons, those who are rich experience in merchant banking activities.
(f) They should have recognised professional qualification in finance, law or business management.
(g) The registration should be in the interest of the investors.
(h) The merchant bankers or their associates should not be involved in any litigation connected with the securities market.

2. Capital Adequacy Requirement: The SEBI has the authority to grant the certificate of registration to the merchant bankers. They will be granted registration by the SEBI in different categories on the basis of their capital adequacy norms. The capital adequacy consists of its net worth, paid up capital and free reserves. The SEBI has fixed the following net worth values for different categories as follows:

(a) Category I	Rs. 5 crores
(b) Category II	Rs. 50,00,000
(c) Category III	Rs. 20,00,000
(d) Category IV	Nil

The SEBI will monitor the activities of all the merchant bankers on half yearly basis. Every category of registered merchant bankers shall furnish to the SEBI of his half yearly unaudited financial results. They should pay the required fee to the SEBI on the basis of their status.

Registration Fee

Category of Merchant banker		*First two years*	*Third year*
I	Annually	Rs.2,50,000	Rs.1,00,000
II	Annually	Rs.1,50,000	Rs.50,000
III	Annually	Rs.1,00,000	Rs.25,000
IV	Annually	Rs.5,000	Rs.1,000
Renewal Fee			
I	Annually	Rs.1,00,000	Rs.20,000
II	Annually	Rs.75,000	Rs.10,000
III	Annually	Rs.50,000	Rs.5,000
IV	Annually	Rs.5,000	Rs.2,000

SEBI has increased the registration fee to Rs.5,00,000 since 1999. The renewal fee shall be paid before the expiry period of three months. They shall pay the renewal fee as indicated above. If any merchant banker fails to pay renewal fee within the stipulated period of time, his registration may be suspended.

3. Obligations: The merchant bankers shall abide by the code of conduct as specified in the Act. A merchant banker shall conduct his business with a high standard of integrity and fairness in his all transactions. He shall conduct his business activities in a systematic way. He shall render his services to his client at all times. He should exercise due diligence, ensure proper care and exercise professional judgement. He shall behave properly with other merchant bankers. He has to disclose all the information and the possible conflict of duties and interest when he is rendering service to his client. He should make any comment or statement against any act which is harmful to the interest of other merchant bankers while executing any assignment. He should not disclose information about his clients before other clients or press. He should not reveal his capability or influence to render certain services or his achievements before his clients. He should always render the best possible advice to his clients and ensure that all professional affairs must be dealt in very prompt, efficient and cost office way. He should deal with this client company after disclosure of the information to the SEBI. He should also inform the board of directors of the client company regarding the various assignments of the company. The merchant banker should have the following characteristics:

1. He should provide true and adequate information without misguiding the client before taking any investment decision.
2. He should make available the copies of prospectus memorandum of association and any other literature to the investors.
3. He should make adequate steps for the fair allotment of shares and refund the application money without delay to the **Non-allottees.**
4. He must pay proper attention towards investor's grievance. He shall try for settling of their problems as far as possible.

He should not involve particularly in respect of the issue of any securities, to create false market or manipulations or price rigging or spreading of price sensitive information to brokers, or to other market players in the capital market. All these activities are unfair, unethical and undesirable to the investors. He is the most important person in public issue and shall abide by all the rules and regulations framed by the SEBI.

2. Lead Managers

Lead managers have to be associated with the issuing company till the despatch of share certificates of the refund of excess application money to the investors. They will make agreement with the issuing company for setting out their mutual rights, liabilities and obligations relating to such issues. A statement containing all these information is to be furnished to the SEBI atleast one month before the opening of the issue for subscription. The lead managers have to accept a minimum underwriting obligation of 5% of the total underwriting commitment or Rs.25 lakhs whichever is less. If the lead manager is unable to underwrite this amount, it should be assigned to the merchant banker under intimation to the SEBI. The number of lead managers will be appointed according to its issue size. The following provisions may reveal about their appointment:

	Issue Size	*No. of Lead Managers*
(a)	Less than Rs.50 crores	2
(b)	Rs.50 crores – 100 crores	3
(c)	Rs.100 crores – Rs.200 crores	4
(d)	Rs.200 crores – Rs.400 crores	5
(e)	Above Rs.400 crores	5 and more

The lead managers are responsible for the verification of the contents of a prospectus or letter of offer in respect of public issue. After the verification of content he has to submit certificate to the SEBI atleast two weeks before the opening of the issue. He has to submit a due diligence certificate regarding all legal provisions which have been complied by the company in connection with the public issue. The lead managers have to submit the documents to Registrar of Companies and Regional Stock Exchange containing the following information:

(a) particulars about the public issue.
(b) contents of the offer document/prospectus.
(c) other literatures useful to the investors all of the above particulars should be submitted to the SEBI along with the prescribed fee specified below.

Issue size (Including premium)	*Fee per document*
Upto Rs.5 crores	Rs.10,000
Rs.5 crores – Rs.10 crores	Rs.15,000
Rs.10 crores – Rs.50 crores	Rs.25,000
Rs.10 crores – Rs.100 crores	Rs.50,000
Rs.100 crores – Rs.500 crores	Rs.2,50,000
More than Rs.500 crores	Rs.5,00,000

A lead manager/merchant banker is prohibited from acquiring securities of any company on the basis of unpublished price sensitive information during any professional assignment. He has to submit the particulars to the SEBI for any acquisition of securities of a company where the issue is being managed by him within 15 days from the date of the transaction. He has to disclose all the information to the SEBI.

(a) Particulars regarding his responsibilities relating to the present issue.
(b) Any change in previously furnished information to the SEBI while granting the registration certificate.
(c) The other client companies which he is involved in public issues.
(d) The full information about the capital adequacy requirements.
(e) The other information relating to his professional assignments as consultant, underwriter, managers or advisers to an issue.

The SEBI has the right to inspect the books of accounts, records and documents. He has to maintain the books of account as per the legal provisions of the Act. The lead Manager/Merchant banker who fails to comply with the legal provisions, the SEBI has the right to take action against them. It can levy the penalties in two kinds—**(a) suspension of Registration, and (b) cancellation of Registration.** The suspension of the registration can be done in the following situations by the SEBI:

(a) If any violation made by the Merchant banker in relating to the SEBI Act, Rules and Regulations.
(b) If the merchant banker fails to furnish any information as required by the SEBI.
(c) If he furnishes wrong information to the SEBI.
(d) If he fails to submit periodical returns to the SEBI.

(e) If he does not cooperate with the SEBI in any enquiry which is conducted by it.
(f) If he fails to pay the specified fee.
(g) If he involves in malpractices or in price rigging.
(h) If he violates the conditions while granting registration.
(i) If he fails to maintain capital adequacy requirement as per the provisions of the Act.
(j) If he violates the code of conduct of the business.

In the following situations, the SEBI has the right to **cancel** the registration:

1. If he is found in guilty of fraud.
2. If he is involved in conviction of a criminal offence.
3. If he is involved in deliberately at manipulation or price rigging or cornering activities.
4. If SEBI feels that he is harmful to the investors.

The SEBI is a powerful organisation in the primary market to control the activities of different kinds of intermediaries. It has the power to cancel or suspend the registration. It also imposes penalties where the merchant bankers are in non-compliance of conditions for registration. The defaults made by them generally can be categorised as follows:

(a) Major defaults.
(b) Serious defaults.
(c) Minor defaults.
(d) General defaulters.
(e) Default in prospectus.

(a) Major Defaults (3 points): The primary market consists of various financial intermediaries. The Merchant banker is one of the most important intermediaries in public issues. The issuing company has a little role to play in the market. The following activities will be treated as major default by the SEBI. This kind of default attracts 3 penalty points—

(a) **fails** to take up mandatory underwriting;
(b) deploying excess number of lead manager than permitted by it;
(c) involvement of unauthorised merchant banker in a public issue.

(b) Serious Defaulters (penalty points): The SEBI is the watchdog of the capital market. It observes all the intermediaries and regulates the market. If any merchant banker fails to cooperate with the SEBI in furnishing desired information or documents will be treated as serious default. This type of default attracts 4 penalty points. If any merchant banker violates the code of conduct will be viewed as serious default. Any merchant banker who reaches cumulative penalty points of 8 leads to cancellation/suspension of registration. But there will be a chance to take corrective mistakes by them. The maximum penalty points are restricted to 4.

(c) Minor Defaults (2 penalty points): The primary market is a combination of number of financial intermediaries. The success of the public issue depends upon many factors. But the merchant bankers will take an important role in the issue process. If the following mistakes are made by the merchant bankers, it will attract two penalty points:

(a) Any advertisement material not being prepared in compliance with rules and regulations may be treated minor default.
(b) If fails to attempt the investor's grievance promptly.
(c) If any delay made in refund of application money.
(d) If any failure provides adequate and fair disclosure to investors about the risk factors in prospectus.
(e) Failure to verify the contents of prospectus.
(f) Failure to non-disclosure of substantial matters in highlights to the issue in prospectus.
(g) Exaggerated information incorporated in the contents of the prospectus or in any press conference, investors conference, brokers conference to market the issue of shares.

(d) General Defaults (1 penalty point): Usually the merchant bankers dominate the public issue process. They occupy key role in the process of an issue. They should coordinate many things in post or pre-issue situation. In this capital market every player shall move according to the strict rules and regulations. Every movement of the every intermediary will be observed by the market surveillance system of the SEBI. Therefore, the following activities which are made by the merchant bankers will be attracted one penalty point:

1. If the lead manager fails to submit the draft prospectus to the SEBI before filing with the Registrar of companies or stock exchanges.
2. If the merchant bankers fail to submit the certificate of minimum subscription to the issue.

3. Fails to despatch the share certificates, refund orders and filling listing application by the Issuer.
4. If the merchant banker fails to submit the diligence certificate in a proforma to the SEBI before opening of the public issue.

(e) Default in Prospectus: Prospectus is the constitution of public issue. It is the basic document, which the investor makes investment decision on the basis of description in the prospectus. Therefore, the prospectus can be described as **"Manifesto"** of the political party. If the merchant banker fails to disclose the risk factors in the prospectus he attracts negative points. If any content disclosed in the prospectus as extraneous and absence of listing will attract negative points. The grading points will be made as follows:

(a) Grading points of prospectus can be 10.
(b) Prospectus scoring greater than or equal to **8 points** are classified as **"A"**.
(c) Prospectus scoring with **6** or less than 8 points will be categorised as **"B"**.
(d) prospectus scoring with **4** or less than 6 points will be treated as category **"C"**.
(e) Prospectus scoring with less than **4 points** can be categorised as **"D"**.

3. Underwriters

Public issue involves number of intermediaries in the primary market. Underwriter is another important intermediary in the new issue market. They agree to take up securities. They provide assurance to the issuing company that the issue may be subscribed either by others or by themselves. Underwriting is not mandatory after April 1995 but its importance cannot be ignored. It is just like insurance for public issues. They are appointed by issuing in consultation with the merchant bankers to the issues. A certificate should be issued by the lead manager in relating to underwriters financial capacity and this information should be disclosed in prospectus.

SEBI is the regulator of the primary market. It has the right to grant the registration to the underwriters in accordance with the provisions of the Act. An intermediary who wants to act as underwriter, a certificate of registration must be obtained from the SEBI. While granting the certificate of registration, the SEBI will examine the following factors:

(a) Adequate infrastructure equipment and manpower to smooth functioning of the activities.
(b) The past experience in underwriting business.
(c) Employment of atleast two persons with rich experience in underwriting.
(d) The persons who have been applied previous to the SEBI and found rejected are not eligible to grant the registration.
(e) Any person who has been previously taken disciplinary action against such person under the SEBI Act or rules and regulations.
(f) The net worth should be **Rs. 20,00,000** (Capital + Resources).

The underwriter who has been granted registration, will have to pay a fee to the SEBI **Rs. 2,00,000** for the 1st and 2nd years and **Rs. 1.00 lakh** for the 3rd year. A renewal fee should be paid Rs. 20,000 for every year. After 1999, the SEBI raised the **Rs. 5,00,000**. The registration will be in force, a renewal fee of **Rs. 2,00,000** every three years from the 4th year from the date of initial registration is payable. If any person fails to pay the required fee leads to suspension of the registration. The underwriter who has been granted registration should follow the following guidelines:

(a) General Responsibilities
(b) Code of Conduct

(a) General Responsibilities: The underwriting is a process of insurance to the public issues. The issuing companies do not need to worry about the response for their issue because the issue is fully assured by the underwriters. Therefore, they will play an important role in the capital market as per the provisions of the Act, the underwriters shall get benefit from underwriting commission only. He should not be benefited either directly or indirectly. An underwriter can oblige underwriting agreements should not exceed **20 times** to his net worth. He has to subscribe for underwriting the securities within **45 days** of the receipt of intimation from the issuing company. An underwriter shall enter into an agreement with his client company. The agreement contains all the information about both parties. Full particulars should be discussed and it should be incorporated in the agreement. The SEBI has the right to inspect the books of accounts and other documents of the underwriter. An inspection of the records if he fails to comply with the legal provisions, the SEBI has the right to take action against him. It has the right to cancel the registration or suspend the registration of any underwriter. The punishment will depend upon the situation.

(b) Code of Conduct: The person who takes the responsibility of non-subscription shares by the public is known as underwriter. He is the most important intermediary in the public issue. Underwriting is an activity of profession. Therefore, the underwriter shall follow the professional code of conduct. He should at all times abide by the code of conduct. He has to maintain a high standard of integrity, dignity and fairness in all his dealings with his clients and fellow professionals. He has to ensure that all the ethical manners should be adopted in issue of capital. He has to render high standard of service and exercise due diligence and adopt independent professional judgement. Any underwriter should not wilfully make untrue statements. He should not make any false representation in the market. He shall disclose to the issuing company about his potential areas of conflict of duties and interest of other underwriters. He should not disclose any information about the issuing to any other company. If any information came to his knowledge and deal in securities shall inform to the SEBI immediately.

4. Bankers to an Issue

The success of a public issue depends upon many factors. The primary market consists of number of intermediaries. Every intermediary has his own role in the issue process. Banker is one of the important intermediaries who collects the application money from the investors through his wide network of branches they will collect the application money along with applications and in turn it will be transmitted to the company. The SEBI is the most powerful organisation in the primary market and having the authority to grant the certificate of Registration to the bankers. Every banker must obtain a certificate from the SEBI. It grants the registration on the basis of all the activities relating to the banker for an issue with reference to the following requirements:

(a) The banker should have the necessary adequate infrastructure and manpower to effectively discharge his activities.
(b) The banker must be a scheduled bank.
(c) The grant of a certificate must be in the interest of the investors.
(d) The banker should not be involved in any litigation of any economic offence.

The Registered banker to an issue shall apply for the renewal of his registration 3 months before the expiry of the registration. The SEBI has the right to collect a fee of **Rs. 2,50,000** for the first two years from the date of registration and **Rs. 1,00,000** for the 3rd year to keep the registration in force. He has to pay renewal fee annually for the first two years. It is **Rs. 1,00,000** and **Rs. 20,000** for the third year. The registration fee has been changed from **1999**, a fee of **Rs. 5,00,000** as initial registration fee and **Rs. 2,50,000** renewal fee every three years from the fourth year from the date of registration. The banker to an issue should follow guidelines in the following aspects:

(a) General Responsibilities.
(b) Code of Conduct.

(a) General Responsibilities: Usually a banker, who has been appointed as banker to issue, shall have to follow the guidelines which are issued by the SEBI. If any violation is made against the guidelines he will be liable to pay penalty. A banker to an issue has to furnish the following information to the SEBI:

(a) His past experience as a banker to an issue.
(b) The number of public issues handled by him.
(c) The number of applications collected by him.
(d) The amount of application money collected by him.
(e) The dates on which the applications are received from the investors should be forwarded to the Registrar to an issue.
(f) The particulars about the refund to the investors.

The SEBI has the authority to call for any information from the bankers. The bankers to an issue are required to maintain the books of accounts, records and documents for a minimum period of 3 years after the closing of the public issue. He should maintain the books of accounts containing about the number of applications received, amount collected, forwarded dates etc. The registered banker shall enter into an agreement with the issuing company. The agreement contains full information about the number of collection centres and the process of forwarding the same to the Registrar of issue. It also contains the full information about the daily statement during the public issue period. If any violation is made by the banker, the RBI will take disciplinary action in relation to issue payment and it should be informed to the SEBI. If the banker is prohibited from these activities, the SEBI registration is automatically deemed as cancelled or suspended according to the situation.

(b) Code of Conduct: Banking is a highly respectable profession. The banker has to follow the professional code. He should conduct his business in a dignified way. He should maintain a high standard of integrity and fairness in all his dealings. He should not do any harm to other professionals. He should not make any exaggerated statement to his clients about his capability to render the services in this aspects. He has to render best possible advice to his clients. His professional dealings must be in prompt, efficient and cost effective manner. He should not reveal the confidential information about the client to the public or others. He should follow all the legal provision, rules, regulations, guidelines, resolutions and notifications. The RBI has the authority to inspect the banker on request from the SEBI. The purpose of inspection relating to books of account, records, documents and investor's grievances. On completion of inspection, The SEBI has the authority to take action against the banker according to the situation. Any failure made by the bankers will have to face the penalties and fines. The SEBI is empowered to suspend or cancel the registration. The following activities lead to suspend the registration of banker to issue:

(a) Fails to furnish the required information
(b) Furnishes false information
(c) Fails to resolve the investor's complaints
(d) Involved in guilty of misconduct
(e) Fails to pay required fee
(f) Fails to carry out his obligations.

The following activities lead to cancellation of registration:

1. Repeated defaults leading to suspension:
2. Conduct of the business adversely affect the interest of the investors.
3. Found guilty or conceited in a criminal offence.

5. Brokers to the Issue

Brokers are one of the financial intermediaries in the public issues. They are mainly concerned with the mobilisation of share capital from the investors. The brokers will be selected in consultation with the concerned stock exchanges. The inexperienced and unknown agencies into this field are discouraged. The letter consent given by the broker should be submitted to the Registrar of Companies. The prospectus should disclose the names and addresses of the brokers. The brokerage is fixed at **1.5%** for all the types of public issues. The expenses for distributing the application forms should be borne by the stock-brokers. The company will not reimburse the expenses incurred by the brokers. The brokerage for private placement of capital is fixed at a maximum rate of **0.5%**. The brokerage is not allowed in respect of promoters quota or renounced by the existing shareholders. Brokerage is not payable when the application is made by the institutions. The brokerage should be paid by the company within two months from the date of allotment to the broker. The brokerage rate should be disclosed in the prospectus.

6. Registrars to an Issue

The Registrars to an issue is one of the intermediaries involved in the primary market. He carries on the activities such as collecting applications from the investors, preparing records and receiving money from the investors. He assists the issuing company for making allotment in consultation with the stock exchanges. He is involved in processing, despatching allotment letters, refund orders, certificates and other related documents related to public issue. The Registrar also performs the function of share transfer agent. The share transfer agent is a person who maintains the records of holders of shares on behalf of the company. He deals with the matters connected with the transfer of shares. He must get the registration certificate from the SEBI. It may also be renewed every year by the SEBI on the basis of performance. He must abide by the rules and regulations which are issued by the SEBI from time-to-time.

PRIMARY MARKET (SERVICES)

Introduction

The asset formation is the basic function of the primary market. The development of a country depends upon the activeness of this market. The SEBI is most powerful organisation to monitor the activities of the different services rendered by various intermediaries public issue involves participation of many organisations to make success the issue. Though the success of public issue depends upon mainly on **good reputation, well-known** and financial discipline of the issuing company. But we cannot ignore the services which render the services during the issue period. All formalities should be fulfilled by all participants. The public issue involves two activities—**(a) pre-issue, and (b) post-issue**. All activities commencing with the planning of a capital issue till the opening of subscription list is classified as **pre-issue activities**. After the commencement of subscription list is known as **post-issue services**. These services are more important and require to follow the SEBI guidelines at every moment. Every service is closely monitored and reviewed by the SEBI. There will be penalties and fines if any intermediary violates the SEBI guidelines and government regulations. The aim of the close observation by the SEBI is to protect the investors from the indiscipline companies. At present the investors are cheated by some duped companies. The issuing companies are also required to follow the company law requirements in relation to the issue of shares. We must remember that the SEBI will control the service of the issuing company those are to be listed on the recognised stock exchanges. The company law guidelines are applicable to only unlisted company/deemed Public Limited Company/Private Limited Company. Therefore, the issuing companies have to be followed many rules and regulations as stipulated by the acts and provisions. The post-issue activities will cover in detail under the unit of financial services of this book.

B. MONEY AND CAPITAL MARKET

Introduction

Money market is the market for lending and borrowing of short-term funds. It is the basis for an effective monetary policy. Monetary policy deals with the monetary system of a nation. It is associated with monetary decisions and measures. It controls, directs and guides the methods of cost and use of money and credit. According to **Paul Einzig** "Monetary policy is the attitude of the political authority towards the monetary system of the community under its control".[34] It is the most important element in framing economic policy. It is also used to control the supply of money in the economy. The basic objectives of monetary policy is (a) price stability in the economy, (b) price stability in foreign exchange, (c) provision for full employment, (d) achieving the economic growth. It plays a vital role in the economic development of a nation. It has been utilised in the forms such as **Issue of Currency, Credit Control and Foreign Exchange Regulation.** Issue of currency notes and credit control is the part of monetary policy. Bank rate will be used as a weapon to control the volume of credit flow. It encourages savings attitude in the society. Foreign exchange regulations have been changing as per market fluctuations. The RBI has a separate wing to control foreign exchange for the purpose of procuring reserves. Fiscal policy is an important instrument of economic policy for achieving stability in economic growth.

C. DEVELOPMENT FINANCIAL INSTITUTIONS

Introduction

The expansion and capital formation of the industrial sector depend upon the availability of adequate financial resources. The development of financial institutions provide long-term capital needs to agriculture and industrial sectors. They are established specially to provide assistance for the development of proposed projects. They provide loans and assistance directly and indirectly. Indirect method of finance, they help the industries by providing long-term loans. They also contribute share capital to the forthcoming units. The development financial institutions provide indirect finance by underwriting of shares and providing guarantees for term loans. They are specialised financial institutions to promote banking business as well as economic development. They do not accept deposits from the general public unlike commercial banks. They provide long and medium term finance but the commercial banks provide short-term loans. They are development oriented banks. They participate in fulfilling the social objectives of the government. The social objectives will play an important role in the development of a nation. In India, the structure of development banks can be categorised as follows:

A. Industrial Development Bank of India
B. Industrial Credit and Investment Corporation of India
C. Industrial Finance Corporation of India

A. INDUSTRIAL DEVELOPMENT BANK OF INDIA (IDBI)

Introduction

The Industrial Development Bank of India was established in 1964. It has been empowered to finance all types of industrial concerns. It provides direct and indirect finance to the corporate sector. As direct financier it renders assistance to the corporate sector in the following ways:

(a) Sanctioning term loans and advance.
(b) Underwriting the issue of shares or debentures of the companies.
(c) Sanctioning third party loans to business.

The direct financial assistance is usually granted for purchase of fixed assets, for expansion and modernisation of existing units. The direct financial assistance is the most useful to the large scale manufacturing units. As an indirect financier it assists in the following ways:

1. Refinancing of industrial loans provided by the commercial banks and SFCS.
2. Providing financial assistance to the financial institutions by subscribing the shares and debentures of them.
3. Rediscounting of bills.
4. Refinancing of export credit sanctioned by commercial banks to exporters.
5. Readers consultancy services to the corporate sector.

The bank provides loans which are normally repayable over a period of 10 years. The authorised capital of the IDBI users is Rs. 2000 crores. It can be further increased to Rs.5,000 crores. The main sources of the fund for the IDBI are:

1. Borrowing from Central Government and RBI
2. Issue of shares and bonds
3. Grant and loans from World Bank

Management: The IDBI is managed by the Board of Directors. The Board of Directors consisting of 22 persons including the Chairman and Managing Director. The Chairman and Managing Director are appointed by the Central Government. The other members of the Board comprise a representative of RBI, a representative each of the All India Financial Institutions, two officials of the Central Government, 3 representatives from each public sector bank and SFCs, 5 members having special knowledge and experience of industry. The Board of Directors has constituted an Executive Committee which consists of 10 members.

Role: IDBI was set up as the principal financial institution for the industrial development in the country. Now it is playing an important role in the capital market. The role of the IDBI for the purpose of exposure can be categorised into three phases:

(a) I Phase
(b) II Phase
(c) III Phase

I Phase (1964-75): The IDBI was set up as a statutory corporation in July 1964. It was a wholly owned subsidiary of the RBI. The ownership of the IDBI was transferred to the Government in 1995. The IDBI Act was amended to provide greater operational flexibility. The amendment of the Act was made during the dynamic phase of the bank. The lifecycle of the IDBI started from 1964 to 1975 as first phase. The transformation of the IDBI took more than 35 years. The first phase was the most important stage in the life of the IDBI. The first phase had been concentrated towards industrialisation of the nation. The bank had focused on establishing the core industries such as textiles, fertilisers, chemical products, basic metals and machinery. The industrialisation strategy was also required to encourage the small ancillary industries to create more employment opportunities in the country. At this point of time SFCS, SIDCS were already in place to promote and encourage these segments of the industry. The IDBI took over the activities of the Refinance Corporation in 1964. Therefore, it started providing financial support to the SFCS and others primary lending institutions in the country by refinancing facility. The IDBI had introduced the rediscounting of machinery bills scheme to encourage the capital goods industry. Hence the IDBI fully involved in direct project loans. Refinance and bills rediscounting schemes to the industries.

The IDBI played an important role for the development of exports sector, balanced regional development and coordination between financial institutions. The IDBI started a scheme during this phase for financing project exports and export of capital goods on deferred payment basis. It actively participated in the formation of Export and Import Bank of India. The IDBI played an important role in achieving the balance regional development strategy. It initiated steps to conduct surveys for identifying industrial potential in backward areas and other specific locations. It played an important role in setting up of technical consultancy organisation in collaboration with other financial institutions. The Central Government provided long-term loans to the IDBI at concessional rate of interest. The RBI created a separate national industrial credit fund to meet the long-term operations of the corporate sector. The IDBI received loans from this fund at concessional rate of interest. The Government had exempted from income tax, which are issued by IDBI due to this recognition of development role. It also focussed on developing linkages with other financial institutions.

II Phase (1976-85): The second phase started from 1976 to 1985 because the IDBI was delinked from the RBI on 16.2.1976. It was accorded principal financial institution, wholly owned by the Government of India. This period was the most important in the life of the IDBI. The RBI had transmitted its all responsibilities to the IDBI. It also transferred the initial capital of the SFCs was also transferred to the IDBI by the RBI. It was an autonomous institution during this period. It actively involved in the process of industrialisation and upgradation of technology. It had achieved a certain degree of maturity during the second phase. The IDBI introduced a soft loan scheme during this phase. The scheme was designed to meet the modernisation programme in industries such as jute, cotton, textiles, sugar, cement and engineering goods. Later a revised modernisation package was introduced for all industries. The Central Government created a Special Technical Development Fund for modernisation of industries to boost the process of technology upgradation. According to this scheme, the IDBI provided concessional assistance for the import of balancing equipment acquiring technical know how and consultancy services for upgrading existing technology of the approved units. It also actively participated to provide assistance to the sick units. It had taken various measures during this period to meet the requirements of small village and cottage industry. It initiated package of refinance to small and medium sectors towards meeting the modernisation requirements. The technology upgradation required a higher amount of foreign currency. It diversified its resources base and borrowed the foreign currency from the global markets.

The term lending is an important aspect of industrial financing system. It is the oxygen for promoting of the industrial growth. The term lending widens the entrepreneurial base and the related infrastructure, services, etc. The industrial activities will be increased only when the entrepreneurial base widens. Therefore, the IDBI took initiative to educate the entrepreneurs by setting up a number of institutes for entrepreneurship development in association with other financial institutions. It encouraged the entrepreneurs by introducing of a scheme, which is known as seed capital scheme.

III Phase (1986): The third phase was one of the tremendous growth in activities of the IDBI. It provided several new challenges due to economic restructuring programme initiated by the Government. During this period, the IDBI introduced new product to meet the growing needs of entrepreneurs. It also focussed on balanced regional development of the country's sectoral growth of the industries and capital market in India.

The Central Government announced the technology of selected capital goods industries. It was assigned to formulate the system for this scheme. It also established in 1986 a Textile Modernisation Fund to provide a point for modernisation efforts in the industry. The World Bank helped the IDBI in the modernisation of cement industry.

The IDBI introduced an export incentive scheme in 1986. It encouraged the export units by providing incentives in the form of rebate of interest on rupee loan. The IDBI established a Venture Capital Fund in 1986 to provide financial assistance for industrial concerns. It was also giving top priority to energy conservation sector and environment audit aspects. The World Bank provided a special assistance to the pollution central projects.

The IDBI played a major role in the development of the capital market in India. It took initiative steps to set up several subsidiaries and associate concern. These concerns offered a wider range of products and services. It set up the Stock Holding Corporation of India in 1987. It provided depository services to the financial institutions. The Central Government had also assigned the responsibility of setting up the SEBI. The NSE was also established by the IDBI with the instructions from the Central Government. The NSE provided nation-wide screen based trading system. It had thrown a challenge to the Bombay Stock Exchange. The BSE has the competitor of the NSE. The IDBI promoted/established the following institutions with the directions from the Government:

(a) National Securities Depository Ltd.
(b) Credit Analysis and Research Ltd.
(c) IDBI Capital Market Securities Ltd.
(d) IDBI Investment Management Company Ltd.
(e) IDBI Bank Ltd.
(f) North Eastern Development Finance Corporation Ltd.
(g) Infrastructure Development Finance Company Ltd.
(h) Over the Counter Exchange of India (with others).
(i) Tourism Finance Corporation of India (with others).
(j) Shipping Credit and Investment Corporation of India.
(k) Bio-Tech Consortium of India Ltd.

The IDBI decentralised its officers and processing of projects to meet the competition from the market. It devised a host of new products to meet the needs of the modern corporate sector. It also empowered to manage its own foreign currency.

B. INDUSTRIAL CREDIT AND INVESTMENT CORPORATION OF INDIA

Introduction

The Industrial Credit and Investment Corporation of India was incorporated on 5.1.1955. It was founded by the Government of India, World Bank and others. It was promoted as a public limited company. It has been established for the purpose of assisting industries in the private sector. The aim of setting up of the ICICI was to provide foreign currency finance to the industrial projects and promote industries in private sector. It provides financial packages for R&D, commercialisation of technology, venture capital, pollution control and environment protection. It had diversified into a number of other activities. It had also been managing United States Agency for international development and World Bank and funds through its technological financing programmes.

The ICICI's principal business was to provide medium and long-term project financing, underwriting to shares, guarantees to suppliers of equipment and foreign lenders. It has entered into new areas of business like commercial banking, investment banking, non-banking finance, broking, investor servicing, venture capital financing and infrastructure financing. It operated in accordance with the guidelines of RBI/SEBI. It had the status of a public financial institution. This status is useful in getting the benefits of taxation. Its bonds were treated as public securities for investment by trusts.

Financial Resources: The resources of the ICICI comprised two kinds:

(a) Foreign Currency Resources
(b) Rupee Resources

The resources of the ICICI consisted of interest free loan from the Government of India and an advance in foreign currency from the World Bank.

The rupee resources of the ICICI comprise the following components:

(a) Share Capital
(b) Reserves
(c) Borrowings
(d) Public Deposits

(a) Share Capital: It started with the initial resources of about Rs.17.5 crores. At the end of March 1996, their paid up capital amounted to Rs. 376.3 crores and reserves and surplus amounted to Rs. 2059.4 crores. A large part of the capital was held by public sector institutions such as banks, LIC, GIC and its subsidiaries, IDBI, UTI, etc. It issued ADRs and GDRs and a significant change was resulted in its shares ownership structure.

(b) Reserves: It has been consistently building up a large chunk of reserves. Reserves are the most important element for the financial companies. The higher amount of reserves is the financial strength of the company. The reserves consist of capital reserve, capital redemption reserve, share premium account, general reserve and special reserve.

(c) Borrowings: It mobilises the funds from domestic and foreign markets. The domestic borrowings by the ICICI are from:

(a) The Government of India
(b) Institutional borrowing
(c) Government backed bonds
(d) Public issue of bonds
(e) Miscellaneous

The foreign currency resources consist of the following borrowings:

(a) Multi-lateral borrowings
(b) Commercial borrowings

The multilateral borrowings have been from the multilateral institutions. The World Bank played an important role in setting up of the bank. It had been providing financial assistance from various foreign agencies.

Commercial borrowings played an important role of the financial architecture of the ICICI. It had diversified its resource base with a view to establish in the global market. It raised a public issue of SF8 million bonds in the Swiss market in 1973. It depends upon the increase of the commercial borrowings. The commercial borrowing from various countries made their financial stability to survive in the global market.

It borrowed the commercial borrowings in the following ways:

(a) Euro credits and other loans
(b) Bond issues in Switzerland
(c) Private placements in Japan
(d) Euro convertible debt market

It received strong support from the international banking and financial community. It also achieved its objectives of interest and currency diversification by borrowing in various markets in dollar, swiss franc, yen, pound, sterling. It had been constantly searching for financial assistance in the international markets. It launched a global medium term note programme in 1996-97 to facilitate borrowing in small amounts of competitive rates.

(d) Public Deposits: It started an accepting public deposits from 1979. It is only a management source of funds. It also invited public deposits from the public by offering competitive rate's interest.

Business Operations: The business operations of the ICICI can be categorised into 5 kinds:

(a) Lending operation
(b) Capital market operations
(c) Advisory Service
(d) Sponsorship
(e) Subsidiaries

(a) Lending Operation: Lending is the basic operation of only financial institution. This activity refers to the business concerns. The lending operations generate income to the ICICI by charging different rates of interest from the corporate sector. The lending operations of the ICICI consist of the following activities:

(a) Project finance
(b) Technology finance
(c) Non-project finance

Project finance is the most important activity of the bank. It grants the loans to business concerns in the form of rupee and foreign currency loans. Underwriting and direct subscription to issue of shares and debentures. It also provides financial assistance for the modernisation, expansion of manufacturing and processing units. The rupee project loans are involved in financing the purchase of equipment and machinery. It also finance under this scheme towards cost of land, construction of factory and preliminary expenses etc. The rupee currency loans dominated the portfolio of loans disbursed by ICICI. The share of rupee loans in the total financial assistance is provided by the bank increased substantially. Foreign currency project loans are provided to finance the purchase of imported capital goods. The World Bank channelises foreign currency resources for the private industry through ICICI. It did not sanction any foreign loan during the commencement of its operations. It started financing the foreign currency loans from 1958 with the emergence of foreign currency loans exchange crisis. After 1971 the component of foreign currency loans declined substantially. This was due to the recessionary state of the economy. At present the Indian companies are directly by accessing international capital markets through the issue of

GDRs. It started guaranteeing loans from the private investment sources. It charges 1% p.a. on the outstanding balances of guarantee issued in rupees and 1.8% in case of foreign currencies. It also offers assistance to corporate by underwriting the issue of shares and debentures. Now it has been following a policy of direct subscription of shares to the extent of Rs.1 crore.

Technology financing has emerged as one of the sources of finance. The ICICI is the largest financiers of technology in India. This source of finance runs with the help of United States agency of International Development and World Bank. They are providing funds for various schemes of financing. It offers a wide variety of financial packages for R&D commercialisation of technology. It also offers package relating to pollution control and environmental protection. The following schemes are offered by the ICICI:

1. SPREAD
2. ACE
3. TEST
4. PACT
5. PACER

Sponsored Research and Development Programme (SPREAD) is one of the schemes which is offered by the ICICI. It encourages Indian corporate sector to set up their R&D activities. It links up the technology and industry. The package offers for the projects which are involved in the development of new product or process. The product modification will also be considered by this package. The package allows activities like preparation of feasibility studies, laboratory, trails and pilot plant operations. The project under this scheme should have feasible and quantifiable objectives. The project should to take larger than two years to be completed. The company should bear 50% of the total cost of the project. The remaining amount will be granted as eligible project. Specific expenses which are included equipment facilities, materials payments to consultant fee payable to technology institutions, project related travel and overhead expenses. The financial assistance provided by the ICICI will be charged with an interest rate of 6% during the implementation period of the R&D project. The repayment period is up to 10 years. At the final stage of the project, the rate of interest will be increased to 15%.

The Agricultural Commercialisation Enterprise (ACE) is another programme which is funded by the ICICI. This scheme is formulated for the development of agribusiness in India. It provides financial assistance for setting up innovative projects in horticulture, floriculture, mushrooms fruits, essential oils, herbal products, enzymes etc. This projects activities involve looms to private sector providing technical assistance and conducting travels. It conducts field trips to members of industry for observing and knowing the technical aspects.

The ICICI is conducting another research based programme which related to commercialisation of energy. It provides funds for the development of the technology in India towards energy sector. The financial assistance is provided for the technology development of energy such as renewable sources of energy, energy conservation, fossils.

The ICICI is also financing Indo-US joint ventures in R&D for the development of the technology process in specified areas. The scheme is applicable to agriculture, health and other areas. It aims at improving. The availability of quality products and services in the segments of child health, AIDS and reproductive health. It also finances for the technology development of the environmental and pollution control.

The ICICI is also providing non-project finance to the industry with medium and long-term maturity period. It provides short-term loans to the corporate sector to meet working capital needs. It provides assistance to the corporate sector number of schemes.

(b) Capital Market Operations: The ICICI mobilises funds through debt and equity. It actively involved in capital market operations. It encourage entrepreneurs by making investments in their companies by direct subscription to public issues. It participates in the capital market operations by taking up right issues of the companies conversion by option of loans assisted companies, participating in private placement of the corporate sector and provide rehabilitation package for the sick industries. It does not acquire securities in the secondary market. The investment operations of the ICICI have been increasing at present. It also offers fee based services to its clients. These activities are advisory in nature providing consultancy services. It has been offering project advisory services since 1991 to PSUs, and private sector companies. It acts as trustee for the holders of convertible and non-convertible debenture issues. These financial instruments are issued by the companies to the public in the form of rights issue, private placement etc. It offers comprehensive custodial services since 1992. Its clients include FIIs overseas depository banks.

The ICICI has been actively involving in promoting a number of institutions which are strengthening the institution structure of the money and capital market. The Credit Rating Information Services of India Ltd.

had been established in association with UTI in 1987. It provides quality of consultancy services to the corporate sector CRISIL involved in rating various types of financial instruments that are offered to the investing public. It is also instrumental in promoting the following institutions:

1. Technology Development and Information Company of India Ltd. (TDCI)
2. Over the Counter Exchange of India Ltd. (OTC)
3. Stock Holding Corporation of India Ltd. (SHCI)
4. Discount and Finance House of India (DFHI)
5. Management Development Institutes (MDIs)

After the liberalisation, privatisation and globalisation, the ICICI entered new areas of business like investment banking, assets management, commercial banking etc. It has set up specified subsidiaries which are presented below.

1. ISEC Ltd.
2. ICICI Brokerage
3. ICICI Banking
4. ICICI Infotech
5. ICICI Personal Financial Service Ltd.
6. ICICI Capital Services Ltd.
7. ICICI Venture Ltd.
8. ICICI International
9. ICICI Properties

Merger of ICICI with ICICI Bank: The ICICI has merged with ICICI Bank on 28.3.2002. The universal bank plans major thrusts on the retail and international fronts. The ICICI and ICICI Banks have been moving towards a merger for over two years now the formal announcement was made on 25.10.2001. There has been frantic activity in the ICICI group to conform to the statutory obligations to turn into a universal bank. The merger process required the ICICI to show Rs.23,000 crores by the way of SLR for the combined entity. The ICICI Bank already has Rs.5,000 crores in its SLR portfolio, an additional Rs.18,000 crores was required from ICICI. Then the ICICI mobilised the fund through a combination of relation retail deposits and assets swaps, the remaining Rs.10,000 crores was brought in by the way of retail deposits. The merger regulations did not allow merged entity to have any subsidiary that was involved in non-banking activities. The swap ratio has been fixed at one share of the ICICI Bank for every two shares of ICICI. Therefore, the final 2:1 ratio falls within the audit of all the valuation norms. The aim of the post merges was aggressive capital management optimal size technology, intensive multi-channel delivery architecture world class skill basis and enduring customer relationship. The post merges will bring several advantages. ICICI itself get access to cheaper retail funds. The merged entity is focusing on the new avenues. They are fee income, trade finance, for remittances cash management services dividend management, agri-business, small and medium enterprises, consumer finance, auto loans, credit and debit cards, housing finance, personal loans, internet banking, retail business, third party products, mutual funds insurance, pension products, smart cards and fund transfer.

Recently it introduced "e-cheque" system in fund transfer process. According to the scheme the customer can transfer money to any account in any bank in any of 14 cities. Another services has been launched in Delhi. Any cell phone owner can tap up with the ICICI ATM. It also focuses on cross selling instead of individual marketing. The major advantage of cross selling is that the customer acquisition cost comes down massively. Customer loyalty and satisfaction is reflected in across selling. The other major thrust area is the international division. The international business provides 10-15% of ICICI banks turnover and profits in the forthcoming 5 years. But today, it identified five geographic setting up representative offices in the US, UK, Dubai, Singapore and London. The international division will be setting up a consultancy to provide services to banks and other financial sector players internationally.

The Indian economy requires large banks to cater its requirements. The ICICI merger will create a significant player. The merger is clearly a reflection of the overdue consolidation of the banking industry needs.

A Merger Snapshot

(Rs. in crores)

	Account on September 2001			
	ICICI	*Bank*	*Merged*	*March 31, 2000*
Assets				
1. Total credits	61235	11660	72895	65000
2. SLR Investments	489	5400	5889	23500
3. Cash Reserves		1450	4500	4500
4. Other Assets	12650	2290	14940	15000
5. Total Assets	74374	20800	95174	108000

(Contd.)

(Contd.)

	Account on September 2001			
	ICICI	*Bank*	*Merged*	*March 31, 2000*
Liabilities				
1. Equity capital	786	220	613	600
2. Reserves	7996	1224	9612	9600
3. Borrowings	59668	685	60353	60000
4. Deposits	–	17515	17515	32000
5. Other Liabilities	74374	20800	95174	1108000

The expressions by the analysts and experts are that the new merged entity may be sitting on mountain of non-performing assets that may come home to roost their conclusion is that its loan portfolio cannot be too different from that of IDBI or IFCI. All of them were lending to the same sectors and companies with similar profiles. ICICI comes with net NPAs at around Rs.3,000 crores or 5.3%. The ICICI bank has net NPAs at 1.36%.

C. INDUSTRIAL FINANCE CORPORATION OF INDIA

Introduction

The Industrial Finance Corporation of India was set up in July 1948 by the Government of India. It was established under the IFCI Act, 1948 with the basic objective of providing finance to the industries in private sector. At present it is also providing financial assistance to cooperative joint, public sector units. It provides loans for expansion, diversification and modernisation of existing units. It also underwrites and directly subscribes to industrial securities, merchant banking services and lease finance. It renders financial assistance both in rupees and foreign currencies to the corporate sector.

The small scale industries, proprietary and partnership concerns were not eligible for financial assistance from the IFCI. It did not grant assistance for the purpose of working capital. It did not provide assistance for the acquisition of capital goods for commercial or trading purpose. It did not grant loans in foreign currencies purchasing of raw materials imports or payments of royalties, interest and dividends. The IFCI Act was amended in 1986. The authorised business of the IFCI was presented in the following:

(a) It provides technical administrative assistance, legal and marketing assistance to any industrial concern.

(b) It provides consultancy services in and outside India.
(c) It appointed as administrator.z

Financial Resources

The sources of the funds are share captal retainment. Repayment of past loans and scale of investments, borrowings from IDBI borrowings from foreign lending institutions, foreign capital markets and public deposits.

The paid up capital of the IFCI was held directly by the Central Government and the RBI. The holdings of the two concerns were transferred to the IDBI. The balance of the paid up capital was contributed by the commercial banks, insurance organisations and cooperative banks. It made a first public issue of equity shares in December 1993. The authorised capital has now been increased to Rs.339.1 crores. It had consistently increased and built up sizeable reserves. The reserves of the IFCI consists of the following elements:

(a) General reserves
(b) Reserve fund
(c) Benevolent reserve
(d) Special reserve
(e) Specific grant from the GOI
(f) Share premium account

It mobilises the funds from the sale of bonds. It grants rupee currency and foreign currency loans, the rupee currency loans are met from the domestic market and foreign market respectively. The IFCI policy is to reduce its dependence on the government. It focussed on market borrowing by issue of bonds. The bonds are guaranteed by the Government and redeemable at par at coupon rates ranging from 8.75% and 13.5%. It depends on bonds which are privately placed and issued to public. The issued bonds to the public carry and maturity of 7 to 30 years. The privately placed bonds have a maturity of one to 27 years. It offered a variety of innovative bonds targeting different segments. It also issued deep discount bonds, education bonds, gift bonds, retirement bonds, floating millionaire bonds, etc.

It was authorised in **1952** to borrow in foreign currency. It had been borrowing from foreign agencies/financial institutions. It was allowed to borrow from global market. It obtained financial assistance from **USA,**

Germany, France and UK. The borrowings from the international capital market are from:

(a) Euro currency market
(b) Germany market
(c) Japanese capital market

It diversified its resources base by raising short-term funds through certificate of deposits and commercial papers. It reduced its dependence on GOI and RBI. Its main funding source is market borrowings through a variety of innovative family bonds.

Business Activities: IFCI actively participated in industrialisation of the country. It provided financial assistance to corporate sector through different schemes. The industrial financing activities consist of two segments. They are:

A. Project finance
B. Financial services

Project finance covers the entire funding new projects, expansion, diversification and modernisation in the form of foreign currency and rupee term loans. The project finance is the main activity of the IFCI. The projects will be financed through the term loans. The IDBI directly subscribes to equity shares of smaller new companies to encourage the new breed of entrepreneurs.

It also involves in the capital market operations. Its investment portfolio consists of acquisition of shares for underwriting obligation direct subscription to shares basis issues, subscriptions to right shares conversion of convertible debentures proportion, conversion of dues into shares or debentures. It also guarantees to finance the amount to the industry. IFCI now also provides indirect finance for leasing companies. It has started providing short-term loans to corporates for meeting the working capital financing.

Financial services is the secondary activity of the IFCI in order to improve its profitability the financial services include fund based, fee based, project counselling, issue management, loan syndication, financial restructuring, mergers and acquisitions, debentures, trusteeship, equipment leasing etc. It provides financial assistance to enterprise in the private sector. It actively participates in sugar cooperative, the government directed the IFCI to continue the support to textile industries also the assistance given to the industrial cooperative has in all cases been in the form of loans only.

The financial assistance to the cooperative sector has substantially declined over the years. The IFCI sanctioned loans to the private sector. Its assistance to the private sector projects has increased substantially over the years. It has been providing financial assistance to PSUs, government companies, since 1969. The financial assistance has been provided for the expansion and diversification of the following:

(a) public limited companies
(b) had declared a maiden dividend
(c) had built up sufficient internal resources
(d) should not have approached for budgetary support

It provides financial assistance to wide variety of industries. The sanctioning of loans depends upon changing conditions of national priorities. Initially it has given preference to sugar and textile projects. It has also diversified its investments strategy and concentrated in power generation, telecom services, textiles electronics, synthetic, resins, plastics, fertilisers, basic chemicals petroleum refining and cement. It provides finance to industrial enterprises. This has spread over to Andhra Pradesh, Gujarat, Maharashtra, Tamil Nadu, Madhya Pradesh and West Bengal. It has been providing assistance. It has initiated measures to achieve the balanced regional development.

It actively involves in promotional activities like project identification, formulation, implementation and operations. It provides consultancy fee subsidy scheme and interest subsidy scheme and assistance schemes.

The consultancy fee subsidy scheme providing services to industrial units which are identified as the small, tiny and ancillary units. The scheme is applicable to small entrepreneurs in rural, cottage, tiny and small scale sectors to new entrepreneurs for meeting. The cost of market survey. Interest subsidy scheme is to provide encouragement to the unemployed youth and women entrepreneurs. This scheme is implemented through SFAs. It is also providing assistance scheme to the existing industrial projects in the medium and small scale sector.

It encourages professionalism in management to improve the quality in day to day management. The IFCI sponsored in 1973 the Management Development Institute to provide training and research in the field of banking. It established in 1977 a Development Banking Centre as its autonomous wing. The MDI and DBC have been continuously working for the development of managerial manpower in public private, joint and cooperative sectors in the industry. It diversified its business activities in the following areas:

1. Merchant Banking,
2. Project Counselling,
3. Credit Syndication,
4. Consultancy to Sick Industrialisation, and
5. Sponsoring of Financial Institutions.

FINANCIAL INSTITUTIONS

Introduction

Financial institutions are the active players in the capital market. These organisations provide long-term loans as easy instalments to the corporate sector. They help in promoting new business enterprises expansion and diversification of the existing companies. In underdeveloped countries there is a strong need for the establishment of the financial institutions because of a large number of industrial organisations. A number of financial institutions have been set up all over India and at regional level for accelerating the growth of industries.

They involve in the mobilisation of funds and in channelising the savings towards the productive way. These institutions provide credit to the commercial enterprises. They provide a wide range of services to the public. They deal with the financial assets like deposits, banks and securities. They mobilise the saving either directly or indirectly from the financial markets. They deal with the financial market. The financial institutions are a part of the financial market. They always rotate in a business environment. The pace of the industrialisation of a country depends upon the disbursements of loans by these institutions. They play an important role in the development of a nation for the following reasons:

Lack of organised capital market
Low rate of savings
Low capital formation
Lack of entrepreneurial spirit
Low rate of the GDP
Altitude of the investors
Lack of the financial facilities to the mega product

The financial institutions do not directly add to the volume of the real capital formation. They are only the intermediaries between the savers and to user they encourage savings. They are classified into the following categories:

(a) Regulatory
(b) Intermediaries
(c) Non-intermediaries
(d) Others

The financial institutions may be categorised as banking and non-banking. They completely involve in the money and finance aspects of the entire nation. Banking institutions are based on service basis. They can create money and finance. They are the creators of wonderful sculptor of a new economy. They create the wealth of a nation. They çomprise commercial banks and cooperative banks. The non-banking institutions involve in the indirect finance of the corporate sector. They actively participate in the capital market. However, the non-banking financial institutions have a financial muscle and vast resources at their disposal. They will fulfil the needs and objectives of the socio-economic and political aspects in a mixed economy. The examples of the non-banking institutions are LIC, UTI, IDBI etc. All the insurance companies were nationalised and renamed as LIC in 1956. The Unit Trust of India was started in 1964. The IDBI was established in 1964 as a subsidiary to the RBI.

The financial institutions are further classified as intermediaries and non-intermediaries. The intermediaries involve in the mobilisation of the deposits from the customers to dispose the funds at interest for various purposes. They provide deposits, grants, loans to the needy sector. They disburse the loans in the form of short, medium and long-term loans. All banking institutions belong to the intermediaries. The non-intermediary institutions lend the money from their own resources. The non-banking financial intermediaries, IDBI, IFCI are the best examples. These institutions are established to provide the financial assistance for the specified purposes, sectors and regions. They are established by the Government of India by introducing an Act in the Parliament. The structure of the intermediaries is presented below:

Intermediaries

Banking

- → R.B.I.
- → Commercial Banks
- → Co-operative Banks
- → Urban Co-op Banks
- → Post Office Saving Banks

Non-Banking

- → Provident Fund
- → Small Savings
- → LIC
- → GIC
- → UTI
- → Mutual Funds
- → Investment trust
- → Housing Dev Finance
- → Investment Companies
- → Manufacturing Cos.
- → Finance Companies
- → Venture Capital
- → Leasing Companies
- → NHB
- → Hire Purchase Cos.
- → HUDCO
- → Chits Nidhis

RESERVE BANK OF INDIA

Introduction

The Central bank plays an important role in the monitory and banking structure of a nation. It supervises, controls and regulates the activities of the banking sector. It has been assigned to handle and control the currency and credit of country. In olden days, the Central banks were empowered to issue the currency notes and bankers to the Union Government. The first Central bank in the world was Bike bank of Sweden which was established in **1656**. The Bank of England was established in 1694 for advancing money to the Government. It led to the development of the Central banks in other parts of the world. The Bank of France was established in **1800**. The Bank of Netherlands was established in 1814. The National Bank of Austria was instituted in **1817**. The Bank of Norway was established in **1817**. The National Bank of Denmark was set up in **1818**. The National Bank of Belgium was formed in **1850**. The Bank of Spain was set up in **1829**. All these ones were the landmarks in the history of the Central Banking. The Bank of Russia was established in **1860**. The Reichs Bank of Germany was instituted in **1875**. The Bank of Japan was established in **1882**.

The Central bank has the responsibility of managing all the economic and monitory affairs of the nation. The Central bank looks after the welfare of the population. Central bank has been defined by R.P. Kent "as an institution charged with the responsibility of managing the expansion and contraction of the volume of money in the interest of the general public welfare".
According to De-cock the Central Bank has been defined as "A Central bank being generally recognised as a bank which constitutes the apex of the monitory and banking structure of its country and which performs as best as it can." On the national economic interest it performs the following functions:

1. The regulation of the currency in accordance with the requirements of business and the general public for the purpose of which it is granted either the sole right of note issue of atleast a partial monopoly thereof (R.P. Kent, *Money and Banking*) p. 551.
2. The performance of general banking and agency services for the state.
3. The custody of the cash resources of the commercial banks.
4. The custody and management of the nations reserves of international currency.
5. The granting of accommodation in the form of rediscounts and collateral advances to the commercial banks, bill brokers dealers and other financial institutions and the general acceptance.
6. The settlement of clearance balance among the banks.
7. The control of credit in accordance with the needs of business and with a view to carry out the broad monitory policy adopted by the state.

A further requisite of a real Central bank is that it should not to any extent perform such banking transactions as accepting the deposits from the general public and accommodating regular commercial customers with discount and advances.

The Central bank is not profit making enterprise. But they earn much profit through it functioning. The Central bank monitors the operations of commercial banks, industrial banks, agricultural banks and investment banks. The Central bank is controlled by the Central Government. The bank has certain relationship with the commercial banks. It has no authority to accept the deposits from the public. The Central banking system has been playing an important role in the economy. It plays a more positive and dynamic role in the development of a country. The financial muscle of a nation depends upon the soundness of the policies of the Central banking. The objectives of the Central banking system are presented below:

1. The Central bank should work for the national interest of the country.
2. The Central bank must aim for the stabilisation of the mixed economy.
3. It aims at the stabilisation of the price level of average prices.
4. Stabilisation of the exchange rate is also essential.
5. It should aim for the promotion of economic activities.

The Central bank is the nucleus of the Indian financial system. It is the apex institution. Since the inception of the economy, it has been guiding, regulating, controlling and monitoring the Indian financial system. It is the oldest among the other developed countries banks. The functions of the Central bank as mentioned by De-cock are as follows:

1. **Bank of Issue**
2. **Banker to the Government**
3. **Bankers bank**
4. **Lender of the last resort**
5. **The controller of credit**

The regulatory framework of the financial sector in India is formulated by the Ministry of Finance and the GOI. The Ministry of Finance administers the Companies Act, 1956, the Securities Contract Regulation Act, 1956, the RBI and the SEBI, the IRDA, the Stock Exchanges and the apex financial institutions. The RBI and the SEBI have a special role and responsibility. At first let us discuss about the RBI.

The Reserve Bank of India (RBI) is the Central bank of the country. It has been occupying an important role in the Indian financial system. It started its functioning from April 1, 1935. It was set up under the RBI Act, 1934. The RBI till January 1949 was under the management of the private shareholders. The private institution became a state owned institution under the RBI Act, 1948. The Act empowers the Central Government to issue the direction in the interest of the public. The Central Government has the authority to guide, regulate and monitor the activities

Government has the authority to guide, regulate and monitor the activities of the RBI. It has the authority to appoint the governor and the deputy governor of the RBI. The RBI is managed by a Board of Directors. It consists of the governor, 4 deputy governors and 15 directors nominated by the Central Government. The Board of Directors consists of 4 local boards of director and a committee. The local boards are set up for giving advices to the Central board on specific matters. It is also required to perform the duties delegated to them. The Board has the supreme authority to control the activities of bank. The internal organisation of the bank structure may change from time-to-time depending upon the volume of work. It has been working on the basis of the functional specialisation with adequate coordination for the smooth functioning of the RBI, it has been divided into 20 departments and the training establishments besides banking and issue departments.

Functions

The RBI functions are based on the mixed economy. The RBI should maintain a close and continuous relationship with the Union Government decision will be final. The main functions of the RBI are presented below:

1. Welfare of the public.
2. To execute the financial transactions safely and effectively.
3. To develop the financial infrastructure of the country.
4. To maintain the financial stability of the country.
5. To allocate the funds effectively without any partiality.
6. To regulate the overall credit volume for price stability.

Authorities

The RBI has the full authority in the following aspects:

1. Currency issuing authority
2. Monitory authority
3. Banker to the Union Government
4. Foreign exchange control authority
5. Promoting authority

1. Currency issuing authority: The RBI has the sole authority to issue the currency notes and coins. It is the fundamental right of the RBI. The coins and one rupee notes are issued by the Government of India and they are circulated through the RBI. The notes issued by the RBI will have legal identity everywhere in India. The RBI issues the notes in the denominations of Rs.**500, 100, 50, 20** and **10**. The RBI has the authority to circulate and withdraw the currency from circulation. It has also the authority to exchange notes and coins from one denomination to other denomination as per the requirements of the public.

The notes issue department: The currency notes are handled by the issue department. The currency may be distributed throughout the country through its 15 full pledged offices and branch offices and more than 4000 currency chests. The currency chests are maintained by different banks in various locations. The RBI issues currency notes based on the availability of balances of gold, bullion, foreign securities, rupees, coins, GOI securities and permitted bills. The RBI notes are backed by 100% asset security. At present, the RBI is following a minimum value of gold coin, bullion and foreign securities as a part of the total approved assets.

2. Monitory Authority: The RBI has the full authority to control all the aspects of the banking system in India. The RBI is known as the Bankers' Bank. The banking system in India has worked according to the guidelines issued by the RBI. The RBI is the premier banking institution among the commercial banks. All the commercial banks, foreign banks and cooperative urban banks in India should obey the rules and regulations which are issued by the RBI from time-to-time. The RBI controls the deposits of the commercial banks through CRR and the SWRs. Every bank should deposit a certain amount in the RBI. The commercial bank has the power to borrow the money from the RBI where they are in need of finance. Hence it is known as lender of the last result. The RBI has the authority to control the credit supply in the economy and monetary system of the nation. The RBI has the following powers with regard to the banking system:

(a) It has the power to grant the licences for the establishment of the new banks in India.

(b) It has the power to grant the licences for the branch expansion of commercial banks.

(c) It has the power to inspect the commercial banks and its branches in India and abroad.

(d) It has the authority to fix the norms regarding the paid up capital, reserves transfer of reserve funds, maintenance of cash reserves and other liquid assets.

(e) It can check the commercial banks organisational set up branch expansion, mobilisation of funds, credit portfolio management, regionwise performance, profit planning, training, appraisal etc.

(f) It has the authority to conduct the enquiry, investigations against complaints, irregularities and frauds in the banks.
(g) It has the authority of mergers and acquisition among the banks.
(h) It has the authority to appoint the CEOs of the private banks re-appointment and termination of the chairman also has with it.
(i) It also controls the methods of operations of the banks.

The Narasimhan Committee (1991) recommended that for the suspension of the commercial banks a separate department should be created on the basis of the recommendations. The Government of India has created a separate department of suspension on 22nd December, 1993. The RBI had set up a particular department on the eve of the securities scam for monitoring the activities of the financial sector. The Board of Financial Suspension was formed on 16th November, 1994. The Department of suspension took the responsibility of conducting the inspection from 1995. It also surprises All India Financial Institutions and NBFCs. The Board of Financial Supervision has a full time Vice-Chairman and 6 other members. The RBI Governor is the Chairman. He has the power to supervise and inspect banks, financial institutions, NBFCs. A five member advisory council has been formed for rendering the reserves. The Department of Supervision assists the Board of Financial Supervision. However, all these bodies failed to curtail the visiting number of frauds and irregularities in the financial sector. Therefore, the Department of Supervision should have the full frauds and irregularities in the banking sector.

3. Bankers to the Union Government: Generally in any country all over the world the Central bank dominates the banking sector. It advises the government or monitory policies. The RBI is the banker to the Union Government and also the State Government in the country. It provides a wide range of banking services to the government. It also transfers the funds, collects the receipts and makes the payment. On behalf of the Government, it also manages the public debts. The Government will not pay any remuneration and brokerage to the RBI for rendering the financial services. Any deficit and surplus in the Central Government amount with the RBI will be adjusted by creation and cancellation of the treasury bills. The treasury bills are known as the "*Adhoc* Treasury Bills".

The RBI has the authority to maintain the ways and means advances to both the Central Governments and State Governments. The ways and means is a divice to the governments for borrowing the money from the RBI. The RBI will make temporary advances to bridge the gap between the receipts and payments of the State and Central Government affairs. The maximum maturity period of these advances in three months. The Central Government will issue the *adhoc* treasury bills for adjusting the deficit in the ways and means account. The ways and means advances to the State Governments are subjected to certain conditions. They are—

(a) clean advances
(b) secured advances
(c) special advances

The clear advance means the advance is made by the RBI to various State Governments without any collateral security. The secured advance is made by the RBI to the State Governments against the pledge of the Central Government securities. The special advance is a facility granted by the RBI to the State Government. These advances are offered by the RBI to various State Governments on interest basis which will change from time-to-time.

The RBI sanctions not only the ways and means advances but also overdrafts to various State Governments. The overdrafts are the excess limits of the ways and means. On the overdrafts the RBI may charge interest above the bank rate. Almost all the States have been utilising this facility. The major function of the RBI is to issue the management and administration of the public debt. To render this services the RBI charges a commission from to Central and State Governments.

4. Foreign exchange control authority: The RBI's another major function is to control the foreign exchange reserves position from time-to-time. It maintains the stability of the external value of the rupee through its domestic policies and foreign market. The RBI has the full authority to regulate the market as presented below:

(a) to monitor the foreign exchange control
(b) to prescribe the exchange rate system
(c) to maintain a better relation between rupee and other currencies
(d) to interact with the foreign counterparts
(e) tó manage the foreign exchange reserves

It administers the FERA. In 1973 it is replaced by the FEMA (Foreign Exchange Management Act) which would be consistent with full capital account convertibility with the policies of the Central Government.

The RBI administers the control through the authorised forex dealers. The RBI is the custodian foreign exchange reserves. The foreign exchange is previous and it takes the responsibility of the better utilisation.

5. Promoting authority: The RBI's function is to look after the welfare of the financial system. It renders the promotion services to strengthen the banking and financial structure. It helps in monitoring the savings and diverting them towards the productive channel. Thus the economic development can be achieved after the nationalisation of the commercial banks. The RBI has taken a number of series of activities in the following sectors to develop the economy of the nation:

(a) Agriculture Sector
(b) Industrial Sector
(c) Lead Bank Scheme
(d) Cooperative Sector

The agriculture sector has been facing the financial problem. It occupies an important role in Indian economy. The RBI has been rendering the services to the agriculture sector by providing the credit flow. The RBI Act also emphasise the need to support the agriculture sector for the better output of the commodities.

The RBI appointed a Deputy Governor especially for providing the rural credit. The RBI has conducted an in-depth analysis on the problems of the rural credit. It has conducted an All India Rural Credit Survey in 1954. It was followed by studies of India Rural Credit Review Committee which was formed in 1986. The RBI fully involves in providing short-term finance at a concessional rate for seasonal agricultural operations and marketing of crops. It contributes to the debentures of Land Development Banks. It helps the agriculture sector through the cooperative institutions for the long and short-term finances in the form of the National Agricultural Credit and Fund (long-term) and the National Agriculture Stabilisation Fund. It established especially for the agriculture sector in July 1963, a separate entity known as the NABARD. The NABARD was established for providing the medium and long-term finance for the agriculture sector. The agricultural finance corporation was established by the RBI to look after the welfare of the farmers.

The RBI has been playing an important role in the industrial sector. The RBI has established all the special development institutions to undertake the welfare of the industrial sector at Central and State levels. It has been rendering the services for promoting several financial institutions. The RBI took initiative steps for the establishment of the Unit Trust of India. A number of institutions have been established and also they have been rendering services such as guarantees, technical consultancy etc. only because of the efforts of the RBI.

The Head Bank Schemes were proposed and implemented by the RBI. It has been acting as a leader in sponsoring the scheme. The RBI has the statutory authority to grant the licences. Therefore, it has been expanding the branches with an appropriate geographical distribution of bank branches.

The RBI has taken a step in 1962 to ensure the security of deposits with the banks. Hence, it took an initiative in the setting up of the Deposit Insurance Corporation.

Monetary Policy of the RBI

Every nation government objective is to stabilise the economy by framing the policy matters. The RBI treats the monitory policy as a weapon. The aim of the planning is growth. Social justice and stability are the most important factors in a planned economy. The objective of the monetary policy is to alleviate the economic development of a country. It has been encouraging the sectoral and overall development of the social justice. It is concerned with the control of credit and money supply with reference to the seasonal requirements for credit. The credit expansion process will be undertaken by the light of price irritations without considering the industrial output. The monitory policy is able to avoid the waste resources and it creates an environment for the better employment opportunities. The policy also helps to eradicate poverty and regional imbalances. It strives from the self-sufficiency.

Monetary policy aims to boost the exports. The policy had done a programme of food procurement operations. The steps have been taken to deregulate the interest rates. The policy concentrates for introducing flexibility, encouraging, diversification, promoting more competitive environment and importing greater discipline.

Techniques of the Monitory Control

The monitory policy is basically concerned with the regulation of money supply and interest rates. The policy describes various control and techniques to stabilise the Indian economy. The techniques are presented below:

1. Open market operations,
2. Refinance and rediscounting,
3. Bank rate,
4. Credit planning,

5. Regulation of interest rates,
6. Credit norms,
7. Credit authorisation scheme,
8. Selective credit controls,
9. Credit rationing,
10. CRR, and
11. SLR.

The above techniques were not used equally and actively in the past some of the important techniques are eradicated here.

1. Open market operations: The Open market operations are actively used in USA, UK and many other countries. Open market operation deals with the purchase and sale of government securities. The RBI has the authority to monitor the reserve positions of the banks yield on government securities and cost of bank credit. This technique is a powerful weapon in the hands of the RBI. The RBI may not restrict the quantity and maturity of the government securities in buying and selling and to hold it. The bank has the authority to conduct the open market operation in treasury bills, Central Government securities and State Government securities. But actually the transactions are carried out in the name of Central Government securities. It does not purchase them against cash. It purchases and sells the government securities from time-to-time with surplus funds of the IDBI, NABARD and EXIM bank. The open market operations are performed according to the objectives of the monetary and fiscal policy. The objectives of the policy are presented below:

(a) to control the reserves of the banks,
(b) to maintain stability in the government securities market,
(c) to make bank rate more effective,
(d) to facilitate the government borrowing programmes,
(e) to provide smooth flow of credit in seasonal requirement basis.

The open market operations are carried out by the RBI for the purpose of debt management. But the government securities market is not well-organised. The RBI has recognised the open market operations as one of the important monetary policy tools in stabilising the Indian economy. The RBI has taken a large number of measures to develop the open market operations. Therefore, the coupon rates of the government securities have been raised and thus made the market more competitive. The open market operations have helped in regulating the flow of bank credit to the private sector more effectively.

2. Refinance and bank rate: The RBI is the premier bank in India and it provides the financial accommodation to the banking sector—The industrial finance sector and cooperative banks sector. It provides the finance provision in the form of rediscounting bills, promissory notes, loans and advances etc. The bank rate is the most important factor in refinancing and rediscounting the facilities. The bank rate is defined by the RBI Act, Section 49 as "the standard rate at which the banks prepared to buy and rediscount bills of exchange or other commercial papers". In the olden days the financial accommodation was made by the RBI to the banking sector at the bank rate. The bank rate is charged by the RBI for various sectors at different rates. The bank rate and cost of refinance are used to regulate the volume of resources of the banks and other financial institutions. The refinance policy has to be kept in mind about the seasonal requirements of funds for various sectors. The major changes will arise in the refinance policy of the RBI from time-to-time.

3. Cash Reserve Ratio (CRR): The commercial banks should follow the guidelines issued by the RBI from time-to-time on various aspects. As per the norms every bank should keep a fraction of their deposit liabilities in the form of liquid cash. The system is known as the "Fractional reserve banking system". The RBI utilises the CRR as a weapon to ensure the safety and liquidity of deposits of the banking sector. The CRR has become an important tool for regulating the lending capacity of the banks. The RBI uses the two important financial weapons for controlling the credit control in the country. These two financial weapons are known as "Cash Reserve Ratio and Statutory Liquidity Ratio". The Cash Reserve Ratio means, the cash which banks have to maintain with the RBI as certain percentage of their demand and time liabilities. The RBI has the authority to change. The CRR from time-to-time according to the market situations. The CRR is also applicable to various NRI deposits account. The RBI has the power to impose penalty interest rates if any banks fails to the requirement of the prescribed CRR. The RBI disallows the refinance and rediscount of bills for the defaulted bank in the CRR.

4. Statutory Liquidity Ratio (SLR): Another financial weapon to control the credit flow in an economy is Statutory Liquidity Ratio in the hands of the RBI. The RBI frequently uses this ratio to monitor and control the banks. The SLR is the ratio that every bank keep cach in hand, balance in current account with the SBI, the balances with other counterparts and the RBI. It also includes gold and approved securities. The SLR is the most important ratio in the banking sector. The SLR is also applicable to the cooperative banks and non-scheduled banks and regional rural banks. The norms are applicable to foreign currency accounts (non-residents) and non-residents rupee account (external) deposits. The RBI has the authority to change the SLR according to the market movements. An increase in the SLR is possible only through the expenditure of the private sector. The SLR involves in distribution of the bank resources in favour of the government sector.

5. Credit Planning: The credit plan was introduced by the RBI in 1967-68. It is an innovation tool for the credit management. It is made as a product of economic planning. It is aimed to work as a tool in the macro credit management of the economy. It works in a specified environment. It is unique tool of credit management. The objectives of the credit planning are presented below:

(a) to facilitate the flow of funds to a desired level.
(b) to facilitate the flow of funds to desired sectors, specified areas, purposes, uses.
(c) the quantum and qualitative aspects of a fund flow.

The credit plan is an input from the national monetary plan, fiscal plan and economic plan. The credit plan will be prepared at national levels, and district level. The process of credit plan involves at the bank level. Every bank is required to prepare the realistic annual credit budget incorporating the estimates of volume and growth of deposits and demands for credit. The budget is revised in the light of changes in credit policy and banking trends. All the banks, their budgets are submitted to the RBI for its finalisation. The credit budget will be finalised in every May/June of the year. The RBI makes continuous monitoring and control of these budget aspects.

6. Regulation of interest rates: The RBI has the authority to directly regulate the interest rates on bank deposits and credit. The bank rate technique has been very weak till 1999. Basically a change in the bank rate is reflected in all market rates of interest and help to achieve the objects of the monetary policy. The bank rate has lost its significance. It used to solve the situation by regulating the market rates of interest directly. The RBI has been fixing all the deposits rate of interest directly. The RBI has been fixing all the deposit rates of commercial banks and their lending rates. The cooperative banks deposits rates have come under the regulation in 1974. The 1991 policy has changed the entire picture of the market with the introduction of the deregulation of interest rates.

7. Credit norms: The RBI has undertaken the responsibility for the direct administration of the interest rates in the economy when the bank rate technique weakened. The monetary policy objective is to quantify the control of credit and credit ceiling. The credit technique was introduced in November 1973 by the RBI. The RBI has been stipulating certain targets for the credit distribution to various sectors.

8. Credit authorisation scheme: The RBI has introduced credit authorisation scheme in November 1965. The scheme was promoted to regulate the heavy amount of borrowers. The scheme is aimed to sanction the financial assistance for short-term needs of the corporate sector. The objectives of the scheme have been presented below:

(a) to regulate the credit to control the inflation.
(b) to impose the financial discipline on the commercial borrowers.
(c) to provide the credit for the productive ways.
(d) to ensure that the credit is supplied in accordance with the planning.
(e) to curb the monopolistic ways for the credit sanctions.

The scheme is applicable to the commercial banks, public sector banks, cooperative banks and private sectors. It is also applied to the long and short-term loans. It operates for more than 20 years and the RBI decided to withdraw after the review of its working. It is replaced by a new scheme known as Credit Monitory Arrangement. According to this scheme, a credit proposal for Rs.5 crores and above should be submitted to the RBI. As a working capital more than Rs.2 crores should also be submitted to the RBI for the term loans as a credit proposal.

9. Selective credit control: The selective credit control is a popular technique. It is widely used in our economy. The seasonal nature of our environment and the inflation pressure have made it useful in our context. The selective credit control technique changes the composition of the credit. These controls are used to reduce the supply of credit and prevent the speculative holdings in sensitive commodities. The commodities such as paddy, pulse, oilseeds, vanaspati, cotton and sugar influence the speculation on motives. These credit controls are applied in the credit given for trading in shares. These credit controls are now applied both to commercial and cooperative banks. These techniques are applied to the private sector trading but the public sector trading is not covered by these control techniques. The RBI applies these controls in three forms:

(A) Fixation of margin requirements
(B) Fixation of separate minimum lending rates
(C) The fixation of ceiling on flow of credit

The assets and liabilities of the RBI are presented below:

(Rs. In crores)

Assets and Liabilities	1990-91	1999-2000	2000-01	2001-02
Issue Department	53807	1,92,532	212937	2375
Banking Department	66884	168654	172028	1729
	120691	353188	384965	4104

The break-up values of other particulars are presented in the preceding pages:

Assets and Liabilities of the RBI (Issue Department)[35]

(Rs. in crores)

Liabilities	1990-91	1999-2000	2000-01	2001-02 (Up to Jan.)
1. Notes in circulation	53784	192483	212858	237484
2. Notes hold in banking department	23	51	79	31
Total Liabilities	53807	192534	212937	237515

(Rs. in crores)

Assets	1990-91	1999-2000	2000-01	2001-02 (Up to Jan.)
1. Gold coin and bullion	6654	10598	10324	11242
2. Foreign securities	200	72700	91700	123700
3. Rupee coin	29	102	78	107
4. Government of India	46924	109134	110835	10246
	53807	192534	212937	23751

Assets and Liabilities of the RBI (Banking)

(Rs. in crores)

Liabilities	1990-91	1999-2000	2000-01	2001-02
1. Deposits	38542	85551	87828	70618
2. Central Government	61	500	100	101
3. State Governments	33	41	41	41
4. Scheduled banks	33484	77781	76939	60854
5. Scheduled State Cooperative Banks	244	816	978	1099
6. Non-scheduled Cooperative Banks	13	45	61	42
7. Other banks	88	246	918	1276
8. Others	4619	7122	8791	7206
9. Other liabilities	28342	74102	84199	102338
	66884	160654	172028	172956

(Rs. in crores)

Assets	1990-91	1999-00	2000-01	2001-02
1. Notes and coins	23	52	80	31
2. Balances held at abroad	4008	52313	92600	99161
3. Loans and Advances				
(a) Central Government		982	-	922
(b) State Government	916	7519	4395	8035
(c) Scheduled Banks	8169	9513	5980	1927
(d) Non-Scheduled Banks	38	15	27	25
(e) IDBI	3705	1740	1440	1110
(f) NABARD	3328	5884	6580	585
(g) EXIM Bank	745	697	617	53
(h) Others	1616	11541	9104	420
4. Bills discounted	41670	62660	43127	3668
5. Other assets	2666	7738	8078	617
	66884	160654	172028	1729

BANKING INSTITUTIONS

Introduction

Bank deals mainly with money and credit. They are the manufacturers of money. Industrial and economic evolution would not have accrued in the absence of banks. They play the significant role in the shaping and in the advancing of modern societies. They have contributed a lot in advancing the developed countries. They are the architecture of the digital economy. This serves the country in a number of ways. They help in the proper use of surplus funds. They encourage trade and industry. They provide the habit of thrift, create credit and capital. They distribute the funds equitably, reduce cyclical fluctuations. The industrial development will not be possible without the help of the banks. They purchase and sell money and credit. Creation of credit is a special function of banks.

Banks are the oldest, biggest and fastest growing financial mediators in India. They provide the various types of financial services to customers. Their objective is to make profits. They deal in other peoples money. They are working for the principles of profit maximisation and liquidity management. They predominantly follow the liquidation approach. Their business is subject to seasonal variation.

Banks have been defined by several authors. Some of the definitions are given below.

According to Section 5(b) of Indian Banking Act, 1949, "Banking means the accepting for the purpose of lending or investment of deposits of money from the public repayable on demand and otherwise and withdraw able by cheques, draft orders and otherwise".

Sayer has defined the bank "Bankers are not merely traders in money, but also important manufacturers of money".

According to Prof. Hart, "A banker is one who in the ordinary course of his business, receives money which he repays by borrowing cheques of persons from whom or on whose account he receive it".

According to Section 5(c) of Indian Banking Act, 1949, "Banking company means any company which transacts the business of banking".

Characteristics: The Bank accept deposits from the public and grant loans. The main characteristics of bankers are given below:

(a) Bank accepts deposits of the savers.
(b) The deposits are advanced in the form of loans.
(c) The money will be disbursed through credit instruments or in other modes.
(d) They render utility services to the customers.
(e) They must have a geographical place to carry their business.

Functions: The function of banks are classified as:

1. Basic functions
2. Agents functions
3. Other functions

Basic Functions: The functions are the main income sources of money. Every bank must follow these functions. The basic functions of a bank:

(a) Accepting of deposits.
(b) Advancing of loans.

Deposits are the most important element in the banking sector. They collect surplus money from the public. The deposits will be mobilised by banks. The money collected from the public are presented by banks and interest will be paid by the banks. The depositors are benefited and their amount of money is safe at the banks. In this situation the banks can earn a sum of money on the amounts, collected by them. The banks create credit on the basis of deposits. The level of creation of credit depends upon the amount of deposits. The banks have introduced different types of deposits to suit the various requirements of the depositors. The types of deposit schemes are briefly discussed below:

(a) Fixed deposits
(b) Current account
(c) Savings Bank account
(d) Money multiplier account
(e) Other accounts

Under this scheme the bank mobilises the deposits which are repayable after the expiry of three months to five years. The banks are free to use the deposits for a certain period. They grant higher rate of interest on these certain period of time for more remunerative purposes. The small savers will get more benefits from this scheme. The small customers are unable to make investments in the industrial securities market. They do not want to take risk from the securities market. A large number of savers prefers this mode of investments. The fixed deposit has become more lucrative as rate of interest has increased up to 10%. At present situation they offer only 8% rate of interest. The customers can earn more by combining the fixed deposits account with recurring deposits account. The interest as FDR will be credited to the recurring deposit account.

The amount of fixed deposit cannot generally be withdrawn before the expiry of the period of deposits. However, bank can advance money of the security of fixed deposits if fixed depositors are not willing to withdraw the amounts deposited. Recently some banks have introduced various types of other deposits which are a slight modification of the fixed deposit. The rate of interest is higher than that of other deposits in case of "whole life deposits".

The fixed deposits are also known as term deposit. Fixed deposits have grown in importance and popularity in India during recent years. These deposits constitute more than half of the total bank deposits. The rates of interest and other terms and conditions are regulated by the RBI. The RBI revised the rate of interest on fixed deposits several times. The main object of the step was to make bank deposits more attractive as compared to other savings instruments.

Current account is more beneficial to those who withdraw several times from the account of deposits. No interest is paid on this account. Cheques are generally used for withdrawing a certain amount from the deposits. Current accounts are more useful to the businessmen. They can produce this account as an evidence of revenue for the assessment of income tax. The businessmen are not required to keep with them a large amount of money. He will make payments by issuing cheques to the parties. The cheques can be transferred to any person for the settlement of dues. The current account is opened subject to the conditions. Generally no interest is paid on the amount of deposits, balances and no charges are required for maintaining such account. Current accounts are more useful to the businessman, firms, companies and individuals.

Savings Bank Account: Savings bank account is useful to middle and low income groups. They can save certain amount during a certain period. It is a flexible account. In this account the depositors can withdraw money about thrice a weak The account-holder can deposit money at any time. The interest is calculated on the minimum balance maintained each month. A person wishing to open savings bank account will have to fill up a form. He has to furnish his specimen signature. A pass book will be issued to the account holder. If the depositor wants to withdraw money he must fill up a withdrawal form and must present his book for payment. Now some banks extended the cheques facility to the savings bank customers.

Money multiplier account: The persons who are interested to deposit money for more money at short period of time. Under this scheme the amount of interest is higher on this deposit. The depositors can withdraw the accumulated money after the stipulated period. The depositor can withdraw the whole amount either lump sum or instalments. If the depositors opted for instalments higher amount is returned to the person. This is most suitable for old age provision.

Other accounts: There are so many saving deposit accounts like recurring deposits accounts, private savings accounts and special savings accounts. Recurring deposits accounts are more popular in India. A fixed amount is deposited at a regular interval and it attracts accumulated at compound rate of interest. Under this scheme the interest and the principal amount is returned to the depositor after the fixed period. The rate of interest is higher that of S.B. account and lower that of fixed deposits account. It is a great source of stimulating short deposits. These schemes are designed to meet the requirements of education and marriage.

Advancing of loans: Bank deals with money of other persons. Bank does not lend its own money. It is the others, money in which it deals. The advances of bank may be granted in the form of loans, overdraft cash credit, credit discounting bills of exchange. The bank advances loan more than the amount of deposits, because all the loans are not withdrawn immediately. Therefore, the loan creates deposits. The bank creates loans and loans create deposits while advancing loans. The bank gives priority to safety and next profitability. In advancing loans the principles of investments safety, liquidity and profitability, diversification and social objectives are considered. Generally the bank advances in the following ways:

(a) Loans
(b) Cash credit
(c) Overdraft
(d) Discounting of bills

(a) Loans: Loans are important element of the profitability of the banks. They are made by debiting the customers loan account and crediting his current account. The customers are allowed to withdraw the loan amount by instalments. The regular customers are permitted loans by crediting to their accounts. Proper care is taken while granting the loans. All of the loans require a proper security or mortgage. Sometimes only the personal security is required for advancing the loans. The interest is charged on the loan amount. Loans involve low operating cost than any other kind of loans. Loans are given against the securing of movable and immovable assets.

(b) Cash Credit: Cash credit is the another method of advances made by banks. In this method the banker grants his customer to borrow money upto a certain sanctioned limit. The bank requires security of certain bonds, promissory notes, shares, other commodities. Sometimes commodities are kept in the possession of the bank in its godowns. The borrower is charged interest on the amount of advance. Generally the cash credit system provides adequate amount for meeting essential expenditures of the business. The large amount of credit is granted through credit system because the whole amount of credit is not required to be withdrawn at once. It is the best method to suit the requirements of the business community. Generally raw materials are purchased on the basis of this credit. This type of loans are mostly short-term credit. The borrowers can withdraw the sanctioned loan according to their convenient. The interest will be charged on the dates of withdrawals of the amount.

(c) Overdraft: Bank overdraft is allowed to current account holders. The current account holders may be allowed to overdraw. The overdraft facility is more advantages to the customers because interest is charged only on the amount withdrawn. There is no need to provide collateral security for the facility of overdraft. It can be used at anytime of requirements. It is used for long-term purposes. It is the most useful form of loans to commercial and industrial units to avail from time to time.

The overdraft will be granted by the bank with the mutual agreements with the customer and bank. This form of advances has undoubtedly more benefits.

(d) Discounting of bills: It is the one of the methods of advances made by the banks. The banks involve in discounting of bills. They discount only clear and reputed bills. Generally the goods are sold on the basis of bills of exchange which are drawn by.

Other functions: It involves a number of miscellaneous functions. They act as a catalyst, underwriters mediators of their customers in business. Knowing of the financial position of the parties is very common whenever any person is willing to know about the financial position of a business unit. The concerned bank can furnish necessary information. Bank also acts as underwriter of shares and securities of their customers. Banks collect various information and statistics of the nation. Banks protect the valuable ornaments, jewels, documents, deeds for safe custody to protect the articles from theft and fire. Banks issue letters of credit for their customers. The banks also help in foreign exchange market.

The Role of Bank in Financial System: The role of banks would be easily assured from the progress and development of the globe. The industrial and economic evolution would have occurred with the presence of banks. Banks played an important role in the shaping and designing of modern in societies. Banks have contributed a lot in advancing the developed countries. Banks serve the country in different ways. Banks in increasing productivity advancing business and in the proper use of idle funds. They encourage industry and trade, create and educe cyclical fluctuations. The industrial development will not be possible without the existence of banks. We cannot imagine the existence of the present society without banks seller of goods and is accepted by the purchaser. Therefore, the purchaser accepts the credit conditions and pays the amount of dues after due period. In this situation if the seller is willing to discount the bill he can do so from his bank and obtain the amount of discount. Sometimes bills of exchange can be made by Railway receipt bills of lading. This form of loans is becoming very popular in India. The commercial banks can rediscount these bills of exchange from the RBI. The bills of exchange can be transferred from one bank to another. There is no need of collateral security in discounting the bills of exchange. The bill market is increasing gradually as the industrial activities are increasing.

Agents Function: The banks are the agents of their regular customers. They act as trustees, attorneys, administrators of their customers. The banks collect and pay their cheques on behalf of their customers. They collect subscriptions, rents, income tax, insurance premium of their customers. A nominal commission is charged for these services. They act as brokers for purchasing and selling of securities on behalf of their customers. They get commission for this purpose. They advice on legal matters. They act as administrators. They also collect the interest and dividend of their customers. The banks plays an important role in the construction of a modern community. The following factors will help us about the importance of the banks:

1. Increase productivity
2. Helpful to industry and trade
3. Better use of funds
4. Expansion of business
5. Reduces regional disparities
6. Cultivate saving habits
7. Creates credit
8. Capital formation
9. Economic development

The natural resources of a nation will be fully utilised with the help of banks. The bank helps the society to produce wealth by lending money to producers. The banks provide adequate supply of funds to acquire raw materials machines for maximising the production. Banks may divert the idle funds for productive purposes.

The banks are always helpful to industry and trade by providing loans and advances. They arrange the required credit as demanded by the corporate sector. The cheques, hundies, promissory notes and bills have provided adequate funds for better functioning of industry. These credit instruments are properly handled by banks. The business community will get the funds from the banks when their funds are locked up and are not in a position to settle the transactions. The finished goods and raw materials can be used as securities for obtaining loans. The banks provide adequate amount for short-term and long-term requirements of industries. The banks help in promoting the new business enterprises. The new enterprises are facing the financial problem to obtain raw materials and labour etc. Some sectors are given priorities in securing loans. The industries depend mostly on banks for their developments.

The surplus funds of the community are channelised towards productive purposes by the banks. They invite various types of saving scheme. The surplus cash balances pooled by banks capital are circulated to the community. The financial circulation of funds provide the industry more flexible to reduce their financial costs. The demand for the funds depends upon the seasons. The banks will grant the loans according to the seasonal situations to different units. The funds of the society flow from one individual to another, one geographical area to another according to the needs of the persons of the society.

The banks provide sufficient funds to the business community therefore, the trade and industry will expand their activities with the help of banks. Banks provide more funds to purchase the raw material and to pay other expenses of the expansion of credit creates the full employment. It leads to inflation. If the credit supply reduces the business and economic activities decline the increase of financial resources the corporate sector is able to acquire more raw material semi-finished goods or finished goods. Therefore, the business community can sell more goods than they can originally sell from their resources. There is a relationship between bank credit and economic activities. The bank can accelerate with a faster speed of the business activities. In the absence of the banking system it would have been slower in the business activities. The accelerated trade cycle leads to higher profit to the corporate sector.

The banks will provide the financial assistance to the corporate sector irrespective of their location of industries. The banks provide assistance to all areas. The regional disparity is a bridged. The disparity will be minimised by operating the new branches and advancing loans. The surplus funds of developed centre are flown to the centres of deficit. The less and ignored developed areas get the opportunities of development. The banks will distribute the fund equitably to all areas. The funds are transferred to where it can be more utilised and effectively deployed. The balanced development of a nation is possible only with the support of banks.

The banks can cultivate the habit of savings among the public. The banks are more powerful in attracting the small savings by a wide network of the branches. The small amounts from the millions of account holders will make crores of rupees. These amounts of funds are available at the disposal of the banks. The persons who are unable to utilise their funds in a proper way can get higher returns by depositing in the banks. The banks provide safety, liquidity and profit to their funds. The banks are just parking place for idle funds of the community. The idle funds are properly utilised by banks. The depositors are encouraged for savings by paying a higher rate of interest for their savings.

The banks create credit on the availability of their deposits and loans. The creation of credit level depends upon the level of deposits with them. The banks invite more deposits by allowing higher rate of interest. The bank can create credit not only on the basis of deposits but also on the volume of loans. Because the total advances are not granted in cash at a time. The loans amount will be credited to the individual account and they are permitted to withdraw the money at the borrowers flexibility. The loan deposits are created in exchanges of debts. The banks are more powerful in creation of credit.

Banks are the financial nerves of the business community. They utilise the fund of other persons for granting loans to another. They invite the deposits from the savers and lend the money persons. They invest the accumulated funds of the society in a productive way. The bank credit provides more financial muscle to industries and business community. They invite saving at remunerative way. The idle funds are mobilised and in active capital of the society is perished. The unused resources are canalised for more productive purposes. The capability of production of the society is enhanced. The financial and economic development of the nation is accelerated. The financial resources are properly utilised. The banks generally provide assistance to the new enterprises by way of capital formation. The capital formation is the most important element in the economic development of a country.

A developing country definitely gets a maximum assistance by the banks. The unutilised resources are fully utilised with the help of the bank. Credit regional disparities are minimised production and employment activities are carried on by an accelerated peace economic activities are reached to the peak level to boost the development of industries. The banks can open branches even in remote areas. Rural and semi-urban areas are developed. The expansion of the banking facilities influence the total structure of the nation. The new entrepreneurs get the chances of establishing new productive units.

Kinds of banks: A single bank is unable to serve all the needs of the country. Therefore, the various types of banks have formed for selling different needs of society. The specialisation has also been required by the banking industry. Specialised banks have been established to fulfil the need of persons. Some banks serve the various purposes of the community. Some banks have been specialised in short-term loans. Others are interested in foreign trade and others are related to agriculture or industry. There are different kinds of banks which are discussed below:

1. Commercial Banks
2. Industrial Banks
3. Agricultural Banks
4. Exchange Banks
5. Central Banks
6. Savings Banks
7. Miscellaneous Banks

1. Commercial Banks: Commercial banks are engaged in performing the basic banking business. They accept the deposits of public and grant loans and advances. They mainly grant the short-term loans only. They unable to grant the long-term loans because the depositors may call their money at any moment. Their aim is to protect the interest of the depositors. The commercial banks also known as public banks. The commercial banks deal with them for their deposits and short-term borrowings. The commercial banks are the most important kind of banks and collect the idle funds of the public. They fulfil the needs of the commercial class. At present the time deposits have been encouraged by offering attractive rates of interest. Therefore, they were able to grant long-term loans. The long-term loans create the possibility of bad debts. Therefore, they discourage the long-term finance to avoid the bad debts. The banks are competent in providing of short-term loans. The traders and businessmen can get short-term loans to purchase the raw materials and machines. The regular financial requirements are fulfilled by the commercial banks.

The commercial banks accept the deposits and grants the loans. They occupy an important role in the development of a country. These will fulfil the objectives of achievement of balanced growth. Balanced growth will be achieved by through reducing the regional disparities. The functions of commercial banks will be different according to the needs of the country. The commercial banks are free to grant loans and advances to the agriculture sector after nationalisation of commercial banks. But they have to maintain proper balance between safety and profitability. The political and economic climate of the country determine the direction of role of the functions. The commercial banks always invest fund in non-speculative activities. In some situations the commercial banks permit loans for those activities which may provide more profits. Therefore, the commercial banks should avoid these activities because the confidence of public may be lost. The credibility is the most important factor in the banking industry. If the public looses its credibility in a particular commercial banks it will suffer heavily. Therefore, the consequences are declining deposits and lending capacity of a bank will go down. The bank will be collapsed. The commercial banks can create credit. They issue credit instruments, which will be treated on par with currency by masses. They are known as bank money. The commercial banks will settle the transactions without payments of the cash but with the help of cheques. All the cheques are not paid at the bank counter. They nullified and settled on the basis of book keeping entries. They are able to provide more credit than the amount of deposits held by them.

2. Industrial Banks: The industrial banks are also known as development banks. These banks meet the requirement of different industries. They deploy the funds in long-term loans. Therefore, commercial banks are unable to grant the long-term loans. Therefore, these development banks have been established for this purpose. These banks have got long-term deposits and can deploy the funds on long-term basis. They provide the financial resources to the industrial community. They have financial experts to study the object, investment proposal and render the advisory services to the banks. They can understand the intricacies of the long-term investments to the industries. These banks are appointing the experts as the nominee director in the board of directors of the industries to which loans are permitted by the banks help. The industries by permitting loans directly to them by underwriting their shares and debentures. Therefore, the capital and loans are provided by the industrial banks. These banks are funded with their own shares capital and issues debentures and bonds. They also get the financial support from the Government of India and international financial institutions. They have mutual agreements with other financial institutions at the time of disposal of loans. These banks are playing an important role in rapid industrialisation depends upon the country. The peace of industrialisation depends upon the speedy disposal of these banks. These banks evaluate the projects, appraise the projects and give suggestions to the industrialists. They will submit the feasibility reports for consideration of financial assistance to the board of directors. The banks inquire and investigate the future of the industry soundness of financial investment and utilities of the projects. The industrial units also approachs these banks for underwriting of their issue of shares. If the shares and debentures are not fully subscribed by the public within a limited period. These banks will come into the picture and take up the residual amount of share and debentures which are not subscribed by the public. The new industrial organisations are benefited through underwriting of securities and direct financial aids. These banks advise the industries, financial and non-financial areas because they are experts in those matters. These banks assist financial support as well as they suggest various types of sources for raising funds. They can explain where the funds are available? At what rate of interest? At what time to refund the debt? They have been specialised in financial matters and able to render valuable suggestions to the corporate sector. The functions of these banks can be divided into three kinds:

1. Accepting of long-term deposits.
2. Deployment of funds on long-term basis.
3. Advices and consultancy.

The fundamental functions of any type of bank is to accept the term deposits. The term deposits are the oxygen to banks. These deposits are attracted by paying higher rate of interest. The deposits of the public and other financial institutions are often invited. These banks are mainly established for providing financial assistance to the industrial sector. They grant direct financial aids to the industries. These banks are established for granting long-term loans generally on the mortgage of land machine and other fixed assets. But in some situations they also grant the loans for short-term credit. These short-term loans will be utilised for purchase of raw materials and fulfilling short-term commitments. These banks have first hand information about the financial and economic climate of the nation at the macro and micro level. These banks are well-competent to give advises in the financial and non-financial areas of the corporate sector. These banks are more popular in USA, Germany and Japan. These banks also contributed a lot to the economic development of the country. For Example : IDBI, ICICI, IFCI, SFCs etc.

3. Agricultural Banks: The commercial banks are unable to cater the needs of agriculture. The commercial banks concentrate on the financial needs of the business community. Therefore, there is a need to concentrate towards agriculture sector. Agriculture banks have been set up to assist the agriculturists the cultivation of land is full of risk. The investments in agriculture does not always yield better returns. Hence there should be certain specialised institutions which may endeavour to meet the financial requirements of agricultural machinery equipments like, tractors, pump sets in long-term investments. These assets will be purchased through long-term loans as the land development and buying more land requires long-term investments. The short-term credit is required to meet general requirements like buying of seeds and manure and payments of labour expenses. The cooperative banks and land mortgage banks were established. These banks are assisting agriculture banks which caters the financial requirements of the entire agriculture sector in India. The agriculture sector needs are fulfilled by the following banks:

(a) Cooperative banks, and
(b) Land mortgage banks.

Cooperative banks are established to fulfil the needs of agriculture sector. The short-term needs are cater by the cooperative banks. In India there are three forms of cooperative banks exists. They are presented below:

(a) State cooperative banks,
(b) Central cooperative banks, and
(c) Primary credit societies.

The above banks are functioning at state district and village levels respectively. In past the financing of agriculture sector was made by the money lenders and indigenous bankers. But there were a number of defects in such financing. No other institution came for assistance to provide short-term finance to the farmers. The agriculture finance involves inherent risk. Therefore, the cooperative banks came to the rescue of the farmers from the clutches of the money lenders and indigenous bankers. The cooperative societies are the association of the borrowers. They pool their resources and can borrow from the mobilised funds on the personal securities. The cooperative society gets the power to raise the funds from the open market. Basically the primary societies borrow from the Central cooperative banks. Therefore, the Central cooperative banks borrow the money from the state cooperative banks. The primary cooperative societies get sufficient funds to cater the need of their members. But the societies are not in a position to continue for ever and they should have an independent powers and authorities. The Central cooperative banks are in such a position to help the members and non-members according to their situation. These banks are useful in other ways. They mobilise the deposits from the rural areas. They encourage to saving and train them for self-development. The role of central cooperative banks has been expanded and diversified. They can borrow the funds from the commercial banks, state cooperative bank, central bank at a lower rate of interest. Therefore, they accumulate adequate funds for the advancing to the agriculture sectors. At present the cooperative banks are sanctioning the loans to small scale industries and export institutions. The cooperative banks are emerging as financial nerves of the digital economy.

The land development bank is also known as Development Bank. The bank grant primarily loans as the mortgage of land for the purchase of land and development of land. The bank acquires funds from the government and public issuing shares and debentures. The debentures issued by the bank backed by the securities. The bank sanctions the loans for productive purpose. Only the financial experts of the bank evaluate the project thoroughly and reasonably. The bank will charge a reasonable rate of interest from the farmers. The other banks and financial institutions do not take the liabilities of granting loans at the mortgage of land, real estate, houses etc. These assets involve a complicated formalities and legal hurdles in the evaluation and transfer of these assets. These hurdles are taken up by the development banks. These banks are very useful in agricultural societies.

4. Exchange Banks: Exchange banks deal mainly with the foreign exchange. These banks are helpful in international trade. They will undertake the responsibility of settlement of foreign exchanges and make the foreign business. They involve in foreign exchange bills and manage it. They have opened the branches throughout the globe, an important locations to purchase foreign exchange. The commercial banks and other financial institutions are not able to conduct at this business transactions. These exchange banks know the intricacies of the foreign exchange (forex) market. They do perform the functions of commercial banks and also tactfully handle the foreign exchange business. The foreign exchange banks do arrange shipment, insurance and settlement of transactions. The exchange banks are highly specialised to handle the international transactions very smoothly. These banks purchase bills from the export oriented units and sell them to the importers will be realised in the form of bills. These bills are discounted by the exchange banks. The exporters will get the whole proceeds excluding the discounting commission from the exchange banks. The exporters need not wait till maturity of the bills. These banks carry on their business through their branch offices which are located throughout the globe. The transactions of the banks are made easy with the assistance of their branches. The importance of these banks are very crucial in minimising the fluctuations in exchange rate. The commercial banks are also now undertaking the business of forex market. They also opened branches or representatives in foreign countries to increase the business volume and smooth functioning of the transactions Foreign banks were dominating the business of forex markets in India. The forex market now dominated by the State Bank of India and other commercial banks.

5. Central Banks: The Central banks are the most important banks to govern national economy. They are fully involved to direct, guide, take steps, measure the economy of a nation. The economy of a nation depends upon the efficiency of the Central bank in that country. The Central bank was established to discharge functions of issue of notes and coins. They also involved in framing the monetary policies of the Central Government. The Union Government will implement its policies through the Central bank. The Central banks were primarily responsible for the issue of currency notes and coins. They were assigned the power of banks of issue or national banks. The Bank of England was the first bank to act as a Central bank. The Central bank got the momentum following the recommendations of the Brussels Conference in 1920. The Central bank act as bankers to the Central Government. They work as financial advisers to the government. These Central banks have vested the responsibilities of achieving full employment and the economic development of the nation. They are guiding force of the national economy and they are responsible for the development of money and the capital market in the country. The Central banks are required to strengthen the liquidity slovenly and proper functioning of the banking system in the country.

Saving banks deal with people deposits. These banks mobilise small savings from the community. The saving banks cultivate the habit of savings among the public. They encourage to increase the savings of the public. They are not permitted to grant the short-term loans like commercial banks. They need not maintain certain portion of their assets in liquid form. They usually invest their funds in the government securities. Every citizen is allowed to deposit their small savings in the savings bank. The depositors are provided a pass book. The pass book contains each and every transaction made by the customer. The account holders are not permitted to withdraw their amounts. The savings bank allows withdrawal twice a week. If the depositor wants to withdraw more than a specified amount the branch manager permission is required. The depositors are allowed a nominal rate of interest. The savings banks are the commercial banks in our country which allow with the facilities of time deposits. Post offices are also doing the same business in India. They cover rural and remote areas also.

7. Miscellaneous Banks: There are various other banks which render the specialised services to the public. The miscellaneous banks are categorised in:

(a) Investment Banks
(b) Acceptance Banks
(c) Merchant Banks
(d) Discount Houses

Investment banks deal with the controlling and distribution of capital. They were established in USA. They are very popular in western countries. The acceptance houses are highly specialised institutions. They were established in UK. The acceptance houses fully involved in discounting of bills. They accept the bills and provide finance to the business community. The merchant banks are involved into look after the welfare of the businessman. The merchants are selling goods in foreign countries. The international trade requires a highly specialised skills to handle the transactions very smoothly. The trade involves high risk and complications are available at every stage. All of these hurdles are easily met by these banks. The general businessman does not know these intricacies of the foreign trade. The discount houses are another specialised agencies. They are engaged in discounting the commercial bills. The discount houses discounts the commercial bills for very nominal commission and provide immense services to the business community. They are fully involved in bill of exchange of different businessman community. They are fully involved in bills of exchange of different businessmen of several countries. They issue shares and debentures to get adequate funds for smooth functioning of the business. They enjoy sometimes the arbitrage of discounting rates. They do their business throughout the globe through their branch offices and their business representatives.

Types of Commercial Banks: Commercial banks have been categorised into various categories of the banking system. They are classified into different ways. One classification of banks is presented below:

(a) Branch Banking
(b) Unit Banking

Another classification of banks are:

(a) Group Banking
(b) Chain Banking

They are also classified on the basis of merits:

(a) Deposits Banks
(b) Investment Banks/Mixed Banks

(a) Branch banking: Branch banking means a number of branch offices scattered throughout the country to look after the banking business. It refers to that banking system which assumes each bank as a single entity having one board of directors and one group of shareholders in the hole of the branches. In some situations, the branches may extend beyond the territories of the country and may spread over different countries. The policies and instructions are laid down by the head office and the branches are instrumental to implement the instructions. The branches undertake the business and perform the functions. In this banking system a single bank is able to transact the banking business in a broader way. At present the branch banking has become very popular. USA and European nations have developed branch banking system. In India it has also become very popular. All of the major commercial banks have opened their branches in rural and remote areas. The branch banking system has the following advantages:

1. They are involved in extensive coverage of business.
2. They are doing the business more efficiently without risk.
3. They do the business in large scale.
4. Rationalisation and scientific management is possible.
5. Investments can be made in diversified areas.
6. The personal bias and favouritism is avoided in this system.
7. The diversification of investment reduced the risk.
8. Non-performing assets may be reduced substantially.
9. The economies and operations are available in this system.
10. The financial stringencies are possible with the system.

Disadvantages: The branch banking system suffers from the certain disadvantages which are presented below:

1. This system ignore the needs of people.
2. The head office sometimes unable to understand the local.
3. The regional disparities will be increased.
4. Partiality will be shown while granting the loans.
5. The small customers may be ignored.
6. There is no proper control on branches.
7. Head office is holding all the powers.
8. The red-tapism and delay of decisions.
9. It leads to concentration of economic power in few.
10. Speculative activities may develop and favouritism may be exercised.

(b) Unit Banking: Unit banking refers that the business operations are carried out through a single office and at one place. The units are working within a limited area. The banking business is not carried on through the wide network of branches. Unit banking was very popular in USA. Branch banking operates through only one office. Unit banks are separate entities and have their own capital board of directors and shareholders. The area of the operation is very small. The unit banks understand the needs of the local people. These banks give first priority to the local requirement and their investment in the government securities. The local funds are used for local developments and the funds are not transferable to any other areas. The unit banks know the pulse of the local customers and know better to cater the needs of the local business community. The local industries agriculture get the opportunities for their development. Individual entrepreneurs are given personal attachment by the unit banks. The unit banks are very small, do not exist any problem relating to the management and control of the business. In unit banking there is no chance for frauds and irregularities. Unit banking also suffers for limited resources. The unit banking cannot expand their business. The banks are unable to earn maximum profits because of the scarcity of resources. The unit banks are liable to work in a limited area. The possibilities of survival are least. The cyclical fluctuations of business may severely hit the business. The economies of large scale are not available in this system. Unit banks are unable to achieve balanced growth. The unit banking system neglects the backward people where the financial assistance is much required to develop the nation. These banks suffers from the local influence to patronage the unworthy of the credit are granted. They suffer from numerical disadvantages.

(a) Group Banking: Another classification of banking system the commercial banks may be known as Group banking. The group banking has some special distinctive features. These banks are the direct outcome of the effects of the unit banking. In this system two more banks are brought directly or indirectly under the control of holding company. The holding company will coordinate all the things of the affairs. Group banks are very common in the USA. The group banking system has been emerged with the combination of the advantages of branch banking and unit banking. Each member bank maintains its identity and functions economically without losing the confidence of people. Each bank has its own board of directors and officers. The member bank can enjoy the experience and technical expertise of the holding company. The business can be expanded and profitability can be increased. The holding company provides the advertisement, support and standardises the accounting pattern. the member bank can avail of the services of the holding company. The member banks will get instructions from the holding company to carry the business very smoothly and effectively. Therefore, there are some intricacies in the group banking system. The grouping bank system operates as the principles of centralisation. Every decision will be taken by the holding company and there may not be any freedom to member bank. The member bank is only an instrumental to implement the policies of holding company. The holding control does not impact as the functioning of the member bank. In the group banking these will be possibilities of manipulation and speculation are higher. The failure of the member bank will adversely affect on other banks.

(b) Chain Banking: The chain banks were emerged in America and were very popular up to **1920**. In this banking system the individual banks are incorporated and brought under common control. There is no existence of holding company. Some persons are directors of two or more banking companies. The ownership is common in India. The managing agents were playing an important role and these were utilised by the resources chain members. The chain banking system enjoys the advantages on par with the group banking. It also suffer from the problems as in the case of group banking.

Deposits Banking: The another classifications of commercial banks are two kinds. They are categorised on the basis of deposits and investment. They are presented below:

(a) Deposit banking
(b) Investment banking
(c) Mixed banking

Deposits banking is the type of banking where the deposits are mobilised from the public. These banks are known as deposits banks. The deposits banks sanctioned the loans for the short-term loans. These loans are sanctioned to meet the needs of working capital of the industry. These banks have grown up in England. These banks cannot freeze their funds in long-term investments. They were sanctioning the loans for only short-term basis. They were not granted the loans for long-term capital investments. These banks were to provide working capital for currents and seasonal requirements.

The deposit banks are acting as trustees of the depositors. The depositors are the main customers of the banks. The business of the bank depends upon the credibility. The depositors hard earned money should be preserved. The depositors may demand their money at any time. Therefore, the bank should maintain the liquidity position. Therefore, these banks are invested towards short-term finance to the corporate sector. These banks are providing finance to the industrial sector and to small or medium type industries.

Investment banking is mainly interested for providing long-term finance to the corporate sector. The investment banks are also known as "Industrial banks". These banks are advancing loans on long-term basis. The commercial banks are unable to provide long-term finance to the industries. The investment banks are very popular in Germany. These banks were established to promote industrial development. These banks did not accept the deposits initially. But later on, they mobilised the resources from the public. Several banks were formed as consortium or syndicate. They took the responsibility of financing to industrial units. These banks were closely related with the industries. The investment banks enjoyed the mutual cooperation of the industries. The promotion of new industries and development of established industries were developed by the mutual assistance of the banks and other related industries. The banks were expertised in the mobilisation of resources and sanctioning loans to the industries.

Mixed Banking: The mixed banking involves in mobilisation of deposits and grant term loans to the corporate sector. It developed in UK after Frist World War. Industrialisation, competition, mass production encouraged the mixed banking system. They functioned as investments banking. In India the mixed banking system was emerged on the recommendations of Central Banking Enquiry Committee (1931). The Shroff Committee also recommended indirect participation of banks in industrial finance. The demand of industrial financing through commercial banks have been increasing tremendously. The IDBI was established in 1964. It took initiatives to finance the industries. The RBI also encourages the commercial banks for increasing the term lending. The term lending was very popular in USA and is taking important position in India. There are several industrial financial institutions which have been established to look after the welfare of industrial sector. These institutions were established by the Parliament by making an Act. They are **IFCI, ICICI, IDBI, IRCI** etc. The term lending finance has extended from industries to agriculture after nationalisation of banks in 1969. The commercial banks in India are turning to mixed banking.

Commercial Banking in India: The nature and significance of the emerging trends in Indian banking system can be studied since the early 1950s. The evolution of Indian banking system can be divided in 3 phases.

(a) From 1951 to 1964 – I Phase
(b) From 1965 to 1990 – II Phase
(c) From 1991 onwards – III Phase

I Phase: The first phase of the banking sector is to consolidate its position on the eve of independence. The banking structure at the initial stage was faced by a number of problems like unsound economic practices, frauds and malpractices etc. The system failed to attract the public confidence. The banking system had lost its credibility. The failures were a frequent occurrence. There is a strong need for the promotion of sound banking. The evolution of banking system in the 1st phase can be studied on the following elements:

(a) Structure of the system
(b) Credibility
(c) Banking policies

(a) Structure of the system: The banking structure should be stable and strong to meet the growth of the economic development of a nation. The structure should be able to prevent the frauds failure and to restore the public confidence. The Banking Regulation Act, 1949 expressed for the promotion of sound banking. The Act was replaced with Banking Companies Act. The objectives of the legislation was to weed out:

(a) Non-variable units
(b) Small-banking units

The Act has also tone up the administration by eradicating unsound practices and great protection to depositors. The RBI took a decision to amalgamate the small and non-viable banking units with stronger units. Therefore, the banks were reduced to 108 in March 1966 from 566 in 1951. The RBI had taken a strong measures to strengthen the system.

(b) Credibility: The Government of India took a decision to provide public confidence on the banking system with the aim of restoring public confidence. The deposits insurance was introduced in 1961. The protection for small deposits have been provided under the "Deposit Insurance Corporation Act, 1961". The Deposit Insurance Corporation was set up in January 1962, to provide protection to the depositors under this Act. The insurance cover was upto Rs.1,500 at initial period. Later it was raised to Rs. 5,000 in January 1968, and Rs.10,000 in April 1970. The insurance cover was raised at present upto Rs.1,00,000.

(c) Policies: The changes in policies and practices of Indian bank have been raised to:

(a) Credit
(b) Diversification
(c) Priorities sectors
(d) Regulation of bank credit

(a) Credit: The first phase of the evolution of the banking structure is consolidation and charges in the banking policies and practices. There is a strong to integrate the banking operations and policies. The RBI had modified the monetary and credit policies in the form of instruments. The instruments such as credit control and macro type control to encourage the banks to finance the industry. Prior to this, the banks mainly grant the loans to trade and commerce. After the commencement of second five year plan, there is a rapid industrialisation occurred in the country. The industrialisation leads to increase in the bank financing of industry. The banks credit to the industry have been increased tremendously. The credit rose by an average of about Rs.14 crore per year during the First Plan period (1951-55), Rs.68 crores per year during the Second Plan period (1956-61) and Rs.164 crore per year during the Third Plan period (1962-66). The upsurge in the bank credit to industry during this period shows the raising importance of credit as a main source of finance to the corporate enterprises.

(b) Diversification: The commercial banks in India were encouraged to enter the new mode of financing based on the two factors:

(a) Term lending
(b) Underwriting

The term loans are occupying an important portfolio in their loans and disbursement programmes of the commercial banks. Prior to this period the banks were restricted to provide short-term loans only. The commercial banks traditional role have been changed and they are actively participating in the development of the industrial growth. During the Second Five Year Plan there were modifications in the existing pattern of financing to the industry. There was a strong need for expansion of institutional credit facilities for the small and medium sized enterprises. Therefore, the government encouraged the commercial banks to involve in term lending to the industry and designed a specific scheme for this purpose in 1958. According to this scheme the Refinance Corporation of Industry Ltd. had been created for the purpose of refinancing facility. The new scheme reveals that the commercial banks which were lending the term loans to the industry will have refinancing facility against approved term loans from the RCI. The RCI was merged with the IDBI on 1.9.1964. The flow of bank credit was encouraged as being in conformity with the policy of industrialisation in the country.

Underwriting is the another innovation during this phase. The entry of commercial banks in the area of underwriting of new issue has created a new dimension in this sector. The entry of commercial banks towards underwriting activity had been suggested by the Indian Central Banking Enquiry Committee in 1931. The same activity was also recommended by the Shroff Committee in 1953. The Committee also recommended the formation of joint underwriting consortium of banks and insurance companies. The commercial banks not only sanctioning term loans, involving underwriting activity but also entered in the financial services sector. They are actively involved in providing finance to the corporate sector partly through direct subscription to the shares and debentures. A seminar was organised by the RBI at Hyderabad in 1958. The RBI had taken initiative steps to provide finance to the neglected sector of SSI.

Secondly, in pursuance of the problems focused by the seminar, the Government of India formulated a "credit guarantee scheme". The scheme was finalised in consultation with the Reserve Bank in July 1960. According to the scheme the Central bank will guarantee the major part of the advance given by Bank to the SSI. The credit guarantee scheme was administered by the RBI. The guarantee was given by the Central Government. The RBI had appointed a working group to examine the provisions of this scheme in detail. The working group has also suggested some modifications in the scheme with effect from 1.2.70. The aim of the scheme was to provide financial assistance to all eligible advances on an automatic basis. Every eligible institutions have been entered into agreement with the credit guarantee organisation. The approved institutions were provided bank finance and guarantee cover was up to 75% of the amount defaulted or the amount guaranteed whichever was lower. The CGS covers all credit facilities allowed to small units. The maximum amount recoverable from the CGS was Rs. 7.50 lakhs for working capital advances and a further sum of Rs. 2.50 lakh in respect of the term loans per borrower. The CGS helped the banks in taking more responsibilities in the financing of small scale enterprises and partly through their lending against such securities. The commercial banks are helping the corporate sector by subscribing shares and by underwriting the public issues therefor, the growth of corporate sector depended upon the commercial banks.

(c) Priorities sectors: Some of the sectors of the Indian economy have been neglected by the authorities. These sectors were identified during this phase and the commercial banks were directed to channelise their resources towards neglected areas. These neglected areas were identified the small scale industries, exports and agriculture. These small sectors received very little credit from the banks. Previously, the policy and institutional measures to stimulate bank credit to the following sectors are described below:

1. Small Scale Industries
2. Exports
3. Agricultural Finance
4. Institutional Sector

1. Small Scale Industries: The small scale industries is one of the most neglected sectors in the Indian economy. The government has taken a policy to provide financial assistance to this sector. The provision of finance to this sector depends upon three steps:

(a) Systematic study of problems
(b) Credit guarantee of problems
(c) Credit policy

At the first step a systematic study of SSIs problems involved was studied in depth by the small scale industrialists and bankers were brought together to sort out the probiems for replying the solution.

Finally, the credit policy contains the facilities to stimulate bank credit to the small scale sector. The RBI introduced in 1962 a policy of granting additional rights to the banks to borrow from it concessional rates if they sanction excess quantity of amount. These concessions were provided to the commercial banks by the RBI in different forms. The RBI arranges the refinance at bank rate. The rediscounting of bills under the new bill market scheme. As a consequences of these measures there was a tremendous rise in the quantum of credit expanded to the small sector by the banking industry.

2. Exports: The export sector is another one of the neglected sectors in the Indian economy. The Government of India has taken an important measure to provide finance for exports. For this purpose the Central Government had established the Export Risk Insurance Corporation in 1957. It was promoted to offer insurance to exporters against exchange control. There is no clear information available regarding the credit worthiness of importers. The Export Risk Insurance Corporation was renamed as the Export Credit and Guarantee Corporation (ECGC) Ltd. It extended guarantees to the commercial banks providing financial assistance to the reporters and also it covers the insurance to the reporters. The ECGC providing concessional rates of interest were fixed export credit by the banks.

3. Agricultural Finance: The agricultural sector was totally ignored by the banking sector. To improve the credit facilities to this sector, the Agricultural Refinance Corporation Ltd. (ARCL) had been established. It was set up as a subsidiary to the Reserve Bank of India. It was established in 1963 for providing long-term finance to eligible banking and financial institutions. It will be provided refinance facility for promoting the development of agriculture and allied activities. The ARCL financed to agricultural projects could not be financed by any other existing credit agencies.

4. Institutional Credit: The RBI introduced this scheme in November 1965, to regulate the bank credit to institutional borrowers. According to this scheme the commercial banks were directed to secure the RBI for granting the cash credit limit more than one crore to any single party. Every commercial bank shall get the permission of the RBI to grant the cash credit to institutional borrowers. But actually there is no need to get approval from RBI for sanctioning the cash credit facility. The scheme is popularly known as "Credit Authorisation Scheme (CAS)". The objective was to control the institutional borrowers as well as to align the credit facilities of the banks. The CAS was modified to suit the needs of customers by the banks. The CAS was now replaced by Credit Monetary Arrangement.

II Phase (1964-90): The second phase of banking (1964-90) may be described as the innovative banking period after 1964. There was a radical changes in the country. During this period there was increasing concern about the problem of concentration of economic power in few hands. This period had also witnessed a widening economic disparities. These problems have been studied by several officials and the following development desire to be presented in this context:

(a) The Mahalanobis Committee, 1964
(b) The Monopolies Inquiry Commission, 1965
(c) R.K. Hazari Committee, 1966
(d) The Patel Committee, 1966

(e) The R.K. Hazari Committee, 1967 (Licensing Policy)
(f) The Dutt Committee, 1969

The Mahalanobis Committee had been appointed for studying about the distribution of income and level of living. The Monopolies Inquiry Commission has been set up to study about the concentration of economic power in few hands. In 1966, a Committee was formed to study about the concentration of private cooperate sector and its ownership and control. The Committee was headed by a well-known expert Shri R.K. Hazari. In the same year another Committee has been established for inquiring about the affairs of managing agency system. The Hazari Committee had been appointed to look into the matters of industrial licensing policy. The Dutt Committee was made inquiries regarding industrial licensing policy in 1969. These Committees have framed the guidelines to change the Indian banking system. The main objective of the Committee is to look after the equitable distribution of bank credit to all classes of borrowers. It was found that the large scale industries, institutions borrower, big corporate houses had almost enjoyed the bank credit. It was also found the commercial banks have been entirely neglected the sectors such as small scale industries, agriculture and exports. No bank credit had been available to these sectors. These Committees had been provided abroad setting for the radical changes in the structure operations and policies of the Indian commercial banking system during this phase. The main features of second phase were presented below:

(a) Community control
(b) Organisational changes

During this second phase, the RBI had been enforced the rigorous control to strengthen the banking system. The banking system has been continued to suffer in terms of credit coverage. The large network of branches covered only a small segment of the community. The bank credits have been enjoyed by a portion of population mostly in the big cities, almost completely excluding the rural areas and the smaller towns. However, there were substantial credit gaps to sub-sectors, agriculture and small scale industries. It was found that some steps have been taken to provide finance to the artisans, retail traders, self-employed persons. All of these community members did not enjoy the facility of institutional credit. The banking system has been controlled by the big industrial houses in order to look after their welfare. It was the most important element in the banking system. Therefore, the Government of India introduced the scheme of social control at the end of 1967. The bank credit was an important element of achieving socio-economic objectives of the state policy. The socio-economic objectives are to achieve a wider spread of bank credit to all priority sectors, preventing its misuse, directing large volume of credit, flow of developmental activities of the country. The government had been decided to remove the control of big business houses over banks without removing their ownership. Therefore, it was sought to be achieved by bringing reforms to the banking sector. The concepts and goals of the banking system have been changed dramatically. The elements of community centres were:

(a) Structural Changes
(b) National Credit Council
(c) Agricultural Finance

Structural changes is the basic step under the scheme of community control. According to the structural change, the changes in the board of directors of bank have been made accordingly. The board was reconstituted by introducing the person with the specialised knowledge or practical experience in agriculture and rural economy, cooperation, of SSIs and banking. The bank chairman was replaced by an expert of banking finance business administration or economics. Therefore, the entire structure of the banking system had been changed to meet the socio-economic objectives of the state economy.

National Credit Council has been established in February 1968. The creation of NCC is to achieve the objectives of providing bank credit to priorities sectors on all India basis. The basic functions of the credit council were presented below:

(a) to estimate the demand for bank credit to the various sectors of the economy.
(b) to determine the priority sector for providing financial assistance.
(c) to ensure the optimum utilisation of resources by coordinating the lending and investing policies of the banks.

Agriculture Finance Corporation: The Agriculture Finance Corporation was established for the purpose of financing agricultural project. It was set up as a joint venture by leading commercial banks. This corporation was set up to help the banks to participate actively in developing the agricultural sector in our country.

The commercial banks were advised by the Corporation to adopt the specific areas/projects in consultation with the concerned State Governments. The aim of the programme was to expand the agricultural credit in order to maximise the benefits to the sector. The benefits which are available to this sector such as supply of inputs, marketing, processing, procurement operations, storage and transportation.

The objective of the socio-economic system is to provide equitable allocation of bank credit to all the priorities sectors. Therefore, the National Credit Council appointed two Committees in October 1968. The first Committee was headed by Prof. D.R. Gadgil to study about the organisational framework for the implementation of social control objectives. The Committee probed into the credit gaps. The another Committee was appointed to the study on the extent to which credit needs of industry and trade are likely to be inflated and how such trends can be checked. The Committee was headed by Shri V.T. Dehejia to examine the problems of an unduly large proportion of bank credit by big industrial houses.

The first Committee report addressed the task of identifying the credit gaps and made suggestions to provide adequate institutional credit could be made available to the neglected sectors of the economy. The Committee was also found that bank credit was unevenly distributed among different states of the country. The Committee provided a solution of an area approach for branch expansion. The individual banks would select particular areas for intensive development and in the process expand the deposit mobilisation to finance the agriculture and small scale industries. Therefore, the lead bank scheme was finalised by the RBI towards the end of 1969. According to this scheme the 336 districts in India with the exception of metros were allotted among the major scheduled banks to provide finance in their concerned territory. The allotments were made on the basis of size of bank. The size of the resources cluster area, regional orientation of the bank, the requirements of each state etc.

Nationalisation: The banking system had taken several measures for achieving the social economic objectives. The Government of India had changed the ownership of commercial banks to satisfy the socio-economic objective. **Therefore, the Government of India nationalised 14 major banks with individual deposits exceeding Rs.50 crore on 19.7.1969. The aims of the nationalisation were:**

(a) to control the heights of the economy
(b) to serve better the needs of development of the country
(c) to provide a great impetus to new orientation to the banking system.

The post-nationalisation period made significant changes in the operational policies and practices of the banks. There were more and more Committees appointed to study the various problems of the banking sector. The Committees such as Narasimhan Committee, Tandon Committee, Chore Committee, Marathe Committee have been appointed.

III Phase: The liberalisation, privatisation and globalisation policies have changed the banking sector tremendously. The post-1991 era of Indian banking is essentially a phase of profitable banking/variable/ prudential. The Narasimhan Committee has been established to look after the financial sector. The Narasimhan Committee (II) had been appointed to look after affairs of the banking sector reforms 1998. The banking system in India has grown tremendously in this III Phase. In this phase the implementation and recommendations of the Narasimhan Committee played an important role in the transformation of traditional banking into modern banking in the digital economy.

The following financial institutions provide finance for the development of industries in the country. They are:

1. Export and Import Bank of India
2. National Bank for Agriculture and Rural Development
3. Shipping Credit and Investment Corporation of India
4. Tourism Finance Corporation of India
5. Risk Capital and Technology Finance Corporation
6. Industrial Reconstruction Bank of India
7. Insurance Regulatory Authority
8. The Stock Holding Corporation of India
9. The Discount and Finance House of India
10. Technology Development and Information Company of India

All of the above financial institutions are covered in this Unit.

EXPORT AND IMPORT BANK OF INDIA

The Export and Import Bank of India was established on 1.1.1982 for **promoting the foreign trade. It renders the financial assistance to the corporate sectors in export and import business. It also coordinates the working of other financial institutions which engage in foreign trade. It functions as an apex body by assisting and developing the export business sector. It undertakes the promotion activities and provide counselling services to the persons and institutions. The bank renders financial assistance to different types of schemes. The bank rediscounts the export** of bills of banks for a period of 180 days only. It is an indirect finance to boost the export business. It also arranges the refinance in respect of post shipment credit facilities the bank grants the finance in the form of term loans. The financial assistance should be for exports of plants, equipments, machinery etc. The bank also contributes the equity investment to the Indian promoters in joint ventures abroad. The bank participates with the commercial banks to the guarantees issued in foreign currencies on behalf of the Indian exporters and importers. The bank offers the credit directly to the buyers for importing the capital goods. The bank also offers advisory services to the exporters.

During the year 1993-94 bank offered new and varied services to the exporters. It has been approved only as an agency in India to facilitate the forfeiting transactions. It offers the Indian exporters an alternative trade financing mechanism. The banks relationship with the European Commission is strengthened through the sponsorship of the joint venture project in India.

NATIONAL BANK FOR AGRICULTURE AND RURAL DEVELOPMENT (NABARD)

The National Bank for Agriculture and Rural Development was established on 12.7.1982. It was established for the purpose of financing agriculture sector. The major functions of the agriculture credit department of the RBI was taken over by the NABARD. All the assets and liabilities of the National Agriculture Credit Fund were transferred to the NABARD which has the full authority to refinance and inspect the Regional Rural Banks (RRBs). It is the premier institution in the sphere of the rural credit. It has emerged as an Apex National Institution. It fully involves in refinance, loans and advances to the state cooperative banks, land development banks, RRBs and other approved institutions. It looks after the financing functions of production, marketing and investments activities relating to the rural development, small scale industries, village industries and handicrafts.

The NABARD has a share capital of Rs.100 crores. It was subscribed equally by the RBI and the Government of India. It also borrows from the RBI and the Central Government. The lending rates and deposits rate changes from time-to-time. The interest chargeable to the ultimate beneficiaries in very less for farmers and small farmers. It also sanctions the loans to the agriculture sector on medium and long-term basis. It charges different rates of interest for different purpose. However, the less rate of interest will be charged for agricultural purposes.

SHIPPING CREDIT AND INVESTMENT CORPORATION OF INDIA (SCICI)

The Shipping Credit and Investment Corporation of India was set up in 1973. It is the youngest and highly performing financial institution. It plays a pivotal role in financing the infrastructural development. The aim of the institution is to finance the green field and export inducing projects and infrastructure financing. It commits to provide the finance to the major power projects. They include the Enron Project, Torrent Project in Gujarat, Valley Project in Orissa and two projects in Andhra Pradesh. Most of the projects are being funded in a consortium basis and the maximum lending will be facilitated.

The SCICI has been encouraging the entrepreneurs to invest in funding national highways. However, the return on the investment would be poor privatisation in the transport segment should take off initially with small projects. It thinks about the viability of funding the national highways by diverting the funds from other financial institutions. The funds come from financial institutions, insurance companies, public structure and restructuring process.

It has been riding on a wave of success with its operations and performance. It becomes the envoy of other financial institutions. It has completed the assignments for restructuring the plan for the ONGC. The funds will be mobilised from the market.

TOURISM FINANCE CORPORATION OF INDIA (TFCI)

The Tourism Finance Corporation of India was incorporated as a public limited company in 1989. It has an authorised share capital of Rs.500 crores of which Rs.67.42 crores is paid up. The institutions hold nearly 75% of the equity. The nationalised banks hold 15.04%.

It provides the financial assistance to the enterprises for setting up and developing the tourism related activities, facilities and services such assistance is extended for setting up new projects as well as for expansion, diversification and modernisation of the projects. It extends rupee loans guarantees for deferred payment and credits raised in India and abroad, equipment finance, equipment leasing, suppliers credit and advisory services. It also coordinates and formulates the guidelines and policies relating to finance such projects.

It provided the surplus amount to the Government of India during the financial year that on March 31, 2001. It had earned a profit of

Rs. 137.53 crores from the operation of business during the year that ended on March 31, 2000, it earned a net profit of Rs.141.32 crores.

RISK CAPITAL AND TECHNOLOGY FINANCE CORPORATION (RCTFC)

The Risk Capital Fund was sponsored by the IFCI. The Corporation was established in 1975. It was set up to provide an assistance to the entrepreneurs. It encourages the medium sized industrial projects. It provides assistance to the entrepreneurs in the form of equity capital. It is popularly known as the RCTFC. It is aimed to encourage the high technology profitable venture which involves innovative products. It also encourages venture capital firms. It floated a venture capital firm in July 1991. It also entered in non-fund based activities. It also acts as a financial intermediary to it assisted units it obtained the membership from the O.T.C. The company perceives itself the role of sponsor primarily for the units assisted by it.

The RCTFC manages a venture capital scheme known as the VECAUs-III. Venture Capital Unit Scheme III was floated by the UTI, the VC firm has been established by the IFCI and the UTI. The world bank also supports the RCTFC. The financial assistance will be facilitated by the World Bank through the IFCI.

INDUSTRIAL RECONSTRUCTION BANK OF INDIA (IRBI)

The Industrial Reconstruction Bank of India was set up in 1985. It was established as a statutory body under the IRBI Act. It was empowered to reconstruct the sick industrial units. Its objectives are to revive the sick industrial unit. Its objectives can be fulfilled by assisting them in their expansion, modernisation, diversification, reorganisation and rationalisation.

Functions

The functions of the IRBI are presented below:

1. Provides loans and advances to the corporate sector.
2. Contributes/subscribes to equity/debentures of the companies.
3. Provides consultancy services.
4. Provides hire purchase facilities.

5. Provides merchant banking facilities.
6. Provides legal, technical and financial assistance to the mergers and amalgamations units.
7. Provides infrastructure facilities.

The RBI has right to take over the management of the assisted companies. It acts as a coordinator in securing the assistance from the bank and financial institutions. It is aimed to solve the labour problems immediately when the assisted firm approaches. It also offers advises on product mix and allied matters. The IRBI involves in corporate and financial restructuring. The corporate restructuring made it as a government company. Its name was changed as Industrial Investments Bank of India. Financial restructuring involves its conversion of dues transferred to the IRBI Ltd.

INSURANCE REGULATORY AUTHORITY (IRA)

Introduction

Insurance organisations are the repositories of the public trust. Before the nationalisation of life and general insurance, LIC and GIC dominated the market. These institutions were regulated under the provisions of the Insurance Act, 1938. The Act was administered by the Controller of Insurance. The Insurance Regulatory Authority is set up as a statutory body. It is similar to the SEBI. It should have a full time chairperson, two full-time and some part time members. The Chairman and board members should be familiar. They should have integrity, ability, rich experience in finance, insurance, law, administration and other relevant disciplines. One of the board members should have a strong background in general insurance and another must be in life insurance. The IRA should discharge its functions in a free and transparency manner.

Functions

The functions of the IRA are as follows:

(a) The IRA should observe the provisions of law about capital adequacy, solvency margins and other norms.
(b) It has the authority to grant the registration of certificate.
(c) It should look after the interest of the consumers.
(d) It has the authority to modify the rates, terms and conditions.
(e) To monitor the performance and quality of re-insurance.

(f) To ensure high standards of accounting and transparency.
(g) It has the power to detect badly managed unhealthy or failing insurers.
(h) It has the power to rectify consumer's grievances.
(i) It has the power to prepare the annual report on the state of the insurance industry.
(j) It has the power to ensure a variety of insurance products in a transparent manner.
(k) It has the power to design the new product to meet the needs of the rural populations.

The authority has the right to levy 0.5 per cent of the premium income of insurance companies, which they collected from policy holders. The Controller of Insurance was replaced by the IRP on September 6, 1995. The Ministry of Finance has taken over the overall control in the insurance sector. It has been entrusted with the task of assigning the responsibilities.

Salient Features

The salient features of the IRA are presented below:

1. The chairman of the IRA is the COI.
2. It has the authority to think about the introduction of privatisation in the insurance industry wholly and partially.
3. It has the power to regulate, promote and control the activities of the insurance industry.
4. The Chairman of the IRA has the status of an Additional Secretary to the Government.
5. The board should consist of seven members.
6. Three board members should be full time nominated by the Central Government.
7. The board may continue until the pleasure of the Central Government.
8. The Government should provide adequate grants for financing the expenses incurred by the IRA.
9. It would deal with all the matters relating to the promotion and growth of the insurance industry.
10. It has the power to call for records, returns, notes, memorandum, data and any other information relevant to its working from official and non-official bodies.

11. It has its own procedure and powers.
12. It has the responsibility to submit a periodical report to the Government of India on various aspects of insurance industry.
13. It is also responsible for the submission of specific matters as desired by the Government from time-to-time.

THE STOCKHOLDING CORPORATION OF INDIA

Introduction

The Stock Holding Corporation of India was established in July 1986. It was incorporated under the Companies Act, 1956. It was promoted by the All India Financial Institution. The promoters involve in the formation of the Corporation. They are IDBI, ICICI, UTI, GIC and IRBF.

It was established to eliminate the paper work in relation to the transactions in shares, debentures and securities by introducing the books entry system for the transfer of scrips. Transferring the scrips through immobilisation and dematerialisation of securities. It facilitates the elimination of frauds and errors. It creates greater liquidity of investments in scrips. The main objective of its formation is to provide comprehensive custodial services. It facilitates fully automated infrastructural facilities for trade, clearances, settlement and depository services for the securities. It offers its services to the institutional investors. It works out the clearance function of the NSE for their wholesale debt market segment. The secondary market trading in India has been creating waves in the market with the help of information technology. The Information Technology makes India to reach the world standard in trading methods. It has recently formulated the framework for a national clearing and depository system. It will act as the founder of development secondary market trading in India, national clearance and depository system comprises national trading report, system, national clearing system, national depository system. The NTRC creates the terms and conditions of a contract after the execution of a trade in the market. The NCS takes place nationally on a standard basis. The NCS makes the transfer of scrips with the physical movement of scrip.

THE DISCOUNT AND FINANCE HOUSE OF INDIA (DFHI)

The Discount and Finance House of India was incorporated in April 1988. It was promoted on the basis of the recommendations of Shri N. Vaghul Committee. The paid up capital of Rs.100 crores was contributed by the

RBI (51%), public sector banks (33%) and financial institution (16%). The basic aim of the Corporation is to provide liquidity to the money market instruments in the market. It deals with the short-term instruments. The sources of the finance of the Corporation are paid up capital, refinance with the RBI and credit limit to PSBs for Rs.200 crores.

Functions

The functions of the Corporation are presented below:

(a) It involves in buying and discounting of 91 days and 364 days treasury bills.
(b) It actively participates in the inter-bank call money market.
(c) It discounts and rediscounts the short-term commercial bills for the financial institutions and banks.

It develops the money market mutual fund. It actively involves in the call money market. The RBI had allowed the entry of any mutual fund and any entity during 1991. The DFHI operates the money market. It is a vehicle for operations of the RBI in the money market. It also involves in purchasing and selling of commercial bills, commercial papers and certificate of deposits. It also quotes bid and offer rates for the repositive buy-back transactions. Its presence in the money market stimulates the secondary market. There has also been a significant improvement in the number of participants. The DFHI was converted into a primary dealer in 1995. The setting up of the primary dealers and satellite dealers made the money market more liquid and broadens the primary dealers and the liquidity and the satellite dealers makes the market broadens.

TECHNOLOGY DEVELOPMENT AND INFORMATION COMPANY OF INDIA (TDICI)

Introduction

Technology Development and Information Company of India Ltd. was established in January 1988. It was promoted by the ICICI and the UTI. It started India's first Venture Fund, the VECAVS Venture Capital Unit Scheme, with a corpus fund of Rs.20 crores. It has been rendering the service to 37 small and medium enterprises. It also provides financial assistance to the software companies.

It works now as a venture capital institution and provides technical services to the information technology companies. It provides marketing services to the export oriented units. At present it concentrates on high tech and low tech industries for financing the projects investments decisions and always depends upon the coverage of the entrepreneur. It takes interest to fund the high risk investment projects.

The high risk project generally generates high returns and leads to a high rejection rate as much as 90% of all proposals. It gives top priority to the close ended companies. They provide finance to those companies which have no access to the public issue and to the unknown ones. It will nominate a number as the board of director in the assisted companies.

It provides financial assistance to the companies ranging from software foods, power generation and art, painting etc. A large number of firms are located in Mumbai, Pune, Nasik and Chennai.

INTEREST

Introduction

Interest is a payment for the use of capital. It is a price for surrendering liquidity preference. It is necessary to induce people to save the money. The concept of interest depends on the interest theory. The classical theory of interest is believed as payment for the use of capital goods. Just as rent is a payment for the use of land, similarly interest is a payment for the use of capital. Just it is the price of capital. It is expressed as a **percentage** return on capital invested excluding risks. It has been defined by **Marshall** as "the price paid for the use of capital in any market".[36]

The interest rate charged on the industrial business usually reflects the market situation. Generally the people assume that interest is the price of the service of capital. It is also known as **Gross interest**. Gross interest is the total amount which the debtor pays to the creditor. Hence, the borrower pays the cost of fund to the lender as per the agreed rate of interest. Gross interest consists of the following elements:

(i) Pure interest
(ii) Risk
(iii) Safety

Pure interest is a payment only for the service of capital. The borrower will pay the amount of interest to the lender for the supply of money.

Risk is a chance of loss. The fund supplier is exposed to risk when he lends money. The lender will face the risk in two situations: (a) The lender may not know about the unreliable character of the borrower, and (b) trade risks. Trade risks are depended upon the fortunes of the performance of the business sector in which the money is invested. Therefore, the lender may fear about his money until it is refunded to him safely.

Safety is the most important element in the world of finance. The lender always thinks about the safety of his disposed money. Lending money means parking of idle fund in a safe place. For this parking time, the lender will be paid in the form of **interest** when a person lends money, he loses control over it for a fixed period. He is unable to make investment during this period. He may also slip good opportunities for investment during this time period.

Keeping all these elements in mind the lender has to face many problems. The return on government securities is an example of **pure rate of interest**. In money market the borrowers are charged different rates of interest which depends upon the supply of money and demand. It may be remembered that the pure interest trends to be the same when calculated over the same period of time in the same money market. The actual differences that prevail are differences in gross interest. The pure interest may be different in different investments and the market will not be in the same situation due to many factors. The interest rates are different in India because the people are more willing to deploy their fund nearer to home. They are not willing to lend their money at a long distance. This situation may create differences in supply and demand of money. Generally the people will invest for a fixed period of time to meet their commitments. They think if money is lent for very short periods and has to be re-lent again and again. The rate of interest decreases as the amount of loan increases usually the lender prefers to lend his money towards liquid securities which will carry a lower rate of interest. The difference in interest rates is influenced by the **maturity period** of the loan. The long-term loans will carry higher rates of interest than do short-term loans. In financial market **goodwill** enhances the capacity of raising financial resources. Therefore, a large nationally reputed corporation can mobilise the higher amount of fund from the market.

The differences in **gross interest** may be due to the following elements:

(a) Reputation
(b) Profitability

A business concern with better reputation can raise financial resources at lower rates. Usually the people will not lend their money to **unknown organisations** or persons. Another factor in differences in gross interest rates is profitability of the sector where the fund is deployed. In speculative sector, the fund earns usually more rate of interest than any other sector. We cannot say all sectors provide equal profit to the producers. Some sectors will facilitate higher returns. Hence the fund carries maximum rate of interest in that specified industry. The productivity of capital may differ in various industries accordingly.

Theories of Interest

Interest is the cost to the borrower while lender earns income as the deployment of fund. Therefore, it occupies an important role in the economy. The theory of interest must reveal two things: (a) the process of interest arises, and (b) determination of the rate of interest. Some theories explain only one of the aspects and others reveal both. The cost of interest is explained by the following theories:

(a) Productivity theory
(b) Waiting theory
(c) Agio theory
(d) Fisher's time preference theory

The determination of the rate of interest is explained by the following theories:

(i) Classical theory
(ii) Neo-classical theory
(iii) Keynesian theory

Productivity theory was explained by older economists. They thought that the capital might be productive in case of goods such as land for crops. They treated the interest as the part of productive expenses. The production activities are carried out with the aid of capital. The capital will be available in the market for a specified rate at a specified time in a specified place. But some arguments were there that the interest would not be a cost factor. If the people were willing to lend unlimited fund without charging interest. The business would expand up to a certain point. Therefore, the commodity price in the long run must cover all the costs including interest.

Waiting theory approaches the supply of money. It reveals that saving involves a sacrifice and is an act of abstaining from consumption. It is necessary to reward those people who sacrificed their desires. They will be paid in the form of interest. This theory is widely criticised on the basis of positive discomfort. Usually the rich people are the main suppliers of the capital who save without the least inconvenience. The savers do not refrain from consumption for all time, they postpone to prevent consumption to a future date. For this period of time they have to wait. Hence, the majority people do not like to wait. It is necessary to encourage this postponement of consumption.

Agio theory was first submitted by John Rae in 1834. This theory is also known as **"psychological theory of interest"**. The final shape was completed by Bohm Bawerk who was an Australian Economist. It was slightly modified by Fisher and later became popular. This theory refers the attitude of the people towards the reward for the deployment of financial resources. It assumes that one bird in hand is said to be worth two in the bush. It is associated with the future satisfaction of the savers. The future satisfaction will be discounted from the present situation. The discounted factor is called as interest. It must be paid in order to induce people to lend money or to postpone the present satisfaction to a future date. The interest equates the future satisfaction with the present satisfaction. The people are willing to save the money because the future is less clearly perceived than the present. The future is uncertain. The demand for the present goods is more than that for the future goods. The present goods have a technical superiority over the future goods.

Fishers time preference theory was based on the time factor. The individuals are impatient to spend their income at present. Their savings depend upon the size of income, their desire for enjoyment in the future and the temperament. Therefore, the people who earn large income presently consume goods than in future. The poor people are fully satisfied in the future than at present. The distribution of income overtime depends upon three elements. The individuals income may be stable throughout the life or increase with the age or decrease with the age consequently. If the individuals income is uniform, the spending attitude will be determined by the temperament of the individual. The attitude of the individual is also influenced by the time factor.

Classical theory explains the determination of the rate of interest. It refers to the demand and supply theories. The rate of interest is determined by the demand for saving to invest. The rate of interest is highly influenced by productivity and thrift. This theory indicates that the rate of interest depends upon the demand and supply of savings. The demand for the capital goods comes from the business concerns to produce the consumer goods. The capital has marginal revenue productivity. The demand for the capital goods rises as the rate of interest falls in the market. The supply of savings is available for those who save from their current income. The individuals will save the money by postponing their current consumption. For sacrificing their desires, they must be offered some reward in the form of interest. We must remember that, if the savings are increasing. The people postpone their current consumption. Hence, there will be decrease in the demand of goods. The rate of interest at which the demand for capital and the supply of savings are in equilibrium will be the rate determined in the market. This theory is criticised by **Keynes**. He pointed out that this theory is based upon the following assumptions:

(a) full employment of resources
(b) more investment will curtail consumption
(c) changes in income level was ignored
(d) position of savings will vary with the level of incomes

The other theory in determination of interest is **neo-classical theory**. It is also known as loanable funds theory. It explains how the interest rates arise. According to this theory interest is the price paid for the use of loanable funds. It reveals that the rate of interest is determined by the equilibrium between the demand and supply of loanable funds in the financial market. It indicates that the funds are available in four basic sources such as savings, bank credit and structural changes. The individual and household savings basically depend upon the size of their income levels. The business concerns also save undistributed profit in the savings of the corporate sector. A high rate of interest is likely to encourage the business savings as a substitute for the borrowings from the financial market. Bank credit is another source of supply of funds. The banking system provides loanable funds to the corporate sector. They advance loan to the business community. They can also reduce the amount of money by contracting their lending. The additional fund created by the banks adds greatly to the supply of the loan funds. The loanable fund is available to the market due to the structural changes in the existing technology of the corporate sector. The higher amounts of funds are demanded by the corporate sector due to the replacement of old machines and technology. The replacement of the technology requires a lot of money for the new technology which stimulates the productivity of industrial output. The latest technology, sophisticated machines may definitely enhance the productivity.

The demand for funds comes from three sources such as business sector, consumption, profitability. Generally, all the business enterprises borrow money from the market for their smooth functioning of their operations. They procure funds from market when they purchase capital goods. The corporate sector demands more funds when they are in expansion or diversification. The corporate sector will make purchase of larger amounts of capital goods when the rate of interest declines. Another demand for the loanable funds comes from the individuals are households to make the purchases of consumer durable goods such as automobiles, refrigerators, radios etc. If the market provides lower rate of interest, the loanable funds will encourage some increases in the consumer borrowings. At higher rate of interest, people will hold less money and lent more money due to the profitability. The people will take advantages of the higher rates. **The liquidity preference theory** is known as **Keynes theory**. He gave a new view of interest. He said that interest was the reward for parting with liquidity for a specified period. Every individual would save a certain proportion of his given income. He must decide himself how much of amount would be held in the form of cash. Liquidity preference theory means the demand for money to hold or the desire of the public to held cash. According to **Prof. Meyer** "Liquidity preference is the preference to have an equal amount of cash rather than of claims against others".[37] Liquidity preference of an individual depends upon several factors.

(a) transaction motive
(b) precautionary motive
(c) speculative motive

(a) Transaction Motive: Usually people will hold some of the proportion of their earnings in the form of liquid cash for their current needs. They hold cash in order to bridge the interval between the receipt of income and its expenditure. This cash amount will depend upon the size of the individuals income. The corporate sector also hold ready cash in order to meet their current needs of various kinds. They need money all the time for purchase of raw material wages, transport, salaries and other production expenses. These situations may require ready cash for the smooth functioning of industrial activities. The amount of ready cash will depend upon the turnover of the business concern.

(b) Precautionary Motive: Generally the people will keep some amount of money for unforeseen contingencies. They hold a certain amount of money to provide for the danger of sickness, accidents, unemployment etc. The quantum of amount of money will depend upon the individuals living conditions.

(c) Speculative Motive: Speculative transactions require a high specialised talented skill. Commonly all people will not involve in these activities. Some people will hold financial resources in the liquid form in order to take advantage of the market movements regarding the fluctuations in the rate of interest. The stored money is used to make speculative gains by dealing in the debt instruments whose price fluctuate. When the rate of interest falls, the speculator will buy bonds to sell if the prices later rise. They know perfectly when to buy and when to sell in the market with the stored money. They perform the transactions with expectations of their past experience. The amount of money to be kept by them will depend upon the market situation. Therefore, the demand for money determine the **rate of interest**. According to the market situation, the money supply may be adjusted by the **Central bank**. The shifts in the liquidity function may be either downward or upward depending on the market situation. According to **Keynes**, it has been pointed out that the rate of interest is not purely a monetary phenomenon. The real forces may play an important role in determination of the rate of interest.

The Keynesian Theory assumes an equilibrium with less than full employment. This theory regards money as stock and it is an independent variable and is not affected by changes in the rate of interest. Therefore, the banking system can influence the rate of interest by expanding credit.

Modern Theory of Interest: All of these theories discussed above are put forward from time-to-time according to the market situation. These theories suffer from various drawbacks. Modern economists accepted the monetary and real factors. **Prof. Hicks and Hausen** made a study about the determination theory of interest. According to him, the effect of changes in certain variables such as, the saving pattern, the supply of money, investment habits, liquidity preferences on the rate of interest. This theory explains the following elements in the determination of the rate of interest:

(i) money supply
(ii) savings pattern
(iii) government expenditure
(iv) liquidity

(i) Money Supply: Money supply occupies an important role in determination of the rate of interest. If the supply of money has been increased by the Central bank, more money will be diverted for the speculative transactions and the interest rate will come down. If the Central bank has reduced the money supply, the speculative transaction will come down and the rate of interest will be higher.

(ii) Savings Pattern: In the determination of the rate of interest, the savings attitude of the public occupies an important role. If the public desire to save less amount of money, it affects increase in the current consumption of goods. As a result, the level of national income stimulates at each level of rate of interest. In this situation the rate of interest automatically increases. If the people desire to save more amount by postponing their present consumption. It leads to fall in interest rates.

(iii) Government Expenditure: In the economy, the spending capacity of the government will pay a vital role in increasing or decreasing the money circulation. The supply of money plays an important position in the economy. If the government expenditure increases the national income will rise. If the government expenditure reduces, the supply of money will be reduced in the economy and the level of national income will go down.

(iv) Liquidity: The public will keep some amount of money towards the contingent commitment or unforeseen situation. Usually every business enterprise will also hold some amount of money for meeting their unforeseen situation. Therefore, the stored money kept by the society influence the circulation of money. If the public maintains higher liquidity position the money circulation will be declined and the rate of interest increases. As a result the level of national income lowers. If the people are not interested towards the liquidity the supply of money increases and there will be a lower rate of interest. As a result the national income will be stimulated.

All these above factors will influence the rate of interest and circulation of money. The government is also in a position to influence the level of economic activities by the monetary and fiscal measures. The theory explains that the theory of money is related with the theory of income. It has synthesised the monetary and fiscal policies. These policies can play a useful role in the regulation of economic activities. The modern theory has its own limitations.

Statement Showing the Interest Rates in India During the Period 1972-2001 (%) (P.A.)

Year	*Bank Rate*	*Money Market Rate*	*Lending Rate Government*	*Bond Yield*
1972	6%	4.69%	–	5.65%
1973	7%	6.64%	–	5.65%
1974	9%	13.52%	–	6.04%
1975	9%	10.40%	–	6.35%
1976	9%	11.28%	–	6.29%
1977	9%	10.18%	–	6.32%
1978	9%	8.05%	13.50%	6.37%
1979	9%	8.47%	14.50%	6.45%
1980	9%	7.24%	16.50%	6.71%
1981	10%	8.61%	16.50%	7.15%
1982	10%	7.27%	16.50%	7.59%
1983	10%	8.30%	16.50%	7.99%
1984	10%	9.95%	16.50%	8.65%
1985	10%	10.00%	16.50%	8.99%
1986	10%	9.97%	16.50%	–
1987	10%	9.83%	16.50%	–
1988	10%	9.73%	16.50%	–
1989	10%	11.39%	16.50%	–
1990	10%	15.57%	16.50%	–
1991	12%	19.35%	17.88%	–
1992	12%	15.23%	18.92%	–
1993	12%	8.64%	16.25%	–
1994	12%	7.14%	14.75%	–
1995	12%	15.57%	15.46%	–
1996	12%	11.04%	15.96%	–
1997	9%	5.29%	13.83%	–
1998	9%	–	13.54%	–
1999	8%	–	12.54%	–
2000	8%	–	12.29%	–
2001	6.5%	–	12.08%	–

Source: *International Financial Statistics Year Book 2002*, p. 563

SUMMARY

A well-regulated modern financial sector is essential in a globalised economy. Finance has a tendency towards from bust cycles. Financial system is the base for the capital formation. Indian financial system can be classified into three categories: (a) Indian financial system (Banking), (b) Indian financial system (money and capital market), and (c) Indian financial system (Development Banking Institutes). Money market is the market for lending and borrowing of short-term funds. Capital market is the market for long-term sources of finance. It refers to meet the long-term sources of the requirements of the industry. Primary market is a new issue market. The funds are raised through the sale of new securities flow from the buyers of securities, the issuer of securities.

The expansion and capital formation of the industrial sector depends upon the availability of adequate financial resources. The structure of development banks can be categorised as IDBI, ICICI and IFCI. IDBI has been empowered to finance all types of individual concern. ICICI has been established for the purpose of assisting industries in the private sector. IFCI has been also established for financing to the industries in private sector. It also provides financial assistance to cooperative, joint public sector units. Financial institutions are the active players in the capital market. These organisations provide long-term loans on easy instalments to the corporate sector.

NOTES

1. Ruddar Datt and K.P.M. Sundaram, *Indian Economy,* S. Chand and Co., 1996, p. 274.
2. *Ibid.,* p. 285.
3. Roshini Jayakar, The Stock Markets Future, *Business Today*, Annual Issue, p. 72, BTAI 2002.
4. *Ibid.*
5. *Ibid.*
6. BSE Then and Now, BT, Anniversary Issue, p. 63, 2002.
7. The Mutual Funds Boom, Business Today, Anniversary Issue, p. 69, 2002.
8. Indian Household's Investment Preferences, L.C. Gupta, Society for Capital Market Research and Development Jan. 2000, p. 1.
9. *Ibid.*
10. Indian Household Investment Preferences, All India Investor's Survey, Dr. L.C. Gupta, Society for Capital Market Research, New Delhi, 2001, p. 67.
11 *Ibid.*
12. *Ibid.*
13. S.N. Maheshwari, R.R. Paul, *Banking and Financial Services*, Kalyani Publishers, 2001, p.76.
14. *Ibid.,* p.67.
15. Mithani and Gordon, *Banking and Financial System*, Himalaya Publishing, 2002, p. 149.
16. Current Statistics, *Economic and Political Weekly*, 7-12-02. p. 4878.
17. Some Issues of growth and profitability in Indian public sector banks, *Economic and Political Weekly*, 1-6-2002, p. 2155.
18. *Ibid.*

19. K.B.L Mathur, Public Sector Banks in India, *Economic and Political Weekly*, 8.6.2002, p. 2245.
20. *Ibid.*, p. 2249.
21. *Ibid.*, p. 2245.
22. *Ibid.*
23. *Ibid.*, p. 2253.
24. *EPW*, 1-6-2002, p. 2158.
25. Mithani and Gordon, *Banking and Financial System*, Himalaya Publishing House, 2002.
26. *Ibid.*, p. 228.
27. *Ibid.*, p. 85.
28. *EPW*, August 10, 2002, p. 3311.
29. P. Subramaniyan, *Capital Market*, Kalyani Publications.
30. *Fundamentals of Financial Management.*
31. Household's Investment Preferences, *SCMRD*, Jan. 2001, p. 111.
32. C. Vanhorne, Fundamentals of Financial Management, *PHI*, p. 527.
33. *Ibid.*
34. M.N. Mishra, Money, *Banking and International Trade*, S. Chand and Co. Ltd., 1987, p. 228.
35. *Sources: RBI Bulletin* Feb. 2002, p. S103.
36. K.K. Dewett, *Modern Economic Theory*, S. Chand & Co. Ltd., 1997, p. 282.
37. *Ibid.*, p. 291
38. James C. Vanhorne, *Fundamentals of Financial Management*, p. 91, Prentice Hall of India, New Delhi.
39. L.M. Bhole, *Financial Institutions and Financial Markets*, p. 25.

Unit - II

- Management of Financial Institutions
  (a) Risk
  (b) Commercial Banks
  (c) SEBI

Chapter 1

RISK

RISK AND RETURN

Introduction

The public sector banks already with the burgeoning **non-performing assets, low profit margins and poor management** are now hit by the recent pay order scam gripping the markets. The pay order scam triggered by the **Madhavpura Mercantile Cooperative Bank** has once again brought to light the poor risk management systems of the State. The banks have suffered losses of nearly **Rs.250 crores** on account of transactions with troubled cooperative banks. The risk management procedures of the public sector banks have not changed since liberalisation. Over the last five years, India saw the demise of **non-banking financial companies.** At present it is beginning to see the demise of smaller cooperative banks.

Banks are in the business of financial intermediation and naturally related to various kinds of **financial and non-financial risks.** They have been moving towards centralising risk management with an integrated treasury management function in order to benefit from the information on aggregate exposure, natural netting of exposures, economies of scale and easier reporting to top management. The risks are appropriately managed and typically be vested with the board of directors.

Generally every commercial enterprise is haunted by uncontrolled environment. The business activities is exposed to all sorts of dangers. The business has to face both internal and external threat. Now-a-days, it is highly impossible to run the business without the threats. The business became as adventure. The firm may not be in a position to face the heavy competition. Usually the banking sector faces a hidden threat, that is risk. Risk is arisen when the money follows to get return through business operations. The return is always chased by the powerful element "**Risk**". There will be more changes to risk to the financial institutions because they are doing the business with money. Risk is measurable and it may be expected by past experience. The intelligent entrepreneur will escape the risk and trying to reach the return. The risk can be defined as "The variability of return from those that are expected".[1]

Types of Risk

The financial institutions have the chance for the exposure of risk. There are a number of sources behind risk. The following are the different types of risks which occurred in the normal business environment:

A. Systematic risk
B. Unsystematic risk
C. Financial risk
D. Maturity risk
E. Default risk
F. Call risk
G. Inflation risk
H. Currency risk
I. Country risk
J. Total risk
K. Business risk
L. Interest rate risk

The Systematic risk is known as market risk. It affects the overall market. It does not affect a single firm. It is common to all business concerns to the industry. The market can be influenced by nation's state of economy, such as tax reforms, amendments made by the Parliament or a change in the global environment. The systematic risk can be defined as "The variability of return on stocks or portfolios associated with changes in return on the market as a whole".

Unsystematic risk affects to particular business concern or industry. It does not affect to overall the market. It is also known as **Diversifiable risk.** It may be reduced or eliminated through diversification. It has been defined as that "Risk which can be reduced or eliminated through diversification of security holdings".[2]

The unsystematic risk depends upon the factors such as management capability. Consumer preferences and labour strikes. These factors affect a particular industry or a firm. The investors will find in assessing the risk. **Beta** is an index of systematic risk. It measures the sensitivity of a stock's returns to changes in return on the market portfolio. The **Beta** of a portfolio is simply a weighted average of the individual stock betas in the portfolios. The security with a higher beta that is more fluctuation than the market. The security with a lower than 1 beta would rise or fall more slowly than the market. Beta can be positive or negative. The beta can be arrived by the following formula:

R_s = $a + B_s R_m$
R_s = stimated return on the stock
a = estimated when the market return iso
B_s = measure of stocks sensitivity to the market index
R_m = return on the market index

Financial risk is related with the use of debt financing by companies. The high presence of debt in the capital structure may lead to the insolvency position because the earnings are not sufficient to meet debt payment pressure on the company. The presence of high debt in the capital structure component requires heavy amount of interest payment. It is avoidable risk and the company management have the freedom to decide to borrow or not to borrow funds. The debt financing is also called as trading on equity. A company without debt component in the Capital structure will reflect on Company share holders earnings. The veliance on debt financing is known as financial leurage. The debt financing has the affect on three important factors:

(a) It increases the variability of their returns.
(b) It affects the shareholders expectations regarding dividends
(c) It increases risk.

Maturity risk is associated when the term of maturity of the security happens to be longer. The payment of debt is the term of maturity. The greater the risk the business of the future, forecasting visualising becomes more and more difficult and involves risk.

Default risk is related from the failure on the part of the borrower or debtor. It is associated with non-payment of the principal and interest amount for the time specified in the debt contract. It has the capital and income risk.

Call risk is associated with corporate bonds. The bonds are issued with a particular date of its maturity. The issues of the bond have the right to redeem before maturity. Therefore, the bondholders face the risk by giving up higher coupon bonds. Hence, the bondholder re-investing the proceeds at a lower interest rates and incurring the cost and inconvenience.

Inflation risk is related to fixed income securities. It is also known as purchasing power risk. It is the risk that the real return on security may be less than the nominal return. The fixed income securities since payments in terms of rupees are fixed. The value of the payments in real terms declines as the level of commodity prices increase. There is always a chance that the purchasing power of invested amount will decline or that the real return will decline due to inflation. It is really the risk of unanticipated. It is closely related to invest rate risk. The interest rates generally rise if inflation occurs.

Currency risk is called as Exchange rate risk. It is related to international transactions market. It refers to cash flow variability reflected by business units which are engaged in international trade. It is involved in unexpected changes in exchange rate. The forex is a highly volatile market. The unfavourable changes in global market will adversely affect the profitability of the companies under the fixed exchange rate system. There is no chance to occur currency risk. The currency risk is highest in case of freely floating exchange rate system.

Country risk is referred as related to a risk to an investment within a given country. The risk occurred in respect of an investment in a foreign country is known as country risk. It is a complicated concept. The country risk mainly depends upon the political risk involved in that country. The stability of the government in a concerned country is the most important element. Economic stability of the country is another important element.

Total risk in the summation of systematic and unsystematic risk. It is also known as diversifiable and non-diversifiable risk. Diversifiable risk represents the portion of an investments risk that can be eliminated by holding sufficient stocks. The total risk is uncontrollable. Non-diversifiable risk is external to an industry and is attributed to broad forces such as war, inflation, political events and sociological events. The total risk can be shown as follows

Total Risk = Diversifiable Risk + Non-diversifiable Risk

The intelligent investor can eliminate diversifiable risk by holding sufficient portfolio of securities. The ideal scrips selecting 15 scrips for the portfolio that can be easily eliminated by diversifiable risk. Non-diversifiable risk is an avoidable. Each security possesses its own level of non-diversifiable risk.

Business risk means the uncertainty of cash flows due to the nature of the business. It is a function of the operating conditions faced by a business concern. The variability in income levels of the concern will be reflected in operating income and expected dividend. The level of degree of variation from the expected trend would measure business risk. Business risk is faced by firms with two elements they are:

(a) External business risk
(b) Internal business risk

External business risk is beyond the control of the firm. Each firm in the market faces this kind of business risk. The external factors are too numerous to present in detail.

For example: A cut in defence budget of the government, tariff system of the government policy, demographical considerations, political policies, government policies regarding various sectors. These external factors show impact on sale of retail stores, television manufacturers etc.

International business risk is closely related with efficient operational capabilities of the firm. Every firm has its own set of internal risk. It is controllable by the firm.

Interest rate risk means the uncertainty of future market values occurred by fluctuations in the normal level of interest rates. The variability in return on security caused to changes in the level of market interest rates. The interest ratc risk is directly associated with the length of time to maturity of thc security. If the maturity period of time is very long the market value of the security may fluctuate widely. The interest rate risk consists of two elements. They are: (a) price risk and (b) reinvcstment risk. The price risk will increase if the interest rates increase. There will be inverse relationship between the security price and interest rates. The re-invcstment risk involves from the uncertainty of the interest rates if the normal interest rates increase but the re-investment risk declines. Interest rates risk will be involved in all types of securities. The higher interest rates on debt leads to reduce their demand for equity. When the demand for equity declines it leads to decline in the security prices. If the interest rates increase the common stock prices will be lower.

Return

Gencrally the investors have many motives for investing. Some investors make investments to gain power in corporate sector. For majority of the investor, their interest in investments is to earn a better return on their investment. The most investors not only like return but also they dislike risk. Most of the investors do not invest in few scrips. The other factors may be taken into consideration in the selection process of scrips. The investor will make up his mind about his investment decisions to be taken. He thinks about what securities must purchased and how much amount of money should be allocated to each scrip. All of these decisions will be taken on the basis of two steps. At the first instance the investor should prepare his estimation of return and the risk is associated with the selected securities over a period of holding period. This step is called as security analysis. The second step requires the estimated return risk which must be compared in order to allocate the available funds among this scrips as a continuing situation. This step is known as portfolio analysis, selection and management.

Usually the investors want to maximise their return and minimise the risk. Return is the reward to the investors. It is the oxygen to the millions of investors. It is the strong motivating force behind the investors investment decisions. Return is the most important factor to the investors in comparing alternative investments. Historical return is the important factor for the investors for the estimation of future commonly return and expected return. Realised return is called as historical return. The realised return is enjoyed by the investor from the company. Expected return is a predicated return. It is the return from an asset that the investor has expected to earn some in future. It may or may not occur. Usually the investors may will make their investment decisions for a particular asset if the expected return is adequate. But the investors must understand that their derive may or may not be materialised.

Return on investments consists of two elements. They are: (a) regular return, and (b) capital appreciation. The regular return on securities is available either in the form of interest or dividend. The periodic cash receipt on the investments is known as the dividend or interest the income from an financial asset consisting one or more cash payments paid at specified interval of time. The interest on bonds will be paid semi-annually. The term yield is used in connection with the component of return. Yield is associated with the income component in relation to some price for a security. The yield is not the factor or for proper measure of return from a security. The capital appreciation or loss should be taken into consideration.

TOTAL RETURN = INCOME + CAPITAL APPRECIATION

The above equation is a conceptual meaning for total return. Every investor should remember that security's total return consists of the sum of two components, dividend and capital appreciation.

Return Measurement

While estimating total return, the correct measurement must incorporate both income and capital appreciation. The returns can be measured for a period of time or make comparison from different securities. The total return can be computed as follows:

$$\text{Total Return} = \frac{\text{Cash reward received} + \text{Capital appreciation over the period}}{\text{Purchase price of the asset}}$$

The price change over a period of time is the difference between purchase and sale price. This can be either negative or positive. The total return for each year can be calculated. It is an acceptable measure of return for specific period of time. It can be calculated in two kinds:

(a) Arithmetic Return
(b) Geometric Return

The arithmetic average return is the statistical familiar to the most people. The arithmetic mean can be computed by the formula

$$\bar{X} = \frac{\Sigma x}{n}$$

It is appropriate as a measure of central tendency.

The geometric mean return is another measurement for calculation of total return. It measures compound cumulative returns over time. It is useful in investment decisions to analyse the realised change over in multiple periods. The geometric average is defined as the *n*th root of the product resulting from multiplying a series of return together.

The geometric mean can be computed by the following formula:

$$U = \left[(1 + R_1)(1 + R_2) \ldots (1 + R_n)^{\frac{1}{n} - 1} \right]$$

U = geometric mean
n = number of period

It reflects compound, cumulative returns over a period of time. Return may be categorised as follows:

(a) Yield rate
(b) Bond rate
(c) Expected return
(d) Holding period yield
(e) Basic yield
(f) Current yield
(g) Yield to maturity
(h) Dividend yield
(i) Real return
(g) Earning yield
(h) Required rate of return

Yield rate is also known as internal rate of return. Internal rate of return is the rate of discount which makes the present value of all the cash inflows from the investments that is equal to the total cost of that investments. It is the rate which discounts the cash flows to zero.

It can be computed in the form of ratio as follows:

$$IRR = \frac{\text{Cash inflows}}{\text{Cash outflows}}, \text{ or}$$

$$IRR = \frac{R}{I+V}$$

R = cash inflow
I = cash outflow
V = internal rate of return

or

$$F = \frac{I}{C}$$

F = factor to be located
I = original investment
C = cash inflow per year

Bond rate is also called as coupon rate. The coupon rate of interest will be received by the investor on the face value of the bond or par value of the bond. The bonds are generally issued by the commercial enterprises and the government. Every bond carries its coupon rate. The coupon rate will be filled before the issue. The bonds are usually redeemed either 10 or 15 years. For example: If a company or the government issues a 15 years bond with Rs.100 face value and 10% rate of interest. Therefore, it would be described as 10 per cent bond or debenture. It may also be called as 10% coupon rate bond.

Expected return is also called as predicted return. Return is not a simple concept. It is not guaranteed. It is mostly expected by every investor, business organisation and every being. But it may or may not materialise. Hence the expected return is predicted, desired anticipated which is subject to uncertainty realised return is the actual earned amount by the investors and business community. It is the historical return. It is a post return.

Holding period yield is the total return from an investment during a particular period of time. It is expected that it does not mean that the security is actually disposed and the profit or loss is actually realised by the investor. It can computed as follows:

$$\text{HPY} = \frac{\text{Any dividend required} + \text{Sale price}}{\text{Purchase price of the asset}}$$

Basic yield is the concept of pure rate of interest. It is unique and absolutely risk less. It is the lowest yield actually attained in the market by high grade bonds of a maturity period of time. It is absolutely safety and certainty of principal and income. It is free from losses through changes in commodity prices, interest rates and taxes. It is available on the highest quality of bonds.

Current yield is associated with the bond market. It is the ratio of coupon rate per year to the current market price of the bond. It is also known as the market yield or income yield. It will not take into consideration of the return which was to be realised by the investor due to the appreciation/depreciation in the value.

Yield to maturity is also known as Redemption yield. It is the promised rate of return to the purchased at the current market price and yield till maturity. The consideration which is to be received by the investor from the purchased bond till maturity. The yield to maturity can be calculated by the following formula:

$$\text{YIM} = \frac{\text{Annual interest} + \text{Capital appreciation or depreciation}}{\text{Face value of redemption value}}$$

Dividend yield refers to the ratio of per share expected dividend to the current market price of the share. It is also the ratio of per share prospective dividends gross of tax to the current market price of the share.

Real return is the return which is adjusted for changes in prices.

Earning yield is consisting of gross and net yield. Gross yield refers to the yield which is realised by the investor before paying taxes. The net yield is the remaining amount after payment of the taxes. The net yield can be calculated as follows:

Net yield = Cross yield (1 – Tax rate)

The required rate of return plays an important role in the valuation of asset. It occupies a vital role in financial and real investment decisions. It is the minimum expected rate of return at a accepted level of risk by the investor.

It has two elements (a) the risk free vote of return, (b) the risk premium. The risk free rate of return is also known as the real rate of interest. It is the reward to the investor to postpone his consumption to the future. The required rate of return is the risk free rate of return which is equal to the real rate of return plus inflation premium. The another element of the required rate of return is the risk premium. The premium for risk reflect the uncertainty in investments.

Risk Return Trade off

Generally all the investors are interested towards higher profit. They want to maximise return and minimise the risk. But they should know that where the higher risk, where the higher return available. The common investor always think about the high profit on his investment by ignoring the risk. If the low risk is involved in financial asset, there will be lower profit available to him. The financial markets offer a wide range of assets. They are available in market from very safe to very risk. The intelligent investor will consider the best asset for investing which provides potential return and the risk involved. Usually there will be a high correlation between risk and return over longer period of time. The securities are usually priced at high risk is rewarded with high return, low risk is followed by low return. This relationship is known as risk return trade off. The return is always involved by the risk. The level of degree of risk between return and risk is considered by the market forces. Basically every financial asset having its own range of risk. The rational investor will accept the greater risk only when the additional return is on the asset. If the investors want to earn higher return, they must be ready to assume greater risk. It is further observed that the expectation of higher return is involved by higher risk from that financial asset.

Valuation of Securities

Commonly the buying and selling of securities involve on through understanding of the stock, market operations. Before buying a financial asset we must be able to know its intrinsic value. Then we may buy that asset in a right price otherwise it may be purchased in our price. Valuation of securities is being made by financial analyst for the purpose of stock market operations. Valuation means professional estimating, assessing, determining the price worth and value of a financial asset. The objective of any investment is to get the asset which is worth more than its cost. If you want to take financial investment decision portfolio selection and management, it is necessary to know the process of valuation. The valuation technique provides the investors a benchmark or standard of comparison between financial assets and companies. Before valuation of securities the following concepts should be known by every investor:

(a) intrinsic value
(b) time value of money
(c) book value
(d) liquidation value
(e) market value
(f) terminal value.

Intrinsic value is known as fair market value or investment value. Intrinsic value is equal to the present value of a stream of cash flows expected to be generated by the financial asset. The technique for finding out present value is called discounting. In the perfect market environment the market value of the asset truly reflects the intrinsic value.

The concept of time value of money is that a sum of money received today is worth more than of the same is received after sometime. Because the present consumption is valued.

The book value of an asset of a company is based on accounting reports. It is entirely involved in financial data of the concerned company. The book value of an asset can be computed in various methods. In case of a physic asset the following formula can be applied to find out the value of an asset Book value of physical asset = Historical cost – Accumulative depreciation.

In case of common stock the following formula shall be applied to arrive at the value of a stock:

$$\text{Book value of common stock} = \frac{\text{Net worth}}{\text{No. of outstanding shares}}$$

(Net worth = Paid up capital + Reserve and Surplus)

Liquidation value of a firm refers to the value of the business firm which ceases its business. The liquid value of an ordinary can be calculated by the following formula:

$$\text{Liquidation of an ordinary share} = \frac{\text{Amount realised from the asset credit preference share holder}}{\text{No. of outstanding ordinary shares}}$$

Market value means it is the value of an asset which is traded in the market at particular period of time.

Terminal value means it is their value of the asset or money is the value of today's money at some moment of time in future.

The valuation of assets can be studied by the following methods:

(a) valuation of debenture
(b) valuation of preference shares
(c) valuation of equity shares.

Valuation of Debenture

The valuation of debenture can be calculated through the following methods:

vd = $I\,(ADFI) + F\,(DFF)$
vd = current value of the debenture
I = interest payable on the debenture/bond
$ADFI$ = annuity discount factor applicable to face value
F = face value
vd (i) = A/i
vd (i) value of a debenture (irredeemable)
A = annual interest
I = expected rate of return

$$yd = \frac{Ai}{Mpd}$$

yd = yield of debentures
Ai = annual interest
Mpd = market price of debentures

$$ydm = \frac{Ai + (F - p)/n}{(F + p)/2}$$

ydm = yield till maturity
Ai = annual interest
F = face value of the debentures
p = present value of the debentures
n = period of debenture to maturity

Valuation of Preference Shares

Preference shares carry a fixed dividend rate and hence their valuation can be done on the same basis as that of bonds or debenture. Preference shares further can be classified as Redeemable and Irredeemable shares. In case of irredeemable preference shares the following formula can be applied:

Vp = Dp/Yp
Vp = value of a preference share
Dp = dividend on a preference share
Yp = yield on a preference share

Valuation Equity Shares

There are various kinds of valuation of equity shares. They basically based on two methods:

(a) dividend capitalisation approach.
(b) earning capitalisation approach.

Dividend capitalisation approach is a very sound approach. The value of an equity share is equivalent to the present value of future dividends plus the present value of the price expected to be realised on its resale.

$$Po = \frac{Di}{(1+Ke)} + \frac{Pi}{(1+Ke)}$$

Po = current price of the equity share
Di = dividend per share expected at the end of first year
Pi = expected market price of the share at the end of first year
Ke = the required rate of return or capitalisation rate
Po = De/Ke
Po = current value of an equity share
De = expected annual dividend per equity share

Ke = capitalisation rate
Po = *Fi/Ke* (Earning approach) stable dividend
Po = current value of an equity share
Ke = capitalisation rate
Ei = expected earning per share

Approach and Security Analysis

The basic aim of the security analysis is to estimate the real worth of a security by considering various factors such as earning potential of a firm, state of the economy mortuary, policies of the central bank, corporate laws, social and political environment etc. During the period of economic prosperity the demand for more goods and services of the firm is likely to result in higher profits. The approach to the study of security analysis can be done by the following tools:

(a) Fundamental analysis
(b) Technical analysis
(c) Efficient market theory.

The fundamental analysis reveals the intrinsic value of a security. The intrinsic value is the real worth of a security. The real worth of a security is influenced by various factors.

The technical analysis is used to find out the price of a stock which depends on supply and demand in the market. The technical analysis is the controversial aspect of investment management. The technical analysis is a tool which should be used with fundamental analysis.

The efficient market theory is another approach to find out the worth of a security. All known information is immediately discounted by the market.

All of the above approaches will be studied in depth in the following chapters:

SUMMARY

Security analysis refers to the analysis of trading securities. It analyses about the share prices, returns and the risk involved. Every investment is risky and the expected return is related to the risk. The security analysis contains the elements such as Risk Return. Risk return trade off and valuation risk is a situation where in objective probability distribution of the values, a variable that can take place is known but the exact value is not known. The risk is measurable. It may be expected by past experience and the law of chance. There are various kinds of risks which are generally occurred in the normal business situation such as systematic risk, unsystematic risk, financial risk, maturity risk, default risk, call risk, inflation risk, currency risk, country risk, total risk, business risk and interest rate risk.

Generally the investors have many motives for investing. The investor's interest is to earn a better return on their investment. The investors not only like return but also dislike risk. Return is the reward to the investor. It is the oxygen to the millions of investors. The return may be categorised as Realised Return and Expected Return. Realised return is called as Historical Return. Expected return is a predicated return. The return can be measured by various methods. Valuation means professionally estimating assessing, determining the price worth and value of a financial asset. There are three approaches to find the real value of the security. They are: (i) fundamental, (ii) Technical analysis, and (iii) Efficient Market theory.

Key words

Investments	:	The intention of the investors to enter in a business transaction is known as investment.
Security analysis	:	Security analysis refers to the analysis of trading securities.
Risk	:	Risk is a situation where in objective probability distribution of the values variable that can take place is known but the exact value is not known.
Systematic risk	:	The systematic risk affect the overall market. The market can be influenced by the nations economy, tax reforms or change in the energy situations.
Unsystematic risk	:	Unsystematic risk affect to a particular company or industry.
Financial risk	:	Financial risk is related with the use of debt financing by companies.
Maturity risk	:	Maturity risk is associated when the term of maturity of the security happens to be longer.
Default risk	:	Default risk is related from the failure on the part of the borrower or debtor. It is associated with non-payment of the principal and interest amount for the time specified in the debt contract.

Call risk	:	Call risk is associated with corporate bonds. This risk arises when the bonds are pre-matured.
Inflation risk	:	Inflation risk is related to fixed income securities of inflation occurs the interest rates generally rises
Currency risk	:	Currency risk is related to international trade market. It is involved in unexpected changes in exchange rate.
Return	:	Return is the reward to the investor.
Yield	:	Yield is used in connection with the component of return.
Intrinsic value	:	Intrinsic value is equal to the present value of a stream of cash flows expected to be generated by the financial asset.

Chapter 2

COMMERCIAL BANKS

Introduction

The Indian banking system has been changed in response to the merging socio-political economic environment in India. It has restricted itself to the area of short-term finance for meeting the growing needs of the working capital requirements and of the corporate sector. The banks perform several functions such as lending and borrowing. The advances to customers may be made in many ways: **(a) overdraft, (b) cash credit, (c) discounting trade bills, (d) call money, (e) term loans, (f) consumer credit, (g) miscellaneous.** A commercial bank grants overdraft facility to an account holder. The account holder is allowed to draw an amount in excess of the **balance** held in the account up to stipulated limit. **Cash credit** is one of the lending activities of the bank. They give credit in cash to the business units against the guarantee given by the borrowers. It is the most popular lending activity in the banking systems. **Bill discounting** is another type of lending activity by the banks. They facilitate trade and commerce by discounting the bills of exchange called as **trade bills. Call money** means granting loans for a very short period by the bankers. Generally the banks grant loans not exceeding 7 days to the borrowers. Usually the stock-brokers utilise these sources of finance from the banks. Term loan refer finance to the traders, industrialists and agriculturists against collateral securities. The maturity period of the loan is in between **1 to 10 years**. These loans are useful to the industrial sector for meeting the requirement of the working capital. The business concerns generally require two kinds of capital such as Fixed Capital and Working Capital. **Fixed Capital** will be procured by the companies through the issue of shares and debentures. **Working Capital** can be raised from the banks through various sources of finance. The working capital is the most important factor for the smooth functioning of the business operations without any interruption. The management of the working capital requires an efficient financial planning.

In the modern **digital economy** the banking system has to reorient its lending practices to cope with the financial needs of the industry. The banks in India shifted their focus in favour of industry. They provide financial support to the new industrial enterprises in the form of new financing methods such as **lending, underwriting and direct subscription** to the corporate securities. The Central Government introduced a formal scheme of term loan in **1958.** According to this scheme, the banks were provided with the refinancing facilities against the term loans from the **Refinance Corporation of Industry Ltd.** The RCI was established for this purpose. It merged with the IDBI in 1964. The banks merely acted as the financial intermediaries to distribute the term loans, which was sanctioned by the RCI. Afterward they provide term loans from their own funds. The banks can also participate in the underwriting activity through the permission of the Reserve Bank. The bulk of finance to the industrial sector is still in the form of short-term finance. The RBI constituted from time-to-time a number of expert groups to examine the various aspects of the banking policy relating to the industrial aspects. The Committees such as **Dhejia Committee (1969), Tandon Committee (1974), Chore Committee (1980) and Marathe Committee (1984).** The Committees made recommendations for formulation of framework and for regulation of industrial financing after the mid-seventies. The framework contains the following elements **(mid-seventies)**:

(a) fixation of rules and regulations
(b) mode of finance
(c) surveillance

Fixation of Rules and Regulations

The salient features of the regulations were associated with the fixation of rules for bank lending to corporate sector. The regulations can be categorised into two categories.

(i) Raw material norms.
(ii) Lending conditions.

Generally the companies involved in procuring the raw material according to their convenience. They hold raw material to the maximum level and deploy them for smooth functioning of the production levels. Hence the banks prepared initially the inventory and receivable norms for advancing the loans to the industrial sector. The commercial banks provided finance to the corporate sector accounted for about **one-half** of the funds of their portfolio. They provided finance in respect of 15 major industries. The RBI revised the norms and several industries were added to the list from mid-eighties. The norms were related to raw materials, stock in process, finished goods and receivables. The regulations were based on time element. The financing process would be based on the consumption of the raw material. The time factor stock in progress and cost of production would be taken into consideration. The estimation of finished goods value and receivables and volume of sales would also be taken into valuation. The regulations prescribed for the account receivables were associated only to the domestic sales on a short-term basis. These regulations framed the maximum levels of holding inventory and receivable for all industries. The borrowing parties such as companies, commercial enterprises and manufacturing concerns were not expected to hold more than that level. The assessment of raw materials could be considered by the following factors:

(a) purchase of raw materials with bunched receipts
(b) interruptions in the process of production such as power-cuts, strikes etc.
(c) the length of time period for stock in process
(d) the lock in period for finished goods
(e) the time allowed for debtors or the time lag period for Accounts Recievables
(f) provision of raw material for specific export contracts.

All these factors were based on time factor. These norms were prescribed for different industries in different ways. The borrowers were not permitted to hold more than permitted levels. Hence the availability of bank credit had been subjected to various conditions. The government appointed the following Committees to study about the granting of finance for the working capital:

(i) Dehejia Committee Report, 1969
(ii) Tandon Committee Report, 1975
(iii) Chore Committee Report, 1980
(iv) Marathe Committee Report, 1984

V.T. Dehejia Committee was appointed in 1968 to determine the extent of credit requirements of industry and trade. The national credit council was constituted for examining the credit needs of industry. The Committee submitted its report in September 1969. They found that there was a tendency on the part of the industry to avail excess credit than their requirements. The acquisition of **Non-current Assets.** The Committee made various recommendations to improve the lending system. The Committee recommended that every application must be scrutinised by the banker on the basis of cash flow statement submitted by the borrower. It also recommended that the cash credit should be sanctioned in two portions. They are **hard core** and short-term requirement of credit. Hard Core components such as the minimum level of inventory, finished goods and stores. All these requirements should be financed as **term loan.** The short-term requirements of credit such as increased inventories, tax, dividends and banks payment should be financed in the form of **cash credit.** The Committee made an important recommendation to avoid the possibility of double or multiple financing. The borrower should continue to only one banker. In case of large borrowers it was suggested for the adoption of consortium arrangement.

P.L. Tandon Committee was appointed by the Reserve Bank in July 1974, to look into the matters of bank credit system. It was appointed to suggest guidelines for the commercial banks to follow up and supervise credit facilities. It was also to suggest the type of operational data and other information to be submitted periodically by the banks to the RBI. It was appointed

(a) to make good suggestions for prescribing inventory norms for various industries.
(b) to suggest the corporate sector for better capital structure and good financial soundness in association with borrowings.
(c) to make recommendations for better financing of the minimum working capital.
(d) to suggest suitable modifications in financing process of working capital requirement.

The Committee studied the existing financing of the working capital requirement to industry and identified the following recommendations essentially based on three principles such as **proper financial discipline** has to be followed by the borrower. The bank credit should not be misused. The available bank credit should be a supplement to the borrowers resources to carry an acceptable level of current assets. The Committee recommended for lending banking norms to finance the working capital.

These norms can be divided in two methods:

(a) inventory norms, and
(b) lending norms.

The Committee has suggested norms for 15 major industries such as cotton and synthetic textiles, jute, rubber products, industrial chemicals, fertilisers, pharmaceuticals, cement, engineering, oils, papers, man-made fibre and capital equipments suppliers.

Lending norms has indicated that the financing of bank credit should be a supplement to the borrowers own financial resources.

Chore Committee was appointed in March 1979, to review the working of cash credit system. The Committee was also asked to suggest alternative types of credit facilities which should ensure greater credit discipline to the borrowers. The Committee recommended to continue the existing system of lending such cash credit, loans and bill discounting. It further suggested the banks to streamline cash credit system. It made the following recommendations to the government:

(a) no demarcation of cash credit accounts.
(b) separate credit level to seasonal and unseasonal level requirement.
(c) large borrowers should submit quarterly statements.
(d) the borrowers should not entertain more than the sanctioned limits.
(c) the over dependence on bank credit should be reduced.

Marathe Committee was appointed by the Reserve Bank of India to suggest measures for providing meaningful directions to the credit management function of the Reserve Bank. It indicated five requirements under **Fast Track Scheme.** They are:

(a) Every banker should check about clients past record such as production, sales, other current assets and liabilities etc. The bank should observe the past trends and it is also to be seen that the build-up of investor levels and accounts receivable reasonable.
(b) The bank should verify the classification of current assets and liabilities of the client company as per the guidelines of the RBI.
(c) The banker must observe about the maintenance of minimum current ratio of 1.3:1.

(d) The banker should ensure himself that all the forms are submitted quickly or not?

(e) According to the Fast Track system the borrower should submit his annual accounts regularly and promptly. The banker is empowered to review the borrowers account atleast once a year.

After the completion of careful examination, the banker should forward a certificate to that effect to the Reserve Bank. The banker should gear up their organisational efficiency at various stages of their organisational hierarchy.

Lending Norms

Another category of norms is also related to lending. It is the norms related to the current assets of the client. The corporate sectors current assets should be financed by the trade credit and current liabilities. The difference between current assets and current liabilities is known as **working capital.** It should be financed by the company's own fund and partly by the bank finance. The part of the bank finance should be sanctioned as short-term financé. There are 3 methods to finance the bank proportion to the corporate sector. According to the **first method,** the working capital requirement of the company shall be through short-term credit to the extent of 75% and the remaining amount should be financed through long-term funds. **The second method** stipulates that the company must provide 25% of the total current assets and the rest will be financed by the bank. The total current liabilities of the including bank borrowings should not exceed 75% of the current assets. According to the method the company should maintain the current ratio 1.3:1. According to the **third method** the minimum level of raw materials, stock in progress, finished goods and stores should constitute a fixed element from the total current assets. It has resulted in further reduction in the bank credit and strengthening of the current ratio. Another important factor in the lending norms is the kind of financing. The corporate sector enjoyed the bank finance through the **cash credit system** till mid-seventies. Therefore, it was continued upto 1994. In 1995 it was slightly changed and put a mandatory limit on cash credit and a loan system was introduced. Thus the corporate working capital was financed through the cash credit system to the extent of **60%** and the balance was in the form of **40%** as short-term loans. At present the banks sanction **20%** in cash credit and **80%** as loan component. This sanction of financing the working capital was based on the submission of information by the companies. The banks should furnish four important documents such as **Form I, II, III, and III-B.** All these documents should be furnished as per the prescribed proforma by the companies to the concerned bank. They should furnish as a quarterly basis to the bank. **Form I** reveals about the particulars of production and sales estimates for the current and next quarter. It also includes about the estimates of current assets and current liabilities of the completed quarter. **Form II** should be contained about the details of actual production and sales during the current year and latest completed year. It also includes about actual current assets and current liabilities for the latest completed quarter. **Form III** contains about the information of operating performance for half yearly ended in relation to the estimates provided. **Form III-B** consists of the estimated as well as actual sources of funds and disposal of funds for half yearly ended.

The liberalisation, privatisation and globalisation have created a revolutionary changes in the banking sector. The banks are given full freedom in assessing the working capital requirements of the corporate sector. The RBI is supreme authority in the banking sector. It permits the banks to finance the industrial sector with more freedom. Therefore, the RBI relaxed and modified the rules and regulations to finance the corporate sector. The modified regulations are related to inventory, accounts receivables, maximum permissible bank finance, credit delivery system and monitoring etc. The RBI announced its credit policy in October 1993. According to this policy the banks were permitted to make their own assessment of the borrowers credit fulfilments on the basis of their total business operations. The norms would serve as a broad guidelines for the banks. The RBI has taken several steps to maintain discipline among borrowers for better utilisation of credit. It has introduced a new credit delivery system. Previously the banking sector has provided finance to the corporate sector through a combination different style of finance such as cash credit, loans, bills discounting and commercial papers. The new style of finance system made the banks mandatory to provide 25% of the maximum permissible bank finance as demand loan and the balance could be sanctioned as cash credit for the working capital. The corporate borrowers are permitted to invest their short-term idle funds in the money market instruments. In 1997 the banks are allowed to evolve their own methods and to assess the working capital requirements under the prudential guidelines and exposure norms. Some banks prefer to finance through maximum permissible bank finance. Some other banks prefer finance through **Turnover Method.** The turnover method is based on some limits.

(a) The turnover method is applicable to all corporate borrowers those whose working capital limited up to **Rs.2 crore.**
(b) This ceiling limit is fixed at a higher of the following amounts:
  (i) 20% of projected gross annual sales turnover, or
  (ii) Actual working capital requirement.
(c) The inventory holding level must be
  (i) Five months sales / 45% of gross sales,
  (ii) For industries such food products, vegetables, fertilisers, man-made textiles at level of **four months sales one third of gross sales** or the projected current assets whichever is less fixed.
(d) In case of tea, sugar and construction industries in view of their unique nature of manufacturing operations, they require higher level of current assets. They must hold above **four or five months** level of stock. The banks can take a decision after a thorough analysis of the proposal.
(e) The rules for granting working capital assistance, there will be some partial modifications in the components of current assets items. As per the modified rules margin on letter of credit, guarantees are part of. They are utilised for meeting **current liabilities.** In the light of partial modifications, any liability which is payable within one year is treated as **current liabilities.**
(f) The corporate sector must maintain the required current ratio as **1:33.** In the case of industries which are having a higher level of term loan instalments must keep a minimum ratio of **1:2**
(g) The corporate borrowers can get the eligible financial assistance from banks without any further condition such as **pre-sale or post-sale.**
(h) The unpaid stock amount is also considered as a part of current asset. The borrower should get all approvals before getting the financial assistance from the banks.
(i) The following norms should be fulfilled by the borrowers:
  (a) There must be interest coverage ratio 2.
  (b) The net worth must be **3** excluding NBFCS.
  (c) Borrowers must earn profits continuously.
(j) The banks should take all the precautions to expedite credit delivery by avoiding repeated and extensive process.

(k) The domestic receivables which are outstanding for more than **6 months** must be excluded from the computation of current assets.

(l) The physical verification of current assets should be done atleast once in a year by a reputed chartered accountant firm.

(m) The bank should see the end use of funds. There should not be any diversion of money from one purpose to another.

(n) The banks should take care about the borrowers financial condition by observing the current ratio profitability ratio, total liability/equity ratio.

Credit Monitoring Arrangement

The Credit Authorisation Scheme was introduced in October 1988. it was replaced by **Credit Authorisation Scheme.** According to this scheme guidelines, the banks should take permission of the RBI before financing beyond a specified level of amount to large borrowers. The scheme put rigorous conditions for sanctioning the financial assistance. The motive behind the scheme was to enforce **financial discipline** among large corporate borrowers. The banks will take **8 to 10 weeks** for the assessment of the proposal made by the corporate borrowers. They will take another **three or four** weeks for the disbursement of funds under this scheme. RBI issued guidelines in 1993 towards credit policy which provides a wider choice to the borrowers. As per the guidelines, the companies with total funds requirement exceeding **Rs. 50 crore** have loan syndication or consortium arrangement. **Consortium arrangement** is the system of financing the borrower by two or more banks. The financing banks will complete the scrutiny within **60 days, 45 days and 30 days** on receipt of an application for a fresh loan or renewal. The consortium arrangement has its advantage. The risk is spread between the participant banks. In this method of financing system, the lead bank occupies an important role. It dictates all terms and conditions to the participant banks. This system of financing fosters efficiency as both the banks and companies have more freedom. The participant banks can charge interest according to their own assessment. It helps the banks to manage their funds more effectively and with profitability. Now the corporate borrowers have full freedom for selecting their lending bank.

Financing Mode of Working Capital

The short-term requirements of the corporate is met by the commercial banks. The needs of the industry are fulfilled by the banks under various schemes. The banks will provide the short-term finance to the corporate sector for their **working capital.** The working capital for the corporate sector is provided by the banks in the following methods:

(a) Cash credit/overdraft
(b) Discounting/purchasing bills
(c) Letter of credit
(d) Commercial papers
(e) Loans
(f) Working capital term loans.

Cash credit/overdraft is the system of financing to the commercial enterprises. It is the arrangement of bank finance to the business community. According to this system, the bank specifies a pre-determined borrowing limit to their customer. The customer/borrower has the choice to draw the cash up to the stipulated level of amount. The borrower can withdraw his sanctioned amount according to his needs and convenience. The interest will be charged on the basis of the running balance or actual amount utilised by the borrower. The bank never charges on the sanctioned amount. However, a minimum charge is payable by the borrower for availing this facility. This kind of financing is very popular among the business community due to its advantages. The borrower can repay the due whenever he desires during the period. This system is more convenient to the businessmen. It is sanctioned for a period of one year. But it may be renewable every year. It is highly flexible and the level of limit can be increased or decreased according to the situation. Interest on the **cash credit** is charged only on the actual amount utilised by the borrower. If the sanctioned limit is not at all used **1/4th or 1/3rd** of the portion amount will be charged for interest purpose. A separate account will be opened for this purpose. The borrower can withdraw the amount from this account for the purpose of working capital. **Overdraft** is another facility which is offered by the banks to the corporate sector. It is an arrangement, whereby a customer is allowed to overdraw his current account up to a sanctioned limit. Therefore, **overdraft** is sanctioned to the borrowers in the current account itself. There is no need to open a separate account by the borrowers. It is granted against security. It is a temporary adjustment and cannot be granted on a regular basis. In this method the borrower can withdraw and deposit money from this account according to his situation. The interest will be charged even though the borrower does not utilise the sanctioned amount.

Discounting of bills/purchase of bills is another important form of credit provided by the banks to the corporate borrowers. This system is relatively originated in India. This scheme was introduced by the RBI in 1970. The bank credit is being made available through purchase/scounting of bills to the corporate sector. It is one of the sources for the corporate sector to meet their short-term financial requirement. According to this system of finance, the commercial banks lend money against the bill of exchange or a promissory note. Generally the business transactions are carried out by the credit system. When a transaction arises between two parties, the bill system will exist in the market. A holder of bill has to **wait** upto the specified period. If the holder is in need of money he can make discount the bill with his banker. Then the banker will credit the account of borrower who brings the bill for discount purpose. There is no any other security except bill in this transaction. But it is provided only to the **good-reputed** parties. This kind of financing eliminates the scope for the misuse of credit to other purpose. This form of financing is not popular in India. The bills can also be re-discounted with other banks or RBI.

Letter of credit is an indirect form of finance. It is provided by the banks to the corporate sector for temporary financing. In this method the banks assume only **risk.** The credit is being provided by the supplier himself. The buyer of goods on credit basis will get a letter of credit from a bank. The bank will assure the supplier that in case of default by the buyer, the amount will be paid by the banker.

Commercial paper is another method of financing to the corporate borrowers. It is a short-term unsecured promissory note issued by a corporate entity. The commercial paper is more useful for mobilising large amount of resources, by a good-reputed companies. It is a reliable source for short-term finance to the corporate sector. The cost of commercial paper is very low when compared to other methods of financing.

Loan is another method of financing to the borrowers. In this method of financing system, the banker will credit the current accounts of the borrower with the sanctioned loan amount. After releasing the entire sanctioned amount, the borrow has to pay interest on the whole amount. The borrower is required to repay the loan on periodical instalments. At present the corporate sector utilises this means of financing for its commitments to the extent of 80%. This system implies a **financial discipline** on the part of the large borrowers. **Financial discipline** is the most important element for every business concern or individual or a nation. It enhances the efficiency of a commercial enterprise. It stimulates the goodwill value of the company in the market.

Working capital term loan is one of the methods of financing provided by the banks to the corporate sector. According to this scheme, the loan amount shall be payable by the borrower from **3 to 7 years** on yearly or half-yearly instalment.

All the above methods of financing involve some or other kind of risks. Therefore, the banks will finance the borrowers after taking adequate **security.** Generally the banks will take security on the following basis:

(a) Hypothecation
(b) Lien
(c) Pledge
(d) Mortgage
(e) Charge

(a) Hypothecation: Generally the banks provide different kinds of loans to different borrowers. The banking sector lends crores of rupees to the public. The disbursement of loans will take only after getting a suitable security from the borrowers. Therefore, **hypothecation** is one of the securities required by the banks in order to dispose the loan amount to the borrowers. It is also known as **Mortgage** of movable property. According to **Dr. Hart,** Hypothecation is nothing but "a charge against property for an amount of debt, where neither ownership nor possession is passed to the creditor".[3]

Usually the banks sanction loans to the borrowers against the security of movable property. The inventory of the company will be hypothecated to the bank as a security. Hypothecation is an extended idea of pledge. If the goods are hypothecated to bank, the goods will be in the possession of the owner of these goods. But the bank has the legal right to sell the goods, if the borrower fails to repay the debt. This facility is available only to the reputed firms. Under hypothecation, the ownership always remains with the borrower.

(b) Lien: Lien means the right of the lender parts to retain the goods belonging to the borrowers party till the repayment of his due amount. It is a right to retain the property of the customer, given as security till the loan is repaid. It can be categorised into two kinds: **(i) particular lien,** and **(ii) general lien.** Particular lien means it is a right of the banker to retain goods until the clearance of his due for specified goods. General lien means all dues of the lender will be paid.

(c) Pledge: Pledge is different from hypothecation. Under this method the goods which are offered as security will be transferred to the lender. The goods will be in the custody of the lender. The borrower is known as **pledger,** the lender is called as **pledgee**. The pledge creates liabilities for the lender. The pledged goods should be taken care of it. If the borrower fails to pay the due amount, the bank has the right to sell goods for his recovery of amount. **Section 172 of the Indian Contract Act** defines pledge as "the bailment of goods as security for payment of a debt or performance of a promise".[4] Further the section lays down the following conditions:

(i) There must be bailment of goods,
(ii) The property or goods will be kept as security for the payment of debt, and
(iii) The goods must be returned on receipt of the due amount.

The borrower should deliver the asset to the banker at the time of getting advance. There must be a physical transfer of goods from the pledger to the **pledgee.** Under pledge, there will not be transfer of ownership of goods. The pledger always remains as the owner of the security. The pledge is applied for the existed goods only and not for the future goods. When the loan amount is repaid, the goods which are kept undertake pledge should be **redelivered** to the borrower. The pledge has the most convenient feature because there are no formalities involved with the creation of pledge. It is a simpler form than any other method. Under the pledge system, it will not be possible for getting the **double finance** with a single item of asset. Manipulation is not possible in the pledge system. The banker can recover his amount of due from the insurance company in case of any damage or loss to the property.

(d) Mortgage: Mortgage is another kind of charging method. It will be used in the case of **immovable properties** such as land and building. According to **Section 58 of the Transfer of Property Act, 1882**, "A mortgage is the transfer of an interest in specific immovable property for the purpose of securing the payment of money advanced or to be advanced by way of loans, an existing or future debt or the performance of an engagement which may give rise to pecuniary liability.[5]

The mortgage will be arisen in the case of immovable property and does not mean transfer of ownership. The person who transfers the interest in property is known as **Mortgager.** The person to whom it is transferred is called as **Mortgagee.** The transaction between two parties is effected through **Mortgage deed.** The mortgagee has no right to sell the mortgaged goods without the consent of the mortgager. The banker should always think about his recovery of money from the mortgagee not by selling of the mortgaged goods. It is only the final solution after taking all possible things by the banker. The Transfer of Property Act recognises various types of mortgages such as **Simple Mortgage, Anomalous, English Mortgage, Mortgage by Conditional Sale etc.**

(e) Charge: Generally the borrower should provide sufficient security to the lender. The way by which lender obtains control over the security is known as **charge.** It is the right to retain the property of the borrower as shown security. The property will be returned to the borrower on clearance of the due amount to the lender.

Management of Funds

The fundamental objective of the bank is to carry the business activities with the public money. The banks are doing business with the money. They play an important role in the economy. They occupy a dominant role in the monetary and fiscal polices of the government. Their fundamental duty is to borrow and lend the money. They are earning their profits through difference in the interest rates. They procure duns at cheap rates and lend the money at high rate of interest. In the banking sector, the borrowing of money is essential. They earn the profit by a number of sources such as exchange commissions and rent for safe lockers. But these profits do not contribute a large portion of their total profits. Therefore, they earn major part of their profits through deployment of funds only. Even though their share capital will also be deployed in the business, but it occupies less amount of proportion. Generally they borrow money from the public by way of procuring deposits from the public, issuing bank notes, drawing bills of exchange, issue of bonds, debentures and cash certificates. The main source of supply of funds is in the form of deposits. In India the bank deposits take three forms such as **Time Deposits, Saving Deposit and Current Deposits.** The time deposits are also called as Fixed Deposits. Under fixed deposit scheme, the deposits which are procured by the bank will be repayable after the expiry of a certain period of time. The expiry date will be fixed at the time of money deposit. The efficiency of a bank will depend upon the quantum of amount procured by the bank under FD. These deposits occupy the dominant position in the portfolio of a bank. The time bound deposits enable the banker to invest the money or deploy in the business to earn adequate profit. These term deposits are very popular in India. A good number of small investors prefer to lodge their money in the form of **fixed deposit.** The investors who dislike the stock market will park their fund in the form of time deposit. The banks are playing an intermediary role in the **money business.** They procure the money from savers and lend the money to the needy person. Therefore, they act as only an intermediary in transfer of funds from surplus place to needy place. Hence the banks will take the task for better flow of funds between two parties. The banks procure the funds from deposit holders and they are accountable to them. **The liability** of a bank is to repay the deposits to their customers as per time schedule. **The asset** of a bank is due from its borrowers. Generally the borrowers are customers of the bank. They take loans from the banks for their different needs. The banks are sanctioning loans to different people to meet their growing needs. The **Savings Deposit** is one of the sources of funds to the banks. They are not so important to bankers, because the account holder can withdraw his money at any time. Generally small and middle class families will maintain these accounts. The banks will pay a little amount of interest to the account holders. At present, the Savings Deposits also constitute a substantial part because interest rates on the **Fixed Deposits** have been slashed. Hence, the public is not interested to make fixed deposits in the bank due to low rate of interest. The **Current Account** is another source of funds to the commercial banks. But they do not contribute to the sources of funds. The banks do not allow any interest on the **Current Deposits.** The bank knows exactly in the case of fixed deposits, what maximum amount can be called upon to pay at any given time, but in case of current deposits, it can use only the minimum balances which are kept by the customers could be utilised. Therefore, the banker has to keep larger funds to meet the contingencies. The bank also accepts **Recurring Deposits.** They have started various **daily, weekly or monthly** deposit schemes from the public. They encourage the public to save the money on a regular or recurring basis. On this kind of deposits interest will be paid on par with the fixed deposit holders. These deposits generally range for a period of one year to ten years.

The banks are doing the business with two sources of funds, such as **share capital and borrowed capital.** The banks usually issue the shares to the public whenever they need money. The share capital will be issued on receipt of clearance from the government. Therefore, the bank's own funds will be deployed in the lending activities of the bank. The owned fund includes **paid up capital, reserve fund and accumulated undistributed profits.** The banks borrow the funds from public, from other bankers etc. They could mobilise the funds from IDBI, ICICI, UTI, LIC, RBI and EXIM etc. The banks will prepare balance sheet as in the case of a commercial enterprise. The asset side of the balance sheet contains **liquid assets, investments, advances and fixed assets.** The liquid assets include cash, cash balance with other banks, cash balance with RBI, cash at short notice etc.

The liabilities of the bank include share capital, resources, undistributed profits, deposits from depositors etc. and borrowings from other banks and RBI. The banks could borrow money from the banks **IDBI, EXIM, NHB, DEHI and NABARD** in the form of refinancing and bills rediscounting. The Central bank provides financial assistance to the **scheduled banks** by a number of ways. The RBI extends financial facility to the banks by way of food credit refinance, export oriented refinance pledge of the government securities etc. The terms and conditions for the refinance will be decided by the RBI from time-to-time. In addition to these borrowings, the banks supplement their resources by the issue of certificate of deposits. The CDs are high cost sources of funds to the banks. The process of funds management in a commercial enterprise is a highly adventurous activity. It involves a high skill and manageable talent. The fundamental principle of a business enterprise is **profitability, liquidity, risk and flexibility.** Profitability is the important factor in the management of funds of a bank. The bank generates income by way of earning interest, commission and rent. The profitability in the banking sector can be expressed as **return of assets, return on equity or return on working fund**. **Liquidity** is the most important factor especially for the financial institutions. It refers to the ability to pay all the legitimate demands at a short period of notice. **Risk** is the common phenomenon in every business community. But in Institutions sector risk is always a problematic factor because the bank share capital is low and their borrowing and lending are high. In any failure of its recoveries, its ultimate impact will fall on the depositors. The risk component is an important one to all other financial institutions.

The deregulation of domestic interest rates, introduction of new financial instruments and other government policies has created a question of efficient liquidity within the banks. The RBI has circulated a draft of **Asset Liability Management (ALM)** guidelines for better and smooth function of the banks. The asset side of the bank balance sheet shows the pattern of the deployment of funds in various kinds of assets. The asset creation may be done through liability or its earning. The financial institutions must secure a balance between **profitability and liquidity.** The banks should get profits without loosing their liquidity position. The bank management will fall in dilemma which element could be given more importance. These two factors are the important. Therefore, the bank management should design a best portfolio in order to get more profits to satisfy the shareholders.

The banking sector at present has been rapidly changing. It occupies a key role in the monetary and fiscal policies of the government. The new breed of banking sector has shown an excellent growth in terms of its profitability. The banks are able to provide efficient services to the customers. They provide **ATM service, internet banking, phone banking, issuing of draft at a click of mouse etc.** Now-a-days the customer need not go to bank to make his transactions effectively. This is a revolutionary change in the banking sector due to the new breed of banks.

Assets Liability Management: The financial institution's efficiency can be measured through its **Assets Liability Management.** It can be defined as **maximising the risk adjusted returns to shareholders over the long run**. The basic objective of ALM is minimising risk and maximising returns. However, the return is always **chased** by the **risk** factor. The ALM is the outcome of risk adjusted return. It can also be termed as "**management of total balance sheet in terms of size and quality**". Risk management is the basic function of ALM. It occupies an important place especially in fund based activities organisations. It is a new concept to the world. Its importance was noticed in USA in 1980s. In USA, a number of savings and financial institutions have number of savings and financial institutions have turned **insolvent** due to the mismatch on their balance sheets. The competition is growing at global level and its impact on margins are reduced. The profits are reducing due to the heavy competition in the market and thus unable to match their ALM. The **volatility** in interest rates have fuelled to lower incomes for these intermediaries. Hence, the banks in a bid to shore up their earnings, they have adopted aggressive strategy. These strategies have increased the risk substantially. It led to insolvency. Therefore, the **management of asset and liabilities** is a highly adventurous task before its management. The management of financial institution is different from manufacturing/distribution units. They can be managed in the following ways properly:

(a) Asset Management
(b) Liability Management

(a) Asset Management: The portfolio of assets in the financial institutions is the most important factor. Because, the efficiency of a firm will depend upon the method of deployment of its funds. Banks can take decisions about the fund to be employed in a proper way in order to earn adequate profits. The banks should keep in mind which they are designing their portfolio regarding the **regulator constraints.** The banks shall work under the regulatory environment such as **RBI, Ministry of Finance, SEBI** and other legal bodies. Maintaining an appropriate balance between profitability and liquidity is the big question before the banks. It is the big task for them. For achieving this balance, the banks must maintain a large sum in cash and yielding near cash items in the asset portfolio of the banks. They have to pay whenever a customer stepped into the bank premises for the want of his money. At the same time, it is also necessary to earn profit to bear the cost and operating expenses of the bank. This situation results in a **dilemma** for the bank management. The portfolio of an asset of a bank includes cash, liquid assets, investment in securities or advances and fixed assets. Usually, the advances dominate the asset portfolio of a bank. It is followed by investments in securities. The **fixed assets** normally constitute a small portion of asset portfolio. The management of the banks does not participate in day to day operations of the business. The top level management of the bank will formulate the policy matters for the smooth functioning of the bank activities.

Liquidity is the basic principle while designing the portfolio of a bank. The financial institutions must give priority to the liquidity on par with the profitability. The bank should be always conscious that, if the depositors demand their deposits, it should be able to pay in a position or situation. Then the bank maintains liquidity more effectively and appropriately. It must be remembered that the maintenance of liquidity involves cost. Because the bank will keep its funds in cash and near to cash where there is no generation of income. Hence, the banks should note that maintenance of **much liquidity position** reduces its profitability. If the bank concentrates more on profitability, it may tend to lose the **liquidity position.** Therefore, the art of commercial banking lies in maintaining enough liquidity to avoid crisis but at the same time the profitability of the bank should also be taken into consideration. After maintaining all the regulatory functions, the banks can invest their funds in the money market. **Money market** is an ideal place for parking their funds. The money market provides both the profitability and liquidity to the bank funds. In money market, the banks can invest in a number of ways as they like. Most of the banks invest their funds in **call money, treasury bills, inter-bank participation on and commercial papers.** The banks could also store their fund with the RBI, bills discounting, lending to other banks. The liquidity position of a bank depends upon a number of factors such as **external and internal factors.** The liquidity of a bank is influenced by the national and local conditions of the economic situation. The national economic condition depends upon general economic situation, political certainty, monetary and taxation policy of the government. The local factors are influenced by the stage of the economy, nature of local population with reference to their economic status, their earning capability, their spending capacity and their attitudes. The internal elements of the liquidity situation include banking habits among the population, the deposit system in the banking sector, the portfolio of depositors and the access to money market. The banks can make profits through the money market transactions in addition to their lending income. The liquidity position of a financial institution stimulates the goodwill. The goodwill is the **oxygen** to the banks for procuring the deposits from the public. The liquidity position of a bank can be measured through various ratios. The ratios are the powerful tools in the measurement of the performance. In the banking sector, the performance can be analysed with some ratios such as **cash to total asset ratio, cash to deposits ratio, loan to deposit ratio, loan to asset ratio, current ratio etc.** Cash to total asset ratio indicates the ready cash available as per cent of the total assets. The **higher ratio** reveals that the bank has high liquidity position. The depositors can withdraw their amount at any moment from the banks. The near cash includes cash in hand, cash balance with the RBI, call money in the money market etc. Cash to deposit ratio indicates the extent of liquidity position that is maintained by the banks to meet the demands of the depositors. **Loans to deposit ratio** reveals the position about the portion of its interest earnings assets in loans. The high ratio indicates that the bank advanced more loans from the available deposits. Therefore, the bank earns more profits but at the same time it loses the liquidity position. **Current ratio** is an important tool in analysing the financial performance of a bank. It is a widely accepted measure of liquidity. In financial institutions/banks current asset refers to cash near cash assets, the government securities, accrued interest, taxes paid in advance. Current liabilities include bills payable, interest accrued and adjustments from branches. In financial institutions or banks, the reserves are the powerful factors for the smooth functioning of the institutions. The financial strength of the banks depends upon the quantum amount of reserves. Reserves indicate a healthy situation in the operating efficiency of a bank. The maintenance of the reserve position depends upon the statutory obligations. The banks shall follow the obligations such as **CRR and SLRs**. The banks also maintain non-statutory reserves for the sake of liquidity. These reserves can be utilised by the banks at any time. They are call money, short-term loans to other banks, treasury bills, short-term maturity period of promissory notes, bills purchased and discounted and bonds. These financial instruments help a banker to successfully trade off between profitability and liquidity. The management of these financial instruments rely upon the past experience and expertise.

The asset portfolio of a bank includes investment in securities. Investment in **securities** play an important role in generation of income to the banks. The management of the securities is the most important one in the overall funds management of the bank. The securities value may fall and increase according to the economic situation of the nation. There will be possibility of **risk** due to many factors. In the same way there will be possibility of high **return**. Stock market is a highly volatile market. In this stock market, even specialist may not get returns in some situations. Another **risk** in case of investment in securities is **interest rate risk.** The fluctuation in interest rates in the market may tend the bank either profit or loss. Therefore, the bank shall design an asset portfolio keeping in view of the behaviour of the interest rates to match the liquidity and profitability. Usually, the management of asset and liabilities affairs will be formulated by the top level management of the bank. They formulate the investment policy of the funds of the bank. The board of directors will assign this responsibility to the Investment Committee or the senior officers of the bank. They shall manage the securities after taking careful analysis of various external factors such as **interest rates, RBI guidelines.** There are some internal factors which could be taken into consideration before making the investment decisions. The internal factors such as **risk** bearing abilities, portfolio risk will show impact on the profitability of the bank. The Investment Committee will make the management of securities on the basis of guidelines framed by the board. The guidelines contain about the size of securities portfolio, types of securities, policies about trading in securities, tax management and buy-back arrangements. Once the portfolio is constructed, it requires a continuous evaluation and monitoring otherwise the portfolio will face the risk. The portfolio should change according to the changes in the **fundamental and technical analysis.** A team of stock market analyst constantly reviews the performance of the portfolio. They observe, analyse and give suggestions to enhance the growth value of the portfolio. Generally the banks portfolio is dominated by the government securities and other securities. The shares and debenture of a joint stock companies occupy a small portion in the portfolio. They also invest in short-term treasury bills. The RBI also provides refinance for these instruments. These instruments have become attractive avenue. The composition limits of the portfolio will change according to the market movements.

The bank portfolio generates income, which is the major source of revenue to the bank, this should be constructed with utmost carefulness. The bank lends some amount of money which involves risk a banker can minimise it. The banks should follow the statutory regulations such as SLR and CRR, the remaining portion of the deposits are available for lending to the borrowers. The banks grant the loans as per the guidelines issued by the Reserve Bank. The RBI guidelines reveal that loans should be given on order of priority as specified by it. It indicates priority sector lending, export credit etc. The credit worthiness depends on **character, capacity, capital, collateral and conditions.** The loans should be disbursed according to the RBI guidelines and interest may also be charged as per the direction. The lending rates are now regulated.

(b) Liability Management: The Asset Liability Management is the main task of the bank management. In financial institutions/bank, the management of liability items are the most important and crucial factors in determining the survival of the banks. With growing competition worldwide, profit margins are declining. The profit margins will be stabilised only on efficient management of liabilities. After liberalisation, the banks have increasingly paid attention towards the liability management. The efficient management of Asset and Liability would definitely stimulate the growth of the banks. A good efficient management of funds can satisfy the deposit holders. The liability management comprises two factors such as **management of deposits and capital.** The bank procures deposits from the public in different ways. The deposits are the main sources of funds. These financial resources have to be managed with more attention. The banks can procure demand deposits, savings and term deposits from the public. The interest will be paid on the deposits as per the direction of the RBI. In India every bank should follow the guidelines and instructions of the RBI. The RBI is the supreme authority in the banking sector. The rate of interest on deposits and advances will be decided by the RBI from time-to-time there are several factors which influence the magnitude of the bank's deposits, a number of steps could be taken by the bank management for the deposit mobilisation. At present a number of innovative schemes are introduced by all banks. They are working for their customers. Now the banks are very busy in motivating the staff, marketing various financial products through the media, conducting market surveys introducing marketing personnel for the credit card divisions etc. They are now focusing on the customer needs in view of the heavy competitive environment. The liability side of the balance sheet, every commercial enterprise has

capital. Capital is the most important element in commencing the business operations. No firm will commence the business with the **share capital.** The share capital of the bank is subscribed by its shareholders. The capital includes its reserves. The reserves are built up by every bank in order to meet the unforeseen situations in the future. The commercial banks utilise a high degree of financial leverage than other business enterprises. The issued share capital provides safety against any losses arising due to business operations carried out by the banks. The capital reduces the risk position and increases the **solvency position** of the bank. The liquidity and profitability are the two important factors in the survival of the banking sector. There are various ratios which determine the amount of capital that is necessary for the efficient smoother functioning of the banking operations. Capital to deposit ratio indicates the relationship between capital and deposit of the bank. a high degree of this ratio explains that the depositors of that bank will be safe then they are exposed to **low risk.** Another ratio, **capital to asset ratio** reveals about the relationship between the share capital and its assets. A low ratio explains a lower capacity to absorb losses due to the fluctuations in their assets values. This ratio has some limitations. The other important ratio is **risk asset ratio.** This ratio distinguishes between risk free assets and risk assets. The cash balance in hand, cash with other banks are the examples of risk free assets. But they have low profitability in nature. **The risk weighted asset ratio** reveals about the banks different assets which are involved in various degrees of risk. The balance sheet and off balance sheet items are assigned risk weight according to the specified percentages. These norms will be stipulated by the RBI. As per the risk weighted assets, the bank has to manage its affairs accordingly.

Asset Liabilities Management Practices: The economic reform has been taken to its logical conclusion of deregulation and privatisation. The privatisation and deregulations have forced the banks to move with the wind. The banks have been changed from the traditional position to the modern banking. The modern banking system has created a revolutionary changes in India. Now banking has become as **shopping** for different financial products. The modern banks are required to work more effectively due to the competitive environment in the market. They are required to introduce effective risk management systems in order to reduce various risks. The banks will have to face many kind of risks such as **credit, market and operational risks.** The Narasimhan Committee has also been recommended to improve their efficiency by introducing various innovative schemes. In India, **the Asset Liability Management** practice was introduced in 1.4.1999. RBI introduced ALM system as a part of the risk management and control systems in banks. The ALM process is based upon three elements such **(a) Information system, (b) Organisation, and (c) Process.** Information is the most important element in every field or sector. Information is the base for taking any decision. It is a weapon to each competitor. The information is required to collect from a large network of branches. It will take time for banks to get the appropriate information. They should make analysis as per branch wise regarding their asset liability management from time-to-time. They should also take into consideration the asset liability behaviour with reference to each branch. Generally the banks adopt centralisation process, where the key information lies with the **Head Office.** In centralisation process head office occupies a dominant position with regard to the information. The data will be available at the head office and the information can be procured at the click of mouse at this **digital economy.** In this digital economy everything is possible within few minutes. At present all the banks are making computerisation for the smooth and efficient functioning of the activities. The computerisation makes more effective flow of information. **The Asset Liability Management** organisation is related to its structure of the board management. The **ALM** will be organised with the help of top level management. The top level management is responsible for the overall functioning of the bank. The board generally involves in policy framing exposure of risk maintenance of liquidity, profitability, interest rate and risk from foreign exchange market and equity market. For organising ALM, a committee will be appointed for formulating the business strategy regarding ALM. The Committee consists of top level management such as **Chairman, Managing Director and other Directors.** They should be responsible for ensuring adherence to the limits set up by the board. A special staff will be appointed for the collection of information, analysing, monitoring and reporting. They should also predict the future taking into consideration of the present market trends. The **ALM** process takes into consideration of exposure of risk. It deals with the risk management, funding and capital planning. It also deals with the profitability and liquidity. All these functions will be carried out by the banks as per the regulations and guidelines that are issued by the RBI from time-to-does time.

Chapter 3

SECURITIES AND EXCHANGE BOARD OF INDIA (SEBI)

Introduction

The Government of India set up the SEBI on April 12, 1988 from the regulation and order by function of the capital markets. It is likely to promote the measures for fair trading in the securities and to protect the rights of the investors. The capital market in India has to develop on the right lines for a competent government agency in USA.

Initially, the SEBI was established as an interim body under the administrative control of the Finance Ministry. Later, it was given statutory powers. The **SEBI** is the most powerful organisation in the security industry. It is the **watchdog** of the stock market. The tremendous growth in the capital markets led to the **establishment** of the SEBI. Every company in India is required to register with the SEBI to work under the limitations and rules laid out by the SEBI. Until May 1992, the issue of capital by the companies was controlled by the Central Government through the **Office of the Controller of Capital Issues.** The CCI regulated the pricing of issues. These controls have been removed with the repeal of the Capital Issues (Control) Act on May 1992.

The SEBI has emerged as an important constituent of the Indian financial system. The powers of the Indian financial system have been delegated to the SEBI. Let us start with a brief discussion of those constituents. **i.e., the Companies Act, 1956, the Securities Act, 1956, the Capital Issues Act, 1947.** The Companies Act deals with the financial and non-financial aspects of the corporate sector. The aim of the Act is to develop an integrated relationship among promoters, investors and company management. The Act seeks to protect the interests of the shareholders and their effective participation in the corporate sector. The Companies Act contains specific provisions of the regulation such as **issue of share capital, dividend distribution, capital structure, voting**

rights of share holders. Inter-corporate investments, share holders meetings, format of annual accounts, allotment process of shares, issue of share certificates, issue of shares at premium par or discount, issue of non-voting shares, buy-back of their own shares. The Act is administered by the Department of Company Affairs and the Company Law Board. All these things are working under the control of **Ministry of Law, Justice and Company Affairs.** The provisions of the Companies Act from Section 55 to 68-A are related to the issue of prospectus. If any prospectus is issued against the **contravention** of Section 57 or 58 the company and every responsible person would be punishable with the fine up to **Rupees Five Thousand.** The ROC will not register the prospectus unless it is satisfied with the requirements of **Sections 55 to 58**. The shares allotment made by a company should be in accordance with **Sections 76, 77, 78, 79, 80, 80A, 81, 85, 86, 113** of the Companies Act. **The Securities Contracts Act, 1956** deals with the secondary market operations. Section 3 deals with the recognition of the stock exchanges. Any Stock Exchange for the purpose of reorganisation should apply to the Central Government empowered under section 4 to grant the reorganisation. According to the **SCRA** every recognised stock exchange should submit its annual report before 31st January of every year. The annual report should contain all the activities of the Stock Exchange about its trading securities, chance in rules by laws, change in governing body admission or readmission or resignation of members, defaults, securities delisted, etc. The SCRA lays down the rules and regulations about the listing of securities in the stock exchanges. A company as defined public limited under the Companies Act divisions of getting its securities listed on a recognised stock exchange should apply to the Central Government along with its application and required documents and information. The powers under the SCRA are transferred to the SEBI. The SEBI is empowered to control, regulate and monitor for all the activities of the secondary market. The SEBI is the most powerful organ in the control monitoring and in the evolution of both the primary and secondary markets of the capital market in India.

The Capital Issues Control Act, 1947 has been playing an important role in the functioning of the Indian capital market. Since 1947, its provisions are administered by **the control of capital issues** in the Ministry of Finance, Department of Economic Affairs. The SCRA mainly regulates the secondary market. The primary market is mostly regulated by the Capital Issues Control Act, 1947. The main objectives of the Act are to protect the investors normal-practice by the corporate sector, no undue congestion of public issues to monitor the foreign investment. The Capital Issues Control Act provisions have now became the powerful and functions of the SEBI.

The CICA was repealed and the office of the CCI was abolished in 1992. Certain powers and certain sections of the SCRA and Companies Act were delegated to the SEBI. The regulatory powers of the SEBI have increased the securities laws. The SEBI has now become a very important constituent of the financial regulatory framework in India. The SEBI was established on the same pattern of the **Securities Exchange Commission** USA.

Organisation of SEBI

The SEBI restructured its organisation and has been rationalised. It has divided its activities into the following **seven** departments headed by officials of the rank of Executive Directors. All these departments are further sub-divided into the following division:

1. Primary market department
2. Issue management and intermediaries department
3. The secondary market department
4. The secondary market department (administration)
5. The institutional investment department
6. Legal department
7. Investigation department

The **primary market department** deals with the policy matters, financial intermediaries, investors grievances etc. The issue management takes care of prospectus and registration regulation and monitoring of issues related to the financial intermediaries.

The secondary market department involves in the preparation of policy matters, stock exchange operations, control of secondary market trading activities, development of the new innovative financial products, price manipulations, monitoring, market surveillance, insider trading etc. all the other things related to it. It also involves in the inspection of the non-members intermediaries and stock sub-brokers. **The institutional investment department** concentrates on mutual funds and foreign institutional investment affairs. It looks after corporate mergers and acquisitions. It fully involved in research and publications and international affairs. **The legal department** undertakes all the legal affairs of the SEBI. It guides the SEBI on legal litigations which are faced by it in the routine activities. **The investigations department** works under the direction of chief of investigation. It carries out inspection and investigation activities. The SEBI is the member of the **International Organisation of Securities Commission (IOSCO).** It is an international organisation which connects the other security regulations from over **100 countries.** The SEBI is the active participant in the Development Committee of IOSCO.

Objectives of the SEBI: The SEBI consisted by the Central Government as a supervisory body to regulate and promote the securities market. The objectives of the SEBI are as under:

(a) to promote fair dealings by the issuers of the securities.
(b) to provide a better market place for the corporate sector to raise funds at a low cost.
(c) to provide investors protection and safeguard their rights and interests.
(d) to regulate and develop the skills of the financial intermediaries with a view to make them more competitive and professional in spirit.
(e) to regulate the securities market.

Powers of the SEBI

The SEBI cannot act independently. It is governed by the Central Government. It is obliged to make an annual report of the Union Government every year. The annual reports should be laid down before the Parliament. The SEBI is entrusted with the following specific powers/ functions:

1. Regulating the securities market
2. Regulating the affairs in the stock exchanges
3. Power to call the periodical returns from the recognised stock exchanges
4. Power to call for any information from the stock exchanges
5. Power to grant the approval to the bye-laws of recognised exchanges
6. Registering and regulating the market of the stock-brokers
7. Registering and regulating the work of the bankers, registrars
8. Registering and regulating the work of the merchant bankers, underwriters
9. Registering and regulating the work of the portfolio mangers, STAs

10. Power to prohibit the insider trading
11. Power to promote the investors education
12. Power to levy fee
13. Power to make or amend the bye-laws of recognised stock exchanges
14. Power to prohibit the unfair trade practices
15. Power to regulate the acquisition of shares and take over by companies
16. Registering and regulating the work of depositories, custodians, FIIs, Credit rating agencies etc.
17. Registering and regulating the work of the venture capital funds
18. Power to call for information, undertaking inspection, conducting enquiries and audits of the stock exchanges, financial intermediaries
19. Power to prescribe the maintenance of certain documents by the stock exchanges
20. Compel a public company to list its shares in the stock exchange
21. Power to give directions to the stock exchange
22. Power to suspend the business of a recognised stock exchange
23. Power to grant the recognition to the stock exchanges
24. Power to withdraw the recognition of stock exchanges
25. Regulating and control of the business dealings in spot delivery contracts
26. Power the prohibit the contract in certain cases
27. Licensing the dealers in securities in certain cases
28. Power to declare the applicability of Section 17 of SCRA in any state of area and to grant licence to the dealers in securities

SEBI Act 1992

The SEBI Act provides for the establishment of a board to protect the interests of the investors in the securities and to promote the development and to regulate the market. **Chapter I** deals with the preliminaries and definitions. **Chapter II** deals with the establishment and in corporation of the board, management of the board terms and conditions of the services of the chairman and the members. The removal process of members from the office. The procedure for conducting meetings, the appointment procedure of the offers and the employees of the board. **Chapter III** contains the process of transfer of assets, liabilities of the existing board. The substantive parts of the powers and functions of the board are incorporated in **Chapter IV.** The registration process of stock-brokers, sub-brokers, share transfer agents, banker to an issue are presented in **Chapter V. Chapter VI** deals with the grants provided by the government to the board maintenance of fund. According to procedure and audit of the board, **Chapter VII** contains all the miscellaneous factors regarding the powers of the Central Government to the issue directions and the powers of the Central Government to supersede the board returns and reports delegation of powers appeals savings employees of the board who are treated as public servants, penalties, exemptions from tax as wealth and income cognizance of offences by courts, offences by companies, power to exempt power to make rules, regulations etc.

Constitution of the SEBI: The SEBI as a regulatory and development board has wide and varied powers. Its efforts include measures of efficiency, reforms, transparency in the market. The SEBI is a body of **six** members consisting of the chairman, two members from the Central Government who deals with the **Finance and the Law Ministries**, two members who are professional, experts in the securities market and one member from the RBI. All these members except the RBI nominee are appointed by the Central Government. The Central Government has the full authority regarding the appointment of its members, terms of office tenure, conditions of service, removal of a member from the office etc. The Central Government is the supreme authority to supersede the SEBI in the public interests. The general superintendence, the direction and management of the boards affairs vest in the board of members. The board of members and the chairman exercise all the powers that are done by the board. The chairman and other members should be persons of ability, integrity and have a special knowledge or experience in law, finance, economics, accountancy, administration etc. The term of office and other conditions are prescribed by the Central Government. It has the full authority to terminate the services of the chairman/members before the expiry period. The government by giving him notice of not less than **three** months in writing or three months salary and allowances in lieu thereof and the chairman or a member as the case may be, shall have the right to relinquish his office at any time before the expiry of the period prescribed. The Central Government has the authority to remove a member from his office if he:

(a) is or at any time been adjudicated as insolvent,
(b) is of unsound mind and stands so declared by a competent court,
(c) has been convicted of an office which involves a moral turpitude,

and

(d) has in the opinion of the government, so obsessed his position and as to render his continuation in office detrimental to the public interest.

The SEBI formed **two** Advisory Committees, namely **The Primary Market Advisory Committee** and **Secondary Market Advisory Committee**. These Committees are constituted among the market players, investors associations recognised by the SEBI and eminent persons in the capital market. The Committees are non-statutory in nature and the SEBI is not bund by the advice of the Committee. The SEBI has recently opened its regional offices in **Kolkata, Chennai and Delhi** and the head office in Mumbai. The regional offices help the investors in their complaints and with their issuers intermediaries and stock exchanges in the region. All the approvals are centralised at the head office.

The SEBI endeavours to provide a regulatory framework which would facilitate an efficient mobilisation and allocation of resources through the securities market. The SEBI has issued the following guidelines for the smooth functioning of the securities market:

1. SEBI Guidelines (Disclosure and Investor Probation), 1992
2. SEBI Merchant Bankers, 1992
3. SEBI Debentures Trustee Rules and Regulations, 1992
4. SEBI Stock-brokers and Sub-brokers Rules and Regulations, 1992
5. SEBI Insider Trading Regulations, 1992
6. SEBI Guidelines for FII, 1992
7. SEBI Registers and Share Transfer Agents Rules and Regulations, 1993
8. SEBI Underwriters Rules and Regulations, 1993
9. SEBI Portfolio Managers Rules and Regulations, 1993
10. SEBI Mutual Funds Regulations, 1993
11. Guidelines for Foreign Brokers, 1993
12. Advertising Code Primary Issues, 1993
13. Guidelines for MMMEs
14. SEBI Bankers to the Issue Rules and Regulations, 1994
15. Guidelines for Disclosure and Investors Protection
16. Guidelines Preferential Allotment by Listed Companies to FIIs, 1994
17. Guidelines for Advertisements of Schemes of the Mutual Funds, 1994

18. SEBI Significant Acquisitions and Takeover Regulations, 1994

Registration

The SEBI has the power to grant the certificate of registration to the stockbrokers. Registers, sub-brokers, merchant brokers, underwriters, share transfer agents, lead managers, portfolio managers, investment advisers and such other financial intermediaries. The other intermediaries like depositor, custodian, FII credit salary agency commence their business after obtaining the Registration certificate from the SEBI. No intermediary will be allowed without the certificate from the SEBI.

It has the authority to order suspend or cancel the certificate of registration in such a manner as determined by the regulations.

Financial Support from the GOI

The Central Government will look after the financial needs of the SEBI. The government has the authority to provide sufficient funds for the smooth functioning of the board. It may after the due appropriation made by the Parliament by law on its behalf make the grants to the board. A fund should be constituted as the SEBI general kind. This should be credited by all grants, fees, charges received by the board, penalties realised under the Act and any other sources as decided by the government. The SEBI general fund should be utilised for the payment of salaries, allowances and also for the remuneration of the members, officers and other employees of the board. The expenses should be made according to the specifications of the Act. The SEBI should maintain proper accounts and other relevant records. The board should prepare the annual statement of the accounts in such a format as prescribed by the government. The Central Government may direct the SEBI after consulting the Comptroller and Auditor General of India at a specified schedule. The audit expenses should be borne by the SEBI. The CAG or his nominee has the right to demand for the production of books, accounts concerned vouchers and other documents. The audited accounts should be submitted to the Central Government which in turn submits in the house of Parliament.

Penalties

The SEBI has the whole authority to by penalties impose fines if a personal intermediary fails to obey the specification of the Act. Every financial intermediary/person who is associated with the securities market must honour the rules and regulations issued by the SEBI from time-to-time. If any person who fails to furnish any document, return or report is liable to a penalty not exceeding Rs.150 lakhs for each such failure. If any person fails to file any return or furnish any information looks or other documents within the time specified, he is liable to a penalty not exceeding Rs.5000 per day during which the failure continues.

If any person fails to maintain the books of accounts or records, he is liable to a penalty not exceeding Rs.10,000 per day during which the failure continues.

If any financial intermediary registry with the SEBI but facts to enter into an agreement with his client is liable to a penalty not exceeding Rs.5,00,000 for every such failure. If any financial intermediary registers with the SEBI but fails to redress the investors grievances is liable to a penalty not exceeding Rs.10,000 for each such failure.

Every person should obtain the certificate of registration from the board for commencing the business. Without obtaining the certificate, he is liable to a penalty not exceeding Rs.10,000 for each day from the date of his activities or he should pay Rs.10,00,000 whichever is higher. If any person/financial intermediary registers with the board but fails to comply with the terms and conditions of the certificate, he is liable to pay a penalty not exceeding Rs.10,000 per day and Rs.10,00,000 at a time.

If any person/intermediary fails to make an application for listing its schemes as provided in the regulations governing, such listing is liable to a penalty not exceeding Rs.5000 per day or Rs.5,00,000, if any person who registers but fails to despatch unit certificates of any scheme in the specified manner/he is liable to a penalty not exceeding Rs.5000 per day.

If any person who registers with the SEBI and fails to refund the application money paid by the investors within the period specified in the regulation, he is liable to a penalty not exceeding Rs.1000 per day during which such failure continues.

If any person who registers with the SEBI fails to invest the money collected by him in the same manner, he is liable to a penalty not exceeding Rs.5,00,000 for cash such failure.

If any asset management company of a registered mutual fund fails to comply with any of the regulations, such AMC is liable to a penalty not exceeding Rs.5,00,00 for each such failure.

If any person who registers as a stock-broker fails to issue contract notes in the prescribed manner is liable to a penalty not exceeding five times the amount.

If any broker fails to deliver any security or fails to make the payment for the amount due to the investors he is liable to a penalty not exceeding Rs.5000 for each day during which such failure continues.

If any person who registers with the SEBI charges an excess amount of brokerage as specified in the manner he is liable to a penalty not exceeding Rs.5000 or five times of the excess brokerage charged.

If any insider who deals with the securities of a body corporate on any stock exchange on the basis of any unpublished price, sensitive information or communicates any unpublished price sensitive information to any person then he is liable to a penalty not exceeding Rs.5,00,000.

If any person who fails to disclose the aggregate of share holding in the body corporate before he acquires any share of that body corporate or make a public announcement to acquire the shares at a minimum price, he is liable to a penalty not exceeding Rs.5,00,000.

For the purpose of adjudging the above failures by the concerned persons/intermediaries the board should appoint any officer not below the rank of divisional chief as an adjudicating officer for holding an enquiry. The enquiry should be done in a prescribed manner the adjudicating officer should think about the quantum of penalty after considering the following factors:

1. The repetitive nature of the default.
2. The amount of loss caused to an investor as a consequence of default.
3. The amount of disproportionate gain on unfair advantage.

Appellate Tribunal

The SEBI has acquired the statutory status. The study of various regulations of the Act gives this impression. The Central Government has the authority to establish the Appellate Tribunal. It consists of only one person who is to be appointed through a notification by the Central Government.

The presiding officer of a securities appellate tribunal (SAT) should be a judge of a High Court. He should be a member of an Indian Legal Service and held a post in Grade I for atleast 3 years. He should work as the presiding officer of a tribunal for atleast 3 years. He should hold the office for a trim of 5 years. He should hold the office until he attains the age of 65 years. The tribunal fixes the salary and allowances payable and also the terms and conditions. The presiding officer should not be removed from his office except by an order from the Central Government. He can be removed on the ground of proved misbehaviour or incapacity after the enquiry made by a Judge of the Supreme Court. The Central Government may investigate about the misbehaviour or incapacity of the presiding officer. The staff of the SAT should discharge its functions under the general superintendence of the presiding officer. The SAT should have the discharging functions under this Act. The same power as a civil Court under the Code of Criminal Procedure, 1968 while tying a suit in respect of the following matters:

(a) Summoning and enforcing the attendance of any person,
(b) Requiring the production of documents,
(c) Receiving evidence of affidavits,
(d) Issuing commissions for the examination of witness, and
(e) Dismissing an application for default.

Government Control

The Central Government has the authority to make rules and regulations to monitor the activities of the SEBI. The powers of the Central Government to issue the directions are as follows:

1. Regarding the policy mattes of the SEBI, the Central Government may give directions in writing to it from time-to-time. The board should as far as practicable be given an opportunity to express its views before any direction. The decision of the Central Government is final in any matter.
2. The Central Government considering the publication of a notification regarding superseding the board that
   (a) all the powers, functions and duties may by or under the provisions of this act be exercised on discharged by or on behalf of the board until the board reconstitutes;
   (b) all the members as from the date of suppression vacate their own offices;
   (c) all property owned and controlled by the board should vest in the Union Government until the board reconstitutes.
3. The Central Government may by notification supersede the

board for such period not exceeding six months as specified in the notification.

4. After the expiry of the super session specified in the notification. The Union Government may reconstitute the board by a fresh appointment in such case and person or persons who located their offices under the regulation of the Act should not be deemed disqualified for appointment. The Central Government may take any action before the expiry of the supersession.

Steps taken by the SEBI to reform the Capital Market

The capital market in India has witnessed a spectacular growth during the decade. The trend has been overwhelming till recently. The market is being broadened further with the listing of securities. Therefore, the SEBI has taken several imitative steps to promote, develop and regulate the capital market. These reforms include primary and secondary markets. They are presented below:

1. Abridged prospectus.
2. Proportional allotment might be allowed in case of over subscribed issues.
3. Insider trading is illegal.
4. All the financial intermediaries are to be registered with the SEBI.
5. Credit trading is made compulsory.
6. Underwriting for issues is made mandatory.
7. Department of issue proceeds.
8. Fixation of promoters contribution.
9. Risk factors are to be disclosed in the prospectus.
10. Lock in period for promoters quota shares.
11. Capital adequacy norms are to be prescribed for the stock-brokers.
12. Circuit breaker system should be introduced at the exchange.
13. Forward trading and carry over system are baned.
14. Uniform settlement system.
15. Flexibility in issue pricing.
16. Guidelines for the DFI for disclosures and investors protection
17. Brokers should keep the clients money in a separate bank account.
18. Audit inspection on the books of the stock exchange members.
19. Norms for multiple membership in the stock exchange.

20. Introduction of jumbo transfer deeds.
21. Precautions in the transactions between clients and brokers.
22. Guidelines for preparation of allotment of shares.
23. PSU bonds should be brought under the review of the SEBI.
24. Private mutual funds should be permitted.
25. Constitution of the governing councils of the stock exchanges.

Buy-back Securities

The SEBI has allowed the companies to buy-back its own securities by the following methods:

1. Buy-back through tender offer,
2. Buy-back through open market.

Tender Offer

According to the rules and regulations, a company can buy its securities from the existing shareholders or any others through negotiated deals. A company may also buy its shares through any private arrangement. The SEBI would not permit the insider trading in this aspect. If any company is interested to buy its own securities from any source a special resolution should be made. The copy of the special resolution should be filled with the SEBI and the concerned stock exchanges within seven days from the date of passing the resolution. The notice for the special resolution should be served along with the companies explanation document contains the following matters:

1. The date of approval of the proposal at the board meeting.
2. The situation for the buy-back of the shares.
3. The mode of buy-back of the company's securities.
4. The sufficient provision of money for buy-back the securities.
5. The base point for the fixation of the buy-back price.
6. The number of securities to be purchased by the company.
7. The intention of the promoters regarding this scheme.
8. The details regarding the repayment of loans to FI/Banks.
9. The details regarding the refunding of fixed deposits debentures etc
10. The auditors report addressed to be board of directiors.
11. The details regarding the repayment of preference shares.

12. The assurance of the board of directors regarding the company affairs.
13. The details regarding the general meeting of the shareholders.
14. The board of directors should give assurance that its state of affairs would not become insolvent within a period of one year from that date.

In the tender method of option to buy-back its own securities from the existing security holders on proportionate basis. In addition to the above information they should furnish some additional information regarding the buy-back price of the securities if a company wants to buy-back its shares. It should make a public announcement in atleast one English daily, one Hindi and one regional language. The announcement should contain the following information in the media:

1. Full information about the offer.
2. The schedule time for opening and closing of the process.
3. The details about the authority for the offer of the buy-back.
4. The full details and complete disclosure of all material factors.
5. The environment for the buy-back.
6. The methodology to be adopted for the buy-back.
7. The maximum amount to be invested in this method.
8. Information about the company.
9. The auditors report for the last three years.
10. The full details of the capital structure of the company.
11. The full information about the statutory approval obtained.
12. The lead managers should ensure that the financial data should be latest.
13. The details about the collection and bidding centres.
14. The public announcement data should be confirmed by the board of directors.
15. Present capital structure and the shareholding pattern.
16. The information regarding any change in the management structure.
17. The other disclosures as may be specified by the SEBI from time-to-time.
18. The details about the persons who are in the control of the company.
19. The full information about the escrow account.
20. The information regarding the financial ratios as specified by the SEBI.

21. The listing details of the company's scrip with the stock exchange.
22. The stock marketing data regarding high low and average market price of the scrip.
23. The monthly high and low prices for 6 months from the data of announcement.
24. The information regarding the number of securities are traded on the above (23) period.
25. The market price immediately after the data of approving the buy-back.
26. The volume of securities are traded in each month during 6 months preceding the data of the public announcement.
27. The specified data must be earlier than 30 days and not later than 42 days from the date of the public announcement.
28. the draft letter of offer should be submitted with the prescribed fee to the SEBI.
29. The SEBI will charge the following fee for a proposed buy-back of the securities translations:

Size of the buy-back offer	*Fee*
If the issue size is more than Rs. 500 crores	Rs. 5,00,000
If the issue size is between Rs. 100-500 crores	Rs. 2,00,000
If the issue size is between Rs. 50-100 crores	Rs. 1,00,000
If the issue size is between Rs. 10-50 crores	Rs. 75,000
If the issue size is between Rs. 5-10 crores	Rs. 50,000
If the issue size is upto 5 crores	Rs. 25,000

According to the Companies Act, Section 77A, the company should file along with a draft letter of offer and declaration of solvency in a prescribed manner.

The buy-back of the securities must be opened to the share holders for a minimum period of 15 days and maximum period of 30 days. The buy-back offer should not be earlier than 7 days or later than 30 days after the specified date of the buy-back securities. After the process of completion, a communication should be made within 15 days from the closure of the offer.

Escrow Account

Before the commencement of the buy-back process, the company should deposit some amount in the Escrow Account. It is an account for which the bank acts as an uninterested third party to ensure compliance with the terms of the deal between the two parties only upon the fulfilment of some stated conditions. It becomes operative as soon as the stated event occurs. The banks hold such accounts in which the funds accumulated have to pay **taxes insurance on mortgage property etc.** The escrow Account consists of

(a) Cash deposited with a scheduled bank,
(b) The bank guarantee in favour of the merchant banker, and
(c) A deposit of margin with the merchant banker.

The company should keep the amount in the escrow account and make it available to the merchant banker. The merchant banker is empowered to operate the escrow accounts according to the situation. On payment of consideration to all the share holders who have accepted the offer and after the completion of all the formalities of the buy-back, if any amount securities and guarantee available in the escrow account should be released to the company. The SEBI has the full authority is in case of **non-fulfilment** of obligation. Under these regulations the company **forfeit** the escrow account either in full or in part. The amount of the forfeited sum can be distributed on *pro-rata* basis amongst the security holders who accepts the offer. If there is any balance it should be deployed for the investors protection.

Payment of the Consideration

After the closure of the offer, the company is required to open a special account with a banker and deposit there in such sum together with the amount lying in the **escrow account** must be utilised for the payment of consideration in cash to those security share holders whose offer has been accepted or returned the share certificate of them.

Destruction of the Share Certificates

After the payment of consideration to the accepted share holders, the company may collect the shares physically and **destroy** the security certificates bought back in the presence of a merchant banker/STA/Registrar and the statutory auditor within **7 days** from the date of acceptance of the securities. If the buy-back securities are in the form of **"Dematerialised"** they should be extinguished and destroyed according to the Act of the SEBI **(Depositories and Participants)** Regulations, 1996 and according to the bye-laws. The company should submit a certificate to the SEBI signed by A Registrar/A Merchant Banker and MD with the statutory auditor of the company within **7 days** of extinguishment and destruction of the certificates. The company should maintain a separate account for cancelled and destroyed certificates should be submitted to concerned stock exchanges within **7 days of** destruction of the certificates.

Buy-back from the Open Market

A company can buy its own securities by the method of open market. The shares may be further categorised in the following manner:

(a) Book Building Process,
(b) Stock Exchange,
(c) From odd-lot Holders.

Book Building Process

The buy-back of securities through book building process can be made by the company with a special resolution. The company should pass a special resolution by specifying the maximum price. The company should make a public announcement atleast **7 days** prior to the commencement of the buy-back. The company has to appoint a merchant banker for this purpose. The company has to deposit in the **escrow account** before the date of public announcement. After the announcement of the book building process, the company has to submit a copy to the **SEBI** along with the specified fees within two days. The public announcement should reveal the following matter:

(i) the methodology of book building process,
(ii) the manner of acceptance,
(iii) the format of acceptance,
(iv) details of bidding centres.

The book building process involves with the latest technology and transparent for the book building process. The company should arrange bidding centres with a minimum number **30.** There should be a computer terminal connecting all the bidding centres. The offer should remain open to the security holders for a period of **15 days** and not exceeding **thirty days.** The company should decide the buy-back price along with the merchant banker's opinion. The offer price should be paid to all the holders who have accepted the buy-back method.

Stock Exchange

The shares are also repurchased by the company through stock exchanges. For this purpose, a special resolution has to be passed by the company. The special resolution should specify the maximum offer price. The shares cannot be purchased from the promoters or interested parties. If a company wants to buy-back its shares by the stock exchange process, it should make a public announcement of the buy-back. The company has to appoint the merchant banker. A copy of the public announcement should be submitted to the SEBI within two days along with the specified fees. The public announcement should reveal all the information regarding the details of the brokers and stock exchanges etc. the buy-back should be made only through:

(a) The stock exchange which has an electronic trading facility.
(b) Order matching mechanism.

The merchant banker and the company should furnish the information to the concerned stock exchange on a daily basis regarding the developments of the process. The furnished information should be published in a national daily newspaper. The company identified should appear on the electronic screen. The process for destroying the share certificates will be applicable on **par** with the earlier methods. The company should complete its legal formalities within **15 days** of the payment.

From Odd lot Buy-Back

The rules and regulations pertaining to the buy-back scheme through the odd lot method are applicable in the same manner which the earlier methods followed.

General Obligations

The company can buy-back its own securities either through tender offer method or through open market system. The method to be adopted by the company depends upon the decision of the company. The company should fulfil the obligations in the following manner:

(a) The company should furnish true factual information in a letter of offer or in a public announcement or any other advertisement circular, brochure or publicity material.
(b) The announcement should indicate that the information is true

and the board of directors have to accept the responsibility of the information.

(c) The company should ensure that during the offer period no bonus issue will be made under these regulations.

(d) The company should pay consideration only in the form of cash.

(e) The company should not withdraw the offer if once the announcement is made.

(f) If the company announces the offer to buy-back its own securities through any of the sources the promoter or the person in Central should not involve in the securities of the company in the stock exchange during the offer period.

(g) The Companies Act does not allow the buy-back offer of the companies if the amalgamation method is in pending.

(h) The company should appoint a compliance officer for redressing the investors problems.

(i) The particulars of the destroyed/extinguished security certificates should be furnished by the company to the concerned stock exchanges within seven days of destruction.

(j) The company should not buy-back its own securities in the following situations:

 (i) Locked in securities,

 (ii) Non-transferable securities till the pending of the lock in period.

(k) The company should issue on advertisement in the national daily within two days of the completion of the process by disclosing the following factors:

 (i) The number of securities bought under this offer.

 (ii) The price of securities which the offer is made by the company.

 (iii) The total amount paid in consideration of the securities.

 (iv) The full details of the security holders who have offered their securities under this process exceeding are per cent of the of the total securities.

 (v) The company should also reveal about the consequences of the capital structure before and after the buy-back of the securities.

 (vi) The company should follow all the rules and regulations of the SEBI in addition to the Companies Act and other applicable laws.

Obligations of the Merchant Banker

The merchant banker plays an important role in the buy-back process. The merchant banker is also responsible for fulfilling all the formalities by the offer made company being a client to him the merchant banker has to ensure that:

(a) The offer will be implemented by the company without any hurdles.
(b) The obligations of the company towards the **escrow account.**
(c) Payment of consideration in the form of cash.
(d) The announcement of the buy-back should be done according to the legal formalities.
(e) The letter of offer should be filed with the SEBI.
(f) The contents of information regarding the public announcement should be fair and true.
(g) The compliance of the Sections 77A and 77B of the Companies Act and any other law is necessary.
(h) Fulfilment of the obligations of the **escrow account** must be maintained by the company.
(i) A final report should be furnished in a specified manner within **15 days** from the date of closure of the buy-back offer.
(j) If the merchant banker fails to comply with the obligations of these regulations immediate action should be taken against the financial intermediary.

Penalties and Procedure

The SEBI is the most powerful organisation in India and it controls the activities of all the financial intermediaries like Registers merchant bankers under writers etc. The penalties that are imposed by the SEBI are as follows:

(a) Power to order investigation,
(b) Power to issue directions.

The SEBI has the power to order the investigations on ***suo-moto*** or upon the information received by it to conduct the affairs of any person associated with the process of buy-back. The SEBI is empowered to appoint an officer for the following purposes:

(a) To monitor the activities of any person who involves in malpractice.

(b) To investigate into any complaint of any of these regulations.
(c) The suspected person should produce before the SEBI. The things required, i.e., books, accounts documents.
(d) The suspected person should extend cooperation to the investigating officer for examining the looks of accounts and other documents.
(e) The investigating officer has the full power to summon and enforce the attendance of the person.
(f) After completion of the investigating process, the investigating officer should submit a report to the SEBI.
(g) On receipt of the report from the investigation officer the SEBI takes an initiative action depending upon the degree of guiltiness by such persons.

The SEBI has the power to issue directions in the interest of the securities market and investors.

(a) It has the power to direct the concerned person not to participate in any activitiy which leads to the violation of the Companies Act.
(b) It has the power to direct the concerned person not to involve in any further deal in the securities in any manner.
(c) It can direct the concerned person to direct or sell the shares which are acquired by violating the rules and regulations of the Act.
(d) It has the power to take an action against the registered financial intermediary.
(e) Any person who involves in the insider trading against the provision should be dealt in accordance with the provisions of the SEBI Insider Trading Regulations, 1992 and SEBI (Prohibition of Fraudulent and Uunfair Trade Practices) Regulation, 1995.

Therefore, the SEBI has been set up to protect the interests of the investors. It is the watchdog of the market. It is empowered to look after the welfare of the individual investors, institutional investors, financial intermediaries and corporate sector. It has now full powers to regulate the primary and secondary market.

Takeovers and SEBI Regulations

At present the takeover wave is sweeping the country. It is known fact that there have been a number of takeover lids. It became a quite common phenomenon. It can be defined as the acquisition of another company that may take the form of a friendly or unfriendly merger. The share holders of the target company realise on appreciable increments in wealth relative to the market value of their holdings prior to take over activity. The application in wealth is possible only due to the premium paid by the acquiring company. Once the announcement has been made to the takeover of a particular company, the target company's stock tends to rise in the market. Usually, in the takeover process, the acquiring companies simply pay too much. Therefore, the acquiring company's worth decrease. All acquisitions may not be fruitful but some are worthy because some elements enhance the value of the worth. The combination of these two companies is treated either as a purchase or a pooling of interest.

The benefits of a takeover company depends on the availability of readymade manufacturing facilities, well-established brand market share potential no need of licences and well-planned distribution network. The take over is a dense of the companies which try to enter into the new business areas on expansion in the same time of activity. The various Acts like FEMA, MRTP, IDRA 1961 have further added the needed impetus. It is also known as **"unwanted undertakings"** or buying up their competitors. The BIFR became a facilitator of **MEA** deals. After the introduction of the SEBI regulations, the legal hurdles dismantled. The government is in the attitude of non-interference in the takeover process. The availability of the cheap funds in the global and domestic markets strengthened the takeovers method.

The takeover is a method of amalgamation of companies. In amalgamation one company makes an offer to purchase the shares of another company's members.

The takeover is different from the merger in approach. It is a unilateral step and the offer company decides the maximum price by considering the existing rules and regulations. It takes a less time while the merges requires a time consuming method. Various things influence the takeover decision such as goodwill of the company, large scale production, increase in the earning capacity by acquiring the same line sector company, a high calibre to meet the R&D expenditure. Acquisition is the purchase by one company of a controlling interest in the share capital of another existing company. The acquisition may arise in the following situation:

(a) agreement with the majority shareholders in the company,
(b) buying of shares in the open market,
(c) buying of new shares by private treaty,
(d) payment of consideration in the form of **cash, debentures and issue of shares.**

Amalgamation has been defined by Halsbury as a blending of two or more existing undertakings into one undertaking the shareholders in the company which is to carry on the blended undertaking.

Amalgamations and Mergers Process

Amalgamation means the creation of a new organisation by combining two or more units. In the process of amalgamation two or more companies may liquidate themselves under the law and sell their assets and transfer liabilities to a new company which issues its own stock in exchange for the **new worth** of property received from the amalgamating companies. No one company can exist after the completion of the amalganfations. The merger also known as **Absorption.** The absorbing company retains its identity and expands the size through a merger. **Reconstruction** means purchase of one understanding by the other transfer of shares from one undertaking to the other and an order of the Central Government in regulation of the **Sections 394, 395 and 396** of the Companies Act, 1956. According to Section 391 of the Companies Act, 1956, a compromise should be done with the creditors to carry out the scheme of reconstruction or amalgamation. The court may order for companies for arrangement or by a subsequent order makes provision to facilitate the reconstruction or amalgamation. Section **391** empowers that 3/4th of the value of the creditors.

The following steps are involved in the scheme of amalgamation:

(a) The acquire prepares a scheme of amalgamation.
(b) Defining the transferor and transferee.
(c) Authorised, issued and subscribed capital of transferor and transferee companies.
(d) Basis of scheme, evaluation report, transfer of assets and liabilities specified date, consolidation of capital.
(e) Change of name, object and accounting year.
(f) Protection of employment.
(g) Dividend position and prospects.
(h) Conditions of the scheme.

The mergers, acquisitions and takeovers are regulated by the SEBI. The SEBI regulations 1994 deals with the substantial acquisition of shares and takeovers. The Act contains five chapters indicating the rule position regarding the takeover methodology. **Chapter I** reveals the preliminary aspects such as definitions and concepts of the various terms. **Chapter II** deals with the disclosure of shareholdings as per Regulations 5 to 8. **Chapter III** indicates the applicability of the regulation for takeover process. **Chapter IV** contains the bailout takeover process. The **last Chapter** discloses the information regarding the investigation process as per the Regulations 33 to 40.

Exemptions

According to the Regulations **from 9 to 25** takeover provisions are not applicable to the acquisitions of shares in the following cases **(exempted cases)**:

(a) Application of shares is made in pursuance of a prospectus issued shares (public issue).
(b) Underwriting arrangement.
(c) Shares acquired under Sections 91 and 394 of the Companies Act.
(d) The shares acquired under Section 18 of the Sick Industrial Companies Act.
(e) Acquisition of shares in the general course of business by a registered stockbroker.
(f) The shares of unlisted companies.
(g) The SEBI is empowered to grant exemption.

Minimum Offer Price

The minimum offer price is regulated by the SEBI provisions under **Regulation 19.** It deals with the declaration of the minimum price by the acquirer. The acquired should make the public announcement atleast in one English newspaper and one regional newspaper. An acquired who holds shares carrying **10%** or less voting rights should not acquire further shares from the open market which when taken together with his existing holdings would carry more than **10%** of the voting rights unless he makes a public announcement. When shares more than 10% of the voting rights are held to acquire further shares, the acquirer has to make public announcement. The purchasing offer should be made through a registered merchant banker. The takeover announcement copy should be furnished to the SEBI atleast **24 hours** before its issuance. The Regulation **17** of the SEBI Act reveals that the acquirer should submit the draft of a letter to the board for the approval within **14 days** of public announcement. A certificate is to be submitted by the merchant banker. The acquirer should pay a fee of **Rs.25,000** to the board. The letter of offer should be sent to all the shareholders of the company to the purpose of an acquisition under the regulations. The minimum offer price may be payable in cash or by exchange of shares or combination of both. According to the regulations the minimum offer price is the neglected price or quoted price on the stock exchange which even is **higher** under the Regulation 10 of the Act. The minimum offer price the highest price in the open market or quoted price is on the stock exchange which even is **higher**. The Regulations **21, 23 and 25** deals with the minimum number of shares to be acquired, competitive acquisition and withdrawal of offer respectively. The Regulation **20** indicates the general obligations which are to be fulfilled by the acquirer. The obligations are presented below:

(a) The acquirer company should be able to implement the offer.
(b) The acquirer should submit a letter of offer to the Board of Directors of the company whose shares are being acquired.
(c) The acquire should indicate the period for which the offer should be kept open.
(d) The acquirer should declare accepting the responsibility for the information presented by him.
(e) The acquirer should also give an issue for not making any further public announcement for the acquisition of shares in the succeeding 6 months.

Bailout Takeover

Bail out takeover means the promoter who is taking over a financially weak company in pursuance of the rehabilitation scheme approved by a public financial institution or scheduled bank. The provisions pertaining to bail out takeover would not apply to **sick industrial companies**. The stock industrial companies are governed by the Sick Industrial Companies **(Special Provisions)** Act. The financially weak company may not be a sick company. According to the Regulation **26** of the Act financially weak company means, a company which has accumulated loss at the end of the previous financial year and which has resulted in the erosion of more than **50%** but less than **100%** of its net worth. The net worth of the company is the sum total of the **paid up capita and free reserves.** This regulation excludes sick industrial unit for the better understanding of the context, we must know the difference between sick company and financially weak company. The sick company has been defined by the **Sick Industrial Companies (Special Provisions) Act, 1985** an industrial company (being a company registered for not less than **five years)** which has at the end of any financial year accumulated losses equal to or exceeding its entire net worth.

Substantial acquisition means a total acquisition of not less than **20%** or more of the shares. The Regulation **30** reveals that substantial acquisition held by the public should not be less than **20%** of the paid up share capital of such company. The lead financial institution appraises the company in financial viability, assess fund requirements for revival and drawn up of the **rehabilitation** scheme. The rehabilitation scheme in the acquisition of shares in the financially weak company in the "outright purchase of shares or exchange of shares or a combination of both". According to the rehabilitation programmes the lead institution should invite offers for the acquisition of shares from atleast **three parties.** The lead institution would have to select one party among the three based on the managerial competence, technical capability of the person/party adequacy of financial resources etc. The lead institution should also provide necessary information to any interested person regarding the present management capabilities, technologies range of products share holders pattern financial holding. Five years balance sheets and any other information desired by that person. Thc lcad institution evaluates the birds received with reference to the purchase price or exchange of shares track record, financial muscle, goodwill of the management of the person acquiring shares. After making the evaluation the financially weak company accepts one of the bids. The selection of bid-decision should be informed to the lead institution which in turn invites the acquirer for the determination of offer price. The promoter of the weak company, financial institutions and also other shareholders together determine the offer price by a mutual negotiation between the person acquiring shares and the lead institution.

The acquirer should make a public announcement of his intention for the acquisition of shares. The public announcement should contain relevant details about the offer process. Therefore, the acquisition process should be completed as the procedure laid down in the Act.

The SEBI has the full authority to investigate the affairs of the acquired company as per the SEBI Act. The Chapter V of the SEBI Act deals with the investigation process about the affairs of the acquired company.

SEBI and Insider Trading

Insider trading is an unfair and unhealthy practice. The SEBI prohibited the insider dealing, on trading. It may be defined as "sale or purchase of securities by persons who possess price sensitive information about the company". It dangers the integrity of the market. Insider trading may be the brain child of the brokers and top level management of the corporate sector. The favourable and unfavourable trends of the particular company lead to the insider trading. The favourable trends for a particular company is **takeover, diversification and takeover.** The unfavourable trends are occasions of the poor performance and loss of earnings. The unpublished price sensitive information occupies an important role in the insider trading. For example, financial results, interim and final dividends, right issues, bonus issue, amalgamation, mergers, takeovers. The company executives, journalists, banks, financial institutions, top level management have access towards this information. Insider trading is considered as committing the offence. The SEBI has the full authority to investigate the malpractice on the basis of complains from the investors or intermediaries or ***suo-moto.*** The SEBI can carry on the inspection of books of account, other records and documents of a suspected person. It has the power to issue directions to the suspected person not to involve in the securities in any specific manner. According to Section **24** of the SEBI Act, it has the power to initiate criminal prosecution against the responsible person. The Securities Act also imposes the penalty up to **Rs. 5 lakhs** for indulging in the insider trading. The insider trading can be curbed with any effective enforcement of the Act. The effectiveness can be established through the strict action like **fine withdrawal of licenses, etc.,** and treating such activities like criminal cases. But the criminal case requires a high standard of evidence. Therefore, the insider trading could be watched and controlled by those who hold more than **5 per cent** of stock.

Prohibition of fraudulent and unfair trade practices: The insider trading is extremely difficult to **pin down.** It includes the market manipulation. Market manipulation means no person should buy or sell the securities in a fraudulent manner or no person should indulge in any unfair trade practice. No person should take part or enter either directly or indirectly in the transactions of securities which are likely to have the effect of artificially raising or depressing or stabilising the prices of securities. No person should involve in increase depress or cause fluctuations in the market price of the securities. The prohibition of unfair trade practices are presented below:

(a) No person should engage in any Act which appears as a fraud in connection with the purchase or sale of any securities.
(b) No person should delay the transfer of securities.
(c) No person should indulge in the falsification of his books of accounts and records for the purpose of market manipulation.

The SEBI has the right to investigate the affairs of the suspected person. The board can inspect the books of accounts, records and documents of any person buying or selling the securities. The SEBI has the authority to investigate into the complaints received from the investors or intermediaries or any other person on any matter. The board has also the power to investigate the ***suo-moto.*** The SEBI sends a notice before going to an investigation under Regulation **6** to the concerned persons. Sometimes according to the situation, the SEBI is empowered to investigate the affairs of a person without complaint and notice. With the invest of public, the concerned person should obey the rules and regulations imposed by the Act. The person should submit all the required documents to the inspecting officer for verification. The inspecting officer is empowered to examine or record the statements of any member, director, partner and employee of the concerned person. The inspecting officer submits a report to the board after the verification of the records and facts. On receipt of the report from the inspecting officer, the board takes measures as it may deem fit including issuing directors with the interest of the securities market. The SEBI is empowered to give the directions in the following situations:

(a) The SEBI can direct the person not to deal in the securities in any manner.
(b) It can direct the person to call up any of its officers, employees or representatives to refrain from dealing in securities.
(c) It can prohibit the person from disposing off any of the securities acquired in violation of the regulations.
(d) It can take the disciplinary action against the person/intermediary holding a certificate of registration under section 12 of the SEBI Act.

Procedure of Action in Case of Default

The SEBI is empowered to take the action in case of default by any person/ intermediary. The procedure for action in case of default is presented below:

(a) If any person/intermediary violates the provisions then he is liable to suspension or cancellation of registration or imposition of civil penalty.
(b) The penalty should be imposed after the completion of detailed investigation.
(c) For the purpose of holding an enquiry under section 13, the board may appoint an enquiry officer.
(d) The enquiry officer should issue a notice to the person at the registered office or the principal place of the business of the person.
(e) The person should furnish a reply to the enquiry officer within **30 days** from the date of receipt of such notice.
(f) The person should appear in person or through any authorised person before the enquiry officer.
(g) During the period of enquiry the officer should have the power to sum any person relevant to the subject matter of the enquiry.
(h) If any person neglects or refuses the enquiry, the officer may proceed with the enquiry in the absence of such person.
(i) The enquiry officer will give a chance to appoint a presenting officer on behalf of the board.
(j) The enquiry officer should recommend the penalty to be awarded.
(k) On receipt of the report from the enquiry officer, the board can issue a show cause notice to the person.
(l) The concerned person should submit a reply to the board on receipt of the notice within **21** days.
(m) On receipt of the reply from the concerned person, the board should take the action as early as possible but not later than **thirty days** from the receipt of the reply. The order copy should be sent to the concerned person.

The board has the power to initiate criminal proceedings before the court of competent jurisdiction. The **Metropolitan Magistrate** or Judicial Magistrate of the first class is empowered to punish the concerned person under these regulations of the Act. According to Section **24** of the Act, if any person gives a false explanation in an enquiry he should be imposed **penalty** under this regulation. If any person is aggrieved by an order of the board he may appeal to the Central Government.

SEBI guidelines to stock-brokers/sub-brokers: The entry in to the stock market is not open to the public. The buying and selling of shares and securities are done through the members of the stock exchanges. The financial assets such as **equity, preference shares, bonds, debentures** issued by the companies and bonds securities issued by the government are traded on capital markets. The buyer and seller of the financial asset do not meet directly in an organised stock market. The transactions take place through the broker. The brokers work as agents only. They charge a commission on each transaction which they execute. Stock-brokers play an active role and support the stock exchanges by performing the following useful economic services:

(a) Ready marketability and price stability for the securities.
(b) Contributes the growth of savings.
(c) Contributes the growth of industrial sector development.

The brokers meet in the stock exchange at specified hours for executing the transactions of their clients. All the transactions done on the stock exchange will be entered in the slips and then they confirm. The transactions will be settled through bids and offer. The broker is responsible for the delivery of the share certificates to thc buyers. The sale or purchase of shares procedure is presented below:

(a) Orders are placed with the broker for buying or selling of shares at best rates.
(b) The order price may be inclusive of a broker commission or at market price. i.e., excluding broker commission. The broker commission to be added.
(c) The transactions will be settled through the system of clearing transactions.
(d) The clearing house acts as the coordinator of all the activities between the members of the stock exchange.
(e) The competition among the bidders for buying and selling of the securities may stabilise the securities prices in the market.
(f) The settlement period is generally a week and the transactions made during the settlement period are settled either by payment or by delivery on the specified days of the clearing programme.
(g) After the closing hours of the market every member should

submit his **sauda sheets** to the computer centre that effects the purchase and sale of shares during that day. All the activities of all the brokers will be checked by the computer itself. All the adjustments are made in the computer during the settlement period. A statement of all the saudas thus adjusted is printed out. A **Balance Sheet** for the member in total receivable or payable is also printed out. The sum of the total shares to be delivered should be equal to the sum of the total shares to be received for each security. Every member provided with a statement showing the details of deliveries to be effected by him to others and to him by others. Total transaction report also is prepared after adjusting all the transactions. The details of the unmatched transactions will be printed out.

(h) In case of specified shares, the settlement transactions are settled through **three options.** The broker has to terminate his contract of sale or purchase by a gross contract or squaring **up** to complete the contract by delivery or payment or to carry over the contract to the next settlement.

(i) The settlement system offers a greater liquidity to the authorities in the secondary market.

Registration of Stock-broker

The interested person should make an application for the grant of certificate in **Form A** through the stock exchange. The stock exchange may forward the application form to the SEBI within **30 days** from the date of its receipt. On receipt of the application form the concerned stock exchange, the SEBI will scrutinise the application. It may ask for any such further information or clarifications regarding the dealings in securities for granting a certificate. The applicant or its principal officer, if necessary should appear before the board for personal representation. The SEBI on being satisfied that the person is eligible as a stock-broker it grants a certificate in **Form-D** to the stock-broker and sends an intimation to that effect to the stock exchange. The person who holds the stock-broker certificate should at all times abide by the **code of conduct** as per the Act. Sometimes the SEBI may reject the application form of an interested person for registration. Then the person should follow the following process for the grant of the certificate:

(a) The SEBI may reject the application on the following grounds:
   (i) If the broker has no eligibility.
   (ii) If he does not have the necessary infrastructural facilities.

(iii) If he does not have any past experience in dealing with the securities in the market.

(b) The refusal of granting the registration certificate should be communicated by the SEBI within **30 days** of such refusal to the applicant and concerned stock exchange.

(c) On the receipt of the communication from the SEBI the applicant should apply again within a period of **30 days** from the date of receipt of such intimation for reconsideration of its decision.

(d) Finally, the SEBI may communicate its decision in writing to the applicant and to the concerned stock exchange.

(e) A stock-broker whose application for the grant of a certificate has been refused by the board should not deal in the securities as a stock-broker.

Every applicant who is eligible for the grant of a certificate should pay such fee as specified in the Act from time-to-time. In some moments the board may give time for the payment of fee before the expiry of **six months** from the date on which such fee becomes due. If a stock-broker fails to pay the fee as prescribed by the board may suspend the registration certificate.

Registration of Sub-brokers

The stock sub-broker should apply to the SEBI in **Form-B** for the grant of a certificate. The application for registration should contain a recommendation letter from the stock-broker in **Form-C** along with the recommendation from his banker also. The application form should be submitted to the concerned stock exchange. The concerned stock exchange on receipt of the application should verify the information contained and should also certify that the applicant is eligible for the registration as per the Act. The eligibility criteria for the registration as a sub-broker is as follows:

(a) for individuals,

(b) for partnership firms/body corporate.

In the case of registration for the individuals, the following norms should be fulfilled by the applicant:

(i) the applicant should be **21** years of age.

(ii) the applicant has not been convicted of any offence involving in **fraud or dishonesty.**

(iii) The applicant should have the minimum educational qualification, i.e. **10+2** or its equivalent examination recognised by the government.

In case of registration for **firm/corporates,** the regulations have to be fulfilled. If the board satisfied with the eligibility of the stock sub-broker then it grants a certificate in **Form-E** to the sub-broker and an intimation to the concerned stock exchange. The sub-broker should pay the fee as specified in the Act and abide by the code of conduct. The sub-broker should enter into an agreement with the **stock-broker** for specifying the scope of his authority and responsibilities.

Code of the Conduct of the Stock-broker

The stock-broker is a highly specialised skilful work. It needs talent, knowledge, sincerity, a thorough understanding about the economy, a clear idea about the government policies etc. He must fully acquaint with the latest developments in the national programmes. He should be in a decent manner. He must be a dynamic personality and have his own style of functioning. The broker must be in a good position to maintain relations with all the parties as below:

(a) General relations
(b) Investors relations
(c) Relationship with other colleagues

Relations with General Public

The stock-broker should maintain high standards of integrity, promptness and transparency while conducting his business affairs. A stock-broker should act with due skill care and diligence in the conduct of his business affairs. A stock-broker should not involve in manipulative fraudulent or deceptive or spread rumours with a view of masking personal gains. The stock-broker should not create any false market or indulge in any act detrimental to the investors. A stock-broker should not involve himself in **excessive** speculative business in the market. A stock-broker should abide by all the provisions of the Act and the Rules, Regulations issued by the government, the SEBI and the stock exchange from time-to-time.

Relations with other Investors

The stock-broker should maintain better relations with the investors. The

customer is the king in the market. The broker should possess sincere, mature towards the investors. He should deal with his clients more faith fully in executing the orders for buying and selling of the securities at the best available market price. He should not refuse to deal with a small investor merely on the ground of the volume of business involved. The stock-broker should promptly inform his client about the execution on **non-execution** of an order and make prompt payment in respect of the securities sold and arranged for the prompt delivery of securities purchased by the investors. The broker should issue a contract note to his client without any delay in prescribed form by the stock exchange. The stock-broker should maintain a high confidentiality in the transactions involved with a number of parties. He should not disclose any information to any other person. The broker should not encourage his clients for the sale or purchase of the securities with the objective of generating brokerage or commission.

The stock-broker should not furnish false or misleading quotations or misleading advice or information to the clients with a view to earn commission or brokerage. The stock-broker should not deal or transact for a defaulted client with other brokers. A stock-broker should not make a recommendation to any client or investor. The stock-broker should be adequately trained, skilful, talented staff and make arrangements.

Relations with other Brokers

The stock broking is a highly talented skilful job. It requires a careful handling of the assignments. The stock-broker should maintain healthy relations with the other brokers. The broker should be in a cooperative manner with the other contracting parties while comparing the unmatched transactions. He must be careful in delivery of shares on cooperation in finding **bad delivery**. The stock-broker must cooperate with other brokers in protecting the interests of his clients for their rights to **bonus rights and dividends** related to securities. A stock-broker should maintain the transactions with other stock-brokers should cooperate for smooth settlement of transactions. The stock-broker should advertise only with the permission from the concerned stock exchange. The stock-broker should submit a correct and accurate required returns to the **SEBI** and to the concerned stock exchange.

General Obligations and Responsibilities

The following obligations have to be fulfilled by every registered broker in India. The stock-broker should keep normally the following books of accounts records and documents. All these books should be maintained by all brokers:

(a) Sauda books (Register of transactions)
(b) Clients ledger
(c) General ledger
(d) Journal
(e) Cash book
(f) Bank pass book
(g) Documents register
(h) Members contract books
(i) Margin deposit books
(j) The Register of accounts of the sub-brokers
(k) The duplicates of the contract notes issued to the clients
(l) An agreement with the sub-broker

The stock-brokers who registered with the SEBI should intimate to the officials about the place of keeping the books. Every stock-broker should submit the accounting information after closing the books of accounts to the SEBI not later than **six months** from the closure of the financial year. Every registered broker should preserve the books of accounts and other records for the minimum period of **five years.**

The Procedure for Inspection

The SEBI has the full authority over the financial intermediary. It controls, regulates, monitors, evaluates and directs the market. It can inspect any stock-broker's premises who registers with the SEBI. The board may appoint one or more persons as the inspecting authority to inspect the books of accounts, records, documents of the stock-broker for any purpose. Basically, the SEBI undertakes the inspection for the following purposes:

(a) to check the maintenance of the books of accounts as per the act.
(b) to observe whether the registered broker has fulfilled all the legal formalities or not.
(c) to investigate into the complaints received from the investors and other stock-brokers.
(d) to investigate the ***suo-moto*** with the interest of securities business or investors interest into the affairs of the stock-broker.

(e) the board should give a reasonable notice to the broker before undertaking the inspection.

(f) if the board feels it is necessary to inspect the registered stock-broker, it can commence the inspection without sending any notice to the broker with the interest of the investors.

(g) the stock-broker should be bound to discharge his obligations.

(h) during the tenure of the inspection, it is the duty of every director, partner, officer and employee of the broker to produce the records book of accounts and other documents as inspecting officer may require.

(i) the inspecting authority should submit the inspection report to the board after the completion of the inspection.

(j) on receipt of the inspection report the board should communicate the findings to the stock-broker. Before tasking the action, the board may give him an opportunity of being heard his version.

(k) The board may appoint a qualified auditor to investigate into the books of account or affairs of the broker.

(l) the appointed auditor should have the same powers of the inspecting authority.

Procedure for action in case of default

The SEBI has the power to take the action in case of default by a registered stock-broker in India. If stock-broker fails to comply with any condition subject to which the registration has been granted then he is liable for taking action. A broker who contravene with any of the provisions of the Act, Rules, or Regulations, there is liability to take action against such broker. The broker should strictly follow the rules and regulations of the stock exchange and the securities contracts Act. If he fails to comply with the norms he should be liable to pay the **penalties** as specified in the Act. The penalties in case of default may be either suspension of registration or cancellation. The suspension of registration of a broker may be imposed on the following grounds, if:

(a) the broker violates the provisions, acts, rules and regulations.

(b) the stock does not follow the code of conduct.

(c) the broker fails to pay the fees.

(d) the broker violates the conditions of the registration.

(e) the broker fails to resolve the complaints of the investors.

(f) the broker indulges in the manipulation of share prices.

(g) the broker is improper or unbusiness or unprofessional conduct.

(h) the membership of the broker is suspended by the stock exchange.
(i) fails to respond to the board communication.
(j) the broker involved in price rigging or cornering the activities in the market.
(k) the financial position deteriorates the broker.
(l) the broker fails to furnish any information to the board.
(m) the broker furnishes wrong or false information.
(n) the broker does not submit the periodical return.
(o) the broker does not cooperate during the enquiry period.

The stock-brokers registration can be cancelled by the SEBI if,

(a) the broker violates the takeover regulations or any provision of the insider trading regulation.
(b) the cancellation of the membership by the stock exchange.
(c) the broker is convicted of a criminal offence.
(d) the broker is guilty of fraud.

Any broker being aggrieved by an order of the board may appeal to the Central Government under the provisions of the Act.

SEBI and Investors Protection

The investors are the most important persons in the capital market. They came under the purview of **Consumer Act.** Generally in India, they are facing the problems like **non-receipt of refund, allotment order, delay and non-receipt of interest, dividend, non-receipt of brokerage and underwriting commission.** These problems arise due to the negligence of the **corporate bodies** and financial intermediaries. The problems are solved by the regulatory authorities like the SEBI and the stock exchanges. The basic redressal of grievances are done by the stock exchanges and corporate sectors. All the stock exchanges in India have invest or services cell to resolve the grievances. But there are inordinate delays in resolving such grievances. The SEBI initiated various measures to maintain discipline in the financial intermediaries and stock exchanges by issuing guidelines. The guidelines include the aspects like insider trading, inspection of stock exchanges and their records, scrutiny of prospectus for adequate disclosures, credit rating for financial instruments like debentures, deposits. The stock-brokers are also required to disclose the statutory requirements. They should bring transparency in the clients transactions the SEBI has issued guidelines to the companies and stock exchanges with regard to the following aspects:

1. Inspection of books of brokers.
2. Transparency in prices and volume of trade in the stock exchanges.
3. Enforcing the margin norms strictly.
4. Amendments to the bye-laws of the stock exchanges with regard to capital adequacy.
5. Indicating the brokerage and security price separately in contract note.
6. Reviewing and redressing the investor grievances promptly.
7. Amendment to the relevant bye-laws for the issue of contract note by the broker to the client mandatory.

The **Joint Parliamentary Committee** has expressed its opinion for providing the protection to the small investors. The Committee recommended an effective system to handle the complaints and taking of the follow up action within specified time frame. The SEBI has been vested with adequate powers through the ordinance to protect and safeguard the interests of the investors. The following elements cover the investors protection and grievances:

(a) **Investor protection** – SEBI plus Investors associations
(b) provisions of the SCR Act
(c) provisions of the Companies Act
(d) listing guidelines on investor protection
(e) invest or guidance series
(f) investor protection fund
(g) computerised process of redressed of investors grievances
(h) company law amendment
(i) Companies Act anomalies

Investors Protection

The SEBI has the full authority to monitor the stock market activities. It has decided to intensify the efforts to redress the complaints of the investors in collaboration with the recognised investor associations. The recognised investors association is empowered to facilitate the filling of class action **suits** in the consumer courts against the concerned companies. In India the sharing of information is first done with the **Consumer**

Education Research Centre (CERC), Ahmedabad. Section 12 of the Consumer Protection Act, 1986 enables the consumer associations to file the suits in district forums. The suit by the investor associations in the district is based on the information on investors complaints. It implies that saving in the legal cost apart from benefiting a large number of complaints through a single suit. The SEBI publishes the names of the top **twenty** defaulting companies every fortnight. It puts pressures the companies. The SEBI has the power to issue the **show cause notices** and award penalty points under the SEBI guidelines. The SEBI has the power to issue the **No objection certificate** to the companies for releasing of their **one per cent** deposit with the stock exchange emerged as a major check point for complaints. The SEBI has the power to recommend the suitable legal action against the defaulters to the department of company affairs and for suspension of trading of their shares to various stock exchanges from time to time.

Provisions of the Companies Act

The Government of India has been flooded with a number of complaints from time-to-time. The complaints have been made by the shareholders, investors, debenture holders regarding the delay in the transfer of shares delay in the issue of allotment letters and share/debenture certificates or refund of share/debenture application money to non-allottees to the applicants of public issue. The following provisions of the Companies Act imposes various penalties depending upon the severity of the defaults:

(a) Section **113** of the Act indicates that every company within **three months** offer the allotment of shares/debentures has any default in compliance of the provision of law it is punishable.
(b) If any company fails to register the share after transferring such share within two months, then it is liable to punishment accordingly.
(c) The Companies Act, 1956 has issued the listing guidelines in this regard.
    1. According to the listing guidelines the companies must issue the allotment letters or shares certificates to the allottee immediately after the allotment of shares is made but it should not be later than **two months** from the closure of the subscription list.
    2. The company should issue letters of regret along with refund order to the **non-allottees.**

3. The listed company must issue the share certificate within **one month** of the date of lodgement of transfer of shares.
4. If a company refuses to register any transfer of shares to the transferee within **two months** the Section 111 of the Act permits to file an appeal before the **Company Law Board.**
5. After closing the public issue process, Section 73 of the Companies Act imposes condition for the despatch of allotment letters/certificates as to share and debentures within the stipulated period of time.
6. Companies entering the capital market are required to pay to the unsuccessful applicants and liable to pay the **interest** for the delayed period from the date of closure of the subscription list.
7. Section 621 of the Companies Act, 1956 authorises a share holder to file the prosecution against the company and its officers the companies concerned are advised to ensure that they should strictly follow the provisions of the Companies Act otherwise they would be punished.

Provisions of the Securities Contract Regulation Act, 1956

Section **22A** of the Securities Contracts (Regulation) Act, 1956 deals with the registration and transfer of shares. A company fails to register the transfer of shares on one or more of the following situations:

(a) If the transfer of the security is in contravention with any law.
(b) If the transfer of the security is prohibited by any order of any court/tribunal.
(c) If the financial instrument of the transfer is not in proper method.
(d) However, the company should make a reference to the **Company Law Board** on the above ground within **60 days** of the lodgement of the instrument of transfer.

Listing Guidelines in Investors Protection

The listing guidelines on the investors protection has been issued by the **Department of Economic Affairs**. The share holders can take up the matters with the concerned registrar of companies in regard with non-compliance of the guidelines. A reference may also be made to the concerned stock exchange.

Investors Guidance Series

The investors guidance series is issued by the SEBI with the interest of public to educate the investors on the basic features of various investment. They are required to make precautions before choosing an investment or dealing with intermediary. The Indian investors simply depend upon the advises but not on their own assessment. They simply hand over the cheques to the brokers. They do not know how to select a scrip. They do not know the product which is manufactured by the selected company. Even they do not know some basic stock market parameters like **EPS, PE Ratio, Debt equity ratio, Leverage** and about the company's market share, company's expansion or diversification, products life cycle etc. Therefore, they motivate the investors to develop the capital market. The SEBI will create an awareness about the investors rights and remedies. The investors should take their investment decisions in the light of their individual circumstances. The SEBI has issued the following series of guidance to enlighten the investors:

(a) **Investors guidance** (Debentures)
(b) **Investors guidance** (Transfer of securities)
(c) **Investors guidance** (Stock investment scheme)

Investors Guidance (Debentures)

In India some companies are not able to service the debenture holder. The companies are unable to pay the redemption amount because of financial difficulties. Some other companies delay the interest on debenture or may not redeem the debentures on schedule. The debentures are issued by the companies, secured against the assets. The assets are mortgaged on the names of the trustees which mostly **financial institutions.** A trust deed is executed between the company and the trustee. The trust deed contains all the conditions and movements of the two parties. According to the guidelines issued by the ministry of finance the trustees are more powerful in protecting the interests of the debenture holders. The trustees observe the affairs and the activities with regard to debentures aspect the trustees should verify whether a debenture redemption reserve is created or not The trustees have the responsibility in monitoring the activities regarding the creation of security for the debentures and debenture redemption reserves. The India Trust Act indicates that a trustee may do all acts which are reasonable and proper while protecting beneficiary. The following steps are involved in case of complaints:

(a) The Section 113 of the Companies Act deals with the issue of debenture certificate to the debenture holder within the specified period. Every company must within **three months** after allotment of debentures should deliver the certificate.

(b) The company should transfer the registration within **two months** after applying for transfer of registration.

(c) The Companies Act specifies the above schedule for the delivery of certificates and transfer process. The extension of time will be granted by the company law board. Any default in compliance with the provisions is **punishable** with fine under Section 113(2) of the Act.

(d) An aggrieved debenture holder may apply to the **CLB** to direct the company to deliver the debenture certificate.

(e) The investor can also file a compliant before the **Magistrate Court** or forward his complaint to the stock exchange division of the Department of Economic Affairs.

(f) Section 118 of The Companies Act permits the debenture holder to obtain the copies and inspect the trust deeds and other documents.

(g) According to Section 56 of the **Indian Trust Act,** he has the right to ask the trust for the enforcement of the security created in case of default in the payment of interest and principal.

(h) The investor has the right to bring the matter to the notice of the SEBI, stock exchange and also financial institutions for the redressal of the grievance.

(i) The debenture holder can compel the trustees to perform any particular actor duty.

(j) The debenture holder can also approach the civil Court for the recovery of the due amounts. When the company is unable to pay its debts he can file a winding up petition under Section 433 of the Companies Act to a **High Court.**

(k) The debenture holder has the right to approach the Consumer Disputes Redressal Forum (District Forum), a State Commission, National Commission for claims at various levels stipulated by the Act.

Investors Guidance (Transfer of Securities)

This is another set of series issued by the SEBI with public interest to enlight investors on the public features of investors rights and remedies. The major problem faced by the investors is delay in the transfer of securities. The followings are the steps involved in the settlement of the investors problems:

(i) Transfer of securities

(ii) Registration of transfer

Transfer of securities is the obligation to the corporate sector. They are to be delivered through registered post or personally. The Companies Act, **Section 113(1),** reveals that every company has to compulsorily within **2 months** from the date of application make for registration of securities to the buyer party. The company law board has the power to extend the time for not more than **9 months** within the stipulated period to deliver the certificates. A company is required to send the share certificates duly endorsed within **one month** of the lodgement of the transfer deed.

Registration of transfer can be refused by a company by sending the notice to the buyer and seller and giving the reasons for such refusal. The Section 111 of the Companies Act provides that a company can refuse the transfer of registration on some grounds, besides the **Securities Contract (Regulation) Act** provides the following grounds for the registration of transfer of securities, they are:

(a) That the financial instrument of transfer is improper.
(b) That the transfer of financial asset is in contravention with any law.
(c) That the transfer of security is harmful to the existing investors.
(d) That the transfer of financial instrument is prohibited by any court of tribunal.

If the company has no interest to transfer the shares it should intimate to the investor with a reference to the **CLB.** On the other hand if the company has the interest to transfer the securities to such registration it should intimate to the buyer and seller in a prescribed form. A reference has to be made within two months to the CLB and reference copies to the concerned parties. The company should inform to the applicant, whether his application is refused or transferred before two months from the date on which the instrument of transfer is lodged.

Investor Protection and Guidance (Stock Investment Scheme)

The stock investment scheme has been recognised by the **RBI,** the Department of Company Affairs and the Government of India. It has been treated as one of the tools by which the application money for subscription of shares and debentures may be paid. The RBI has issued instructions to all the scheduled commercial banks to make the stock invest scheme a friendly investor. The stock invest may be described as a postal order. It can be used for the payment of money instead of cash in the appraisal of the stock invest scheme. Three persons involve in the process.

(a) Issuing banks
(b) Investors
(c) Registrars

(A) Issuing Banks: At present all the scheduled commercial banks are issuing the stock invest instrument to the investors. While issuing this instrument the issuing bank has to observe careful observations.

(a) Before issuing the instrument should be properly dated and issued under the signature of the authorised signatory.
(b) Every issuing instrument should contain the particulars as to the name and code number of the branch.
(c) It should be marked as non-negotiable/transfer crossed and payable to the banker.
(d) It should contain the name and full address of the purchaser on its reverse.
(e) The issuing bank should have branches or make necessary arrangements to facilitate the payment against the stock invest.
(f) The registrars to the issue are required to return the stock invest duly cancelled to the unsuccessful applications.

(B) Investors: The following steps are needed to participate in the primary market through the stock invest instrument:

1. The investor can approach any scheduled commercial bank for the issue of stock invest in desired denominations for the payment of money while applying for shares in the primary market.
2. The investor should not withdraw the money from the account until the payment has been made on this instrument.
3. The investors should take care about the use of stock invest. Because it should be used within **ten days** from the date of issue.
4. The investor should indicate all the particulars about the stock invest instrument in the specified place of application form.
5. The investor should use only one stock invest along with each application for subscription to an issue.
6. The investor should not make available the stock invest to the third party. It should be utilised by the account holder only.
7. After the allotment it will be sent to the issuing bank through the

controlling branch.

8. The inquiries relating to the stock invest should be addressed to the Registrar only.
9. After closing the public issue the controlling branches of the collecting banks will forward to the Registrar with a clear segregation of the information.

(C) Registrars: The following steps are involved to complete the process of a public issue:

(a) The Registrars should receive the applications for subscriptions accompanied by the stock invest from the controlling branches.

(b) On receipt from the controlling branches, the registrar should give the house number on the back side of the stock invest. The stock invest should be detached from the application and kept in the safe custody.

(c) The Registrar should process the applications. He should work out on the purpose of allotment and despatch of the certificates to the allotters.

(d) The registrar should report to the non-allottees and cancel their stock invest and return to the applicants.

(e) The Registrar should deposit the stock invest duly filled in the bank-wise and branch-wise and thus further the process should be completed.

(f) The Registrar should reject the multiple applications received with a single stock invest.

The registrar should maintain the proper record of applications which are received with the stock invest.

Computerised Process of Redressal of Investors Grievances

The problems of the investors lie with companies and financial intermediaries. In view of the large number of complaints the department of Company Affairs has set up a machinery for handling these complaints. It has also decided to take strict action against the default companies. The procedure for handling the complaints is by introducing a fully computerised system of processing. The information should be furnished by the companies regarding the action taken on each complaint within a stipulated period of time. The senior officials have been carefully observing the progress of action taken on investors complaints. The

Department of Company Affairs has succeeded fully in settling the investor grievances. The **Senior Officers** will hold the meetings of the companies against when large number of complaints are registered. Therefore, the companies may concentrate in solving the problems of the investors by the pressure from senior officials. If the company and registrar show negligency towards the investors complaints, they can directly report to the SEBI for appropriate action against such Registrars. The computer system in the investors protection cell will solve the problem by designing the status system of complaints.

Company Law Amendment

The Company Law amendments are made by keeping in view its benefits to the investors.

(a) The Companies Act has permitted the companies to hold share holders meeting on **Sundays** to attract more gathering.
(b) The share holders, the debenture holders and fixed deposit holders can now enjoy the nomination facility.
(c) Credit rating made mandatory.
(d) Auditing standards would be enhanced to the extent of international standards.
(e) The defaulted companies are prohibited from raising further loans from the market.
(f) The directors of the companies are made more accountability.
(g) The debenture holders can enforce the CLB for the payment of their principal and interest.
(h) The unpaid dividends are transferred to the investors protection fund.
(i) Enforcement of free transferability of shares and debentures.

The advantages of the Companies Act amendment are presented below:

(a) There is no need to disclose the information regarding drawing large remuneration, drawing employees along with the directors report.
(b) The companies can now file all the returns and records through floppy dishes to the department of company affairs.
(c) The share premium amounts will be included in free reserves.
(d) The companies have freedom to convert the loans/debentures in to equity without the approval of the government.

(e) The companies can now issue non-voting shares subject to certain limitations and regulations.
(f) The companies will be happy because they can buy-back their shares and can retain the control on the company.
(g) The companies have the freedom to maintain the records in loose leaf form.
(h) The companies need not submit the full list of share holders particulars along with annual returns.
(i) If the share holders accept the amendment of the objective clause, there is no need to get the approval from the CLB.
(j) The companies can now get the quick approvals for mergers and acquisition from the government.
(k) The directors of the company can now have the tax free payments from the company and their relatives can be accommodated in the board.
(l) The limit for managerial remuneration of directors is increased.
(m) the concept of dewed public company is removed from the Act.
(n) Inter-corporate fundings are increased to a certain level of the specified amount.

Companies Act Anomalies

According to the Companies Act, 1956, **Sections 73 and 113,** the allotment process of the share capital offered to the public company should approach the public for the issue of share capital to get its shares listed within **10 weeks** from the date of closure of the subscription list the company should dispatch. The share certificates within three months from the date of allotment. Therefore, the time gap between the legal formalities logically pushes the share price up. After the despatch of share certificates the investors may increase the supply position in the market. Then automatically the supply of shares in the market becomes more and more, it leads to the decline of prices in the market. The situation will be encashed by the well-experienced market men to book profits by covering their position. These people will never lose money in such deals. Therefore, the legal experts feel that the company should not be allowed.

SUMMARY

Banks are in the business of financial intermediation and naturally related to various kinds of **financial and non-financial risks.** Generally every commercial enterprise is haunted by uncontrolled environment. The financial institutions have the chance for the exposure of risk. The investors have many motives for investing. Return is the reward to the investor. Return on investments consists of two elements (a) regular return, (b) capital appreciation. Usually all the investors are interested towards higher profit. The buying and selling of the securities involves as thorough understanding of the stock market operations.

The Indian banking system has been changed in response to the emerging socio-political economic environment in India. Generally, the corporate sector involves in procuring of raw material according to their convenience. The corporate sectors current assets should be financed by the trade credit. The difference between current assets and current liabilities is known as working capital. The liberalisation, privatisation and globalisation have created a revolutionary changes in the banking sector. The credit authorisation scheme was introduced in October 1988. It was replaced by credit authorisation scheme.

The Government of India set up the SEBI on April 12, 1988 for the regulation and order by function of the capital markets. The SEBI has empowered powers of the Indian financial system. The Companies Act, the Securities Act and the Capital Issues Act make provisions for the smooth functioning of the capital market.

NOTES

1. James C. Vanhorne, *Fundamentals of Financial Management*, p. 91, Prentice Hall of India, New Delhi.
2. L.M. Bhole, *Financial Institutions and Financial Markets,* p. 25.
3. Mithani and Gordon, *Banking and Financial System,* p. 185, Hamalaya Publishing House, 2002.
4. Mithai and Gordan, *Banking and Financial System,* Himalaya Publishing House, 2002, p. 175.
5. Mithai and Gordon, *Banking and Financial System,* Himalaya Publishing House, 2002, p. 178.

Unit - III

- Management of Financial Institutions
  - (a) International Aspects of Financial Management
  - (b) Mutual Funds

Chapter 1

INTERNATIONAL ASPECTS OF FINANCIAL MANAGEMENT

Introduction

After the introduction of liberalisation, globalisation and privatisation policies, there is a rapid change in industrialisation, information technology and economic development process of the nation. Since the beginning of 1991, there has been change in the rules, organisations, scope and activity level in the Indian financial sector. This has encompassed capital markets. The global economy has witnessed several structural changes. Markets have become more open and competitive. Economies have become more inter-dependent and developed in the sphere of international trade and finance. It altered the pace and pattern of international flows of commodities and investment. Rapid technological changes in the information technology are expected to drive economic growth in the next phase of **digital economy**. The digital economy will overtake the traditional economy. The transportation facilities have increased the volume of trade throughout the globe. At present, the **globe** in a village and the countries are living on neighbourhood basis. The nations are becoming a part of global village. The distance has been reduced by modern mode of transport system. There is no horizon between two nations. The people are willing to accept the high quality goods with low prices irrespective of the goods manufactured nation. Therefore, the people are living locally and getting global products. The general customers now become as global customers. Now the companies are making goods in view of the international customers. The business transactions arise between two countries and increased the volume of business.

In case of many business organisations international transactions account for 50% of their earnings. The multi-national company may be defined as an organisation which has investment and sales in two or more countries. These companies are earning 50% of their total profits from global operations. They do require efficient and effective utilisation of their financial resources. The transactions between nations require the problem of currency exchange. They face more complex than those of domestic business organisations. These firms do the business into different business environments.

The business environment of a nation depends upon many factors. It relates to political risk, government policy, foreign exchange risk, investment and industrial policy etc. These are generally related in every nation. These factors affect the activities of global business enterprise. Generally, the corporate sector will make investment decisions only when the expected return is assured. The risk and return is the most important element in making the investment decisions of the global companies. The risk and return of a project depends upon the current exchange rates, tax structure and accounting practices. Every nation will take investment decisions to encourage the foreign companies. The inflow of foreign investment will be definitely useful to the country. The following statement will reveal the foreign direct investments in India:

Foreign Trade[1]

	1996-97	*1997-98*	*1998-99*	*1999-2000*	*2000-2001*	*2001-02*	*2002-03*	*Upto November 2002*
Exports								
Rs. in core	1,18,817	1,30,101	1,39,753	1,59,561	2,03,571	2,10,011	1,59,917	19,954
US $1 mn	33,470	35,006	33,219	36,822	44,560	44,035	32,865	4,135
Imports								
Rs. in crore	1,38,920	1,54,176	1,78,332	2,15,236	2,30,873	2,41,478	1,90,268	25,872
US $ mn	39,132	41,484	42,389	49,671	50,536	50,633	39,113	5,362
Non-Pol US $ Mn	29,096	33,321	35,990	40,664	34,450	36,985	27,384	3,970
Balance of Trade (Rs. in crore)	-20,103	-24,076	-38,579	-55,675	-27,302	-31,467	-30,351	-5,918

Factors for Investing Global

At present the globe is becoming like a village. The geographical and psychological distance has been reduced substantially due to the rapid technology. The transportation facilities have been helpful in increasing the volume of business turnover of the corporate sector. The companies will take decisions to invest in a project abroad, which is based upon a number of factors. The investment decision of the corporate sector is based upon the following considerations:

(a) Low risk
(b) Better returns
(c) Tax advantages
(d) Government policies

(a) Low Risk: Multi-national companies are operating in different nations under various government control. They know which country is providing better returns for their investment. It has been learnt that the international diversification is often more effective than the domestic diversification in reducing the risk with reference to the economic cycles of different countries. They will gain benefits by international diversification.

(b) Better Returns: Generally every business enterprise will work for profits only. Profit is the **oxygen** to the commercial enterprise. Investing in global basis is the expectation of higher return for an accepted level of risk. There may be demand and supply gap in the international market. The **multi-national companies** can tap these gaps which provide better return for their investments and efforts usually MNCs have good efficient management skills to meet the growing needs of the international customers. The MNCs will take the advantage of material cost, labour cost and other associated expenses. They will manufacture the goods where the cost of production is less. This will increase their margin of profits.

(c) Tax Advantages: Multi-national companies are exposed to various tax laws being operated in different countries. The taxation system will differ from one country to another country. Generally underdeveloped nations have lower tax rates. The underdeveloped countries will offer the tax incentives for attracting the foreign investment. The tax rates in advanced countries are high. Hence MNCs will diversify in different countries to get the tax advantages.

(d) Government Policies: The multi-national corporations will work in various kinds of governments. The policy of the government will definitely show impact on the profitability of a commercial enterprise. The policies of the government is the biggest threat to the existence of a multi-national company. The existence of the MNCs is susceptible to whims and fancies of the government. The companies will do their business upto the patronage of the government. Any political risk may adversely affect the functioning of **the multi-national companies**. The

MNCs will have to face problems such as higher taxes, higher utility charges, extra controls that may be imposed upon them at any time. The political instability in a country can seriously impair the functioning of the **MNCs**. Assessment of political risk is the most important factor before taking any investment decision. This can be done by assessing the degree of stability of the existing government and its attitude towards the foreign investment. If the assessment reveals that political risk is high, the MNCs should not take investment decisions even though high returns are available.

The management of Multi-national Corporation requires high talent, skill, dynamism and competency. A finance manager of the MNC has to pay proper attention towards its financial management. The MNCs are working as global basis and their earnings are related to foreign exchange. Their earnings are highly volatile. Though they earn stable income, they are exposed to foreign exchange fluctuations. The business among the countries necessarily involve currency of those countries. **Foreign exchange** fluctuations is the risk due to the relative rise or full of value of one currency with reference to another country's currency. The fall or decrease may affect future sales, costs and remittances of the company. It is the most important area to be managed by the multi-national companies. The **multi-national companies** should take care about the following factors:

(I) Management of foreign currency
(II) Financing system

(a) Management of Foreign Currency: International trade requires all receipts and payments will be done through foreign currency. The external transaction involves problem of payment and pricing. Generally the price is payable to seller's or in buyer's currency or an internationally accepted currency such as **dollars, pounds or yens**. The buyer has to remit the consideration in international currency. The buyer has to purchase the necessary foreign exchange to make his payments. There will be a difference between this currency and international currency. The foreign currency exchange rate is not fixed at all time. Therefore an exchange rate represents the number of currency units of currency that can be exchanged for another country's currency units. **For example 1 US $ = Rs. 50**. This means that for every Rs.50, $ 1 can be purchased. The currencies of the various countries are traded in an active open foreign export market. The price for foreign exchange is determined by the demand and supply factors. The foreign exchange market provides supply and demand of various foreign currencies. The exchange rates are involved in two types of transactions:

(a) Spot exchange transactions
(b) Forward exchange transactions

Spot exchange transactions means the foreign currencies are traded for immediate delivery. The buyer can purchase the foreign currency at the prevailing rates. The buyer should pay the consideration and get his required foreign currency to settle his business transactions. It is a ready market.

Forward exchange transactions means the required foreign currency will be available to the buyer at future. The delivery of currency will be affected in a future date. The contract between buyer and seller will be made for delivery of foreign currency at a future date. The contract will be made for a specific amount of currency at a specific rate of exchange and at a specific future date.

The **MNCs** should manage all these things very cautiously; otherwise, they will be exposed to foreign exchange risk. Generally MNCs may protect themselves from possible losses due to the exchange risk fluctuations. The following measures will be taken up by MNCs to protect their profits:

(a) Forward market
(b) Foreign currency swap
(c) Arbitrage
(d) Time factor
(e) Inflation

(a) Forward Market: Forward market is a tool for the MNCs to reduce their risk from the exposure of foreign currency exchange. It is also known as **future market**. In this market, the foreign currency is available in future. An MNC can protect itself against exchange rate risk by this market. In this market, a contract will be done at an agreed rate of exchange to buy specific currency at specific time. It eliminates the risk likely to arise between two currencies. These transactions are carried out by the international departments of large commercial banks. The banks will involve in buying and selling of foreign currencies on behalf of their customers. The banks will charge a small percentage of fee for rendering these services. If the bank is willing to buy the currency for his customer. The price is known as "**bid price**". If the basic is willing to sell the currency, the price is called as an "**Ask price**". Sometimes the bank will make a contract to buy or sell the foreign currency which is known as "**bid and ask price**". This market is highly volatile. The future exchange rate is depended upon many factors such as **inflation, economic problems, deficit budgets, etc.**

(b) Foreign Currency Swap: It is the method of hedging. Hedging protects from the risk. It is a tool for hedging against foreign exchange risk. In this method there will be an agreement between two parties to exchange one currency for another at a specified future date and at a specified exchange ratio. The **swap** is both spot and forward transactions. Swap is a technique to reduce the risk which is arisen due to the fluctuations in the market. In a swap deal, buying and selling involve the same currency of same value at different maturity periods. The swap may be any of the following kinds:

(a) Foreign currency can be purchased as spot and in forward market.
(b) The banks can also involve in **forward to forward swap**. A bank may buy one month forward and sell three months forward.
(c) Foreign exchange deal involves difference between buying and selling rates. It also involves premium. A foreign currency is available at more cost in forward market than in **spot market**. In some situations the foreign currency is available at low price in **forward market** than in the **spot market** then it is known as **discount**.

(c) Arbitrage: Arbitrage is a method of technique to make profits in foreign exchange dealings. It cannot be treated as a hedging instrument for reducing in foreign exchange risk. Arbitrage means buying foreign currency at lower price, foreign exchange market and simultaneously selling at higher price market. The arbitragers can make profit between buying and selling prices of difference. It will be done in more than one foreign exchange markets. This process requires high talent, vast experience and risk bearing capacity. The arbitrage can be divided into two kinds: **(i) space arbitrage, (ii) time arbitrage**. Space arbitrage means buying and selling of foreign currency in two or more capitals for delivery as the same day. The two physical foreign capital markets are very distance place in buying and selling of the exchange market. The speculator will earn profit of the difference in buying and selling of foreign currencies. **Time arbitrage** means an investor can make profit by executing a spot and a forward contract to buy and sell a foreign currency.

(d) Time Factor: In foreign exchange currency market, the borrower has the responsibility to face any risk arisen due to the fluctuations in the market. It is common to have exchange risk clause in the agreement for borrowing the foreign exchange. The risk or return depends upon the length of time from the time of borrowing to the time of repayment. The speculator will take the advantage of currency value in the foreign capital markets.

(e) Inflation: The speculators or buyers in the foreign exchange market can reduce their risks through various ways. A multi-national company invests in assets in many countries throughout the globe. The business will be carried out as the global basis. The loss in value of these assets will reflect monetary loss to the organisation. Suppose a MNC has its assets in an economy where currency is continuously declining. Then the MNC would like to take some measures to reduce the loss. The MNCs would borrow weak currency which was going to decline and hold strong currencies. The MNC hold inventories as its value would be eroded by inflation. The MNC will also invest available cash in fixed assets in order to strengthen itself.

(II) Financing System: International capital markets will play an important role in financing the corporate sector. Generally the MNCs will approach the foreign capital market to meet their growing needs of their finance. The funds are available in this market throughout thc year. But raising of funds as favourable terms is an important aspect of the financial management. The funds are available to good, reputed, high net worth companies only. The funds for MNCs may be raised either through internal or external sources. Internal sources of funds are available to MNCs such as **share capital, loans from parent company and retained earnings**. The MNCs generally procure their requirement from their internal sources. If the amount of internal sources of finance is not sufficient, then it will approach the external sources of finance. Usually the MNCs have the following external sources of finance:

(a) Loan from international banks
(b) Discounting of bills
(c) Euro currency markets
(d) Development banks
(e) Euroband market

(a) Loan from International Banks: The MNCs will procure their required money from the banks in the form of loans. All banks throughout the world provide foreign currency loans to the corporate sector. These financial assistance will be utilised for their domestic operations. They also provide facilities such as overdraft and other modes. They will charge interest on these facilities. All MNCs will utilise these facilities whenever they need money.

(b) Discounting of Bills: Generally the business transactions involve credit transactions. At present credit is a normal business operation in the market. The corporate sector usually depends upon the bills as a source of short-term finance. This method is more popular in **Europe and Asia**. They used to finance both domestic and international trade. The companies can get the bill amount from the banks through discounting method whenever they need money. The bills are encashed at discount. The discount represents the interest cost charged by the banker for the relevant period. Bills of exchange is a normal course of action in the corporate sector.

(c) Euro Currency Markets: Euro currency means, the currency is deposited outside of origin. For example: Indian rupee deposited outside India, it will be treated as **Euro rupee**. If the American dollars deposited outside, they are called as **Euro dollar**. These deposits are at the disposal of banks in abroad. They are not in the control of origin banks and are not subject to reserve requirements and interest rate restrictions. This situation creates more freedom to the Euro banks to manage their deposits effectively. Therefore, the multi-national companies could enjoy the benefits of funds availability. They can take the advantages of the euro currency markets.

(d) Development Banks: Every country will have development banks for the development of corporate sector. They encourage the exports by way of providing loans. They provide long-term and medium-term loans to the corporate sector. There are many agencies at the national level which offer incentives to the corporate sector within their respected countries or to finance exports. For example: **Export and Import Bank of India** offers various facilities to the corporate sector in order to encourage exports from India. International Finance Corporation is also providing financial assistance to the private and public sector enterprises. The Regional Development Banks also provide financial assistance to the developing countries to increase their exports. All the international finance agencies will support the finance to the corporate sector especially located in developing countries.

(e) Euroband Market: Euroband market is another significant source of finance to the multi-national companies. It has emerged recently in the international capital market. Eurobands are available in countries other than that of the originated country. They are applicable with their rules and regulations on par with the Euro currency. The Eurobands are issued in a different denominations. For example: the bonds denominated in yen but sold in America, Britain, are called as Eurobands. This kind of financial assistance is adopted by the government agencies and reputed global banks.

Channel of Payment in Global Business

International trade is a complex business environment. It is different from domestic trade. It involves high risk and complicated rules and regulations. In every stage there will be some legal hurdles. In a domestic transaction the buyer and seller are close to each other and they can meet, talk, bargain in settlement of their transactions. But in international trade it is not possible to do all the things as such in case of the domestic trade. In the international trade they do not know about the credit worthiness of the buyer abroad. There will be some problems of communication due to the long distance between the parties. All these problems will make the process of settling the accounts more complicated. In business transactions a seller or exporter would prefer to receive cash in advance or on delivery of goods. Therefore, the cash payments in the international trade became complicated. The credit is dominated by the international trade due to so many factors such as **Intensive competition, credit term negotiations** and credit insurance facility. If the sale is made whether it is for cash or credit payment has to be made by the buyer. The buyer will pay the consideration through the following channels:

(a) Book Adjustments
(b) Agents Sale
(c) Instalments
(d) Banks
(e) Bills of Exchange
(f) Letters of Credit

(a) Book Adjustments: It is one of the sources of payment made by the buyer to the seller. In this method, the seller of the goods will debit the account of buyer whenever he sends goods. After receipt of the goods, the buyer will remit the amount from time-to-time to the seller. The account will be settled periodically in accordance with the terms and agreed conditions. The seller sends the documents of title to the buyer. In this process the seller will be saved from the problems of bills of exchange aspect. But some risk is involved. It is suitable only when the exporters and importers have good relations, confidence and trust for a long period.

(b) Agents Sale: It is another source of mode of channel for sales realisation amount. In this method the exporter will appoint his selling agents abroad. The goods are despatched to the agent. The agent will receive the goods without any payment of advance. But the title of the goods lies with the exporters. The sale of goods activities is made by the agent on behalf of the exporters. After the completion of sale of goods, the agent will pay the amount to the exporter. In this method the receipt of sale consideration will depend upon the behaviour of the agent. But it is also involved with some degree of risk.

(c) Instalments: This channel of payment is selected in case of expensive capital equipment or machinery. The buyer of the capital equipment will pay a part of price in advance. The other part of the sale price will be paid by the buyer on receipt of shipping documents. The remaining balance will be payable in periodical instalments spread over to an agreed period of time. The seller of the goods will take bank guarantee from the buyer for the balance amount due by him. Therefore, in this method the seller has some certainty about his sales realisation of the money.

(d) Banks: In this channel of payment, the buyer of the goods will make payments to a local bank in his currency. The local bank arranges for the payment to the seller abroad in the currency of his nation. These transactions will be carried out either by the local branch or a foreign bank. Generally, the local banks will make arrangements for the disbursement of money on global basis for a charge of commission. Usually the banks will transfer the money among the nations through the **Telegraphic Transfer, Mail Transfer or Banker's Draft**. In telegraphic transfer method when the local bank receives the money from an importer, it orders its correspondent branch telegraphically to pay the money to the exporters abroad. This method of transfer process reduces the time which will save the cost of interest. It is the quick mode of remitting funds. This system does not impose any stamp duty. **Mail transfer** is another process of transfer of money among the nations. In this method the buyer of the goods would deposit the amount in local branch. On receipt of this amount the local branch order will be sent to its correspondent branch by post or mail as desired by the sender. This method also does not require any stamp duty. This order will be in the form of cheque which is not negotiable. It is very safe. But in this method there is a loss of interest to the buyer or remitter. This process requires a lot of time. This will result in delays in the payment to the seller. Generally for the delay period the exporter will charge interest. Therefore, the local bank will gain some advantage during this period. The local bank will charge less amount of commission than the telegraphic transfer. **Bankers draft** is another source of method of transfer. In this method the importer would take a demand draft in favour of the exporter asking the corresponding branch to pay the amount to the payee abroad.

(e) Bills of Exchange: Bills of exchange are also used for remittance in the international trade. The procedure in bill of exchange is same in case of domestic trade. The bill is accompanied by shipping documents. The shipping documents include bill of lading, delivery order, export invoice, marine insurance policy, certificate of origin etc. All these certificates together are called as **documentary bill.** It is sent by the exporter's bank to its branch. The exporter would prepare a bill and submit to the importer for his acceptance. On receipt of the bill the importer would accept the bill along with the title of goods. At the maturity period of the bill, the importer has to pay the bill amount. In this kind of financing the exporter may face some degree of risk. The bill may be dishonoured at the maturity period. In order to overcome the financial hardships usually the banks give the discounting facility. The bank has the authority to sell the goods in case of bill dishonours.

(f) Letters of Credit: Letter of credit is a widely practiced method in the business world. The letter of credit is issued by the banks as request made by the importer. It involves a lengthy process of paper work. But the exporter would get his amount safely. The buyers will have to approach their own bankers with a request that they issue a letter of credit in favour of the exporter. On receipt of the request, the banker will ask them to sign a letter to this effect. The buyer will indicate the seller's name, address for issue of a letter of credit in favour of the said party. The bankers after being satisfied will issue a letter of credit in favour of this seller. It may be sent directly to the exporter or banker's agent. The exporters will draw the bill of exchange and completes the process. The letters of credit are available in different kinds to suit the growing needs of different suppliers.

(a) Ordinary and special letters of credit
(b) Clean letters of credit
(c) Fixed and revolving letters of credit
(d) Confirmed letters of credit
(e) Transferable and non-transferable

(a) Ordinary letter of credit indicates a third person involvement in business transaction. It is addressed by the issuing bank requesting that advance be made to a third person by anyone to whom it is shown. These kinds of letters are in general in business transactions. It is useful to businessmen to meet their growing needs. **Special letter of credit** is issued by the banker which is addressed to some specified persons. The specified persons only can advance the money and acquire rights.

(b) Clean letter of credit provides finance without security of any document. It is an open letter of credit. The issuing bank will honour the bill. This letter of credit will be issued by the banker only at the request of customer. This facility will be offered to only reputed and sound financial position and high integrity.

(c) Fixed and revolving letters of credit is another sources of finance. In fixed letter of credit method the issuing banker would allow the beneficiary to avail the finance facility upto a specified period. In case of revolving credit the issuing banker specifies the total amount. Afterwards the exporter has the limit available stands temporarily reduced to the balance amount.

(d) Confirmed and unconfirmed letters of credit means a letter of credit from the exporters. Country bank will take over the liability at the request of issuing bank. It is known as confirmed letters of credit. Unconfirmed letter of credit refers that the advising banker will not give any takeover the liability of the issuing bank.

(e) Transferable letter of credit means the exporter may request the importer to arrange for a bill to somebody else. This can be done only when letter of credit has been specially designated as transferable. If the letter of credit is not transferable to anybody it is known as non-transferable letter of credit.

Foreign Capital

Foreign capital plays an important role in development of a nation. It occupies a dominant role in the corporate financing in India. The inflow of foreign funds will definitely enhance the production of a nation. There are so many sources of avenues available to invest in our country by foreign companies. The following sources of avenues available to our country:

1. Foreign Direct Investment
2. Foreign Institutional Investors
3. Euro Issues
4. Venture Capital Fund

5. Offshore Fund
6. NRI Investment

1. Foreign Direct Investment: The foreign direct investment depends upon the government policy. In this source of finance the investment comes to direct contribution to the equity capital of the corporate sector. It is useful to technology upgradation and getting for sophisticated machinery etc. The globalisation policy stresses the need for foreign investment. It was allowed in India on a priority sector till July 1991. According to the New Industrial Policy 1991, foreign investment has been separated from technology transfer. It is required in a wide range of industries. Any foreign investment in India should come through the following agencies:

(a) RBI
(b) Central Government.

(a) RBI: RBI is the supreme authority in the banking sector and giving approval for foreign investment in India. Foreign investment in India is subject to regulation under the **Foreign Exchange Management Act**. Any foreign investment agency should get clearance from the government and the RBI. Then the investment should get FEMA regulation which will be granted by the RBI. The Reserve Bank approved foreign investment upto July 1996 under automatic approval to the extent of **51%** foreign capital in 35 high priority industries. The Industrial Policy 1991 permitted to invest upto 50% in mining sector subject to conditions. The following table reveals the inflow of FDI from August 1991 to July 2002[2]:

FDI in India (August 1991 to July 2002)

(Rs. in million)

1.	Maharashtra	488952
2.	Delhi	338472
3.	Tamil Nadu	234758
4.	Karnataka	219847
5.	Gujarat	184538
6.	Andhra Pradesh	130939
7.	Madhya Pradesh	92347
8.	West Bengal	88515
9.	Orissa	82292
10.	Uttar Pradesh	47950
11.	Haryana	35194
12.	Rajasthan	30052
13.	Punjab	19684

(Contd.)

(*Contd.*)

14.	Kerala	15281
15.	Pondicherry	12423
16.	Himachal Pradesh	11739
17.	Goa	9707
18.	Bihar	7397
19.	Chhatisgarh	6328
20.	Chandigarh	1620
21.	Jharkhand	1438
22.	Uttaranchal	1257
23.	Dadra & Nagar Haveli	1240

The RBI has the authority to grant automatic approval to the following:

(a) Investment upto 50% in mining sector.
(b) Upto 51% in 48 high priority industries.
(c) Upto 74% in basic metals, electricity generation and transmission, land transport, storage, warehousing, non-conventional energy etc.
(d) 100% upto a ceiling of Rs.1,500 crores in respect of hydro electric, coal, lignite, oil, gas based thermal power plants, maintenance of roads, highways, vehicles, bridges, toll roads, tunnels, harbours and ports.

The Government made in February 2000 automatic approval in almost all sectors except few sectors in the negative list. The following sectors have not been permitted to invest by foreign investors.

(a) Alcohol, cigar, defence related equipments.
(b) Reserved for SSI items.
(c) Proposals falling outside notified sectoral policy.

The Reserve Bank is the official agency for technology collaboration agreements. It will accord automatic approval to foreign technology agreements in high priority industries subject to conditions and terms. It will not give permission to those which are reserved for SSI, EOUs, SIPs sectors. The extension of foreign technology agreements are approved by the Central Government.

(b) Central Government: All foreign direct investments should get Central Government's approval for investing in the corporate sector. The non-priority industry sector investment should be cleared by the Government. The Government for this purpose constituted a **Foreign**

Investment Promotion Board to clear the agreements. It has the authority to sanction the projects by foreign investors. It will clear the investment proposal within a period of 6 weeks. The foreign investor should also be required to get the permission under **Foreign Exchange Management Act**. The FIPB was the nodal agency for speeding up the foreign investment approval process in India. The priority areas for FDI include infrastructure, large scale employment, exports and social sector projects.

Foreign Investment Implementation Authority has been established in 1999 to facilitate one step service to the foreign investors. It would help the investors to get various clearances and set out operational problems. It can also provide services for any kind of problems faced by the foreign investors. It will also continuously monitor the progress of various sanctioned projects. It will coordinate all the things including administrative ministries, state governments, pollution control board, regulatory authorities, tax authorities and company law board. It will continuously meet for every month to dispose the various projects for implementation. It also makes recommendations from time to time any issue relating to the foreign investors project.

Foreign investors can make their investments in **100% export oriented units or EPZ units**. They should also get automatic approval from the concerned authorities. The automatic approvals can be given subject to the rules and regulations from time-to-time. The government recently permitted the setting up of export processing zones in the private sector and NRIs. They permitted to invest in trading companies engaged in export activities. Foreign investors engaged in manufacturing and trading houses can establish their branch offices in India. Reserve Bank has permitted their branch offices for the smooth functioning of its business activities.

Foreign investors are permitted to invest in the specified sectors as follows:

(a) Power sector
(b) Basic telecom services
(c) Roadways
(d) Telecommunications
(e) Drugs and pharmaceuticals
(f) Banking services
(g) Value added services
(h) Telecom equipment
(i) Ports and shipping

(j) Hotels and tourism
(k) Small scale sector
(l) Real estate

Power sector is the major area where India is looking for foreign investment. The foreign investors are allowed to set up power generation units with 100% equity participation. They can establish power projects in thermal, wind or solar energy sectors without any restriction on the investment. They are permitted to sell or distribute power to state electricity boards. They are allowed a debt equity ratio upto 4:1. The promoter should contribute 11% of the outlay. The public and financial institutions should not be allowed more than 40% of the total outlay. They are also eligible for five years tax holiday for profits. They are allowed licences for 30 years. The state governments are empowered to grant licences for setting up of power plants.

Basic telecom services is another thrust area in India. It requires more investment in this sector. The National Telecom Policy 1994 provides guidelines for private sector participation in this sector. In this sector **49%** of foreign investment is allowed. The licences will be granted as circle basis. Each operator will be allotted one circle. The operators services are available in each circle in addition to **BSNL services**. Therefore, the customers are getting a wide range of services in these sectors. The Central Government established an autonomous body. **The Telecom Regulatory Authority of India** to regulates the telecom sector in all activities. It set standards for the industry, regulate prices, provides technical assistance, protects consumer interests and settles the disputes between operators. It is the supreme authority in the sector.

Roadways is another important area where India is looking for development of infrastructure. The Government is encouraging private sector participation in the highway sector under the **BOT** (Build, Operate and Transfer) concept. In this sector, the Foreign Direct Investments are allowed upto **74%**. They are also allowed upto 51% in case of support services such as **land transport, operation of highways, bridges toll road etc.**

Telecommunication sector has to be developed more in order to modernise the facilities in the country. The Government of India has prepared a comprehensive policy for attracting private, foreign investment in telecom equipment production and in basic services.

Drugs and Pharmaceuticals is one of the important sector. It needs foreign capital for the development of R&D technology. Foreign investment is allowed upto 51% in this sector. In case of bulk drugs, intermediate and formulations are granted automatic approval by the RBI. The Central Government will give clearance for the non-automatic approval list.

Banking sector has to be developed in tune with the liberalisation, privatisation and globalisation policies. In this sector, the government permitted foreign investment upto **20%**. The RBI stipulated rules and regulations for investment by foreigners.

Value added services such as electronic mail, voice mail, data services, audio text services, video conferencing are encouraged by the government. All foreign investment approvals in these services require specific approvals from the Central Government. Foreign investors are allowed upto **49%** of the equity in cellular mobile, paging, VSAT and other wireless services. The Government permitted 51% in the other value added services.

Telecom equipment is another area where India has huge potential for a wide variety of equipments. Initially this sector was reserved for public sector. But the Government permitted all the players in this segment. The items of telecom equipment require automatic approval for foreign technology agreements. The Government permitted **51%** of equity in this area.

Ports and shipping sector needs a proper attention by the government. The government has taken many steps to develop this infrastructure. The government encouraged private and foreign sector to develop this field. They are permitted to invest upto **74%** in the construction of ports and harbours. For support services such as operation, maintenance, loading and discharging of vessels is allowed upto **51%**. The shipping sector has also been liberalised and encouraged to the investment by the government. The ship building and ship repair centre also offer many opportunities to the investors.

Hotels and Tourism Sector is one of the areas where the government is looking for private and foreign investment. In India there will be shortage of hotel rooms in all categories. There is much demand for tourism related services such as transportation, travel and tour operating agencies. The RBI will grant the sanctions for establishing hotels and tourism related industries. The term hotel includes among others, restaurants, beach resorts, tourist complex providing accommodation, catering and food facilities to tourists. The tourism related industry such as **travel agencies, tour operating schemes, transport operating**

agencies, adventure tourism, surface and water transport facilities providers, amusement, leisure, entertainment health units, conventions and seminar units and organisation.

Small Scale Sector has to be developed in India. The government encourages this sector by providing facilities and incentives under various schemes. The foreign equity is allowed upto **24%** of the total investment outlay. This sector has been provided to access the capital market to encourage modernisation and technical upgradation.

Real Estate is one of the growing sectors in India. It occupied an important role in the development of a nation. The RBI is the regulatory authority to give permission for entering this segment. It is empowered to grant general permission to invest in this segment. A declaration should be submitted to the RBI by the foreign investor after acquiring property within 90 days of the date of acquisition. All these assets acquired by the foreign investors should be used for residential purpose only subject to some conditions and terms.

2. Foreign Institutional Investors: Foreign institutional investors are one of the players in the Indian capital. They occupy a dominant role in the market. The government has allowed the **FIIs** to invest in all the securities traded on the primary and secondary markets. They are permitted to participate in all stock exchanges including **over the counter exchange. They include institutions such as pension funds, mutual funds, investment trusts, asset management companies, nominee companies and incorporated institutional portfolio managers**. They can purchase all securities such as share, debenture warrants and the schemes floated by domestic mutual funds. They are also permitted to acquire new financial instruments from time-to-time basis. Finance Ministry issued guidelines to the FIIs on 14.9.1992. According to the guidelines issued by the government, FIIs can invest upto 24% of issued share capital for the total holdings of all registered FIIs in any one company. The ceiling includes the consideration of FCDs and PCDs issued by the company. The holding of a single FII in any company would also be subject to a ceiling of **5%** of issued capital. The guidelines stipulated that FIIs would be required to obtain an initial registration from the SEBI. The FIIs should take initial permission from SEBI before buying any share from the stock exchange. Similarly they should sell the securities through stock exchange only. They are permitted to sell the shares through the counter exchange. The FIIs should apply for registration to the SEBI in a prescribed form forgetting the approval of commencing the business. The guidelines reveal that there would be no restrictions on the volume of investment for the purpose of entry of FIIs. There is no lock in period prescribed for the purpose of entry of FIIs. FIIs are getting some tax exemptions on their dividend profits. SEBI is the regulating authority in the field of FIIs. Every FII should apply to the SEBI for getting sanction of approvals. On receipt of the application made by the FIIs, the SEBI will scrutinise the form and inform its decision to the applicant. It will sanction the permission based on the track record, professional competence, financial strength, experience and such other criteria etc. Its certificate will be valid for five years. The certificate may be renewable for further five years. The FIIs should also get clearance from the RBI under **FEMA**. The clearance from the RBI provides the following facilities:

(a) FIIs can open foreign currency denominated account in a designated bank.
(b) It can also open a non-resident rupee account.
(c) The NR Rupee account is useful to collect all the inflows of the FIIs.
(d) It can transfer the amount from foreign currency denominated account to the NR Rupee account.
(e) The profit after tax will be repatriable from the rupee account to the foreign currency account.

All the foreign institutional investors are not permitted to participate in any short selling in securities. A registered FII can appoint a custodian for settlement of all the business transactions. The appointment of custodian is also to get the SEBI approval. The custodian is the accountant of FII. The custodian shall report to the RBI and SEBI as half yearly basis and disclose all the required information as per guidelines. The foreign institutional investors are liable to pay tax on capital gains. **Section 115 of the Income Tax Act** reveals that all the foreign investors are liable to pay tax at the rate of 20% on capital gains. For this purpose, securities have been defined shares, scrips, stocks, bonds, debentures, marketable securities, government securities, interest in securities. They should pay tax on long-term capital gains at the rate of **10%**. The income from short term capital gain attracts **30%** of the tax. All these taxes will be applied as the gross income without allowing for any deduction. Income of FIIs from securities is subject to deductions of tax at sources.

SEBI Regulations

SEBI is the most powerful organisation in the capital market. It is the regulatory body to control, monitor the activities of all the FIIs. The SEBI regulated the following areas to monitor the FIIs activities:

(a) Registration
(b) Investments
(c) Obligations
(d) Penalties

(a) Registration: According to the guidelines issued by the Finance Ministry, every FII should apply for registration with the SEBI. SEBI is the sanctioning authority to grant the licence. The guidelines also laid down certain minimum and basic criteria to be taken into account by SEBI before granting registration to an FII. SEBI would grant the registration after considering the past experience and professional competence. The FII should get the approval of foreign exchange management act of the RBI. The applicant should be incorporated abroad as **a pension fund, mutual fund, investment trust, AMC, bank, portfolio management, university fund, endowments, charitable trusts and societies.** If the SEBI is satisfied with all the documents shown by the applicant, the certificate would be granted within **three months** after information is furnished. The registration fee is **US $ 10,000** payable within 15 days from the date of intimation by the SEBI. The certificate is valid for 5 years. It can be renewed for a five years period on the payment of fee. The renewal of certificate can be done subject to the conditions.

(b) Investments: The FIIs are permitted to invest in securities such as shares, debentures, warrants and unit schemes of mutual funds. It can enter into primary and secondary market operations. SEBI has the authority to impose penalty if any FII violates the rules and regulations. They are also permitted to invest in the equity and debentures include the government securities. They must follow some additional conditions while entering into secondary market operations:

(a) They would not be permitted to trade in derivatives market.
(b) They are prohibited from short selling activities.
(c) They are not permitted to trade in carrying forward transactions.
(d) They are permitted to trade with the register broker only.
(e) They are permitted to trade in the government securities as per the regulations laid down by the RBI.

(f) They should settle the accounts only through **dematerialised system** for more than Rs.10 crores aggregate worth of securities.
(g) The purchased securities should be in the name of FII.

(c) Obligations: The FIIs are required to prepare and maintain accounts as per the rules and regulations. They should appoint a domestic custodian for looking after the acquisition and sale of shares and debentures. They can appoint more than one custodian with the SEBI's prior approval. The custodian should monitor the investments made in India. The custodian should report to the SEBI on daily basis any transactions entered into by the foreign investor. The custodian should keep the records for a period of five years relating to the activities of foreign investor. Any information called by the SEBI should be furnished by the custodian on behalf of foreign investor in any time. The foreign investor has to appoint a branch of bank for his accounts operations. Every foreign investor should maintain the books of accounts and preserve them for five years. The following records should be maintained:

1. Investment particulars
2. Receipts and payments
3. Bank statement of accounts
4. Contract particulars regarding all purchases and sale of securities
5. Records with custodians

The foreign investor should inform the SEBI regarding the place of books and records available for inspection. He should furnish information to the SEBI and RBI.

(d) Penalties: Any violation of act or regulations made by the foreign investor is liable to punishment. The SEBI has the authority either to suspend or cancel the licence of the foreign investor. The following situation may cause for **suspension of certificate of registration**:

(a) If the foreign investor furnishes any false information.
(b) If the foreign investor does not cooperate in any enquiry or inspection conducted by the SEBI.
(c) If the foreign investor indulges in fraudulent transactions in securities.
(d) If the foreign investor fails to submit an information as desired by the SEBI/RBI.

The SEBI has authority to **cancel the** licence of foreign investor in case of the following situations:

(a) If the foreign investor violates the insider trading regulations.
(b) If he is involved in manipulation of security prices or in price rigging or cornering activities.
(c) If he is found guilty of fraud or in criminal offence.
(d) If he fails to meet the eligibility norms of the SEBI regulations.
(e) If he is found guilty of repeated defaults.

3. Euro Issues: The Indian corporate sector developed a global vision. These companies until now were restrained themselves to only the domestic finance available at higher rate of interest. They never utilised the foreign capital which was available at cheaper rate of interest in **Europe, Asia and America.** At present they realise the need of foreign capital and approach whenever they require. The globalisation policy stressed the importance of foreign capital for the development of our economy. The government cleared the permissions to enter into the global foreign capital markets. The Indian companies can float their stocks in foreign market. The following financial instruments are floated by the Indian companies. They are:

(a) Global Depository Receipts (GDRs);
(b) Foreign Currency Convertible Bonds (FCCBs).

The above two issues are known as **Euro Issue**. An euro issue is an issue made by a company on international basis. The securities are sold globally to corporate and private investors in different countries. It is issued in foreign currency denomination. An euro issue is different from a foreign issue. Euro securities are transferable. They are to be underwritten and distributed by a syndicate. Euro market was first developed in **Europe**. It has the geographical location of **London**. The London market draws attention of participants, issues, underwriters, investor from all over the world. Euro market facilitates funds at a lower cost. They are issued at par or even at a slight premium. International listings can provide increased liquidity for the securities.

(a) Global Depository Receipts (GDRs): The concept of Global Depository Receipts originated in the western capital markets in 1927. It is a negotiable instrument. It is created for an investor who purchases share of a foreign company in the domestic stock market and the same is deposited with a custodian of a depository. The depository issues receipts in respect of such shares and such receipts represent a depository receipt. It can be traded publicly. The issuer company can collect the issue proceeds from the market in foreign currency. The foreign currency can be utilised by the companies for payment of their commitments such as purchase cost, repayment of foreign currency loans, and other payments. GDRs is denominated in US dollars. There is no exchange risk for the issues. The GDR also gives a holder option to convert the same into underlying shares and holds equity shares of the company instead of GDRs. A holder of GDRs does not have any voting rights and so the company does not have the fear of loosing management control. The issue of GDRs is permitted through automatic route without the approval of the Ministry of Finance. The following conditions should be fulfilled by the issuing company:

1. The issue of GDR by Indian companies through registered stock exchange only.
2. The issue related to business reorganisation or merger or demerger as per guidelines of August 17, 1998.
3. If the issue process through **private placement**, it must be approved with the securities and exchange commission in the USA or financial services act in the UK or the regulatory authority in **Japan, Singapore and Europe**.

Every issuing company should get automatic approval prior to approval under the Companies Act and from the Central Government. The issue fluctuation cost are subject to a ceiling of 4% and if any additional cost involve approval from RBI is necessary. The issuing company should report to the Finance Ministry and the RBI after completion of the issue process. The issue proceeds must be used for the said purpose. The issuing company may not be allowed for diversion of funds for other purposes.

Foreign Currency Convertible Bonds (FCCBs): Foreign currency convertible bonds are issued by the companies for restructuring their external debt. It is a long-term maturity financial instrument. Its issue proceeds must be utilised as per the sanction of its approval. The company should fulfil the norms as issued by the government from time-to-time. It has a flexible conversion period. The non-converted portion should have a minimum average tenure of five years. The issue proceeds of the amount, 25% may be utilised for general corporate restructuring including working capital.

4. Venture Capital Fund: Venture capital is one of the emerging sources of finance in international capital market. This facility is mostly useful to the small companies, unlisted companies etc. this facility is allowed with effect from September 1995. The venture capital investment has a minimum lock in period of **three years**. The investment is unlisted company should not be exceeded to **40%** of its paid up capital. The offshore investors can be invested with the approval of **FIPB**.

Venture capital means risk money. The money is used in risky enterprises. The money will be invested either as equity or as **capital**. The business which is involved in high technology and innovative sector is risky. Therefore, the investment in this risky sector is known as **venture capital**. Generally these kinds of business sector is unattractive to the bankers. The bankers usually are not willing to promote these types of business enterprises. Hence, the venture capitalists provide the necessary funds in addition to managerial and marketing assistance. The venture capitalist sells his shares in the stock market at a hefty premium, when the company generates adequate profits. The venture capitalist provides financial assistance for **product development, during gestation period and post-commercialisation, expansion and turn around of sick units.**

5. Offshore Fund: Offshore fund is also known as mutual fund. These kinds of mutual funds collect the money from the residents abroad. The mutual fund facilitates the transfer of capital of the host country. They provide investment opportunities for the individual and institutional investors on global basis. These schemes facilitate tax exemptions. The offshore funds should get approval from FIPB before making investment decision. They are allowed directly to invest in the shares of unlimited companies.

6. NRI Investment: In India, non-residents are permitted to make direct investment in sole trading and partnership kind of business system. They can also be subscribed to share or debenture of private or public limited companies. They can be deposited money in corporate sector as fixed deposits. The direct investment can be made by them in two kinds. They are:

(a) Non-repatriation
(b) Repatriation

(a) Non-repatriation: The non-resident Indians are allowed to invest in new issue of shares or debentures. The Reserve Bank issued a notification for investing by NRIs as non-repatriaton basis. The Reserve Bank has granted permission to NRIs on non-repatriation basis subject to the conditions. They can acquire rights and bonus shares of the corporate sector, subject to the approval of RBI. They can also be invested in mutual funds floated by **public sector banks or financial institutions.** They require permission of Reserve Bank for purchasing shares of Indian companies through private arrangement. NRIs are allowed to invest in shares/debentures of companies through stock exchange under **"portfolio-investment scheme"**. This investment is allowed both on non-repatriation as well as repatriation basis.

(b) Repatriation: The non-resident Indians are allowed to invest as **repatriation** basis through the following ways:

(i) Investment in new issues of Indian companies upto **Forty percent scheme.**
(ii) Investments in priority industries under **100%** scheme.
(iii) Investment in 100% foreign equity in other industries.
(iv) Investment in sick industries.
(v) Investment in non-convertible debentures.
(vi) Investment in housing and real estate sector.
(vii) Investment in air taxi operations.
(viii) Investment in portfolio scheme.

NOTES

1. Current Statistics, *E.P.W.*, Feb. 1, 2003, p. 419.
2. *Andhra Jyothi*, 10.12.2002, p. 7

Chapter 2

MUTUAL FUNDS IN INDIA

Introduction

The investment preferences of households have changed dramatically. In India, the household sector accounts for over **80 per cent** of the **GDP** which plays a significant change in their investment preferences. The investors investment preference may show an impact on the economy. In the emerging economic environment of competitive markets. The investment pattern has been changed all over the financial landscape as a result of financial liberalisation. The household sector is the main provider of savings in the economy. Hence, the direction into which such savings are channeled determines the direction of growth of the financial sector. The financial development occurred because of the technical invention and through the mode of popular joint stock company. **The Joint Stock** form made the large scale industry possible by collecting large amounts of capital. Subsequent financial innovations have carried the process further the risk reduction and liquidity. The capital is generated out of savings leading to investment which is a part of the financial system. The organised financial comprises **money market, capital market, new issue market, stock market** etc., led by RBI, DFHI, banks, financial institutions, mutual funds, merchant banks and all other intermediaries regulated by the **SEBI** and the **RBI**. There are specialised investment institutions which help those savers who do not understand the functioning of the capital market and remain away from the capital market because of the complicated procedure involved in analysing and interpreting the investment opportunities. These institutions which act as investment, conduits, pool the savings of many individual investors and combine them into a fairly large and well diversified portfolio investments. All these features are available in mutual fund. Mutual funds are an investment vehicle for the investors to enjoy the expert management skills of professional and maximise the return with an accepted risk. There are the trusts for the public savers to pool their savings. In the entire globe, the trend has been for the individual investor shifting from the direct investment in equities to the mutual fund route.

Definition

Mutual fund can be defined as "a form of collective investment that is useful in spreading risks and optimising returns".[1] A mutual fund offers safety, it provides the services to the investors and offers a wide variety of securities within the reach of the most modern investors. Mutual funds are fast developing into magic wands for the retail investor. Mutual fund has been defined "Mutual fund is a non-depository, non-banking financial intermediary which acts as an important vehicle for bringing wealth holders and deficit units together indirectly."[2] —Pierce, James L.

According to **Weston J. Fred and Brigham**: "Mutual fund is a corporation which accepts money from the investors and user the same way to buy stocks, long-term bonds, short-term debt instruments issues by the issuers."[3]

The SEBI has defined mutual funds in Section 2(m): "Mutual funds means a fund established in the form of a trust by a sponsor to raise money by the trustees through the sale of units to the public under one or more schemes for investing in securities in accordance with these regulations."[4]

Concept

A mutual fund is an investment company or a trust that pools the resources of thousands of unit holders and invests on behalf of them in security markets. The mutual funds have been functioning as an agent to mobilise the resources from various investors the **Unit Trusts, Investment Trusts, Mutual Funds,** banks, investment companies, real estate, investment trusts, trust companies, personal trust funds etc., all their names contain some common characteristics. The Investment Trust is an investment holding company and very popular in **U.K.** This Investment Trust will be incorporated under the Companies Act. It has the same type of capital structure like the Industrial Company. The **Unit Trust** is established and is obliged to buy back units wherever an investor wants to sell them. But investment trust cannot buy back its shares and the investor has to sell his shares on the stock market. Investment trust can raise long-term debt and can retain a part of its income. The Unit Trust cannot do either of their things. The unit trust always maintains a direct relation between the value of the unit and the value of the fund. **Mutual savings** banks are popular in **USA.** They offer professional fund management entrusted to them by pension plans of business and institutions. Mutual funds are very popular in **USA, Canada** and **India**. Mutual fund is a trust at law. A mutual fund performs the basic function of buying and selling securities on behalf of its unit holders. Mutual fund provides opportunity to the investors to secure a better rate of return on their savings by utilising the benefit of professional management of portfolios. Mutual fund helps the small investors to obtain **high return-low risk** combination from their scientifically managed portfolios. Mutual funds are convenient and efficient investment vehicles. They can take a portfolio of securities including the blue-chip companies. The mutual fund cult has spread much faster and over a wider area than the equity cult within a very short period. **The Society for Capital Market Research and Development** conducted a study regarding the investor's preference towards the mutual funds, the study finally concluded that there are **2/3rd** of middle class households in India. The study further reveals that the shift towards mutual funds has resulted in the declining popularity of certain other financial assets like LIC policies, bank fixed deposits, National Savings Certificates and Company Deposits. The Unit Trust is basically a pure intermediary which involves the capital appreciation. The small investors cannot directly invest in the instruments such as **Certificates of Deposit, Commercial Paper and Treasury Bills** because they require heavy amount of investment. Mutual funds provide continuous supervision, analysis, investment consultancy, judicious investment decision, expert, experienced, professional management at low costs. The investors have to pay expenses like administrative fee, management expenses and transaction costs forgetting these services.

Advantages

The advantages of the mutual fund relative to the stock market are as follows:

1. Low transaction costs.
2. Benefits of high talent and expertise.

3. Diversification.
4. Tax deductions.
5. Low risk and better returns.
6. Investor's protection.

1. Low Transaction Costs

The mutual fund is a specialised institution which acts as an investment intermediary and channelises the savings of a large number of people. The mutual funds are able to get the economies of large scale because of pooling of the large amount at their disposal for investment in the market. This reduces the costs in the form of brokerage fee, commission etc. Thus, a small investor gets the benefits of economies.

2. Benefits of High Talent and Expertise

The investors in India have no knowledge about the stock market operations. They are unable to know the position of market situation. They do not know about the economy, per capita income, demand, consumption, companies operations, efficiency, their earning capability, profit booking etc. The stock market is a highly volatile and even sometimes the experts may fall in confusion. The entire stock market depends upon many factors. The common investor has no observation about all these movements. The stock market is a **heaven** for those with high expertise, in-depth knowledge, scientific analysis, thorough understanding about the industry, company and pulse of the customer, dynamism, courage, mental stability, financial muscle etc. The Indian investors are highly influenced by the **broker's decision**. They do not take any investment decisions regarding a particular scrip. They simply handover the cheque to the broker on their recommendations. They do not know **when to buy, when to sell, what price, at what price** the scrip should be sold etc. The buying price of a particular scrip in the stock market is the most important factor in determining the profits. The sale price/disposal of a financial asset in the market is also a very important element in designing and constructing a portfolio. The portfolio management is a highly specialised skilful activity. It requires a continuous monitoring and evolution. A small investor cannot be an expert in the portfolio management. If the investor invests in mutual funds, he gets all the benefits of the above said factors. All these activities are performed by the mutual funds. They will appoint a high talented, specially trained experts in the portfolio management, equity analysts, fund managers etc. To achieve the targeted return assured by the fund to the investors. The funds can be professionally employed through the mutual fund ensuring good returns. The fund managers have extensive research facilities at their disposal. They are able to analyse the performance and prospectus of various companies and take good decisions in making the investments fruitful.

3. Diversification

In mutual funds a large number of investors small savings can be pooled. The investor can also buy shares of one or two companies. Therefore, the mutual funds can be used to buy shares of many different companies. Diversification reduces the risk of a portfolio. Diversification requires an additional amount of investment. In diversification, sometimes more risk may be evolved. Thus the portfolios construction, expansion and diversification is very easy in the mutual funds.

4. Tax Deductions

The Income Tax Act of 1961 provides some tax deductions and exemptions to the mutual funds. The mutual funds can be designed to suit the tax payers needs. A large number of mutual funds has come up with the schemes ensuring tax benefits to the subscribers. Generally the tax payers contribute in these funds. According to these schemes, the investors are required to keep the money in the fund for a certain period called **"lock up"** which at present is **3 years**. These funds distribute the profits among the unit holders. The units will be repurchased by the fund at **current** NAV. The pooled amount is used to acquire shares and debt instruments. The NAV of the Units varies with values of the financial assets held by the mutual fund.

5. Low Risk and Better Returns

A mutual fund will be operated by the efficient Fund Managers. The Fund Managers have basic and extraordinary skills in their areas. They are well versed with the market movement. They know how to move in a highly volatile market. They are able to reduce the risk factor and increase high return to the unit fund. A small investor on the other hand, may not be in a position to minimise such risks. Therefore, the mutual funds can reduce risk and maximise return to the holders.

6. Investor's Protection

Mutual funds in India are regulated by the **SEBI**. The SEBI regulations of 1996 provide better protection to the investors. The mutual funds activities are also monitored by the **SEBI** (Mutual Funds) regulations. The SEBI regulations import a great degree of flexibility and facilitate competition.

MUTUAL FUNDS IN INDIA

The first Mutual Fund in India was started in 1964. The Unit Trust of India was set up under a special UTI Act in 1963. All Mutual Funds have to be registered with the **SEBI**. The UTI is involved in mobilising small savings and channelising them into productive avenues. The Government of India permitted the Commercial Banks to launch mutual funds in India by Amending the Banking Regulation Act in **1987**. A number of Commercial Banks have started mutual funds to mop up savings in the society. The **SBI** has launched a mutual fund called **The SBI Mutual Fund** in 1987. The first scheme launched was known as **"Magnum Regular Income Scheme"** and another scheme was **"Magnum Monthly Income Scheme"**. It had also introduced **"Magnum Tax Savings Scheme"** with a tax benefit under **Section 80cc** and **"Magnum Regular Income"** with **12 per cent** minimum assured rate of return per annum. The **Canara Bank** formed the Canbank Mutual Fund with the objective of housing investment expertise for the benefit of investors. It had also started two schemes **Canstock** and **Canshare** in 1987. The object of these schemes was a long-term capital appreciation by adopting strategies. The objective was to secure a regular income and growth. The **Indian Bank** had also established a mutual fund called the **Indian Bank Mutual Fund** in 1990. It floated schemes such as **"Swarna Pushpa, Ind Ratna, Ind 88A, Ind Jyothi, Swarna Jyothi"**. Ind 88A was a tax saving growth scheme. The Punjab National Bank set up a mutual fund called The PNB Mutual Fund in 1990. It had floated a PNB Regular Income plus scheme. It had buy back facility after one year. The Bank of India introduced rising monthly income scheme schedule with an objective of doubling the amount after 5 years period. The LIC Mutual Fund was set up in 1989 by the LIC. It had introduced open schemes such as **"Dhanaraksha 1989, Dhanavriddhi, Dhanasahayog and Dhanavidya, Dhanashree, Dhan 80 CCB, Dhan Tax Saver, Dhanasamridhi etc"**. The GIC Mutual Fund was set up in 1990. It had launched schemes like **GIC Safe, GIC Rise**. The

Government of India allowed the private sector corporates to join the mutual fund sector on 14.2.1992. Afterwards a number of private sector companies had approached the **SEBI** for permission to set up private mutual fund. The **Alliance Capital** had set up the Alliance Equity **(D)(G).** The Birla Mutual Fund had introduced **Birla Advantage, Birla MNC (D)(G). The ING** Mutual Fund had set up **IG portfolio (D)(G),** ING Income Portfolio. The Templeton Mutual Fund had introduced **Templeton India Income,** Templeton **MIP.** The Tata Mutual Fund had set up **Tata Income (D/G).** The Sun Mutual Fund had set up **Sun F and C Money.** Kotak Mahindra Mutual Fund had set up **K-30, K-Tech, K Gilt, K Liquid.** Chola Mutual Fund had introduced **Cholagilt Saving, Cholagilt Investments.** The Pioneer Mutual Fund had set up **Pioneer ITI Blue-chip (D)(G), Pioneer ITI Prima Plus (D), Pioneer (IT Index).** The DSP Mutual Fund had set up **DSPML Balanced (D)(G).** The JM Mutual Fund had introduced JM India Bond **(D)(G).** JM Income Bond **(D)(G),** Reliance Mutual Fund introduced **"Reliance Income (DH)(DY),** Sundaram Mutual Fund has set up **Sundaram Bond Savers (D)(G)** Schemes, Zurich Mutual Fund introduced **Zurich India** Prudence D, Zurich India Prudence-G scheme, Prudential, ICICI Mutual Fund has set up **Prudential ICICI MP, Prudential ICICI MP(G), Prudential Liquid Plan.** The IDBI Mutual Fund introduced **IDBI Principal, IDBI Income Scheme,** Grindlays Bank has set up Grindlays SSI, Grindlays SSI DQ Schemes. HDFC introduced HDFC Income (D) (G), HDFC (Liquid) schemes etc. All of these mutual funds have entered the market with the liberalisation of rules and regulations by the Government. In November 1995, the Government has permitted private sector mutual funds to set up **Money Market Mutual Fund. The SEBI** mutual fund regulations of 1996 provides registration, constitution, management and schemes of mutual funds in India. Money market mutual fund emerged in the **US** in 1972 and is now coming up in many countries. MMF are established for the purpose to purchase large pools of short-term financial instruments. In abroad the average maturity period of investments is about **40 days.** The investors will use the **MMMF** with the prior approval of the RBI and SEBI. Since 1.4.1996 the MMMF is available to only corporates and mutual funds. The maturity period of MMMF has also been reduced. Bank of Madurai, Amro Bank, UTI, IDBIMF were given clearance to set up **MMMFs.** The first MMMF established by the **Kothari Pioneer** in 1997 did not succeed. The UTI started its MMMF on 23.4.1997 and collected about **Rs. 30 crores.** The scheme is offered to resident individuals, HUFs, trusts, societies and corporates. The MMMF is involved in buying and selling of money market instruments only. They will construct the portfolio with treasury bills. Government securities, call money, commercial paper, commercial bills, certificates of deposits etc.

The period **1996–98** was the worst in the history of the mutual funds. But several AMCs used the opportunity to restructure their portfolios and were ready for the 1999 boom in equities. In the year 1999–2000, the value of assets under the management swelled to Rs. 107946 crores[5] then the equity melt down. At present there are **34** mutual fund houses managing 614 schemes and **Rs. 94,571 crores** in asset. All of them will not survive, but performance and transparency will prove in the long run.

Year	*Corpurs fund (AMC) (Rs. in crores)*
1964–69	65
1969–74	172
1974–79	402
1979–84	1261
1986–87	4563
1987–88	6739
1989–90	13456
1990–91	19111
1991–92	23060
1992–93	37480
1993–94	46988
1994–95	61301
1995–96	75050
1996–97	80539
1997–98	68984
1998–99	68472
1999–2000	107946
2000–2001	90587
2001–	94571

Private sector funds recorded higher fresh sales as compared from **May 2000–July 2001**. Redemptions were also higher than in June. It resulted in a net inflow of **Rs. 2430 crores**. Private sector funds utilised this period to increase their product offering. **Tarus Mutual Fund** launched a debt and gilt fund. Bank sponsored funds a net inflow of **Rs. 61 crores**. Institutions backed funds also saw a sharp full in net inflows. Mutual funds can be classified as **"by category" or based on functioning of schemes**. The relevant data for the period May 2000 to July 2001[6] for mutual funds (category) was presented in below.

Mutual Funds by Category

(a) UTI mutual fund.
(b) Private sector mutual funds **(excluding UTI, banks sponsored and institutions).**
(c) Bank sponsored mutual funds **(BOB, BOI, Canbank, PNB, SBI).**
(d) Institutions backed mutual funds.

(Rs. in crores)

Particulars	*May 2000*	*June 2000*	*July 2000*	*May 2001*	*June 2001*	*July 2001*
(a) UTI Mutual Fund						
Sales	1224	1410	774	376	1858	237
Redemption	1100	557	134	2302	2265	87
Net sales	124	853	640	–1926	–407	–630
(b) Private Sector Mutual Funds (excluding UTI, banks sponsored, institutions backed)						
Sales	5015	3931	4208	6815	9886	1125
Redemption	4034	3528	3580	4030	6787	880
Net sales	981	403	628	2785	3089	2430
(c) Banks Sponsored Mutual Funds						
Sales	95	101	373	389	835	332
Redemption	161	92	90	136	187	271
Net Sales	–66	9	283	253	648	61
(d) Institutions backed Mutual Funds						
(a) Sales	95	105	66	357	561	531
(b) Redemption	216	91	117	245	225	397
(c) Net sales	–121	14	–51	112	336	134
(e) All Mutual Funds (including UTI)						
(a) Sales	6429	5547	5421	7937	13140	1235
(b) Redemption	5511	4268	3921	6713	9464	1037
(c) Net sales	918	1279	1500	1224	3676	198

Mutual Funds by Schemes

The mutual funds can also be classified according to the schemes:

(a) Growth schemes.
(b) Income funds.
(c) Balanced funds.
(d) Liquid and money market funds.
(e) Gilt funds.
(f) Equity linked savings schemes.

(Rs. in crores)

Particulars	*May 2000*	*June 2000*	*July 2000*	*May 2001*	*June 2001*	*July 2001*
(a) Growth Schemes						
(i) Sales	1018	741	1325	87	112	59
(ii) Redemption	482	481	960	190	80	135
(iii) Net Sales	536	260	365	**–103**	32	**–76**
(b) Income Funds						
(i) Sales	2043	2068	1423	2909	6297	3759
(ii) Redemption	1963	1400	1003	1074	496	368
(iii) Net Sales	80	688	420	1835	4801	78
(c) Balanced Funds						
(i) Sales	698	517	499	64	43	9
(ii) Redemption	285	290	98	1725	2105	115
(iii) Net Sales	413	227	401	**–1661**	**–2062**	–10
(d) Liquid and Money Market Funds						
(i) Sales	2147	1847	1850	4348	5991	8074
(ii) Redemption	2247	1573	1387	3378	5550	6038
(iii) Net Sales	**–100**	274	463	970	491	2036
(e) Gilt funds						
(i) Sales	481	363	318	526	695	489
(ii) Redemption	522	513	466	152	258	390
(iii) Net Sales	**–41**	**–150**	**–148**	374	437	99
(f) Equity Linked Savings Schemes						
(i) Sales	42	11	6	3	2	3
(ii) Redemption	12	11	7	194	25	11
(iii) Net Sales	30	0	**–1**	**–191**	**–23**	**–8**

Funds Flow by Category

All mutual funds taken together recorded a net inflow of **Rs. 1,989 crores,** while fresh sales fell to **Rs. 12,359 crores** redemption increased to **Rs. 10,370 crores.**

The Unit Trust of India saw another month of net outflow. The redemption also fell subsequently to **Rs. 873 crores**. There was a net outgo of **Rs. 636 crores. The private sector mutual funds** recorded higher fresh sales as compared to June. Redemptions were also higher than in June and this resulted in a net inflow of **Rs. 2,430 crores**. Private sector funds utilised this period to increase their product offerings. **Tarus Mutual Fund** launched a debt and gilt fund. Banks sponsored funds saw a net inflow of **Rs. 61 crores**. Institution backed funds also saw a sharp fall in net inflows. The amount in this case was **Rs. 134 crores.**

Funds Flow by Type

The mutual funds can be classified as **Growth schemes income funds, balanced funds, liquid funds, gilt funds and equity linked savings fund**. All of these schemes have been discussed in preceding pages. Debt funds saw fresh sales fall by **40 per cent**. Redemptions on the other hand were higher by **46 per cent**. The net result was that net sales fell to double digit levels. The fresh sales were dismally low, reaching single digit levels. In US64 had fully closed the exit route in July. There were no redemptions from this fund. Liquid and money market funds were the winners during the period **May 2000–July 2001**. The fresh sales increased by **Rs. 2000 crores** over June. Redemptions increased by a little over **Rs. 500 crores** on the whole, this type of fund received a net inflow of **Rs. 2036 crores**. This is a record for the analysis period the strong inflows into liquid and money market funds could also be an indicator of investor's perception that the rally in bond markets is coming to an end. Gilt funds saw fresh sales of **Rs. 489 crores**. The Redemptions stood at **Rs. 390 crores** and the net result was an inflow of **Rs. 99 crores**. Most funds were moving into medium tenure paper and gilt funds can also expect returns to slow down, tax saving funds continued to remain due. Inflows were minimal and there was a net flow of **Rs. 8 crores**.

Investment Trust

The Investment Trust is a financial institution. It collects a small amount of investible funds from a large number of investors. The trust pools the amount of **savings and invests them in stock market** by constructing a suitable portfolio. A small investor may not have large funds to purchase the securities in many companies. It is fully authorised to deploy the funds as it likes. It is very usual in the stock market, the prices are highly volatile, then there is a danger of loss due to fluctuations. Diversification is the process of risk reduction. The portfolio risk can be reduced by diversification. The investment trust collects the funds from the public by selling the shares of trusts. The trust deploys the funds in the market as it desires. The selection of securities is decided by the Trustees. The trust distributes the income among its members in the form of dividend. The trust will make investments from the consolidated fund created from the subscriptions of various members of the trust. The first investment trust was established by the Royal family of **Belgium**. Scottish American investment trust was established in 1873. In USA the investment trust was established during **1925–1929**. The investment trusts were established due to the substantial expansion of finance area and speculative spirit in that period.

Industrial Investment Trust in India

The first Industrial Investment Trust was established in **1933** by M/s Premchand Roychand in **Mumbai.** After the establishment of this fund the number of other trusts were formed, such as Investment and Finance Company, Kolkata, General Investment and Trust Company, Kolkata, Tata Investment Trust, Mumbai. Most of the Investment Trusts are established by the industrial groups. These trusts try to make managerial control of the companies whose securities they are going to purchase. The trusts are organised as private companies. The investment trusts are used as a tool to control more and more unity by owning and controlling the shares. The investment trusts are categorised into two types: **(a) Management Investment Trust, and (b) Fixed Investment Trusts.** The management investment trusts have full freedom over the funds which they collect the **fixed investment trust** is confined to a fixed list of securities. The management of the fund is not empowered to change the portfolio except in unforeseen situation. The fixed investment trust is better than the trust. Fixed Investment Trust is also known as **"Unit Trust".** The objective of the fund is to protect the investors from managerial manipulations. These trusts suffer from a number of drawbacks. There is no opportunity for diversification of investments. All of these funds are kept in few companies scrips only. The expenses for running the trust are very high. At present there is no existence of fixed investment trusts. These trusts are almost obsolete in these days. The Trusts in India can play an important role in the economy. The trusts should be regulated properly for better management.

Mutual Fund Organisation

The mutual funds in India are regulated by **SEBI**. The SEBI has the authority to register both public and private sector's mutual fund. The Mutual Funds set up by **LIC and GIC** are regulated by the Investment Division, Ministry of Finance. All intermediaries and players in the capital market are brought under the **SEBI** authorisation and regulation. If the mutual funds are started by the Commercial Banks, they should get the RBI permission also. The SEBI has taken over the responsibility of regulating, inspecting and controlling the activities of all the mutual funds except **MMF**. The mutual funds in India have five key parties involved. They are:

(a) The Sponsors.
(b) The Board of Trustees.
(c) The Asset Management Company.
(d) The Custodian.
(e) The Chit holders.

The Sponsors are the important party in establishing a mutual fund. Every mutual fund is formed by a Sponsor. According to the **SEBI** guidelines, Sponsors can be defined as "Sponsor means anybody corporate who is acting alone or in combination with another body corporate, establishes, a mutual fund after completing formalities there-of". The Sponsors could be a registered company or a scheduled bank or all India or state level financial institution. The Sponsors must have a good track record, a positive networth and consistent record of profitability and a good financial standing during the last 5 years. **The Board of Trustees** is another party which plays an import role in the formation and management of the mutual fund. According to the guidelines issued by SEBI. It has defined as **"Trustee** is a person who holds the property of mutual fund in trust for the benefit of the Unit holders". The trustee eligibility is determined on the basis of eligibility and suitability will be examined from the composition of the board of directors. The SEBI will examine and approve the **"Memorandum of Association"** of the trustee company. SEBI has the authority to examine and approve the draft of the trust deed. **Asset Management Company** means a company formed and registered under the Companies Act, 1956 and was approved by the Board under Regulation **20**. The approval of the **AMC** was based on good track record, professional experience, net worth etc. **The Custodian** means a person carrying on the activity of safe keeping of the securities or participating in any clearing system on behalf of the clients to affect deliveries of the securities. The Custodian is an independent organisation delinked with the sponsors, the trustees and AMC. The SEBI would approve the custodian when granting the authorisation for setting up mutual fund as a part of the composite authorisation. The custodian is responsible for the coordination with the brokers, the actual transfer and storage of stocks and handling the property of the trust. The custodian is answerable to the **AMC**. The AMC conducts the research and based on it, manages the fund or portfolio. The **AMC** is responsible for floating, managing, redeeming the schemes etc. It receives the fee for the services rendered by it. The guidelines of SEBI should be implemented by the trust board. The AMC has to report on a quarterly basis its activities, investments and operations through AMC. It should report to the trustees and to the SEBI separately in respect to their operations and results. The mutual fund should prepare an annual report and submit to the investors of the fund and to the SEBI. The board of trustees is governed by the **Deed** and the policy in respect of each scheme should be laid down forgetting the approval from SEBI. The management of mutual fund is a top decision making function which rests with the board of trustees as per the latest guidelines of the SEBI. The brain of the mutual fund is the trustees and it is governed by a trust deed. The experts and specialists will be on the board of trustees. The AMC will look after the routine functions of fund. All mutual funds should be managed by the experts, high talented skill fund managers and professionals. The experts in this area are **Finance Professionals**. The AMC will manage the funds by making investment decisions. The fund to be invested in major categories which are regular income investments, growth oriented and money market instruments. The mutual fund should concentrate before taking decisions about the fundamental analysis of the economy, industry and company. The fund can invest towards research and appoint experts, investment analysts, portfolio managers and a host of other specialists.

Organisation Structure of Mutual Fund

The Mutual Funds in India are regulated by **SEBI**. The SEBI has the authority to register both public and private sectors mutual fund. The mutual fund set up should be done according to the norms of the SEBI. The SEBI has provided **"Four-tier"** system for managing the affairs of the fund. The mutual funds are designed to suit the needs and preferences of the investors. The choice of the fund will be determined by the investor himself. The investor should frame his investment objectives regarding whether he expects a regular income or capital appreciation or high earnings or low risk etc. Then the objective will help to choose the best fund among different alternatives. The mutual funds will adopt different strategies to meet the investor's objectives. In India the mutual funds can be classified into **Five categories**. The classification of funds can be based on various factors:

(1) based on ownership status,
(2) based on schemes of operation,
(3) based on portfolio objectives,
(4) based on location,
(5) others.

(1) Ownership Status

The MFs in India can be established by either public sector or private sector. The public sector mutual fund has been functioning since 1963–64. The **UTI** has been functioning since 1964. In **1987** the second public sector mutual fund was launched by **SBI**. SBI MF was the first among all the Commercial Banks. The Government has given the permission to PSBs for entering the MF sector to curb the monopoly of the UTI, Canbank, BOI, PNB, GIC, LIC. Mutual funds have joined operations in the business at a short span of time. Private sector corporates have been permitted by the government on February 14, 1992. Since then a number of private companies have approached SEBI for the approval of mutual fund. The SEBI has provided the guidelines for registrations, constitution and management of the mutual funds. They can be classified on the basis of their operations. The mutual funds can be divided into **3 categories,** i.e., open ended, close ended and open-*cum*-close ended schemes.

(2) Scheme of Operation

1. *Open Ended Schemes*: A mutual fund which offers units for sale without specifying any duration for redemption. An investor can subscribe it at anytime, the scheme will be opened throughout the year and investor can redeem his holding at anytime. The enter and exit of the scheme is very easy. The MF repurchases the units at periodically announced rates. The repurchase prices are based upon the **Net Asset Value.** The NAV of the scheme will depend upon the stock market prices. The open ended funds provide high liquidity to the investors. The sale price of units is also announced by the fund from time-to-time for subscription. For example, **US–64, ULIP** of UTI **Dhanavridhi, Dhanaraksha;** Magnum Balance Fund, Magnum Insta Cash Fund of the SBI.
2. *Close Ended Scheme*: A mutual fund which offers units for sale to the public only at the time of initial issue. The scheme is also offered to the investors at a specified period of time. After closing the time, the investor cannot subscribe to the scheme. A close ended scheme of mutual fund, the period of maturity will be announced in advance. The investor can buy or sell the units of the scheme in secondary market. The price in the secondary market is determined on the basis of demand and supply. The close ended scheme can be easily managed by the

fund managers. The fund manager can evolve long-term investment strategies depending upon the life of the scheme. **Mastergain-92, Grand Master of UTI, Dhanasamridhi, Dhanasree of LIC MF**, Can Double, Canstar, Cangrowth of Canara Bank, Ind Jyothi, Swarna Jyothi of Indian Bank are some of the examples of close ended schemes.

3. *Open*-cum-*Close Ended Scheme*: The scheme offered by the mutual fund is kept open for a specific interval and it runs the scheme as a close end scheme. The scheme is a combination of both open and close ended funds. This kind of schemes are permitted by SEBI in recent years only. In offer document the scheme rules and regulations will be announced. The units of the scheme may be listed in stock exchange. These units may be traded in the stock exchange regularly.

(3) Portfolio Objective

Mutual funds can be classified on the basis of portfolio. The schemes are classified as follows:

(a) Balanced funds.
(b) Equity funds.
(c) Bond funds.
(d) Growth funds.
(e) Tax benefit funds.
(f) Specialised funds.
(g) MMMF.
(h) Leveraged fund.

Balanced Fund means the amount collected from this scheme is deployed in the market by purchasing equity and fixed income bearing securities. The combination of both the financial assets will be fixed MF. Some MFs spent some amount on the equity preference and debentures. Therefore, the situation may ensure certain amount of interest and dividend. Some MFs maintain a ratio between equity and preference share in **50:50**. The balanced fund ensures both the capital appreciation and regular return in the form of dividend and interest. The investors have advantage both in return and capital appreciation. It is also known as **Income and growth funds**. Examples for balanced fund schemes are: Cantriple of Commercial Bank—Canara Bank, Dhanaraksha 1989 of LIC, ULIP 1971, Unit Scheme 95(D), HDFC

Balanced Fund, Tata Balanced Fund, Prudential ICICI Balanced Fund, Alliance 1995 etc.

Equity Fund Scheme units will be offered to the investors by the mutual funds. This scheme proceeds will deploy for purchase of shares. According to this scheme objectives, the funds will be spent for the acquisition of the blue-chip company shares. The fund undertakes risks associated with the investment in equity of the reputed companies. The scheme is also further classified as income fund and growth funds. Examples for equity fund scheme are: **UGC 10000, UTI Pharma and health care, UTI Service sector**, UTI software, K-Tech Alliance Millennium, Magnam IT, Prudential ICICIFMCG etc.

Bond funds proceeds will be spent for acquiring bonds. The bonds ensure fixed and regular income. It ensures regular income to the investors. The bonds are available in the market at lower prices in some situations. Therefore, the net income on these bonds will go higher. Some companies offer non-convertible bonds including shares. Any investor who subscribes for the share will have to take up bonds also. **Example: UTI bond, UTI Mahila Unit Scheme, UTI NRI, Tata Income, Alliance Income Fund 5U EAD, IDBI Principal, K-bond deposit, K-bond wholesale, Sundaram Bond Saver, Templeton Income Fund,** IDBI Principal Deposit, Chola triple fund, Alliance Income Fund, Prudential ICICI, Pioneer ITI Income builder, LIC bond-G, Sun FEC Money value bond.

Growth funds objective is to provide capital appreciation for the value of investments. The scheme concentrates on value appreciation of securities. The risk involved in this scheme is very high. The scheme will not give preference for regularity of income. Growth fund is also called as long haul investments. The scheme is a long-term based fund.

Perhaps Tax Schemes are designed to meet the tax payers needs. The investor who contributes the scheme is entitled to get the tax concession in Income Tax. The lock in period is **3 years**. The scheme distributes the profits among the chit holders. A large number of mutual funds have come up with many schemes. These schemes provide benefits like income, capital appreciation and tax concessions. The proceeds of these shares would be deployed to acquire equity and debentures. Usually all the tax payers will contribute for these funds. **For example: Magnum tax gain, Pioneer ITI tax shield.**

Specialised fund/sector fund invests in a particular type of securities. The scheme objective is to make investments in a particular area or industry. If any investor wants to invest in a particular security he will prefer a fund which deals in such securities. Example: **Birla**

MNC, UTI Pharma, K-Tech, Magnum IT, UTI Software, Pioneer ITI.

Money Market Mutual funds is a scheme which has been set up with the objective of investing in money market instruments. The fund involves in buying of instruments from the money market like Treasury bills, call money, commercial paper, commercial bill, certificate of deposits, Government securities. The maturity period will be less than 1 year for all these instruments. The MMMF constitutes the only portfolio of **MMMF**—Example, UTIMMMF, IDBI principal, Money market fund.

The aim of **Leveraged portfolio** is to maximise the capital appreciation to the investors. In this type of scheme, the financial assets will be purchased by borrowing the fund at a cost. The cost of interest and the gain from holding shares is the profit of leveraged fund. Leverage funds involve in speculative activities to earn more and more profit.

(4) Based on Location

Mutual funds may be categorised on the basis of location where they mobilise funds as **Domestic fund and offshore funds**. Domestic funds mobilise savings from public within the country. Offshore mutual funds are the mobilised funds from abroad for investment in India.

Other types of mutual funds such as **Loan funds and Non-loan funds**. These funds are not very popular in the country.

Objectives of a Mutual Fund

The objectives of the mutual fund are presented below:

(a) To provide a better opportunity to low income group investors.
(b) To provide a better expertise, talent, skilful, scientific approach towards stock market activities.
(c) To manage small investors portfolios that provide regular income growth safety liquidity and diversification.

Importance of Mutual Fund

The mutual funds mobilise a large amount of savings from the small investor's savings. The fund attracts resources mainly from middle class families. Their savings potential is very high in India. The pooling of the large amount of resources, operating and the ability to commit the large sums of money for long periods. The mutual funds will enjoy ample resources at their disposal by mobilising from various investors. The mutual funds gain a lot of significance from the investors. It has been proved in the case of **Master gain–92** scheme of the Unit Trust. The scheme has mobilised **Rs. 4500 crores** from the market and created history in the market. But the Unit Trust failed to manage that scheme. In India, the investors do not have any basic knowledge about the portfolio management. Therefore, the investors are investing in mutual funds. They are important due to the following reasons:

(a) The mutual funds have been functioning like financial intermediaries in mobilising the savings of the public.
(b) The mutual funds invest in a variety of securities where there is a demand.
(c) Mutual funds appoint experts, to get the benefits of speculation activities.
(d) Mutual funds lead to a general prosperity to the investors.
(e) The mutual funds will handle the investors fund with utmost care and try to fulfil the needs of unit holders.
(f) The fund managers will apply all the stock market techniques to enhance the fund of the NAV.
(g) The mutual funds will attract foreign investments by offering **offshore funds.**
(h) The per capita income of rural and urban middle class people is increasing and their savings are channelised towards mutual fund sector. The fund diverts the resources towards industrial undertaking units by acquiring the financial assets of various companies.
(i) The mutual funds have tremendous scope for growth in the country.
(j) The liberalisation and industrial policies gave a scope for the growth of the country. The Government should prepare an agenda about the utilising of the vast resources available with the mutual funds. There are certain areas to be developed such as **water resources, roads, agricultural, etc.** The Government of India can divert the resources towards construction of dams, watersheds and creation of irrigational facilities, development of agriculture sector, development of cooperative service sector, benefits will pass to the farmers. The mutual funds may also enter into power sector to improve the production of power by providing large amounts of savings. In future the

mutual funds may be like **UTI (Agri), UTI (Power), UTI (Roads), UTI (Housing)** etc.

Regulatory Framework

The Mutual Funds in India are governed by the UTI Act of 1963, Indian Trust Act of 1882, Companies Act of 1956, Securities Act of 1956, and the other tax laws. The overall monitoring and supervising are done by the **Ministry of Finance**, the RBI and the SEBI. The RBI had issued guidelines for the bank sponsored mutual funds in 1987. Afterwards it also received the guidelines from the Ministry of Finance in 1991. The SEBI also issued guidelines in 1991 and a comprehensive set of regulations in 1993. After the successful growth of the mutual fund industry, it became necessary that all mutual funds in India should follow uniform norms for the valuation of investments and accounting practices. This leads to better comparison for the valuation of fund performance. The SEBI issued new mutual fund regulations in December 1996 based on the recommendations of the mutual fund **2000 report**. All mutual funds in India including the UTI are regulated by the SEBI. The **offshore** funds are governed by the Ministry of Finance, the Government of India and the RBI. **MMMFs** are governed by the RBI. The SEBI regulations aim at facilitating competition, transparency, investor's protection etc.

Registration of Mutual Fund

According to the SEBI guidelines, the following process is involved for the registration of a mutual fund:

1. Every mutual fund should be registered with the SEBI under Regulation 9.
2. An application for registration should be made in **Form A** by the fund sponsor and shall be addressed to the SEBI.
3. Notwithstanding anything contained in sub-regulation **(1)** any application made by a sponsor prior coming into force of these regulations containing such particulars are mentioned in the form shall be treated as an application made in persuance of the sub-regulation **(1)** and should be dealt with accordingly provided that the fee payable in respect of the application made under sub-regulation shall be the same as is referred to in the sub-regulation of Regulation **4** every application for registration

under the Regulation 3 shall be accompanied with an application fee as specified in **Schedule II** by means of a cheque or bank draft in favour of the SEBI payable at **Mumbai.**

Regulation 5

The SEBI regulation indicates that subject to the provisions that under sub-regulation (3) of Regulation 3, any application which is not complete in all aspects and does not confirm to the particulars specified in the form, shall be rejected provided that, before rejecting any such application, the applicant shall be given an opportunity to remove within the time specified, such objections as may be indicated by the board.

Regulation 6(1)

The Regulation 6 deals with the furnishing information clarification and personal representation. The SEBI may require the sponsor to furnish such further information or clarification as may be considered necessary for the grant of registration. The sponsor should appear before the SEBI for personal representation.

Regulation 7

This regulation indicates the consideration of application. The board on the basis of information furnished in the application and after obtaining such further information as may be required should decide on the application for registration not more than 3 months from the date of receipt.

Regulation 8

This regulation deals with the conditions for the registration of a mutual fund. For the purpose of granting the registration the board should take into account all the matters which are relevant to efficient and orderly conduct of the affairs of a mutual fund and in particular the following:

(a) The sponsor must possess a sound track record and experience in the relevant field of financial services for a minimum period of **5 years**. He should possess professional competence, financial soundness and general reputation of fairness and integrity in his business transactions **"sound track record"** means networth, dividend paying capacity and the profitability of the sponsor.

(b) Mutual fund is in the form of a trust and the trust deed has been approved by the board.
(c) An Asset Management Company who holds an approval of the board has been appointed to manage the affairs of the mutual fund and operations the schemes of such funds.
(d) The sponsor contributes atleast **40 per cent** to the net worth of the **AMC**.
(e) The sponsor or any of its director or the **principal officer** is to be employed by the fund. The management looks after the affairs of its business at any time when it is convicted for any offence involving moral **turpitude** or guilty of any economic offence.

Regulation 9

It deals with the grant of registration. The board on being satisfied that the application is complete in all respects and all particulars sought have been furnished and that the mutual fund is eligible for registration may register with fund subject to:

(a) Receipt of registration fee indicated in **Schedule II** of the Act in a manner specified by the Board.
(b) The terms and conditions specified in Regulation **12**.

Where a mutual fund is found to be eligible for grant of registration, the board shall grant a certificate in **Form B**.

Regulation 10

(a) According to the regulation every mutual fund registered under these regulations, should pay annual fee for every financial year, from the year following the year of registration as specified in **Schedule II.**
(b) The annual fee should be remitted to the board in the manner specified in sub-regulation **(1)** of Regulation 4 before the beginning of each financial year.

Regulation 11

(1) The regulation deals with the failure of the payment of fee by the mutual fund. If any fund fails to remit the annual fee as provided in sub-regulation **(2)** of regulation **10**. The board may prohibit the mutual fund from launching any new scheme till the fee has been remitted.

(2) Without prejudice to these regulations, the board may, on being satisfied with the reasons for the delay and subject to such conditions as it may deem fit, permit the sponsor to pay the annual fee at anytime within 2 months from the commencement of the financial year to which such fee relates.

Regulation 12

According to the regulation every fund which is granted registration is subject to fulfil the following terms and conditions:

(a) Complying with the provisions of these regulations.
(b) Informing forth with the board, as soon as it comes to the knowledge of the sponsor or the trustees that any information or particular previously submitted to the board were either misleading or false in any material respect.
(c) Informing forth with the board of any material change in the information or particular previously furnished, which has a bearing on the registration granted by it.
(d) The sponsor, the **AMC** trustees and the custodian should comply with the provisions of the regulations.
(e) Allowing examination of the directors, officers and other employees in the course of inspection and extending full co-operation on its behalf.
(f) Agreeing to produce books of accounts, documents and such other information as sought for by the board in the course of inspection.

Regulation 13

It deals with the situation procedure where registration is not granted by the SEBI. The following process involved while denying registration:

(i) Where an application does not satisfy the requirements mentioned in Regulation **8**. The board shall reject the application.
(ii) The information about the rejection of application will be communicated to the applicant in writing, stating therein the grounds on which the application has been rejected.
(iii) The applicant, who is aggrieved by the decision of the board under sub-regulation **(2)** may within a period of **30** days from

the date of receipt of such intimation can apply to the board for reconsideration of its decision.

(iv) The board shall as soon as possible, in the light of the submissions made in the application and whenever necessary, after giving an opportunity for personal hearing, convey its decision in writing to the applicant.

Regulation 14

According to this regulation, it deals with the constitution and management of the mutual fund. The mutual fund shall be constituted in the form of a trust in accordance with the provisions of the Indian Trust Act, 1882.

Regulation 15

The regulation informs about the appointment procedure of the trust. The process for the appointment of the trust is as follows:

(1) A company shall be appointed as a trustee to manage the mutual fund provided that the board may regarding the special circumstances can permit the appointment of a board of trustees, as trustees of a mutual fund.

(2) The appointment of the trustees should be subject *inter alia* to the following conditions, namely:

   (a) the trustees are persons who have experience in financial services and are not found guilty of any economic offence;
   (b) the names of the trustees should be forwarded to the board;
   (c) any change in the appointment of the trustees should be subject to the approval of the board;
   (d) no trustee should retire unless another person is appointed in the place of retiring trustee;
   (e) no person should be a trustee or a director of a trustee company in more than one mutual fund;
   (f) atleast 50 per cent of the trustees should be independent members and no such trustee should be an affiliate or subsidiary of the sponsor;
   (g) an AMC, any of its directors, officers or employees should not act as a trustee of any mutual fund.

Regulation 16

(1) The regulation deals with the process of registration of a deed under the Registration Act. The investment of the trust shall be in the form of a deed duly registered under the provisions of the Indian Registration Act of **1908** executed by the sponsor in favour of the trustees named in such instruments and shall contain such clauses as mentioned in **Schedule III** and such clauses which are necessary for safeguarding the interests of the unit holder.

(2) No trust deed shall contain a clause which has the effect of—

   (a) Limiting or extinguishing the obligations and liabilities of the trust in relation to any mutual fund or the unit holders; or
   (b) Indemnifying of the trustees or the Asset Management Company for the loss of damage caused to the unit holders by their acts of negligence or acts of commissions or omissions.
   (c) The trust deed should be made available for the inspection by any member from the public at the registered office or the principal place of business of the mutual fund and if so desired, a copy of the same should be made available to any person on payment of a nominal fee as decided by the mutual fund.

Regulation 17

(1) The section deals with the obligations of the trustees as per the law. The trustees shall have a right to obtain from the **AMC** such information as relevant to the management of the affairs concerning the operations of the trust and may also call for periodical reports from the **AMC**.

(2) Where the trustees have reason to believe that the conduct of the business of the mutual fund is not in conformity with these regulations. They should forthwith take such remedial steps as necessary to rectify the situation and keep the board informed of the same with full particulars.

(3) The trustees should take the steps to execute all the documents, which are necessary to secure the acquisitions disposals. It also assures the transactions that are entered into by the AMC are properly made in accordance with these regulations.

(4) The trustees should be responsible for ensuring that the AMC complies with these regulations.

(5) The trustee should enter into an agreement with the AMC which contains the clauses as specified in the **Schedule IV** and such other clauses which are necessary for the purpose of investment of the funds of the mutual fund then such agreement will be approved by the board.

(6) The trustees should be accountable for and be the custodian of the property of the respective schemes and should hold the same in trust for the benefit of the unit holders in accordance with these regulations and the instruments of the trust.

(7) The trustees should take steps to ensure that the transactions concerning mutual funds are in accordance with the provisions of the trust deed and **Schedule III** of these regulations.

(8) The trustees should be responsible for the calculation of any income due to be paid to the fund and also of any income received in the mutual fund for the holders of the units of any scheme in accordance with these regulations and the trust deed.

(9) The trustees should receive a quarterly report from the **AMC** and submit a **6 monthly** report to the board on the activities of the fund.

(10) The trustees should call for the meeting of the unit holders

  (a) whenever required to do so by the board in the interest of,
  (b) on a requisition of **3/4th** of the unit holders of any scheme or of all the schemes together, or
  (c) when the majority of the trustees decide to wind up or prematurely redeem the units or modify any scheme.

Regulation 18

The regulation deals with the process of setting up of the **AMC**. According to the rules and regulations the following steps are required for the approval of the **AMC**:

(i) The application for the approval of the **AMC** shall be made in **Form A**.

(ii) The memorandum and articles of association of the AMC shall be submitted to the board along with the application for approval **under the sub-regulation (i).**

(iii) The provisions of regulations **5, 6 and 7** should apply to the applications made under sub-regulation **(1)** of this regulation as they apply to the application for registration of a mutual fund.

Regulation 19

(1) The regulation explains the process of getting of an appointment of the AMC. The act indicates that the sponsor, the trustee, should appoint an **AMC** who is approved by the board to manage the affairs of the mutual fund and operate the schemes of such fund.
(2) The appointment of an AMC can be terminated by majority of the trustees or by **75 per cent** of the unit holders of the scheme.
(3) Any change in the appointment of the AMC should be subject to prior approval of the board.

Regulation 20

The regulation deals with the approval of the AMC. For the grant of approval from the AMC. The board may take into account all the matters, which are relevant to efficient and orderly conduct of the affairs of the AMC and in particular the following, namely:

(a) The existing AMC has a sound track record, general reputation and fairness in transaction;
(b) The directors of **AMC** are persons of high fame and stand having at least 5 years of professional experience in the relevant fields, such as **portfolio management, investment analysis, financial administration**;
(c) The board of directors of the AMC has atleast **50 per cent** directors, who are not affiliated or associated in any manner with, the sponsor or any of its subsidiaries or the trustees;
(d) The chairman of the **AMC** should not be the director of a trustee company or trustee of the board of trustees;
(e) The AMC shall have a minimum net worth of **Rupees Five crores.**

Regulation 21

The regulation explains about the terms and conditions of approval of the **AMC**. The grant of approval of the AMC under Regulation 20 shall be subject to the following terms and conditions, namely:

(a) the AMC has professionals with adequate experience in the management of mutual funds;
(b) any director of the AMC shall not hold the position of a director in another **AMC** or of a trustee in any mutual fund;
(c) the AMC shall forthwith inform the board of any material change in the information or particulars previously furnished, which have a bearing on the approval granted by it;
(d) no change in the management of the **AMC** shall be made without prior approval of the board;
(e) the AMC undertakes to comply with these regulations.

Regulation 22

This section deals about the situation, if the approval is not granted to an AMC:

(1) When an application made under regulation 18 for grant of approval does not satisfy the requirements laid down in Regulation 21 the board may reject the application.
(2) The decision to reject the application shall be communicated to the applicant in writing stating the grounds on which the application has been rejected.
(3) The AMC which is aggrieved by the decision of the board under sub-regulation (1) may within a period of **30 days** from the date of receipt of such intimation, apply to the board for reconsideration of its decision.
(4) The board shall as soon as possible in the light of the submission made in the application under sub-regulation (3) and whenever necessary after giving an opportunity for personal hearing, communicate its decision in writing to the applicant.

Regulation 23

The regulation inform about the restrictions on business activities of the AMC. No asset management company shall:

(a) act as trustee of any mutual fund,
(b) undertake any other business activities except activities like financial services consultancy, exchange of research on commercial basis as long as any such activities of one not in conflict with the activity of the mutual fund,

(c) act as an AMC for any other mutual fund to hold the position of a trustee in a trust or act as a director in any other AMC,

(d) permit any director of the AMC.

Regulation 24

The regulation defines the role and obligations of an AMC. The following process tells us about the rule position regarding the obligations of the AMC:

(i) The AMC shall take all reasonable steps and exercise all due negligence and ensure that the investment of funds pertaining to any scheme is not contrary to the provisions of these regulations and the trust deed.

(ii) The AMC shall be responsible for the acts of commission and omissions by its employees or the person whose services have been obtained by the company.

(iii) The AMC shall submit to the trustee, quarterly reports on March 31, June 30, September 30 and December 31 on its activities and the compliance with these regulations.

(iv) The AMC shall be expected to meet all its expenses and make provisions for:

  (a) office space, personnel including **security analysts** and **portfolio managers,**
  (b) regulatory compliance and reporting services,
  (c) preparation and distribution of the funds prospectus, annual and periodic reports and other investor's communications,
  (d) advertising and other sales material,
  (e) accounting services and preparation of tax returns, and
  (f) insurance coverage and other services.

(v) The trustees of the mutual fund may terminate the assignment of the AMC at any time after receiving a reasonable notice in writing from the **AMC**.

(vi) Notwithstanding anything contained in any contract or agreement, the **AMC** or its directors or the officers shall not be absolved of any civil liability to the mutual fund for their acts of commissions and omissions, while holding such position or office.

Regulation 25

The mutual fund shall have a custodian. He is not associated with AMC in anyway.

Regulation 26

The regulation explains about the process of **approval** of custodian,

(i) The custodian shall make in application in **Form A** for registration.

(ii) The provisions of 5, 6 and 7 shall, so far as may apply to the application made under sub-regulation (i) of this regulation.

(iii) For grant of approval of the custodian, the board may take into account all matters which are relevant to efficient and orderly conduct of the affairs of the custodian and in particular the following, namely—

  (a) the existing custodian has a sound track record, general regulation and fairness in transaction,
  (b) the applicant himself or the employees or the persons who have experience in providing custodian services,
  (c) the applicant has the infrastructure, office space and personnel to provide custodian services,
  (d) the applicant or the director or the partners are not found guilty of any economic offence,
  (e) the applicant is not the sponsor or trustee, of any mutual fund.

(iv) The grant of approval to the custodian shall be subjected to the following terms and conditions, namely—

  (a) the custodian or its directors, partners will not in anyway be directly or indirectly affiliated or associated with any AMC,
  (b) the custodian will not act as sponsor or the trustee of any fund,
  (c) the custodian will not act as a custodian of more than one mutual fund without the approval of the **SEBI**.

The rules and regulations framed by the SEBI. Every mutual fund in India has to follow the rules and the regulations from **27 to 39** which indicates about the schemes of the mutual funds.

Regulation 27

It deals with the procedure for the announcement of schemes.

Regulation 28

It reveals the contents of publicity material.

Regulation 29

It contains the rules regarding misleading statement.

Regulation 30

It indicates about the steps involved enlisting of the schemes with the concerned stock exchange.

Regulation 31

This clause explains about the minimum amount to be raised from the market through various schemes. Close ended **Rs. 20 crores** and open ended **Rs. 50 crores.**

Regulation 32

This section tells us that the schemes should be kept open for the public subscription for a period of **45 days.**

Regulation 33

It indicates about the process of refund to an investor when the mutual fund scheme fails.

Regulation 34

It reveals that the allotted applicant should receive the unit certificates from the fund within **10 weeks** in case of close ended schemes and **6 weeks** in case of an open ended scheme.

Regulation 35

This provision deals with the transfer process of unit certificates.

Regulation 36

It indicates the winding up process of a mutual fund.

Regulation 37

It tells the effect of winding up of the schemes.

Regulation 38

It explains the procedure and manner of winding up of schemes.

Regulation 39

This provision deals with the declaration of winding up of scheme.

The regulations from **40 to 46** indicates about the investment objectives and valuation policies of the mutual fund. The rules from **47 to 65** tells about the general obligations of the mutual funds on various aspects. **Regulations 65 to 75** inform about the procedure for an action in case of default regarding various conditions.

RBI Guidelines

The Commercial Banks are considered to follow the guidelines which are issued by the RBI on certain aspects as indicated below:

- Every mutual fund should be constituted as a trust under the Indian Trust Act and the sponsoring bank should appoint a board of trustees to manage it. The board of trustees should have at least two outside trustees.
- The trustees in addition to ability and integrity should have the proven capacity to deal the investment decisions and investors protection.
- The overall direction, control, superintendence and management of the affairs and business should vest in the board of trustees.
- The routine functions of the schemes should be looked after by a full pledged executive trustee.
- The executive trustee should not discharge any other responsibility in the concerned bank.
- A healthy relationship should be maintained between the sponsor and the board of trustees.
- Care should be taken so that there will be no clash of interest between the trustee board and the concerned bank.
- The sponsor bank should contribute the corpus fund and specified by the RBI. No additional contribution should be made by the sponsor bank to the corpus without the prior approval of the RBI.
- The sponsor bank should contribute in addition to the corpus fund and maintain in each of the funds schemes by the way of

its stake, an amount equivalent to 1 per cent of the amount outstanding.

- The banks should obtain the RBI's prior approval before announcing any scheme of a mutual fund.
- The investment objectives and policies of the mutual fund should be laid down in the trust deed and every scheme launched by the fund must be in accordance with such broad objectives and policies.
- The mutual fund should make a clear statement while inviting the public about the investment objectives of the fund and its policies.
- The subscription amounts collected by the mutual funds are primarily intended to be channelised into the capital market instruments.
- The mutual funds should not undertake direct or indirect lending portfolio[6] funds management, underwriting, bill discounting, money operations etc., which are essentially banking/merchant banking functions etc.
- There is no objection to the mutual funds in investing the amounts initially collected for a scheme in the money market instruments, re-discounting of bills or bank deposits for a period of not exceeding **6** months.
- The mutual funds may also invest their temporary surplus fund in similar instruments upto not more than **25 per cent** of their total investible funds. Such short-term/temporary investments can however be made only if they are permissible under the charter of the fund.
- The mutual funds should take delivery of scrips purchased and in the case of scrips sold, give delivery thereof to the purchaser. The scrips purchased should be transferred in the funds name.
- A mutual fund should not make short sale/purchase of securities or carry over the transactions from one settlement period to the next settlement period.
- The mutual funds should not make investments in any other mutual funds of similar collective investment schemes. The funds should not also invest in the shares of investment companies/corporations.
- The mutual funds should not hold under any one scheme, more than **5 per cent** of issued share capital or debenture stock of any company.

- In case the mutual fund operates more than one scheme, the holdings in respect of all its schemes put together should not exceed **15 per cent** of the paid up capital or debenture stock of a company.
- The total amount invested by a fund from any of its schemes in the shares, debentures, of any specific industry should not exceed **15 per cent** of a schemes fund. This provision will not, however, apply to a scheme which has been floated for investments in one or more specified industries and a declaration has been made to that effect.
- The maximum spread between the purchase and selling prices of units/shares of any scheme should not be more than **5 per cent**.
- The total cost of managing any scheme under a fund should be kept within **5 per cent** of the total income of the scheme.
- Income distribution by the way of dividend or capitalisation of gains should not be made on the basis of revaluation of the stock holdings or unrealised capital appreciation.
- The fund should create depreciation on investments held and provision for bad or doubtful debts. The auditors should satisfy before declaring any dividend.
- Further, the fund should create a dividend equalisation fund for each scheme by appropriating a part of its surplus income.
- A mutual fund should maintain separate accounts of each scheme launched by it, segregating the assets under each scheme. No switching of assets between the schemes should take place, except with the prior approval of thc board of trustees and at the prevailing market rates.
- The board of trustees of mutual funds should prepare an annual statement of accounts in respect of each of the schemes which should contain, statements of assets and liabilities and income and expenditure accounts, duly audited by the qualified auditors. Further an abridged version of the annual account together with the reports of auditors and the board of trustees, should be published for the information of subscribers to the concerned scheme.
- The board of trustees of mutual funds should disclose the NAV of each of the schemes and the method of valuation for the benefit of the concerned subscribers.

- The sponsor bank should furnish to the RBI in duplicate, the following reports on a regular basis:
  - — a half yearly report indicating the performance of the mutual fund as a whole as well as each scheme,
  - — audited annual statement of accounts, together with the reports of auditors and the report of the board of trustees,
  - — scheme-wise details of investment portfolio of the funds, value of such investments, changes in the portfolio since the previous annual report and industry-wise exposure.

Company Law Guidelines

Mutual funds generally invest in shares, debentures and other securities of the blue-chip companies and in the money market instruments the guidelines issued by the Government indicate that a mutual fund in a private sector can be sponsored by one or more limited companies having a sound track record. The company or companies which want to establish a mutual fund should establish the fund as a trust under the Indian Trust Act of 1882. The sponsoring company should incorporate an **AMC**. The AMC should have a net worth prescribed by the Government. The sponsoring company should have atleast a 40 per cent stake in the paid up capital of the **AMC**. In order to meet this requirement of **40 per cent** stake, the sponsoring company or companies have to subscribe to the shares of the AMC by complying with the provisions of **Section 372** of the Companies Act (Rule 11). According to the Rule 11(c) the sponsoring company can invest only upto **25 per cent** of the subscribed equity capital. Since the sponsoring company has to invest to the extent of atleast **40 per cent** in the paid up capital of the AMC, the sponsoring company has to get the approval of its shareholders in a general meeting and the Central Government as required by the sub-section **(4)** of Section 372 of the Act for investing in the shares of the **AMC**. As stated above, the mutual fund is required to be established as a trust. Indian Trust Act, Section **(3)** dcfines the term trust as "an obligation annexed to the ownership of property and arising out of a confidence reposed in and accepted by the owner or declared and accepted by him for the benefit of another, or of another and the owner". Section **41(2)** of the Act provides that a person who has agreed in writing to become a member and whose names entered in the register of members shall be a member of the company. A person means a natural person or a corporation. A trust is not a legal entity. It is only a legal arrangement, it is not a person. According to **Section 153** of the Act, no notice of trust shall be entered on the register of members. To overcome, Sections **41** and **153** of the Act, in practice mutual funds get the shares registered with either in the name of the **Sponsoring Company** or in the name of the **Asset Management Company** or in the name of the **Custodian Company**. According to the Government rules and regulations, every mutual fund should avail the services of the custodian. According to the Government regulations every mutual fund should get the shares purchased and transferred to the fund's name and scheme also.

If the shares are not registered in the name of the mutual fund, the mutual fund should comply with **Section 187-C** of the Act by giving the declaration in Form II as prescribed by the Companies Rules of 1975 as contemplated in sub-section (2) of Section 187C of the Act, within **30 days** from the date of registration of transfer of shares should be done by concerned company. Consequently, the company in whose name the mutual funds shares are registered has to file Form No. 1 as prescribed by the Companies Rules, 1975, with the company concerned, within **30 days** from the date of registration of transfer of shares as required by sub-section (1) of Section 187C of the Act. When Forms I and II prescribed under Section 187C are filed with the company, the Company is required to file Form No. III prescribed under the Companies Rules, 1975, with the Registrar of Companies within 30 days from the date of receipt of Forms I and II from the shareholding company and the mutual fund by paying the appropriate filing fees as prescribed in Schedule X of the Act. Section 187C of the Act does not apply to the shares purchased or acquired by the mutual fund since the shares are registered in the company's name and to the account of mutual fund.

Section 153B of the Act provides that where any share or debenture exceeding a certain value is held in trust by any person, such person has to make a declaration to the public trustee appointed by the Central Government under Section 153-A of the Act, within 60 days in Form No. I annexed to Trustees Rules, 1964 and send a copy of the declaration to the company concerned within **21 days** after the declaration is sent to the public trustee. In case of Stockholding Corporation of India, such declaration in Form I shall be made in respect of the shares or debentures held by it as such on or before **31st March**, company-wise, by the **15th** of May every year. If there is any change in the shareholding or debenture holding given in the declaration in Form I, the person who has given the declaration has to send a report in Form II appended to the Trustees Rules,

1964, to the public trustee notifying such change within **30 days** from the date of such change.

According to Companies Act Section 187-B indicates that the public trustee gets all the powers and rights exercisable by mutual fund. The mutual funds and the sponsoring Companies are required to comply with some of the cumbersome provisions of the Companies Act, 1956.

Risk Factors of a Mutual Fund

Risk is the essence of the valuation of a financial instrument. The value of a financial asset depends upon many factors. Risk means, a chance the expected gain, profit or return may not materialise. The actual outcome of the investment may be less than the expected outcome. If the certainty of outcomes expected variance is zero it is called as risk free. Risk can be defined as "the variability of returns from those that are expected"[7]. The actual return on the investment may differ substantially from the expected return. The risk must be considered in determining the value and making the investment choices. Risk and Return are the foundations for **maximising** the shareholders wealth. The Return can be defined as "Income received on an investment plus any change in market price, usually expressed as a percentage of the beginning market price of the investment"[8]. The return comes from two sources **income plus any price appreciation.** For common stock the one-period return can be computed with the following formula:

$$R = \frac{D_t + (P_t - P_{t-1})}{P_{t-1}}$$

D_t = cash dividend at the end of time period t
P_t = stocks price at time period t
R = actual return
t = a particular time period in the past/future
p_{t-1} = stock price at time period t–1

The return which we expect is different from the return which we receive. For highly risky securities, the actual rate of return can be viewed as a random variable subject to a **"probability distribution"**. It can be defined as "A set of possible values that a random variable can assume and their associated probabilities of occurrence."[9] The probability distribution is based on two factors of the distribution: (a) the expected return, (b) the standard deviation. The expected return is a weighted average of the possible returns, with the weights being the probabilities of occurrence. The expected return can be defined as "the weighted average of possible returns, with the weights being the probabilities of occurrence".[10] The expected return can be calculated by the following formula:

$$\bar{R} = \sum_{i=1}^{n} (R_i)(P_i)$$

$\bar{R}$ = expected return
R_i = return for the *i*th possibility
P_i = the probability of a return occurring
n = the total number of possibilities

The another factor which influences the probable distribution is the **standard deviation**. The expected return is based around the dispersion or variability of a financial asset. The conventional measure of dispersion is the standard deviation. Standard deviation can be defined as "A statistical measure of the variability of a distribution around its mean. It is the square root of the variance".[11] The standard deviation of returns depends upon the variability of returns. The standard deviation σ can be expressed mathematically as:

$$\sigma = \sqrt{\sum_{i-1}^{n} (R_i - \bar{R})^2 (P_i)}$$

σ = standard deviation
R_i = return on investment
$\bar{R}$ = the expected return on investment
P_i = probability occurrence of the financial asset

The standard deviation sometimes confuses and sometimes makes to fall in dilemma when compared with the risk of a financial asset. To overcome the limitations of the standard deviation it can be better to find out its coefficient of variation. The co-efficient of variation can be found by dividing the standard deviation with the expected return. The co-efficient of variation can be defined as "the ratio of the deviation of a distribution to the mean of that distribution. It is a measure of relative risk".[12] The coefficient of variation can be calculated by the following formula:

$$CV = \frac{\sigma}{\bar{R}}$$

σ = standard deviation

$\bar{R}$ = expected return

Thus coefficient of variation is a measure of the risk per unit of expected return. The larger the CV, the larger the relative risk of the financial asset. The average investor is averse to risk. The risky investments should offer higher expected returns than less risky investments in order to make the people and hold it. Therefore, the risk averse can be defined as "term applied to an investor who demands a higher expected return the higher the risk".[13] The low risk investments sometimes produce higher returns. Investors usually make their investments in a single financial asset or they deploy their wealth in a combination of two or more instruments. Therefore, this combination of investments are called as **"portfolio"**. Portfolio can be defined as "A combination of two or more securities or assets".[14] Mutual funds performance depends upon the management of portfolio. The NAV is the barometer of performance of any type of mutual fund. The reflection of better management of portfolio is a indication of the high NAV of the units. The expected return of a portfolio is a weighted average of the expected returns of the securities comprising that portfolio. The weights are equal to the proportion of total funds invested in each security. The formula for the expected return of a portfolio can be as follows:

$$R_p = \sum_{j=1}^{m} W_j R_j$$

R_p = the expected return on portfolio
W_j = the proportion of the investments in security *j*.
R_j = the expected return for security *j*.
m = the total number of different securities in the portfolio.

The fund managers of the mutual fund will have to concentrate on many factors like **portfolio standard deviation, covariance, correlation coefficient** etc. The portfolio management also concentrates on the **diversification.** The concepts of diversification is to spread the risk across a number of assets or investments. The meaningful diversification reduces risk. The portfolio risk comprises two components.

Total risk = Systematic risk + Unsystematic risk

The systematic risk means the overall movements of the general market or economy. It is caused by a number of factors. This type of risk is inescapable. The systematic risk is also called as market risk or non-diversifiable risk. The systematic risk can be defined as "the variability of return on stocks or portfolios associated with changes in return on the market as a whole".[15] The diversification cannot reduce this risk. Another risk element is **unsystematic risk**. The unsystematic risk is also called as **"non-market risk"** or **"diversifiable risk"**. The non-systematic risk can be reduced by the diversification. The security's total return is not related to the overall market variability. The unsystematic risk can be defined as "the variability of return on stocks or portfolios not explained by general market movements. It is avoidable through diversification."[16] The unsystematic risk is related to a particular company or industry. Unsystematic risk is independent of economic, political and other factors that affect all the assets in a systematic manner. All the risk associated with the market portfolio is the systematic risk. In this context, the capital market and portfolio theories have developed a critical important concept **"Beta"**. Beta is a measure of relative risk of a security. Beta is a coefficient measuring a security's relative volatility. It indicates the extent of the risk for a given financial asset which is non-diversifiable. It is the co-variance of a security return with that of the market for a security class. Beta can be defined as "An index of systematic risk. It measures the sensitivity of a stock's returns to changes in returns on the market portfolio. The beta of a portfolio is simply a weighted average of the individual stock betas in the portfolio."[17] The security with a higher (than 1) beta is more volatile than the market, and the net asset with a lower (than 1) beta would rise or fall slowly than the market. **For example,** $\beta = 1$ is for everyone percentage change in the market return, on an average, the security return also will change by one per cent.

To understand the financial market in a better way it is necessary to know the value of a financial asset. The value of a financial assets is highly influenced by the return and risk. The fund managers should keep in mind about these components in their portfolios. These two elements can be ignored under any circumstance. The fund managers skill reflects in the risk reduction of a portfolio and enhance the returns to efficient portfolio. The risks may be classified in a number of ways. The following are said to be the major types of risks, which a mutual fund should not be ignored while designing the innovative schemes to meet the needs of the unit holders. They are default risk, liquidity risk, financial risk, maturity risk, inflation risk, currency risk, country risk, business risk, interest rate risk.

Unforeseen risk proves that every long-term stock investors too dump a fund at the worst time. A funds past performance tends to be an unreliable guide except for the worst funds. Volatility in the market is a routine consistent. The fund managers have much more control over the risks than returns. The investor may expect ups and downs in the market and can use the risk indicators to choose a relatively well placed fund. Speculators can bear higher risks for higher returns. The technique reveals the risks that are likely to be most rewarding.

Risk indicators involve mathematics. **Beta** is the most common measure of the risk. A **beta of 1**, matches market risk, less than 1, a fund is calmer than the market. **Alpha** is a performance measure adjusted for the risk. A fund that responds more to the markets advances than the declines has a **positive Alpha.**

Growth funds concentrate on the companies which have rapidly increasing earnings and riskier than the value funds, which hunt for those stocks at low multiple of earnings or book value. To reduce the overall risk a balanced portfolio of funds should be placed across the spectrum with perhaps a slight tilt towards small stocks and value for the long-term invest.

Performance Valuation of Mutual Funds

The SEBI has come out with a standard format of the balance sheet for mutual funds in India. The mutual fund industry does not have a standard accounting policy and comparison may be done after the adjustments. The mutual fund performance is based on the **Net Asset Value**. The NAV of the unit is an important concept and it is the basis for the unit pricing. In the case of open ended and closed end scheme, the NAV can be calculated as follows:

$$\text{NAV} = \frac{\text{Total market value of the assets in the portfolio of the fund} - \text{liabilities}}{\text{Number of funds units outstanding}}$$

In the case of open ended schemes the NAV calculated on daily basis and the sale and purchase are to be made on each day. The following formula can be applied to calculate the sale and repurchase prices of units.

$$\text{Sale price} = \frac{\text{(MVA} - \text{Liabilities excluding CL, ISC, reserve and unit capital)} + \text{Brokerage, Commission, taxes and other example)}}{\text{Number of units outstanding}}$$

$$\text{Repurchase price} = \frac{\text{(MVA} - \text{Liabilities excluding CL, ISC, reserve and unit capital)} - \text{Brokerage, Commission, taxes and other example)}}{\text{Number of units issued or outstanding}}$$

The expected rate of return on units can be calculated as:

$$ERR = \frac{(NAV_t - NAV_{t-1}) + \text{Dividends} + \text{Capital gains}}{NAV_{t-1}}$$

ERR = expected rate of return on units
MVA = market value of assets
CL = current liabilities
ISC = initial share capital
t = current year
t–1 = previous year

The NAV is determined by the stock market prices. The stock market prices are influenced by the supply, the demand and the other factors. The units are discounted to the extent value of the net asset value, and the average discount has been about **25 per cent.** In certain cases the discounts are as high as **30 to 50 per cent**. The following factors may give rise to discounts:

(i) The close ended fund units are very limited trading in value and volume.
(ii) The close ended scheme units floating is very small.
(iii) High administrative expenses and management fee cause low dividend which in turn lower the price.
(iv) The unit prices are very low because the broker offers low prices which they have to hold them for a more time.
(v) On overall the market for these units is limited while comparing with the corporate shares.

The NAV includes dividends, interest accruals and reduction of liabilities, expenses besides market value of investments. The causes for the **Non-satisfactory** performance of the mutual funds are as follows:

(a) poor investment planning,
(b) too much diversification of portfolio,
(c) blue-chip scrips do not yield more than average return,
(d) high turnover of portfolio leads to huge payment of brokerage, and
(e) wrong prediction about income, profitability, interpretation of government policies etc.

Efficiency of Mutual Fund

A good mutual fund always works for the satisfaction of the unit holders. The evaluation of a mutual fund can be done by taking the following factors into consideration:

Liquidity

A good mutual fund should create liquidity to its unit holders in the form of listing on a stock exchange.

Stability

A mutual fund should be stable and offer a wide range of schemes for a long-term period.

Growth

The fund must concentrate on increasing the NAV's consistent growth in dividend and capital appreciation.

Returns

A fund should assure better returns to its unit holders and try to achieve the goal.

Credibility

Previous track record of issuer. An investor before investing should decide and verify the track record.

Management Approach

The management of a fund depends upon many factors, i.e., diversification, risk bearing, return maximisation.

Method of Valuation of the Investments

Every mutual fund in India should value investments according to the following valuation norms:

- **(a) Traded securities.**
- **(b) Non-traded securities.**
- **(c) Rights shares.**

While valuing the **traded securities**, the following factors should be taken into consideration:

(i) The securities should be valued at the last quoted closing price on the bourse.

(ii) If the scrips are traded on more than one stock exchange, generally the AMC is left to select the appropriate stock exchange. The reasons for selection should be recorded in writing. Usually all the scrips can be valued at the prices quoted on the stock exchange where a majority in value of the securities are principally traded.

(iii) In a particular valuation day, if a security has not been traded on the selected stock exchange, the value at which it is traded on another stock exchange may be taken.

(iv) In same situations, when a scrip is not traded on any stock exchange on a specific valuation day, the earliest previous day quotation may be used for consideration. But such date should not be more than 60 days prior to the valuation date.

The **non-traded securities** will be valued in the following manner:

(a) A scrip may be treated as a non-traded scrip, if it is not traded on any stock exchange for a period of **60** days prior to the valuation date.

(b) The **Asset Management Company** has the authority to value the non-traded securities in the following procedure:

   (i) The Board of Directors of the AMC should prescribe the norms for valuation of non-traded securities.

   (ii) The decision of the Board of Directors of the AMC must be documented in the minutes and the supporting data in respect of each security so valued must be preserved.

   (iii) The methods used to find out the value of non-traded security should be periodically reviewed by the trustees of the mutual fund.

   (iv) The Auditors of the mutual funds should be reported as **"fair and reasonable"** in their report on the annual accounts of the mutual fund.

   (v) The Equity Instruments should be valued on the basis of capitalisation of earnings or NAV method.

   (vi) The Debt Instruments should be valued on a yield to maturity basis.

(vii) The value of investments like **call money, short-term deposits, re-discounted bills** should be valued at **cost plus** accrual.

(viii) The value of other money market instruments should be valued at the yield for which they are currently traded.

(ix) The Government Securities should be valued at yield to maturity based on the current market rate.

(x) For the valuation of the non-traded instruments would be valued as follows:
Cost of the non-traded instrument + Interest accrued at the beginning of the day + [Redemption value – The cost (spread over to the remaining maturity period of the Instrument)]

(xi) For the valuation of non-convertible debenture, it will be treated as Debt instrument and Valued accordingly.

(xii) In case of convertible debentures, the convertible component should be valued as an equity instrument.

(xiii) If the financial instruments have been bought on **repo basis,** the instrument must be valued as:
The Resale Price – Interest upto the date of resale.

(xiv) If the Financial Instrument has been sold on repo basis:
Repurchase price – Interest (upto the date of repurchase price) – The value of the Instrument.
If the repurchase price exceeds the investment value the depreciation should be provided. If the repurchase price is lower than the value of the Instrument, adjustment must be taken into consideration.

(xv) In case of valuation of equity, the warrants to subscribe for shares attached to instruments can be valued at the value of the share *minus* the cost of **warrant.**

The value of **Rights shares** should be calculated as:

The price of the rights share may either **"Cum-Right Price"** or an **"Ex-Right Price"**. The cum-right price gives the buyer, besides the ownership of shares already held, the right to apply for new shares offered by the company, while the **ex-right price** gives the buyer only the ownership of the existing shares held by the seller and not the right to apply for additional shares offered by the Company. Ex-right price is quoted either after the rights shares have already been allotted by the

Company or the time to apply for right shares has already expired. The value of the right can be calculated by the following formula:

$$R=\frac{M-S}{N+1}$$

R = value of one right
M = cum-right market price of a share
S = subscription price for a new share
N = number of shares (old) required to purchase one new share.

The valuation of a share ex-right can be obtained by the following formula:

$$P=\frac{MN+S}{N+1}$$

P = theoretical market value of a share ex-right
M = cum-right market price
N = number of old shares entitling to purchase one new share
S = subscription price for a new share.

Alternatively the value of a right can also be calculated by the following formula:

$$R=\frac{P-S}{N}$$

R = value of one right
P = ex-right market price of a share
N = number of old shares entitling to new one share
S = subscription price for one new share.

Alternatively until they are traded, the value of the rights share can also be calculated by applying the following formula:

$$V=\frac{N}{M}\times(P_{ex}-P_{o})$$

V = value of rights share
N = number of rights offered
M = number of original shares held
P_{ex} = ex-right price
P_{o} = rights offer price.

While calculating the NAV of the mutual funds, all expenses and incomes accrued upto the valuation date should be taken into consideration. The management expenses, and other expenses should be accrued on daily basis shall be adjusted. Any change in portfolio of the mutual fund is to be recorded in the books upto a period of **Seven days** following the date of the transaction. The NAV calculation should not be effected by more than **2 per cent.**

The price of the units must be determined with reference to the last determined NAV unless—

(a) The sale price is determined with or without a fixed premium added to the future NAV which declared in advance.
(b) While determining the prices of the units, it must be ensured that the repurchase price is not lower than **93 per cent** and the sale price is not higher than **107 per cent** of the **NAV**.

General Obligations

Every mutual fund in India should work according to the general obligations which were imposed by the Act. Generally, the mutual funds should fulfil the following obligations:

1. **Maintenance of proper books of Accounts.**
2. **Accounting policies and standards.**
3. **Financial year.**
4. **Initial expenses treatment/issue expenses.**
5. **Issue of warrants.**
6. **Annual report.**
7. **Auditor's report.**
8. **Disclosure norms.**
9. **Procedure for action in case of default.**

1. *Maintenance of Proper Books of Accounts*

The important obligation of a mutual fund is to maintain the proper books of accounts according to the sub-regulation (2) of the SEBI Regulations, 1993. The mutual funds should keep the books or accounts to explain its transactions and to disclose it any point of time the financial position of the fund in particular give a true and fair view of the state of the affairs of the fund. The mutual fund shall inform to the

SEBI the place where the books, records and documents are maintained and available.

2. *Accounting Policies and Standards*

The Mutual Fund shall follow the accounting policies and standards to provide appropriate details in the following manner:

(a) The mutual funds should present all investments in the balance sheet at market value.
(b) The mutual fund while determining the holding cost of investment and the gain or loss on sale of investments, the average cost procedure should be followed.
(c) The income of a scheme is generally earned by a mutual fund is in the form of dividend. Dividend income should be recognised by the fund on the date, the share is quoted on an **ex-dividend basis**.
(d) If the shares are not quoted on the stock exchange the dividend income should be recognised on the date of **declaration** by the concerned company.
(e) In case of debt instruments income must be calculated on a daily basis for the concerned period of the time.
(f) The financial statement of the mutual fund should reflect the transactions for the purchase or sale of investments for a particular trade date but not as of the **settlement date**.
(g) While evaluating the income of a scheme, **Bonus** shares are also to be taken into consideration. The original shares are valued on **ex-bonus** basis.
(h) In case of rights entitlements, it should be recognised only when the original shares on which the rights entitlement accrues are traded on stock exchange on an **ex-right basis**.
(i) If the accrued income has not been received beyond due date, the provision should be made in **Revenue account** of the scheme.
(j) In case of **open ended scheme** units are sold if any positive amount is arisen, it should be credited to reserves. And if negative amount found, it should be debited to reserves. The face value will be credited to Capital Account.
(k) If units are repurchased of an open ended scheme, if any **positive** amount is arisen should be debited to reserve and if negative should be **credited to reserves**, the face value being debited to the capital account.
(l) Every mutual fund should maintain an **equalisation account**

for open ended scheme, on sale of the units, an appropriate part of the proceeds should be credited to it. When the units repurchased by the mutual fund an appropriate amount should be debited to equalisation account. The net balance of this account should be adjusted in **revenue account**.

(m) Every mutual fund should maintain capital account for each close ended scheme. In this scheme, if the mutual fund repurchases its units, the par value of the unit should be debited to capital account. If any positive amount is available, it should be credited to **reserves** and if any **negative**, it should be **debited to** reserves.

(n) A proportionate initial expenses should also be transferred to the reserves.

(o) The investment in different financial instruments should include **stamp charges, brokerage charges** etc.

(p) In case of debt instruments, if any discount is found in purchasing moment, it should be reduced from the cost of the investment.

(q) If any underwriting commission received by the mutual fund, it should be treated as **revenue** only when there is no devolvement on the scheme. If there is devolvement, the underwriting commission should be adjusted according to the proportion.

3. *Financial Year*

The Accounting Year for all the schemes shall end on the same date which shall be **March 31**. In case of a new scheme which commenced the accounting year, the disclosure and reporting requirement would apply for the period beginning from the date of its commenced and ending on the last date of the relevant accounting year of the mutual fund.

4. *Treatment of Issue Expenses*

Every mutual fund should identify all expenses clearly and must be appropriate for each scheme. The Asset Management Company **(AMC)** is important organ in mutual fund, it will undertake the functions of buying and selling securities of each scheme. The AMC renders the investment and advisory sources on turn over basis of the schemes. It will charge the **Fee** to mutual fund which is fully disclosed in the offer document subject to the following:

(A) If the net assets do not exceed **Rs. 100 crores,** the commission or fee is **one** and a **quarter** of 1 per cent of the weekly average net assets in each accounting year per each scheme.

(B) If the net assets exceed **Rs. 100 crores, 1 per cent** of the excess amount over **Rs. 100 crores** will be charged.

(C) In addition to the above fee the **AMC** may charge the mutual fund with the following expenses:

(a) Initial issue cost of sponsoring the fund and its schemes.

(b) Recurring expenses such as **brokerage, marketing and selling expenses, Registrar's services** for transfer of shares, agents commission, all of these initial expenses in respect of anyone scheme shall not exceed **6 per cent** of the fund raised under that scheme. In addition to the above expenses, the following expenses may also be charged to the mutual fund:

(i) fee and expenses of trustees,
(ii) audit fees,
(iii) custodian fee,
(iv) cost of funds from location to location,
(v) winding up costs for terminating a mutual fund/ scheme,
(vi) cost of statutory advertisements,
(vii) cost regarding investor communication,
(viii) any such other costs may be approved by the **SEBI.**

The Treatment of Initial Expenses: The initial expenses must be accounted in the books of account of each scheme specified as below:

(i) The issue of scheme can be classified into **two** categories: (a) **load,** (b) **no load basis** or sometimes it may issue as mixed basis. The type of issue should be clearly explained to the investors in the offer document. In the case of a close ended scheme floated on a **load basis** the initial issue expenses should be amortised on a **weekly** basis over the period of the scheme.

(ii) In case of open ended schemes, floated on the load basis. The initial expenses may be amortised over a period not exceeding **5** years. The expenses incurred during the life of an open ended scheme cannot be amortised.

(iii) In case of load basis open end and close end schemes, the unamortised portion of the expenses is to be included in the calculation of **Net Asset Value**. But such portion should not be included for calculation of the advisory service to the AMC.

(iv) If the schemes floated on a **no load basis**, the AMC can levy an additional management fee not exceeding **1 per cent** of the NAV. The AMC is entitled to levy a contingent charges as follows:

   (a) It may be entitled to buy a contingent deferred sales charge for redemption during the **first four years** after purchase should not exceed **4 per cent** of the redemption proceeds in the first year.
   (b) It is **3 per cent** in the second year.
   (c) It is **2 per cent** in the third year.
   (d) It is **1 per cent** in the fourth year.

(v) The distribution charges, in case of load schemes should be borne by the scheme of the mutual fund.

(vi) The distribution charges in case of **no load schemes** should be borne by the **Asset Management Company**.

All the initial expenses together should not exceed to **6 per cent**. If any amount exceeds 6 per cent it should be borne by the **AMC**. The total expenses of the scheme excluding **issue/redemption expenses** but including the investment management and advisory fee are subject to the following limits:

(a) on the first **Rs. 100 crores** of the average weekly net assets **2.5 per cent.**
(b) on the next **Rs. 300 crores** of the average weekly net assets **2.25 per cent.**
(c) on the next **Rs. 300 crores** of the average weekly net assets **2 per cent.**
(d) on the balance of the assets **1.75 per cent.**

Any expenditure exceeding limits should be borne by the **AMC/ Trustee/Sponsor**. The SEBI cannot be approved the expenses beyond the certain level of percentage.

5. *Issue of Warrants*

The issue of warrants or dividends to the unit holders must be despatched within **42 days** of the declaration of the dividend. Repurchase proceeds must be paid to unit holder within **10 days** from the date of repurchase/ redemption.

6. *Annual Report*

Every mutual fund should prepare annual report on scheme-wise basis or an abridged summary. It shall be published through an advertisement within **6 months** from the date of closure of the relevant financial year. The Annual Report or abridged summary shall contain details as specified in **Schedules VII and VIII** of the Act. The Annual Report of every mutual fund shall be made available for inspection at the Head Office of the Mutual Fund. If any member so required, a copy thereof shall be made available on payment of nominal fee as specified by the mutual fund.

7. *Auditor's Report*

The books of accounts of the every mutual fund should be audited by an Auditor. The Auditor shall be different from the auditor of the **AMC**. According to the SEBI regulation **65**, the Auditor may be defined as "Auditor means a person who is qualified to audit the accounts of a Company under Section **224** of the Companies Act, 1956"[18]. An Auditor of the mutual fund should be appointed by the Trustees. The Auditor shall submit his report to the trustees. The Audit Report shall form a part of the annual report of the mutual fund. The Auditor should comprise a certificate to the effect of that

(a) he has obtained all information and explanations which to the best of his knowledge and belief, were necessary for the purpose of his audit,
(b) the statement of accounts has been prepared in accordance with accounting policies and standards as specified by the **SEBI**,
(c) the balance sheet and the revenue account give a fair and true view of the scheme, state of affairs and surplus or deficit in the fund for the accounting period to which the balance sheet or as the case may be the Revenue Account relates.

8. *Disclosure Norms*

The scheme-wise annual report of a mutual fund or its abridged summary thereof should be published through an **"advertisement"**. And an abridged scheme-wise annual report shall be mailed to all the unit holders within **6 months** from the date of closure of the relevant accounting year. The report shall contain all the information as specified by the SEBI. The report should reflect a true and fair view of the operations of the mutual fund. But the abridged information shall not contain full portfolio disclosure but must contain details regarding fund activities. According to the SEBI norms. If any mutual fund publish full accounts in newspapers, the full portfolio disclosure is **not** required. Every mutual fund should submit all the information to the SEBI within 6 months from the date of closure of each financial year. The mutual fund, **AMC, Trustees,** custodian, sponsor of the mutual fund should make such disclosure or submits such documents as they may be called upon to do so by **SEBI.** The mutual fund should furnish the periodical reports to the SEBI as follows:

(a) Copies of the duly audited annual statements of accounts including the balance sheet and profit and loss account for the mutual fund and in respect of each scheme once a year.
(b) A copy of six monthly unaudited accounts.
(c) A quarterly statement of movements in net assets for each of the schemes of the fund.
(d) A quarterly portfolio statement including changes from the previous periods for each scheme.

The sale of units should be done by the Trustees or the **AMC** after providing sufficient information made available for the investors to take a informed decision. The trustees of the mutual fund are bound to make disclosures to the unit holders. It is the response of the trustees to keep the investors informed about all the available information. SEBI is the most powerful organisation in the financial sector of the nation. It has the full authority in the primary market, secondary market, money market and mutual fund industry. All the mutual funds in India shall act as per the guidelines norms issued by the SEBI from time-to-time in force. **SEBI** is the watchdog of the stock market and mutual fund sector. The SEBI is empowered to suspend registration of a mutual fund. If a mutual fund fails in the following situations:

(a) fails to furnish any information,
(b) fails to furnish wrong information relating to its activities,
(c) fails to submit periodical returns,
(d) fails to comply with directions,
(e) fails to resolve investor complaint,

(f) in guilty of misconduct/unprofessional ethics,
(g) fails to pay any fee,
(h) fails to maintain net worth of the Asset Management Company.

The SEBI has authority to cancel the registration of a mutual fund or impose a penalty on the following grounds:

(a) If the mutual fund, Asset Management Company, Trustees of the mutual fund involved in **price rigging or manipulation or concerning activities** affecting the securities market and the investor's interest.
(b) The mutual fund or AMC or Trustees or Custodian is guilty of fraud or is convicted of a criminal offence.
(c) The mutual fund has been guilty or repeated defaults which result in suspension of the registration.
(d) The financial position of the mutual fund deteriorates to such an extent that the board is of the opinion that its continuance is not in the interest of investors and other mutual funds.

Therefore, the SEBI has the full authority in either cancellation of a registration of a mutual fund or suspension of registration of the licence of the fund/**AMC/Trustee**. The suspension/cancellation of a certificate of the mutual fund should be preceded by an enquiry by enquiry officers. The SEBI has the authority to appoint an inquiry officer under Regulation **69** of the Act for holding an inquiry. The enquiry officer shall issue a notice of the MF/AMC/Trustee/Custodian as the case may be at the registered office or the principal place of business of the concerned. The MF/AMC/Trustee/Custodian may within **30 days** from the date of receipt of such notice furnished to the enquiry officer a reply together with copies of documentary or other evidence relied on by him or sought by the board from him.

The enquiry officer shall give to the concerned person a reasonable opportunity of being heard to enable him to make submissions in support of his reply under the sub-regulation **(3)**. The alleged person or any other person on behalf of him should be presented before an equity officer. But no advocate is permitted on behalf of the person. But sometimes, the SEBI will give permission to attend the advocate on behalf of the **MF/AMC/ Trustee**. The enquiry officer shall after taking into account all relevant facts and submissions made by the party submit a report to the board and recommended the penalty to be awarded as also the grounds on the basis of which the penalty proposed in the notice is justified. On the basis of the report, the **SEBI** would issue a show cause notice which the mutual fund must reply within **14 days**. After hearing the reply it would approve the action for default. Every order passed under sub-regulation **(3)** shall be self-contained and give reasons for the conclusions stated therein including justification of the penalty imposed by that order. The board shall send a copy of the order under sub-regulation **(3)** to the mutual fund and Central Government. On and from the date of the suspension, the mutual fund shall **cease** to carry on any activity related to mutual fund during the period of suspension. **On and from** the date of cancellation the mutual fund shall cease to carry on any activity related to that mutual fund. **The order of suspension** or **cancellation** of registration passed under sub-regulation **(3)** of Regulation 71, shall be published in atleast two daily newspapers by the board. **Any person** aggrieved by an order of the board may prefer an appeal to the Central Government.

Winding up of Scheme: In mutual fund, there are basically two kinds of schemes available to the investors. They are categorised as (i) **open ended scheme,** (ii) **close ended scheme.** An open ended scheme shall be wound up, if the total number of units outstanding after repurchase at any point of time falls below **50 per cent** of the originally issued number of units. A close ended scheme of a mutual fund may be wound up

(a) on the expiry of the period of time if any, fixed for the duration of the scheme by that scheme; or
(b) on the happening of any event, which in the opinion of the trustees, requires the scheme to be wound up; or
(c) if **70 per cent** of the unit holders of a scheme pass a resolution that the scheme be wound up; or
(d) if the board so directs in the interest of the unit holders.

If a scheme is to be wound up in pursuance to sub-regulation of the Act, the trustees shall give notice of the circumstances leading to the winding up of the scheme on and from the date of advertisement of the winding up the trustees or the AMC as the case may be, shall:

(a) cease to carry on any business activity;
(b) cease to create and cancel units in the scheme;
(c) cease to issue and redeem units in the scheme.

9. *Procedure and Manner of Winding Up*

The Trustee of the mutual fund shall call a meeting of the unit holders to consider and pass necessary resolutions by simple majority of the unit holders present and voting at the meeting for authorising the trustees or any other person to take steps for winding up of the scheme.

(a) The **Trustee** or the person authorised under the Act shall dispose of the assets of the scheme concerned in the best interest of the unit holders of that scheme. The Trustee or the person authorised under the Act shall dispose of the assets of the scheme concerned in the best interest of unit holders of that scheme.
(b) The proceeds of sale made in pursuance of clause (a) above shall in the first instance be utilised towards discharge of such liabilities as are properly due under the scheme and after making appropriate provisions for meeting the expenses connected with such winding up the balance shall be paid to the unit holders in proportion to their respective interest in the assets of the scheme as on the date when the decision for winding up was taken.

On the completion of the winding up the trustees shall forward to the SEBI and after the receipt of the report, if the board is satisfied that all measures for winding up of the scheme have been completed, the scheme shall **cease** to exist.

Disclosing Through the WEB Mutual Funds Style

Recent Developments

Over the course of the past year, the returns of many equity mutual funds remained in negative territory. This has been largely due to the direction taken by the markets. The fund managers could not give returns due to market situation. The mutual funds now viewed as investments which empower investors to participate in the growth of financial market. Fund investments are transparent as investors are regularly informed about their portfolio. The latest development in the market is, mutual funds are also providing information on websites. The websites of different funds focus on the information required the investors. Daily disclosures of the **NAV**, regular monthly updates and information on dividends and changes in the load structure are the things which all the investors should be aware before investing.

www.alliance capital india.com—Case Study 1

The site provides the first hand information about the Net Asset Value of the fund. The previous days NAV of all the schemes is provided in an easily accessible manner on the site and is updated regularly. The site contains the information such as news about dividend declaration, fund's holdings in its different schemes etc. The quarterly reports also contains the same information. The information about the portfolio usually contains only the top **Ten** holdings of the particular scheme. The website provides the financial data about the funds returns over different time periods as well as the benchmark of the sector.

The site provides **offer document** for all the funds schemes. These can be downloaded in a format. These can also be requested through **e-mail** as well as post. A facility for receiving the **NAV** of the fund's schemes as well as news updates through **e-mail** is also provided on the site.

The site also provides information about the funds as well as its key personnel along with the directors and the trustees. Details about the qualification and the experience of the key personnel are also provided. **Telephone Numbers** and **addresses** of the funds offices in different cities as well as those of its transfer agents are provided. The fund's site has a **learning** centre which has a section of frequently asked questions and an archieve of useful articles from the investment manager. Here also some of the information is outdated. A **Glossary** and a simple savings calculator are also present on the site.

www.pioneeriti.com—Case Study 2

The PIONEER ITI can be reached through above address. The fund is upto the mark by presenting the latest information on **NAVs** of its different schemes. A facility for the daily receipt of NAV through e-mail is also provided.

The portfolio of the funds and different schemes are presented under the heading of the monthly performance reports. Pioneer ITI is among the few funds which provides full disclosure of their portfolios for each month of the year. The information about returns will be provided and is also to be updated on a **weekly basis**.

The fund's site provides a number of tools for the financial planning. These include a savings, networth and inflation calculator. The savings and net worth calculator require detailed inputs and one's financial position. These concerned parameters provide a realistic time frame for developing a saving plan. The inflation calculator is a simple tool to demonstrate the effect of inflation on the current prices.

Forms required for making the investments, redemptions or switches are provided in a downloaded format. These also include the slips for the information about the change of address; change of account number and other routine communication between an investor and the fund.

The **Fund's CEO** communicates with the investors on a monthly basis through the site. This is usually same as the communication as that provided in the monthly fact sheet. This is based on the issues faced by the investor and provides inputs for targets oriented investing. As the proliferation of ranking surveys are being carried out the funds are eager to impress the investors about their performance. This information is also provided by the fund and usually shows the results of the latest ranking exercises. The fund also provide the data of different volatility measures of its different schemes. The significance of these also communicated. The fund provides the detailed information about itself and its sponsors. Information about the fund's key personnel and trustees is also not present. The site's section on the **FAQ** provides a series of questions which take investors through the entire process of investing and the possible questions which arise in an investor's mind. These also indicate general questions on mutual funds and the concept of fund investing. Reports about the funds in different sanctions of the press are included in site. The site provides the addresses and telephone numbers of its offices in different cities.

(1) Basics of Fund Management[19]

The key objective behind every investment is **to get better returns** out of the same, with a moderate degree of risk associated with it. But, in order to reap the benefits from an investment, be it equity, bonds, MFs or FDs.The investor should be better informed and should be in a position to take a call based on certain analysis, and not just be a layman putting the hard-earned money on rumors and information floating around in the market place.

In case of the assets of a mutual fund, which is the poor of assets from the individual investors, the most significant risk is the poor fund performance. While analysing the performance of a fund, Crisil in its research tries to address only portfolio (market) risk and not the credit, counter party, operation and legal risks. In case of pension funds and insurance companies, sufficient research has taken place on asset liability management. In the banking sector, already these exist sophisticated models to measure and manage the risk. In case of a fund's operations, fund adviser's demands are increasing to understand how performance has been achieved for the risks assumed.

For a majority of funds, performance is assessed as against the prescribed benchmarks for the same. A number of methods to assess portfolio risk do exist and many of the funds adopt standard deviations as a measure of risk, along with a few others. For the simple fact that no single model can predict risk accurately. The basic ideas of evaluation of a mutual fund can be implemented more accurately by taking into account the whole organisation. Also, once the Risk Management process is put in place in a fund house, it would prove better for key people: Chief Investment Officers (CIO), fund managers, research analysts, dealers to take conscious decisions based on the set of defined parameters.

In the context of a fund's performance, diversification is in inverse proportion with the risk, within certain limits. The market-linked risk from economy-related factors like fiscal policy, industrial policy, money supply, inflation etc..... cannot be eliminated. Thus, the risk that can be explained by the market conditions is called **systematic risk** and the unexplained residual risk (which could be company or industry or instrument-specific) is called unsystematic **risk.**

(2) Top of the POPS: These are a few of their Favourite Sectors[20]

—Caste Study 3

The scores have changed, so has the popularity. The pharmaceutical sector-riding high on expanding global demand for generic drugs—has emerged as the most popular sector among mutual funds for the quarter ended September 2001. However, even after having lost its sheen during three months, Infosys Technologies still tops the funds' popularity Index chart.

In spite of the ET-Crisil Fund Popularity Index chart, for the September quarter, indicating a 44.8 per cent fall in propensity to invest in Infosys Technologies by Mutual Funds, it still ruled as the most popular stock held by funds.

The propensity to invest finds in pharmaceutical stocks rosé sharply by 37-76 per cent. However, the propensity to invest fell to 55-62 per cent in case of information technology stocks, for the quarter ended September 2001.

During the same period, most funds pared their holdings in Infosys Technology by 23 per cent. The total percentage to Net Asset Value (NAV) of the Scrip in funds slipped 42 per cent to 4.97 per cent even as the price of the scrip fell 26 per cent to 2.4 per cent.

For the same period, stock preferences of private sector mutual funds (excluding UTI) indicator four of the top 20 stocks in their portfolio are pharmaceutical stocks, two information technology stocks and not a single one from the media and telecom sector.

On the other hand, the remaining 14 of these top 20 stocks belonging to core sector like capital goods, engineering, cement, steel, petroleum products and petrochemicals.

Diversification is clearly the new mantras in the mutual funds industry, as is evident from the ET-Crisil analysis of the changing preferences of fund managers. The study excludes all overseas registered Foreign Institutional Investor (FII) without portfolio details as well as domestic mutual funds monolith—Unit Trust of India—due to non-availability of its portfolio for the period ended September 2001.

Analysis of the top equity holding is based on two factors—the number of schemes comprising a particular stock and the simple average of the percentage holdings of each scheme in the particular stock (without considering the absolute value of the holdings). It is, therefore, an amalgamation of how commonly owned. The scrip is and the extent to which the funds are willing to allocate their portfolios (irrespective of the size of that portfolio) to that scrip. We call this the Popularity Index.

The sample size includes 98 equity and balanced schemes which account for over 70 per cent of the total assets of the private sector domestic mutual funds in these two categories (please see accompanying Tables).

The Value-Weighted Holdings

Scrips	*Sept 29, 2001*	*June 30, 2001*	*Chg (%)*
Ranbaxy labs	2.96	0.96	208.84
ACC	2.63	1.32	99.54
Dr. Reddy's Labs	4.93	2.84	73.68
Hero Honda Motors	3.61	2.13	69.55
Cipla	5.79	4.23	36.76
HLL	3.57	2.64	34.97
Reliance Industries	4.74	3.85	23.12
ITC	3.6	3.01	19.74
Grasim Industries	3.19	2.82	13.02
Satyam Computers	2.65	2.47	7.41
MTNL	1.05	0.98	7.06
Avantis Pharma	2.07	2.03	1.86
VSNL	2.16	2.12	1.68
HPCL	1.81	1.82	–0.13
BHEL	2.57	2.66	–3.68
BPCL	2.57	2.66	–3.68
SBI	1.81	1.99	–5.23
Hindalco Industries	1.81	2.05	–11.88
L & T	3.66	4.27	–13.33
Infosys technologies	4.92	8.49	–42.04

So, which stocks are in and which ones are out of favour with fund managers? The Popularity Index of September 2001 has as many as eight new entrants. These include three pharmaceuticals stocks, two telecommunications stocks and one each from automobiles, cement and steel industry. The eight new entrants comprise Grasim Industries (in the 9th position), Dr. Reddy's (10th position), Avantis Pharma (11th position), VSNL (16th position), Hero Honda (18th position) and Hindalco Industries and MTNL taking the last two positions respectively.

Information technology stocks such as Digital global software. HCL Technologies, Wipro and Hughes Software, all of which were among the most sought after stocks by funds for the quarter ended June 2001, have dropped out of the top 20 stocks held by funds during the following quarter. Pharmaceuticals ranked 11th June quarter moved out of the top 20 holdings of funds in the September.

Let us take a closer look at the most popular stocks. At the top, Infosys remains the most preferred stock yet, however, the extent of its popularity has been eroding since December 2000. That evident from the intensity of preference or propensity to invest which is measured by the percentage change in the combined score of how commonly owned, the stocks is and the simple average portfolio allocations to it between two periods.

The propensity to invest in Infosys technologies dropped by nearly 44.87 per cent for the quarter ended September 2001. In fact the intensity of preference for just three stocks of the top ten in the popularity index dipped dramatically for the September quarter. Satyam Computers slipped 60.18 per cent between June-September, while HCL Technologies fell 63.77 per cent.

Realiance Industries dipped 26.95 per cent and Bharat Heavy Electricals fell by 14.87 per cent. A look at the value-volume figures will corroborate this trend. In the case of Infosys, the Private Sector mutual funds shed 23 per cent of their volume holding in the stock.

This, coupled with nearly 36 per cent erosion in the price of stock between June-September 2001 has resulted in a 51.62 per cent decline in the actual value of the fund's Infosys holding, which came down to Rs. 746 mn as of September 30, 2001.

On the other hand, Cipla, the second most popular stock witnessed a 14.8 per cent increase in the propensity to invest by funds in September 2001 over June 2001. Funds shed 0.43 per cent of the volume of their Cipla holdings even as price dipped 2 per cent in the same period.

The Value, Volume, Price Games

Scrips	*Value (Rs. M)*			*Volume (000's)*			*Price (R)*		
	Sept. '01	*June '01*	*Chg. %*	*Sept. '01*	*June '01*	*Chg. (%)*	*Sept. '01*	*June '01*	*Chg. (%)*
Infosys Tech	746.74	1543.46	–51.62	311.14	406.18	–23.40	2400	3799.95	–36.81
Cipla	833.86	901.40	–1.95	792.70	789.32	0.43	1115.00	1142.00	–2.3
HLL	547.77	537.19	1.97	2646.23	2632.66	0.53	207.00	204.05	1.45
L & T	554.56	801.27	–30.79	3532.23	3647.11	–3.15	157.00	219.70	–28.5
Reliance Industries	719.45	921.36	–21.91	2705.72	2481.11	9.05	265.90	317.35	–28.5
ITC Ltd.	550.59	558.94	–1.49	949.78	741.3	28.12	579.70	754.00	–23.1
ACC	398.98	308.37	29.38	3221.45	2259.95	42.55	123.85	136.45	–9.2
BSNL	474.10	685.84	–30.87	3984.03	3853.02	3.40	119.00	178.00	–33.15
HPCL	275.59	297.74	–7.44	2256.20	1878.48	20.11	122.15	158.50	–22.9
Satyam Computers	400.23	590.51	–32.22	3151.41	3485.91	–9.60	127.00	169.40	–25.03
VSNL	328.60	322.79	1.80	1557.73	1010.46	54.16	210.95	319.45	–33.9
SBI	277.38	399.34	–30.54	1681.10	1827.67	–8.02	165.00	218.50	–24.4
Hero Honda Motors	548.75	411.42	33.38	2935.30	2837.38	3.45	186.95	145.00	28.9
Hindalco Industries	276.15	406.65	–31.92	542.17	472.78	14.68	509.35	853.00	–40.6
MTNL	160.47	196.15	–18.19	1263.57	1556.16	–18.80	127.00	126.05	0.75

Sources: *The Economic Times*, dated : 9.11.2002.

The Popularity Index

Base: Sept. = 100 Company	Sept. 2001		June 2001		Index Chg. (%)
	Index	Rank	Index	Rank	
Infosys Technologies	55.13	1	100	1	–44.87
Cipla	49.98	2	43.53	4	14.8
Hindustan Lever	40.45	3	32.11	7	26.29
Larsen & Toubro	38.5	4	34.65	5	11.13
Reliance Industries	37.90	5	52.01	2	–26.95
ITC	37.92	6	16.05	14	105.34
Bharat Heavy Electricals	31.37	8	36.85	9	–14.87
Grasim Industries	29.3	9	27.05	NA	8.35
Dr. Reddy Laboratories	27.62	10	10.38	NA	166.12
Ranbaxy Laboratories	26.82	11	5.11	NA	424.89
Avantis Pharma	24.03	12	17.52	NA	37.2
Bharat Petroleum Corp.	17	13	16.93	17	0.38
Hindustan Petroleum Corp.	16.08	14	13.86	18	15.95
Satyam Computer Services	14.2	15	35.66	3	–60.18
Videsh Sanchar Nigam	13.18	16	7.18	NA	83.56
State Bank of India	13.13	17	10.47	19	25.39
Hero Honda Motors	12.4	18	9.49	NA	30.68
Hindalco Industries	9.09	19	8.53	NA	6.56
Mahanagar Telephone Nigam	8.99	20	5.9	NA	52.2

Source: *The Economic Times*. dated, 9.11.2000, p. 7.

So the pure value of the funds holdings in Cipla, came down by nearly 1.9 per cent to Rs. 883.86 millions. Other pharmaceutical stocks like Dr. Reddy's Laboratories and Ranbaxy Laboratories entered the popularity index chart in September 2001. The sharpest jump in popularity is seen in new entrant Ranbaxy Laboratory. It is the only stock in top 20 list, in which funds value holding jumped a whopping 229 per cent to Rs. 453.4 millions. The same can be attributed to a 147 per cent increase in the volume holdings of the scrip in funds. The share price of the stock rose 33 per cent to Rs. 645 in September 2001.

Mutual Funds Sponsoring Agency

The SEBI was authorised by the Government to register and regulate the mutual funds both in the public and private sectors. All intermediaries and players in the capital market are brought under the SEBI authorisation and regulation. The mutual funds set up by financial institutions like LIC and GIC are regulated by the Ministry of Finance. The SEBI has taken over the responsibility of regulating, inspecting and controlling the activities of mutual funds. The authorisation is a package of approval.

1. The sponsor of the mutual fund is to be a public company, or scheduled bank or all India or State level financial institution.
2. Sponsor means any body corporate, who acting alone or in combination with another body corporate establishes a mutual fund, after initiating and completing formalities thereof.
3. Every mutual fund shall be constituted in the form of a trust in accordance with the provisions of the Indian Trusts Act, 1882.
4. A company shall be appointed as a trustee to manage the mutual fund. The appointment of the trustee shall be subject to the following conditions:

   (a) the trustees must have experience in financial services and are not found guilty of any economic offence,
   (b) the names of the trustees shall be forwarded to the board,
   (c) any change in the appointment of the trustees shall be subject to the approval of the board,
   (d) no trustee shall retire unless another person is appointed in place of the retiring trustee,
   (e) no person shall be a trustee or a director of a trustee company in more than one mutual fund,
   (f) atleast 50 per cent of the trustees shall be independent members and no such trustee shall be an affiliate or subsidiary of the sponsor, and
   (g) An Asset Management Company, any of its directors, officers or employees shall not act as a trustee of any mutual fund.

Registration of the Trust Deed

A mutual fund can be constituted in the form of a trust. The instrument of trust shall be in the form of a deed duly registered under the provisions of the Indian Registration Act, 1908 executed by the sponsor in favour of the trustees named in such instrument and shall contain such clauses as are prescribed in schedule and such clauses which are necessary for safeguarding the interest of the unit holders. No trust deed shall contain a clause which has the effect of:

(a) Limiting or extinguishing the obligations and liabilities of the trust in relation to any mutual fund or the unit holders; or

(b) Indemnifying of the trustees or the Asset Management for loss or damage caused to the unit holders by their acts of negligence or acts or commissions or omissions.

The trust deed shall be available for inspection to any member of public at the registered office or the principal place of business of the mutual fund and if so desired, a copy of the same shall be made available to any person on payment of a nominal fee as may be decided by the muttual fund.

Rights and Obligations of Trustees

The trustees and the Asset Management Company should with the prior approval of the SEBI enter into investment management agreement. The agreement contains the various clauses for the purpose of making investment. The Investment Management agreement contains the following information:

(a) The AMC would be responsible for floating schemes for the mutual fund in various schemes in accordance with the provisions of the trust deed and SEBI regulations.
(b) The AMC would undertake the management of mutual funds only.
(c) The AMC can also be involved such other activities as financial service consultancy, exchange of research and analysis on commercial basis, without the approval of the SEBI.
(d) The AMC should invest only in accordance with the provisions of trust deed and the SEBI regulations.
(e) The AMC should not take any activity with the contravention of the SEBI regulations.
(f) The AMC should not acquire any of the assets out of the scheme fund.
(g) The AMC should not disclose any information without the trustees prior approval in writing.
(h) The AMC can disclose the basis of calculating the repurchase price and NAV of the various schemes of the mutual funds as specified by the trustees or SEBI.
(i) The trustees should have the right to obtain the information from the AMC.
(j) The AMC should comply the provisions in accordance with the trust deed and SEBI regulations.

(k) The trustees have the power to call any information from the AMC.
(l) The trustees would have the power to dismiss the AMC with the approval of SEBI and its regulations.
(m) The trustees should ensure before the launching of any scheme that the Asset Management Company has the best infrastructure facilities such as office space, best talented competent staff and appointment of all key personnel including fund managers, registrars and brokers.

The Asset Management Company should submit the quarterly report about the functioning of the various schemes of the mutual fund to the trustees. The trustees should ensure that the AMC has not given any undue or unfair advantage to any deal with the interest of the unit holders. The trustees should ensure that the mutual fund schemes have been managing independently. The investors benefits should not be overlapped. If the trustees believe that the conduct of business of mutual fund is not in accordance with the SEBI regulations, it should take such remedial steps and inform immediately to the SEBI. The trustees would be accountable for and be custodians of all the properties of the fund. The trustees should take steps to ensure that the activities of the fund are in accordance with the provisions of the trust deed. They should obtain the consent of unit holders in the following circumstances:

(a) According to SEBI norms, it is required to do so, or
(b) The majority of the trustees decide to wind up or prematurely redeem the units, or
(c) The 3/4th of the unit holders to do like, or
(d) If any change in the fundamental attributes of any scheme or the trust.

The trustees should call for the information by the key personal of the asset management company to submit to the SEBI as per the Act. The trustees should review all transactions on quarterly basis carried out between the mutual fund, AMC and its associates. The trustees should also review the networth of the AMC on quarterly basis. If in case of any shortfall, it should make up for the shortfall as stipulated by the SEBI. The trustee should review all service contracts periodically and satisfy themselves that such contracts are executed in the interest of the unit holders.

Trustees Code of Conduct

The trustees of the fund should abide by the code of conduct as presented below:

(a) The schemes should be organised in the interest of all classes of unit holders.
(b) The trustees should provide all information to all unit holders in simple language about the investment policies, objectives, financial position and general affairs of the scheme.
(c) The trustees should avoid excess concentrations of business with broking firms.
(d) They must avoid conflict of interest in managing the affairs of the schemes.
(e) They must ensure scheme-wise segregation of bank accounts and securities accounts.
(f) The trustees should carry out the business and invest in accordance with the investment objectives of the schemes.
(g) The trustees must not use any unethical means in the affairs of the schemes.
(h) The trustees should maintain high standard of integrity and fairness in the transactions of the business affairs.
(i) The trustees should render at all time with high standard of service, ensure proper care and exercise independent professional judgement.
(j) The trustees should submit to the SEBI on a half yearly basis with the required documents. A brief report on the activities of the mutual funds. A certificate indicating that the affairs are carried out properly in accordance with the rules and regulations of the Act.
(k) The trustees should exercise general and specific due diligence as follows:

    1. The trustees should review the desirability of the AMC.
    2. The trustees should ensure that the trust property is properly protected.
    3. The trustees must ensure that all service providers are registered with the SEBI.

(l) The trustees should pay specific attention to the following situations:

    1. any service contract with the associates of the AMC.

2. selection and nomination of individuals to fill vacancies of independent directors.
3. check all the service contracts with all the key persons.

Asset Management Company

The sponsors of mutual funds would appoint the Asset Management Company with the approval of the SEBI. The AMC can be terminated by a majority of trustee or by **75 per cent** of the unitholders of the scheme. The application for the grant of the AMC shall be made in **"A Form"**. The memorandum of association and articles of association of the AMC shall be submitted to the SEBI along with the application. For grant of approval of the AMC by SEBI, the applicant has to fulfil the following conditions.

(a) The AMC should have a sound track record and fairness in transaction.
(b) The AMC should have the directors with adequate professional experience in financial services aspects.
(c) The Directors of the AMC should not have been found guilty or convicted of any economic offence.
(d) The Directors of the AMC shall not hold the position of a director in another AMC or a trustee in any mutual fund.
(e) The AMC should inform any change to the SEBI.
(f) No change in the Management of the AMC shall be made without approval of the SEBI.
(g) The Chairman of the AMC should not be a trustee of any other mutual fund.
(h) The AMC should have a net worth of Rs. 10 crores.
(i) The net worth of the AMC will be calculated as follows:
Paid up capital + Free reserves – Miscellaneous expenses unwritten deferred revenue expenditure/intangible assets.

Grant of Approval of the AMC

For grant of approval of the AMC, the SEBI may take into account all matters which are relevant to efficient and orderly conduct of the affairs of the AMC and in particular the following as:

(a) The existing AMC should have a sound track record and general reputation.
(b) The Board of Directors of the AMC are persons of high repute and standing having atleast 5 years of professional experience in the relevant field.

Restrictions on Business Activities

The Asset Management Company cannot act as a trustee of any mutual fund. It cannot undertake any other business activity. The AMC should engage itself in the activities of financial services like portfolio management services, advisory services to offshore funds, pension funds, provident funds, venture capital funds, financial consultancy, management of insurance funds and exchange of research on commercial basis. If the SEBI accepts, any work can be undertaken by the AMC. The AMC must disclose full information to the unit holders.

Obligations

The AMC must take all precautions in accordance with the provisions of the regulations and the trust deed. It should take care of all the investment decisions. It should be responsible for the acts of behaviour by its employees. The AMC should submit to the trustee about the activities of the fund on quarterly basis. The AMC is required to file with the trustees and SEBI as follows:

(a) A detailed bio-data of all its directors.
(b) The other particulars should be submitted within 15 days of their appointment.
(c) Any change in board of directors.
(d) A quarterly report to the trustees.
(e) A statement of securities holding in the AMC by the Director.
(f) A brief note on investment made by the Directors in other mutual fund organisations.

A mutual fund should not buy/sell securities through any broker who is associated with the sponsors. The mutual fund is not allowed to purchase **5 per cent** or more of the aggregate purchases in all of its scheme for a block of any three months. If the purchases/sales exceed 5 per cent limit a justification report should be submitted to the trustees on quarterly basis. The AMC should not utilise the services of the sponsor or any of its associates for the purpose of business transactions. The mutual fund should disclose at the time of declaring half yearly results: (a) underwriting obligations of the schemes with reference to issue of shares of associate companies, (b) if any devolvement, (c) worked as a lead manager to the issue of shares of the associated companies, (d) any participation in private placement.

The AMC should not appoint any person as key personnel who has been found guilty of share transfer agents. The AMC should assign the processing work to the least charged company. It has to abide by the same code of conduct as specified in the case of **trustees**.

Custodian

The mutual fund should appoint a custodian to look after the custodial services for the schemes. The mutual fund should inform the SEBI within 15 days of the appointment of the custodian. The mutual fund should enter into a custodian agreement regarding the service contract, terms and appointment conditions. The appointment will be confirmed with the approval of trustees.

REFERENCES

1. A. Sudhakar, K. Gangappa, Growth and emerging of mutual funds, "*Financial Services*", Deep and Deep Publications, p. 173, 1997.
2. N. Gopalaswamy, *Inside Capital Market*, Deccan Publications, Chennai, p. III-164.
3. *Ibid.*
4. *Ibid.*
5. *Business Today*, 10th anniversary issue, Jan. 20, 2002, p. 69.
6. Kumar, Amit, *The Economic Times*, 27.8.2001, p. 5.
7. Van Horne, *Fundamentals of Financial Management*, p. 91, 1997.
8. *Ibid.*
9. *Ibid.*
10. *Ibid.*
11. *Ibid.*
12. *Ibid.*, p. 95.
13. *Ibid.*, p. 95, 1997, PHI.
14. *Ibid.*, p. 95.
15. *Ibid.* p. 100, 1997, PHI.
16. *Ibid.*, 100.
17. *Ibid.*, 102.
18. N. Gopalaswamy, *Inside Capital Market*, Deccan Publications, Chennai, p. III-164.
19. *Economic Times* at 9 Nov. 2001, p. 7.
20. *Economic Times*, 9 Nov. 2001, Crisil Fund Tracker, p. 7.

Index